Communications
in Computer and Information Science   1760

More information about this series at https://link.springer.com/bookseries/7899

Sridaran Rajagopal · Parvez Faruki ·
Kalpesh Popat (Eds.)

Advancements in Smart Computing and Information Security

First International Conference, ASCIS 2022
Rajkot, India, November 24–26, 2022
Revised Selected Papers, Part II

Springer

Editors
Sridaran Rajagopal ⓘ
Marwadi University
Rajkot, India

Parvez Faruki ⓘ
AVPTI
Rajkot, India

Kalpesh Popat ⓘ
Marwadi University
Rajkot, India

ISSN 1865-0929   ISSN 1865-0937 (electronic)
Communications in Computer and Information Science
ISBN 978-3-031-23094-3   ISBN 978-3-031-23095-0 (eBook)
https://doi.org/10.1007/978-3-031-23095-0

This Springer imprint is published by the registered company Springer Nature Switzerland AG
The registered company address is: Gewerbestrasse 11, 6330 Cham, Switzerland

Preface

"The number one benefit of Information Technology is that it empowers people to do what they want to do..." - Steve Balmer.

Considering the immense potential of Information Technology (IT) in developing pragmatic solutions to every other field, our initiative with respect to the 1st International Conference on Advancements in Smart Computing and Information Security (ASCIS 2022) started approximately a year ago. Based on the various survey results, the steering committee decided to focus on the following four tracks: Artificial Intelligence, Smart Computing, Information Security, and Industry 4.0 (aka Industry).

In a futuristic list of 10 applications, it is very much evident that the technologies listed above have a major role. Based on this fact, a call for papers was floated to attract original, unpublished papers highlighting some of the innovative research areas in each of the four tracks. We are very much thankful to the editorial board of Springer CCIS who came forward to support us with the proceedings, even though it was our maiden conference.

All of the 200+ papers received were included in the Open Peer Review process and, in the end, 55 papers were shortlisted for the Springer CCIS proceedings (an acceptance rate of approximately 27%). Each submission was reviewed by at least 3 members of the Program Committee. The selected papers either made a contribution in terms of complete and classified surveys or solutions in the form of implemented models or algorithms. The papers belonging to this volume have considered AI and its allied fields and smart computing as the base technologies to govern the solutions of other fields. Research problems in the fields of healthcare, engineering, astronomy, sociology, agriculture, and education were explored and novel solutions were presented by the authors.

The conference, which was held during November 24–26, 2022, started off with a pre-conference workshop on the first day wherein eminent academicians and industry experts were invited to share the future research scope in their respective fields of specialization. On the second day after the inaugural ceremony, papers were presented by the authors under the four parallel tracks in the presence of committee members, research students, and other participants.

This two-volume set titled "Artificial Intelligence-based Smart and Secured Applications" consolidates the papers presented at ASCIS 2022, which describe solutions employing AI and smart computing in different fields and seek to address both theoretical and real-world research problems, including those which demand security solutions.

We believe that this collection will be highly useful for researchers and practitioners of AI and machine learning as well as smart computing .

November 2022

Sridaran Rajagopal
Parvez Faruki
Kalpesh Popat

Organization

Steering Committee

Manoj Singh Gaur	Indian Institute of Technology, Jammu, India
Lalit Kumar Awasthi (Director)	Computer Science & Engineering, NIT Hamirpur, India
Sudeep Tanwar	Computer Science and Engineering Department, Nirma University, India
Parvez Faruki (Head of Department)	A.V. Parekh Technical Institute, India
Sachin Shetty (Executive Director)	Old Dominion University, USA
Mohamed Mosbah (Director)	University of Bordeaux, France
Vijay Laxmi	Malaviya National Institute of Technology, India
Akka Zemmari	University of Bordeaux, France
Vincenzo Piuri	University of Milan, Italy
Ankur Dumka	Women Institute of Technology, Dehradun, India
Sandeep Sancheti (Provost, Vice Chancellor)	Marwadi University, India
Sridaran Rajagopal (Principal Investigator and Dean)	Faculty of Computer Applications, Marwadi University, India
R. B. Jadeja (Dean-Research)	Faculty of Engineering, Marwadi University, India
Shree Naresh Jadeja (Registrar)	Marwadi University, India
Divyakant Meva (Head)	Marwadi University, India

Program Chairs

Sridaran Rajagopal	Marwadi University, India
Parvez Faruki (Head of Department)	A.V. Parekh Technical Institute, India
Kalpesh Popat	Marwadi University, India

Program Committee

A. P. Nirmala	New Horizon College of Engineering, India
Ajay Parikh	Gujarat Vidhyapith, India
Ajay Patel	Ganpat University, India
Ajmery Sultana	Algoma University, Canada
Akka Zemmari	University of Bordeaux, France
Akash Dutt Dubey	Jaipuria Institute of Management, India

Akshara Dave	Indus University, India
Amit Ganatra	CHARUSAT, India
Amit Lathigara	RK University, India
Amit Vadera	Sunshine College, India
Anjali Jivani	MS University, India
Ankit Bhavsar	GLS University, India
Ankit Faldu	CHARUSAT, India
Ankit Subhash Didwania	Gujarat Technological University, India
Anand Sharma	Mody University of Science and Technology, India
Anwar Basha H.	Reva University, India
Apurva Shah	MS University, India
Ashish Rastogi	Indian Institute of Technology, Delhi, India
Ashwin Dobariya	Marwadi University, India
Ashwin Makwana	CHARUSAT, India
Ashwin Raiyani	Nirma University, India
Atul Gonsai	Saurashtra University, India
Balasubramanian Raman	IIT, Roorkee, India
B. Lakhsma Reddy	SJES College of Management Studies, India
B. Muruganantham	SRMIST, India
C. K. Kumbharana	Saurashtra University, India
C. Mahesh	Vel Tech Rangarajan Dr. Sagunthala R&D Institute of Science and Technology, India
C. P. Chandran	Ayya Nadar Janaki Ammal College, India
Chhagan Lal	TU Delft, Netherlands
Chintan M. Bhatt	Pandit Deendayal Energy University, India
Chintan Patel	University of Sheffield, UK
Chintan Thacker	Parul University, India
Chirag Thakar	LD College of Engineering, India
D. Swamydoss	Adhiyamaan College of Engineering, India
Darshita Pathak	A. V. Parekh Technical Institute, India
Daxa Vekariya	Parul University, India
Debabrata Swain	Pandit Deendayal Energy University, India
Deepak Verma	Dr. Rammanohar Lohia Avadh University, India
Dhiren Patel	Gujarat Vidyapith, India
Digvijaysinh Rathod	National Forensics Science University, India
Dimple Thakar	Marwadi University, India
Dinesh Kumar	Marwadi University, India
Dineshkumar Vaghela	Shantilal Shah Engineering College, India
Dipak Ramoliya	CHARUSAT, India
Dippal Prabhudas Israni	R. C. Technical Institute, India
Disha Jigar Shah	GLS University, India

Durgesh Mishra	Sri Aurobindo Institute of Technology, India
Durgesh Srivastava	Chitkara University, India
Dushyantsinh Rathod	Gujarat Technological University, India
Gaurav Singal	Netaji Subhash University, India
Galiveeti Poornima	Presidency University, India
Hardik Joshi	Gujarat University, India
Hardik Molia	GEC, Rajkot, India
Hardik M. Patel	Kadi Sarva Vishwavidyalaya, India
Hetal Thaker	GLS University, India
Himali Ruparelia	Gujarat Technological University, India
Irfan Ahmead	Thassim Beevi Abdul Kader College for Women, India
Ipseeta Nanda	Gopal Narayan Singh University, India
Iyyappan. M.	Adani University, India
J. Lenin	University of Technology and Applied Sciences, India
Jagruti	PM Patel College, India
Jaimin N. Undavia	CHARUSAT, India
Jasminder Kaur Sandhu	Chandigarh University, India
Jatinderkumar R. Saini	Symbiosis Institute of Computer Studies and Research, India
Jay Teraiya	Marwadi University, India
Jaydeep Ramniklal Ramani	Atmiya University, India
Jaykumar Dave	Silver Oak University, India
Jaypalsinh Gohil	Marwadi University, India
Jayshree Nair	AIMS Institutes, India
Jignesh Doshi	LJ University, India
Jinal Tailor	S. S. Agrawal Institute of Management and Technology, India
Jotindra Dharwa	Ganpat University, India
Jitendra Kumar Rout	NIT Raipur, India
Jitendra Kumar Samriya	National Institute of Technology, Jalandhar, India
Jyoti Batra	Banasthali University, India
Kamal Kishorbhai Sutaria	Parul University, India
K. Priya	Marudhar Kesari Jain College for Women, India
K. K. Goyal	R.B.S. Management Technical Campus, India
Kajal Patel	GEC, Chandkheda, India
Kalpesh Gundigara	Swaminarayan College, India
Kedir Lemma Arega	Ambo University, Ethiopia
Karthikeyan E.	Government Arts College, India
Keshav K. Singh	University of Alabama at Birmingham, UK
Krunal Vaghela	Marwadi University, India

Krupa Mehta	GLS University, India
Kumar Chandar S.	CHRIST University, India
Kushagra Kulshreshtha	GLA University, India
Lilly Florence M.	Adhiyamaan College of Engineering, India
Lokesh Gagnani	KSV University, India
Madhu Shukla	Marwadi University, India
Mahesh Podar	Pune University, India
Mallika Ravi Bhatt	S. S. Agrawal Group of Colleges, India
Mamta Chawla	Amity University, India
Mamta Padole	Maharaja Sayajirao University of Baroda, India
Manisha Rawat	Marwadi University, India
Manishankar S.	Amrita Vishwavidyapeeth, India
Manojkumar Bohra	Manipal University, India
Manojkumar Deka	Bodoland University, India
Manohar N.	Amrita Vishwavidyapeeth, India
Mastan Vali Shaik	Malla Reddy Engineering College, India
Maulika Patel	G. H. Patel College of Engineering, India
Mauro Conti	University of Padua, Italy
Mehul Rawal	Ahmedabad University, India
Mladen Konecki	University of Zagreb, Croatia
Mohamed Mosbah	University of Bordeaux, France
Mohammad Wazid	Graphic Era University, India
Mohdshafi Pathan	MIT ADT University, India
Mohit Kumar	Dr. B. R. Ambedkar National Institute of Technology, India
Monika Arora	Amity University, India
Nagaraju Kilari	New Horizon College, India
Nagappan Govindarajan	Saveetha Engineering College, India
Narayan Joshi	Dharmsinh Desai University, India
Navin Chaudhari	National Forensics Science University, India
Neelam Padhy	GITU, India
Neha Soni	SVIT, India
Nidhi Patel	SAL College of Engineering, India
Nilesh Modi	Dr. Babasaheb Ambedkar Open University, India
Nisha Khurana	Gandhinagar University, India
Nour El Madhoun	EPITA, France
N. Noor Alleema	SRMIST, India
P. Naga Srinivasu	Prasad V Potluri Siddhartha Institute of Technology, India
P. V. Virparia	Sardar Patel University, India
Pallavi Kaliyar	NTNU, Norway
Parag Rughani	National Forensics Science University, India

Parag Shukla	National Forensics Science University, India
Paresh Tanna	RK University, India
Paras Kothari	Rajasthan Technical University, India
Pradip M. Jawandhiya	Pankaj Laddhad Institute of Technology and Management Studies, India
Prashant M. Dolia	Bhavnagar University, India
Prashant Pittalia	Sardar Patel University, India
Priya R. Swaminarayan	Parul University, India
Priyank Nahar	Gujarat Technological University, India
Priyanka Sharma	Rashtriya Raksha University, India
Puspanjali Mohapatra	IIT Bhuvneshwar, India
R. A. Thakur	King Khalid University, Saudi Arabia
Rajasekaran Selvaraju	University of Technology and Applied Sciences-Ibri, Oman
Ramesh Prajapati	Shri Swaminarayan Institute of Technology, India
Ravirajsinh Vaghela	Marwadi University, India
Ripal Ranpara	R.K. University, India
Riti Kushwaha	Bennett University, India
Roshan Anant Gangurde	K. K. Wagh Institute of Engineering Education & Research, India
Rutvi Shah	Chimanbhai Patel Institute, India
Sabiyath Fatima	B.S. Abdur Rahman Crescent Institute of Science & Technology, India
S. D. Panchal	Gujarat Technological University, India
Sachin Shetty	Old Dominion University, USA
Safvan Vora	Government Engineering College, Modasa, India
Sailesh Iyer	Rai University, India
Samir B. Patel	Pandit Dindayal Energy University, India
Sanjay Chaudhari	Ahmedabad University, India
Sanskruti Patel	CHARUSAT, India
Satyen Parikh	Ganpat University, India
Satvik Khara	Silver Oak University, India
Savita Gandhi	GLS University, India
Senthil Kumar	Saveetha Engineering College, India
Shikha Maheshwari	Manipal University, India
Suneet Gupta	Mody University of Science and Technology, India
Sunil Bajeja	Marwadi University, India
T. Amudha	Bharathiar University, India
T. Devi	Bharathiar University
Umang Rasiklal Thakkar	Ganpat University, India
V. Asha	New Horizon College of Engineering, India

V. Rashmi	Amrita University, India
V. Bhuvaneswari	Bharathiar University, India
V. Ilango	CMR Institute of Technology, India
V. Vinothina	Kristu Jayanti College, India
Vaibhav Gandhi	B H Gardi College, India
Vijay Katkar	Marwadi University, India
Vimal Parmar	Dr. Subhash University, India
Vinay Kukreja	Chitkara University, India
Vinod Desai	Gujarat Vidyapith, India
Vincenzo Piuri	University of Milan, Italy
Vipin Tyagi	Jaypee University, India
Vipul Vekariya	Parul University, India
Vishal R. Dahiya	Indus University, India
Wafa ben Jaballah	Thales, France
Yogesh Ghodasara	Anand Agriculture University, India
Yogesh Kumar	Pandit Deendayal Energy University, India

Sponsors

CSI

Department of Science and Technology

GUJCOST

ICT Academy

MIT Square

Qtonz Infosoft Pvt. Ltd.

Raj Square

Abstracts of Keynotes

Post-pandemic Applications of AI and Machine Learning

Priti Srinivas Sajja

Sardar Patel University, India

The history of mankind has witnessed many pandemics since its inception. Fortunately, the collective knowledge of mankind has helped us a lot to fight the pandemic and better immune and well-evolved society. The recent pandemic of SARS-Covid-19 pandemic has taught us many things too. Fields such as healthcare, education, production, sales and marketing, and education have suffered a lot during the lockdown and pandemic period. The needs such as working in an independent & isolated way, increased automation in many businesses, quick and secure solutions, and effective control and monitoring became inevitable.

The ubiquitous nature of Artificial Intelligence and Machine Learning (AIML) offers a way to meet the above-mentioned need. Healthcare is the first domain where AIML can help. Starting from tracking patients, finding medical resources such as hospital beds, oxygen, and other drugs, diagnosing diseases to inventing novel drugs & vaccines for the disease, AIML can help. The scarce resources are difficult to manage quickly and efficiently without the techniques such as genetic algorithms, neural networks, and other machine learning methods such as generative networks, decision trees and clustering; to name a few. AIML can also be used in managing big data from health informatics.

Another important domain is training and education. Using many online platforms, education can be continued in a non-traditional manner. However, it cannot distinguish and handle different levels of students and hence customization is needed. Similar challenges arise in monitoring people in work-from-home scenarios. Domains such as production, sales & marketing, planning & designing, military and defense, eCommerce, egovernance, etc. also required the support of AIML techniques to increase degree automation, security, and intelligence. While lockdown, entertainment, web surfing, awareness, and morale-boosting types of applications are also highly needed which are intelligent, learn from data, and offer a significant amount of customization.

The problems and needs within the aforementioned domains are discussed here with the challenges & requirements. The possible solutions through the AIML techniques are discussed with brief solution outlines. Possible research applications in each domain are also enlisted using techniques such as deep learning, generative neural networks, hybrid neuro-fuzzy systems, etc. It is to be noted that, in absence of generalized logic AIML based system can learn from data to provide quick as well as better quality solutions.

Smart and Soft Computing Methods for Prioritizing Software Requirements in Large-Scale Software Projects

Vassilis C. Gerogiannis

University of Thessaly, Greece

Large-scale software projects often have numerous candidate functional requirements/software features needed to be prioritized, under multiple prioritization criteria by various stakeholders, who need to decide which requirements/features will be implemented in the next software releases. Most existing requirements prioritization approaches perform well on small sets of candidate requirements, but suffer from scalability for large number of requirements. Furthermore, all involved stakeholders may do not have enough knowledge to accurately and objectively prioritize all candidate requirements. Particularly in distributed software projects, stakeholders can be geographically dispersed and they often do not have the ability to negotiate and reach a consensus on the final list of requirements' priorities. To support these challenges, we propose the use from smart and soft computing methods (e.g., Intuitionistic Fuzzy Sets, Clustering Analysis and Recommender Systems) to handle stakeholders' uncertainty, minimize stakeholders' information overload, as well as to identify patterns that summarize the stakeholders' preferences on the candidate software features. The suggested methods have been applied to requirements datasets of existing large-scale software projects and to illustrative artificial datasets as well. The results are promising since they indicate that the suggested methods can effectively support multiple stakeholders in order to prioritize sufficiently a large number of requirements, under multiple criteria, while combining scalability and flexibility.

Your Readiness for Industry 4.0

Nitin Bawsay

VP Operations, India at Cin7 Americas

As the world witnesses development, from the wheels to steam engines, to electricity and mass production to digitization - we are NOW at the cusp of adopting the 4th leap into industrialization. We will now witness more and more of the Artificial Intelligence (AI), Robotics, Internet of Things (IoT), Mixed Reality (MR) and much more of volume-based technology aspects in our day-to-day life. The overall industry impact of this will be the single, most obvious thing - Development.

As the world gets ready to embrace this new tech termed Industry 4.0 (or X.0?), it is important that everyone of us gets ready to adapt and adopt to the new. Multiple areas that mark the Industry 4.0 are fascinating and do include:

- Automations
- Cost-saving
- Lower labor
- Unlearning and Relearning
- Capital sensitivity

All this holds value today and will continue to do so. However, adoption to the new tools and technics will be the key to this and this Change will be inevitable. The key to Your Readiness to this Change will make the difference.

We will dig into some instances of change in the Industry 4.0 with the right kind of tools and technology for today and tomorrow.

Securing NexGen Automotives - Threats and Trends

Ramkumar G.

Cyber Security and Risk Leader, Nissan Digital, Nissan Motor Corporation, India

In today's connected world, it is no surprise that new age connected car technologies are targeted by Cyber criminals. There are many instances where hackers specifically target automotive sector – computer networks, applications, factories, Cars exploiting technology and people vulnerabilities. This leads to hundreds of millions to billions of USD in litigation, brand damage, loss of business, and market share decline and damage reputation for automotive original equipment manufacturers (OEMs).

In order to ensure connected cards are safe for people from cyber-attacks, governments' world over are introducing more strict regulations and penalties on automotive OEMs. The business impact of a large cyber-security incident/data Breach at an OEM is significant and could run into Billions of USD including through:

Regulatory penalties, mass recall on multiple vehicle lines, factory refit, decline in sales, etc and Reputation Risk. Given the prevailing scenario, it is imperative for automotive OEMs to have critical focus on our end-to-end cyber security program and have the right tools, processes and people to drive this effectively. The keynote address covers the following aspects related to connected cars cyber security.

1. More Connected Cars = Higher Risks
2. Potential attacks on connected vehicles
3. Top Industry sectors targeted by Hacker groups
4. Key cyber security incidents in automotive sector
5. Affected Automotive Segments
6. Automotive Threats in the Deep & Dark Web
7. Standards & Regulations
8. What OEMs need to do?
9. What Suppliers need to do?
10. What CISOs need to do?

Cyber Attacks Classification and Attack Handling Methods Using Machine Learning Methods

Padmavathi Ganapathi

Avinashilingam Institute for Home Science and Higher Education for Women, Coimbatore, India

Cyber-attacks are predominantly increasing day by day due to the tremendous growth of latest technologies and innovations. There are different kinds of cyber-attacks are evolving in every day to day life. Some of the trending cyber-attacks between 2021 and 2022 include Ransomware attacks, Internet of Things (IoT) attacks, Cloud attacks, Phishing attacks, Malwares, cyber extortion and many more. The goal of the attacker or cyber criminals is to steal the user personal credentials without the knowledge of the user in an illegitimate way. Once, the user access control of the network devices are hacked by the criminals they take over the system control and monitor all the legitimate user activities. To detect the unavoidable illegal intrusions by the attackers through cyber-attacks in various forms are handled by vigilant intrusion detection system. Through, Intrusion Detection System (IDS) mechanism, it must be able to detect and protect the unlawful intrusions through various attacks handling methods. Some of the robust intrusion detection techniques such as signature based, anomaly based and protocol based methods. By incorporating appropriate intrusion detection and prevention system (IDPS) method in an organization will help to detect and mitigate the cyber-attacks effectively. An IDPS is a robust mechanism followed by the worldwide cyber security professionals and network administrators to safeguard the network connected devices. However, IDPS mechanism provides a stout framework to handle cyber intrusions. Similarly, Artificial Intelligence (AI) based attack detection methods using the machine learning (ML) and deep learning (DL) algorithms provides a user friendly automation model to detect the attacks evidently without any human interface.

The Internet of Things (IoT) Ecosystem Revolution in the World of Global Sports

Shamala Subramaniam

Universiti Putra Malaysia

Industrial Revolution 4.0 (IR 4.0) has changed the demographics of multiple significant areas such as robotics, simulation, travel, healthcare, and sports. The emergence and extensive development and deployment of IR 4.0 completely altered the methodologies of sports performance monitoring distinctly. IR 4.0 has seen the birth of multiple new computing.

Paradigms, and tools computer scientists use in the sports sector. This keynote will address the eco-systems in sports and the leverage the Internet of Things (IoT) has in this exponentially growing domain. A detailed discussion on focused on methodologies of sports performance analysis, sport-specific analysis and other technology revolving around sports performance analysis will be done. The talk encompasses detailed analyses on the correlation between the athlete, the sports aspect of their life, the non-sport aspect and the methodologies of sports performance analysis. The development and deployment of an off-field sports performance analysis system developed will be used as a core element in the address the harnessing of IoT in sports. The further integration and enhancements with a comprehensive eco-system encompassing a developed Games Management System will conclude the talk with the discussions on a wide spectrum of open issues.

Orchestration of Containers: Role of Artificial Intelligence

Ramkumar Lakshminarayanan

Assistant Dean for Academic and Scientific Research, University of Technology and Applied Sciences-Sur, Sultanate of Oman

The container is a novel technology that revolutionizes the development of cloud computing in creating and controlling the platforms by bundling the codes of applications with libraries and configuration files. Containers are easily deployable, isolated, have data sharing and are portable. The challenges to be addressed in the orchestration of containerized cloud computing are application portability, performance, and the new architecture development. Machine Learning and Deep Learning-the subset of AI makes it possible to solve the problems in selecting, deploying, monitoring, and dynamically controlling the containerized application. This research presents the difficulties of autonomous container orchestration, along with modern AI solutions and unresolved issues.

Enterprise Cybersecurity Strategies in the Cloud

Andrew Hodges

Senior Security Advisor, Asia Pacific and Japan
Amazon Web Services (AWS)

This session shared numerous insights about the threats that public and private sector organizations face and the cybersecurity strategies that can mitigate them.

During this session the various cybersecurity strategies are examined that have ultimately failed over the past 20 years, along with a few that have actually worked. It gave a very good insight to executives and security and compliance professionals to understand how cloud computing is a game changer for them.

By the end of the session, some examples were shown for how to effectively measure the effectiveness of organizations cybersecurity strategy, the ingredients for a successful cybersecurity strategy, cybersecurity investment roadmaps and efficacy, and how you can help employ and protect your organizations and yourself.

Contents – Part II

Industry

Contents – Part I

Smart Computing

Cyber Security

A Comprehensive Study on Cyber Legislation in G20 Countries

Nisarg Mehta[1]([✉]) [iD], Priyansh Sanghavi[1] [iD], Manish Paliwal[1] [iD], and Madhu Shukla[2]

[1] School of Technology, Pandit Deendayal Energy University, Gandhinagar,
Gujarat 382007, India
nisarg.mmtcs21@sot.pdpu.ac.in, nisargmehta.nm@gmail.com
[2] Marwadi University, Rajkot, Gujarat 360003, India

Abstract. Cyberlaw, often known as Internet law, is a branch of the judicial framework concerned with the legality of internet information technology. It governs the digital transmission of information, shopping-portal applications, and information security. It is associated with justice informatics and electronic components like systems, software, and hardware. This article covers various topics, including the existence and appropriateness of the open Internet, free expression, and online privacy. The standards contribute to a significant decrease in the number of people engaging in asymmetric warfare and also help to restrict their participation by safeguarding illegal access to information, free speech connected to Internet usage, personal space, information exchange, e-mail domains, intangible assets, machinery, and web services, which include data storage devices. As internet traffic increases, so does the number of legal challenges worldwide. Because internet laws differ nationwide, reprisal can range from bedframes to jail, and police agencies can be hard to implement. Cyberlaw protects persons who utilize the Internet or operate an online company. Internet users need to grasp their country's local community and cyber legislation to identify whether behaviors are allowed or prohibited on the network. They can also keep us from engaging in illegal activities.

Keywords: Cyber security · Cyber law · Cyber crime · Privacy

1 Introduction

A computer is a configurable machine that normally stores and processes information according to the user's instructions. In most cases, the user provides these instructions. The proliferation of the Internet and other virtual worlds has made it simpler and more convenient than ever before to transmit data and information across a variety of networks. The internet is used for a broad variety of applications, including as a platform for commerce and financial transactions. Most people who use the internet have some prior computer experience, whether for personal or professional reasons. As a direct result of this, administrators are growing more concerned about vulnerabilities that have not been fixed. Because of this, a new phenomenon known as "Cyber Crimes" has surfaced. As a result, computer crimes, also known as cybercrimes, are defined as offenses

S. Rajagopal et al. (Eds.): ASCIS 2022, CCIS 1760, pp. 3–23, 2022.
https://doi.org/10.1007/978-3-031-23095-0_1

perpetrated with the assistance of a computer system or network and often occur in cyberspace, most notably on the Internet. In their most basic definition, cyberattacks are conducted via the use of the communications or technical infrastructure of the internet. A cybercriminal may exploit a device to access private information belonging to a user, sensitive information belonging to the firm, or secret government papers, or they may do so to delete the information. The illegal sale of private information or data via the internet is an example of cybercrime. Criminals that participate in such actions are sometimes referred to as "hackers," which is a term that describes this sort of offender. As a consequence of this, cybercrime is also often referred to as e-crime, computer-related crime, high-tech crime, online fraud, and new-age crime [45].

Cybercrime has become such a problem today that it is wreaking havoc on people, corporations, and even the government. Many different legal requirements have previously been enacted to address internet-related crimes. The term "Cyber Law" has been disseminated throughout the whole globe ever to encompass that part of the legal system that deals with matters about cyberspace and law, such as concerns with online privacy and safety, among other topics. To put this another way, cyber law might be described as the laws and regulations that regulate cyberspace cyberattacks, digital and electronic signatures, data security and privacy, and other concerns that are addressed by cyber law [45].

2   Literature Review

2.1   Argentina

The E-Signature Law, the Digital Argentina Law, the Telecommunication Law, and the Personal Data Protection Legislation are some of the laws that make up Argentina's cybersecurity system. Other laws include the Digital Argentina Law and the Telecommunication Law, the Broadband Service Law, and the Cyber-warfare Law. It is vital to note that both civilian and military institutions in Argentina are involved in the cybersecurity field. The Defense Ministry, as well as the National Cyber Security Directorate are the two agencies competing in this field. In addition, a National Cyber Security Working Group has been created (ICIC Cert). However, the cyber security sector has no publicly published national standards or certification systems. The argument suggests that Latin American nations that have higher levels of democracy may have less stringent cybersecurity regulations [39] (Table 1).

Table 1. Categorization of laws in Argentina

Law Type	Act Name	Introduce year	Laws Pros [23][24][25]	Laws Cons [23] [24] [25]	Global Ranking[25]
Electronic Transaction Laws	Civil and Commercial Code of the Nation (Spanish)	2014	They have significant growth potential.	They have a less efficient Organizational Measurement.	91
Data Security and Privacy Regulations	Constitution of the Argentine Nation, Law No. 24,430, Enacted on December 15, 1994 (Spanish)	1994		Their Technical Measurement is ineffective.	
	Law 25,326 on the Protection of Personal Data (Spanish)			Cooperative Measures Are Weaker.	
	Decree 1558/2001 (Spanish)			They have a shaky judicial system for punishing offenders.	
	Provision 60 – E/2016 (Spanish)				
	Resolution 159/2018 - RESOL-2018-159-APN-AAIP (Spanish)				
	Agreement 108 approved by Law No. 27,483 (Spanish)				
Computer crime Statutes	Criminal Code of the Argentine Nation – Habeas Data Law 25326, year 2000 (Spanish)	2000			
	Law 26.388 (2008) (Spanish))				
	Law 27411, Agreement on Cybercrime (Spanish)				
	Criminal Code of the Argentine Nation (Spanish)				
	Law 26,388 of Law of Computer Crimes (Spanish)				

2.2 Australia

The computer crime Amendment Act Bill 2011 (the Bill) was adopted by the Australian Parliament. The Bill alters the Telecommunication (Unauthorized access and Accessibility) Act 1979 (the TIA Legislation), the Criminal Act 1995 (the Crimes Act), the Joint Assistance in Criminal Affairs Ordinance (the MA Act), as well as the Telecommunication Act 1997 (the Communications Act) to guarantee compliance with the European commission Convention on Cyber-crime [3]. The Convention urges governments to work together to stop cybercrime by making it a requirement that countries ban four types of online crimes.

– Anomaly Criminal eavesdropping, information leakage, system interference, and device abuse are all examples of offences that jeopardize the availability, integrity, and confidentiality of computer information and services other offences include interception of data without authorization.
– Examples of offences that include the use of computers include forgery and fraud.
– Offences containing material, such as child pornography and.
– Violating copyrights and committing comparable rights violations (Table 2).

Table 2. Categorization of laws in Australia

Law Type	Act Name	Introduce year	Laws Pros [23] [24] [25]	Laws Cons [23] [24] [25]	Global Ranking[25]
Electronic Transaction Laws	Electronic Transactions Act 1999, amended in 2011[19]	1999	To pursue violators, they adopt harsh legal procedures.	They have a less efficient Organizational Measurement.	12
Data Security and Privacy Regulations	Privacy Act 1988	1998	They have significant growth potential.	Their Technical Measurement is ineffective	
Computer crime Statutes	Criminal Code Act No. 12 of 1995 as amended in 2012[11]	1995	They use Cooperative Measures to combat criminals.		
	Cybercrime Legislation Amendment Act No.120/2012				

2.3 Brazil

On the ground, Brazilian law enforcement and military agencies are substantially investing in cyber-security. Despite this, there appears to be a mismatch between the sorts of threats that threaten Brazilian cyberspace and the style of security organization's reactions. Even though organized crime is one of the most serious dangers to Brazil's internet, the country's resources are disproportionately focused on military solutions better suited to the (very uncommon) situation of conventional conflict. Expanding day-to-day law enforcement skills to identify and respond to organized criminal organizations receives less attention. Brazil is adopting an imbalanced approach to cybersecurity due to a lack of a united government perspective on the problem and a lack of trustworthy data. Instead, a tiny group of powerful businesses and individuals are influencing the discussion in ways that will have a major impact on Brazil's cyber-security architecture in the future. The Unit for Combating Cybercrime (URCC) of the Federal Police is the primary law enforcement body in charge of preventing and responding to cybercrime. This responsibility falls under the umbrella of the Unit for Combating Cybercrime (URCC) [41, 48] (Table 3).

2.4 Canada

The federal government of Canada, based in the Parliament building in Ottawa, is responsible for making national laws, which are subsequently implemented across the country's 13 jurisdictions (ten provinces and three territories). The federal government of Canada, which the Criminal Code governs, is responsible for establishing (or repealing) new criminal laws. The provincial and territorial administrations are permitted to draught their laws, but these laws may only be enacted within their national borders. Provincial and territorial governments do not have the authority to enact new criminal laws. Still, they do have the authority to penalize those who violate provincial and territorial laws, such as by fining them or sending them to prisons [26].

In the latter half of 2014, the Protecting Canadians from Internet Crime Act was passed into law to keep the Canadian Criminal Code and the Canada Evidence Act up to date. Police chiefs from throughout Canada have come out in support of the measure,

Table 3. Categorization of laws in Brazil

Law Type	Act Name	Introduce year	Laws Pros [23] [24] [25]	Laws Cons [23] [24] [25]	Global Ranking[25]
Electronic Transaction Laws	Provisional Measure No. 2,200-2, of August 24, 2001, Establishes the Brazilian Public Key Infrastructure—ICP-Brazil and makes other provisions (Portuguese)[34]	2001	To pursue violators, they adopt harsh legal procedures.	They have a less efficient Organizational Measurement.	18
Data Security and Privacy Regulations	Protection of Personal Data Bill 2011	2014	They have significant growth potential.	Cooperative Measures Are Weaker.	
	Internet Act (Law No 12.965, April 23rd 2014). Articles 7 and 8			Their Technical Measurement is ineffective	
	General Data Privacy Law				
Computer crime Statutes	Penal Code Brazil	2008			
	Law No. 12,965, of April 23, 2014				
	Law 11,829/2008				
	Law No. 12,737, November 30th 2012				

Table 4. Categorization of laws in Canada

Law Type	Act Name	Introduce year	Laws Pros [23] [24] [25]	Laws Cons [23] [24] [25]	Global Ranking[25]
Electronic Transaction Laws	Personal Information Protection and Electronic Documents Act, S.C. 2000, c. 5[33]	2000	To pursue violators, they adopt harsh legal procedures.	Their Technical Measurement is ineffective.	8
Data Security and Privacy Regulations	Personal Information Protection and Electronic Documents Act	2000	They have effective organizational measures in place.	Cooperative Measures Are Weaker.	
Computer crime Statutes	Criminal Code of 1985[33]	1985	They have significant growth potential.		
	Evidence Act 2010[33]				

stating that it will assist in the fight against online bullying and non-consensual sexting involving children and that it's time t stop those who harass, threaten, and fear them. The Safeguarding Canadians from Online Crime Act did add new Crimes Act infractions for disbursing and transferring a sexual image of a person without their permission and for recording, storing, and spreading child pornography. It also went after cyber espionage and telecommunications signal theft, just like its predecessor, Bill C-30 [26, 43] (Table 4).

2.5 China

Cyber security was first considered at such a high level in President Hu Jintao's 2012 Work Report to the 18th CCP Congress. A strategy for China's cyber defense has not been made public. Despite this, it has implemented a variety of different data security procedures. The Chinese approach can be implemented above cyber security and incorporates the common aim of data security. Information security, defined by China, is "based on prior information systems and cybersecurity from unauthorized access, use, evaporation, damage, alteration, and ruination in store their integrity, secrecy, and availability." At the national level, a strategy paper would need to be released by President Xi Jinping or perhaps the Communist Party's Federal Congress. In contrast, policy papers are produced at the government level. To achieve this goal, the important announcements made by President Xi have been used as a roadmap to direct the construction of policies implemented at the ministry level. The advancement of the country's information security industry is governed by the 12th Five-Year Transformation Programme of the Information Governance Sector (2011–15), which was publicly released by the Ministry of Industry Technology. This plan establishes goals and targets for the industry and regulates its growth. On the other hand, the report is much more of an industrialization program than a comprehensive plan for protecting sensitive information [38] (Table 5).

Table 5. Categorization of laws in China

Law Type	Act Name	Introduce year	Laws Pros [23] [24] [25]	Laws Cons [23] [24] [25]	Global Ranking[25]
Electronic Transaction Laws	Electronic Signatures Law of the People's Republic of China of 2004[18]	2004	They have significant growth potential.	They have a less efficient Organizational Measurement.	33
Data Security and Privacy Regulations	The Decision of the Standing Committee of the National People's Congress on Strengthening the Network Information Protection, 2012[30]	2012	To pursue violators, they adopt harsh legal procedures.	Their Technical Measurement is ineffective.	
	The Decision of the Standing Committee of the National People's Congress on Strengthening the Network Information Protection, 2012[14]		Cooperative Measures Are Weaker.		
Computer crime Statutes	Criminal Law as amended	1997			

2.6 France

As France continues to expand its cyber capabilities, the ANSSI is increasing its ability to combat cyber threats. Furthermore, the cyber-security policy has emphasized crucial domains of action to achieve the strategic goals of the country, exhibiting a thorough awareness of the issues that have been raised. In addition, the Cyber Defensive Alliance outlines several steps that will increase France's capacity to react to cyber-attacks. To the goals of the national cyber strategy, these activities have been intended to be implemented with the finances that are now available. As a part of the agreement, financial assistance for academic institutions and small and medium-sized businesses will be provided to foster research and innovation in the business sphere. First and foremost, it's important that France can protect its most important resources and national goals, even though technology is changing quickly and there are many different ways to attack online [38, 47].

Because of its substantial economic, technical, and intellectual skills in the sphere of cyberspace, France is a leading actor on the global stage. The current institutionalization

Table 6. Categorization of laws in France

Law Type	Act Name	Introduce year	Laws Pros [23] [24] [25]	Laws Cons [23] [24] [25]	Global Ranking[25]]
Electronic Transaction Laws	Law No 2000-230 of March 13, 2000, adapts the law of the species to information technologies and relates to the electronic signature (French)[29]	2000	To pursue violators, they adopt harsh legal procedures.	They have a less efficient Organizational Measurement.	9
Data Security and Privacy Regulations	The General Data Protection Regulation (Regulation (EU) 2016/679) (GDPR)[35]	1978	They have significant growth potential.	Their Technical Measurement is ineffective.	
	Law relating to the protection of individuals against the processing of personal data		To tackle criminals, they adopt Cooperative Measures.		
	Law 78-17 of January 6, 1978, relating to data processing, files and modified freedoms (French)				
Computer crime Statutes	Law No. 2004-575 of June 21, 2004, for confidence in the digital economy (French)	2004			

process, in addition to supporting regulations and the Information Security Pact, has sped up the formation of French cyberspace security and cyber defense capabilities. This is the case even though political participation in the sector began at a very late stage [38, 47] (Table 6).

2.7 Germany

Cybersecurity. Among the laws addressed are data security and e-privacy rules, forms of intellectual property Laws, client confidentiality Laws, data security requirements, and legitimate constraints. Several German laws govern cyber security. It is widely acknowledged that German Security Act is the most significant legal foundation for cybersecurity [47].

Additionally, there are several essential unwritten IT security principles in Germany. The minimum Baseline for Information Technology Security (BSI), Basic Guidelines for Cybersecurity Evaluation-2012, established as ISO/IEC 15408, and the objective for control of information and associated technology (COBIT) are all contained in this document [47] (Table 7).

2.8 India

The Legislation of 2000, which was modeled after the General Assembly Model The International Law produced the Law on Electronic Transactions Commission Maastricht Treaty (UNCITRAL), is India's major computer crime and e-commerce statute. Originally, the Act was divided into 94 parts including 13 sections and a total of four schedules. The Act is applicable across the whole of India., as well as actions or breaches done by anybody, regardless of nationality, beyond India's borders. The Act grants electronic records legal power and greatly simplifies the remote filing of documents with government agencies [27].

The Information Technology Act of 2000 has four main objectives:

Table 7. Categorization of laws in Germany

Law Type	Act Name	Introduce year	Laws Pros [23] [24] [25]	Laws Cons [23] [24] [25]	Global Ranking[25]
Electronic Transaction Laws	Law to adapt the formal requirements of private law to modern legal transactions (Federal Law Gazette I 2001 p. 1542)	2001	They use harsh legal measures to prosecute offenders.	They have a less efficient Organizational Measurement.	13
Data Security and Privacy Regulations	The General Data Protection Regulation (Regulation (EU) 2016/679) (GDPR)[35]	2016	They took Technical Measurement.	Cooperative Measures Are Weaker.	
	Federal Data Protection Act[20]				
Computer crime Statutes	Network Enforcement Act, 2017[4]	2015			
	German Criminal Code 1986, as espect in 2015 para.202				

- To guarantee legal recognition of digital records.
- To enable the official status of digital signatures. Traditional signatures are vulnerable to fabrication and alteration, making them unfit for use in online transactions and contracts. Digital signatures provide the unique and powerful protection those online transactions demand.
- To give electronic administration legal status. The phrase e-governance refers to a technology-driven government that uses technology to offer services, information, and education more efficiently.
- To impose penalties for cybercrime. The Indian Penal Code of 1860 was insufficient to address the rising threat of cybercrime. These offences were both unique and high-tech, necessitating a new category under the Information Technology Act of 2000 [27] (Table 8).

Table 8. Categorization of laws in India

Law Type	Act Name	Introduce year	Laws Pros [23] [24] [25]	Laws Cons [23] [24] [25]	Global Ranking[25]
Electronic Transaction Laws	Information Technology Act 2000[27]	2000	To pursue violators, they adopt harsh legal procedures.	They have a less efficient Organizational Measurement.	10
Data Security and Privacy Regulations	Bill – Personal Data Protection, 2019[36]	2000	They have significant growth potential.	Their Technical Measurement is ineffective.	
	Information Technology Act 2000[27]		To tackle criminals, they adopt Cooperative Measures.		
Computer crime Statutes	The Information Telecommunication Act of 2000, amended in 2008 – ITA	2000			

2.9 Indonesia

When it comes to ensuring the safety of its computer networks, Indonesia already has a framework and policy in place, both of which are carried out by various government agencies as well as by the general population. The Cabinet of Communication and Information Technology is responsible for cyber security policy (MCI). Three government entities in Indonesia are involved in the field of cyber security. These organizations include the Information Security Coordinating Team and the Director of Indonesia Security Operations Team on Internet Connections and Information Security (ID-SIRTII) [50].

In April 2010, the Internet Security Interoperability Team was created to co-ordinate computer security, with a focus on technology and information competency and practices. The Director of Information Security is important for policy creation and implementation, education, surveillance, evaluation, and reporting in the area of data security governance. Depending on the Ministry of Communications and Informatics Regulatory Oversight No. 8 of 2012, the government established ID-SIRTII to oversee the security of internet infrastructure [50] (Table 9).

Table 9. Categorization of laws in Indonesia

Law Type	Act Name	Introduce year	Laws Pros [23] [24] [25]	Laws Cons [23] [24] [25]	Global Ranking[25]
Electronic Transaction Laws	Law of the Republic of Indonesia Number 11 of 2008 Concerning Electronic Information and Transactions[44]	2008	To tackle criminals, they adopt Cooperative Measures.	They have a less efficient Organizational Measurement.	24
Data Security and Privacy Regulations	Systems Regulation 2016[44]	2016	They have significant growth potential.	Their Technical Measurement is ineffective.	
Computer crime Statutes	Law of the Republic of Indonesia Number 11 of 2008 Concerning Electronic Information and Transactions[44]	2008		They have a shaky judicial system for punishing offenders.	

2.10 Italy

The introduction of the internet in the middle of the 1990s led to an increase in the Italian police's understanding of cybercrime, which in turn caused them to grow concerned about issues related to cyber security. A unit for telecommunications was founded in 1996, and two years later, in 1998, the Postal and Communications Police Service came into being. A task force was established by the Financial and Border Police (Guardia di Finanza) in the year 2001 [40].

In 2010, the House National Council on Intelligence and Security Service of the Italian government issued the first formal public assessment of Italy's national cyber security problems. The Italian government commissioned this study. The concept of asymmetric cyber threats was put up in the paper, which also described cyberspacc as the "new battlefield" of the 21st century and the "scenario of geopolitical conflict." The report focused on four primary concerns: Cybercrime, cyberterrorism, cyberespionage, and cyber-warfare are all examples of cybercrime. According to the study's findings, Cyber security is a strategic problem and a threat to public safety [38]. One of Italy's strengths in terms of its cyber security policy is the presence of police systems specifically designed to fight cybercrime. The enforcement of copyright laws, child pornography on the internet, computer hacking, malware, and fraudulent E-commerce transactions, are the primary areas of concentration for the activities of the Postal and Communications Police Service. Fraud committed through digital means is the primary target of the Guardia di Finanza task force. The Carabinieri has both a cybercrime special investigative branch and a piece of information and communications technology security section [38] (Table 10).

Table 10. Categorization of laws in Italy

Law Type	Act Name	Introduce year	Laws Pros [23] [24] [25]	Laws Cons [23] [24] [25]	Global Ranking[25]
Electronic Trans-action Laws	DLegislative Decree 7 March 2005, n. 82 Digital Administration Code - updated to the expected decree of 13 December 2017, nr. 217 (Italian)	2005	To pursue violators, they adopt harsh legal procedures.	Their Technical Measurement is ineffective.	20
Data Security and Privacy Regulations	Data Protection Code Decree No. 196/2003	2003	They have significant growth potential.	Cooperative Measures Are Weaker.	
	The General Data Protection Regulation (Regulation (EU) 2016/679) (GDPR)[35]		They have effective organizational measures in place.		
	Legislative Decree 30 June 2003, n. 196 - Code regarding the protection of personal data (Italian)				
Computer crime Statutes	Penal Code. (Italian)[10]	2009			

2.11 Japan

Japan ranked fourth among the countries of the Asia Pacific territory relative to the number of people who use the internet in January 2021, with over 117 million them. Security concerns have emerged as one of Japan's most pressing internal challenges as a direct result of the growing significance of digitalization to the country's economy and the people's day-to-day lives. In 1973, the Tokyo District Court was the venue for the hearing of Japan's first case involving a criminal offense employing a computer. This wasn't a criminal case; rather, it was a civil dispute between two parties. However, the theft of data was the primary worry in this instance. Nikkei Shimbun, which is a well-known news organization in Japan, and McGraw-Hill at the time established Nikkei McGraw-Hill. The plaintiff was awarded 2,039,420 Japanese Yen in damages, and the defendant was ordered by the Tokyo District Court to pay a portion of the plaintiff's expenditures and damages [38].

It is now criminal in Japan under the Cybersecurity Act to access the system without authorization. This Law aims to avoid computer-related crimes committed via telecommunication links and to maintain telecommunications network order, as realized through physical access features, by restricting acts of unauthorized computer access and specifying penalties for that acts, as well as additional Encourage regional public safety commissioners to implement preventative steps to reduce the likelihood of similar incidents happening in the future and hence making contributions to the better and healthier development of the nation. This Act was passed to accomplish these goals [38] (Table 11).

Table 11. Categorization of laws in Japan

Law Type	Act Name	Introduce year	Laws Pros [23] [24] [25]	Laws Cons [23] [24] [25]	Global Ranking[25]
Electronic Transaction Laws	Law Concerning Electronic Signatures and Certification Services, Law No. 102 of 2000	2000	To pursue violators, they adopt harsh legal procedures	They have a less effective Organizational Measure.	7
Data Security and Privacy Regulations	Act on the Protection of Personal Information[2]	2003	They have significant growth potential.		
Computer crime Statutes	Unauthorized Computer Access Law, 2013	1999	To tackle criminals, they adopt Cooperative Measures.		
	Penal Code		They took Technical Measurement.		

2.12 South Korea

The incidence of cyber-attacks has risen, and the society of the Republic of Korea is now susceptible to the threats posed by the Democratic People's Republic of Korea. This is because computer networks and information systems play such a significant role in the day-to-day lives of people. Legislation and national strategies that are up to par are required to respond effectively to internal and external cyber-attacks. As part of the Republic of Korea's ongoing efforts to protect the nation, several laws and regulations have been enacted as a direct result of these efforts [42] (Table 12).

Table 12. Categorization of laws in South Korea

Law Type	Act Name	Introduce year	Laws Pros [23] [24] [25]	Laws Cons [23] [24] [25]	Global Ranking[25]
Electronic Transaction Laws	Digital Signature Act No. 5792/1999[28]	1999	To pursue violators, they adopt harsh legal procedures.	They have a less effective Organizational Measure.	4
Data Security and Privacy Regulations	Personal Information Protection Act	2020	They have significant growth potential.		
Computer crime Statutes	Act on the protection of information and communication Infrastructure	2016	To tackle criminals, they adopt Cooperative Measures.		
	Act on Promotion of Information and Communications Network Utilization and Information Protection		They took Technical Measurement.		

In 2002, the Republic of Korea's government passed the Critical Information Infrastructure Protection Act, emphasizing the need of protection as a matter of national security. Critical data infrastructure must be protected from cyberattacks. This law has been in effect ever since. To defend CII from cyberattacks, the Act mandated the creation of a national agency and imposed rules on CII designation, vulnerability assessment and protection measures, cyber incident response, and punishments [42].

In addition, to enhance the nation's overall cyber security, Korean policy-makers and legislators have recently held several hearings, and they have also passed the Cyber Security Industry Enhancement Act. This Act gives Central and local administrations in Korea, as well as municipalities, the ability that devise and carry out policies that promote cyber security, as well as prepare measures to allocate budgets to support those policies [42].

Members of the National Assembly proposed a measure that would solely focus on protecting personal information. The proposal was approved on March 29, 2011, and the Act has been in effect since September 30, 2011. The Act addresses the obligations that must be fulfilled by managers of personal information and relevant ministers of the government [42].

2.13 Mexico

The Mexican Working Group on Combating Cybercrime (CERT-MX) and the Electronic Digital Signature act were both made. Also, Cybersecurity Standards were made, but you don't have to use any of the official certification methods.

This could be because the government doesn't want to "over-regulate" the cybersecurity business. The National Information Security Strategy of Mexico was made by a committee on special information security. This plan was put in place by Mexico (CESI). In official papers in Mexico, the word "cybersecurity" appears sparingly, although the term "information security" appears often. The police force in Mexico is in charge of the cybersecurity of the country. Mexico's role in international cooperation is limited to its commitment to the United Nations and the Organization of American States' fight against cyber-terrorism and cyber-crime [39] (Table 13).

2.14 Russia

Most of Russia's laws about data protection and privacy were passed in 2005 and 2006, so this area of the country's legal code is growing quickly. The Russian Federal Data Protection Law (No. 152-FZ), which went into effect on July 27, 2006, serves as the cornerstone of Russian privacy laws, and data controllers are obligated to adopt "all essential organizational and technological measures needed for securing personal data from unauthorized or accidental access." The Federal Service for the Supervision of Communication, Information and Technology, and Mainstream Media makes sure that everyone is following the rules [42].

Individuals are generally expected to provide their consent before their data is processed; however, this regulation does not apply in cases where the customer is a signatory to an agreement that requires the processing of their personal Federal Service on Telecommunications, which is responsible for data protection and privacy, has declared in the past that appropriate protection only exists among foreign jurisdictions where the Agreement for the Protection of Individuals Regarding Automatic Processing of Private

Table 13. Categorization of laws in Mexico

Law Type	Act Name	Introduce year	Laws Pros [23] [24] [25]	Laws Cons [23] [24] [25]	Global Ranking[25]
Electronic Transaction Laws	Advanced Electronic Signature Law (Spanish)[5]	2012	They have significant growth potential.	They have a less efficient Organizational Measurement.	52
Data Security and Privacy Regulations	General Law on the Protection of Personal Data held by obligated subjects (Spanish)	2010		Their Technical Measurement is ineffective.	
	Federal Law on the Protection of Personal Data Held by Private Parties 2010 (Spanish)			Cooperative Measures Are Weaker.	
	Agreement for the Protection of Persons concerning the Automated Processing of Personal Data and Additional Protocol to the Agreement for the Protection of Persons concerning the Automated Processing of Personal Data, Control Authorities and Transborder Data Flows (Promulgatery Decree) (Spanish)			They have a shaky judicial system for punishing offenders.	
	General Guidelines for the Protection of Personal Data for the Public Sector (Spanish) Regulation Federal Law on Protection of Personal Data Held by Private Parties (Spanish)				
	General Law of Transparency and Access to Public Information (Spanish)				
	Federal Law of Transparency and Access to Public Information (Spanish)				
Computer crime Statutes	Federal Penal Code (Spanish)	2020			

Information has been signed and ratified. However, three key exclusions enable private data to be sent to nations with a lower level of personal data protection or with no obligation at all. On September 1, 2015, a new clause referred to as "Article 18(5)" comes into force, imposing further restrictions on the transmission of data [38].

In Russia, direct marketing, data processing, and management of all data are subject to stringent regulations. Personal data must be adequately protected by applicable laws and the Federal Security Service is currently in the process of formulating required data protection regulations. The regulations mandate the use of encryption to protect any personally identifiable information that is sent outside of Russia, and it is expected that only Russian encrypted software and hardware would be used [49] (Table 14).

2.15 Saudi Arabia

The number of instances of cybercrime has been steadily increasing all over the world. As a direct consequence of this, ensuring cyber security is essential. It is critical to have adequate technological procedures for cyber-security in place. Nevertheless, the

Table 14. Categorization of laws in Russia

Law Type	Act Name	Introduce year	Laws Pros [23] [24] [25]	Laws Cons [23] [24] [25]	Global Ranking[25]
Electronic Transaction Laws	Federal Law No. 476- on Electronic Signatures and protection of the rights of legal entities and individual entrepreneurs (Russian)	2019	To pursue violators, they adopt harsh legal procedures.	They have a less effective Organizational Measure.	5
Data Security and Privacy Regulations	Bill – Regarding Personal Data[21]	2006	They have significant growth potential.	Their Technical Measurement is ineffective.	
	Federal law No. 152-FZ of 27 July 2006 "On Personal Data" (with the latest amendments of 2 July 2021)		To tackle criminals, they adopt Cooperative Measures.		
Computer crime Statutes	Federal Law No. 187-FZ of 26 July 2017[31]	2006			
	Criminal Code of the Russian Federation (with the latest amendments of 1 July 2021), Chapter 28. Crimes in the Sphere of Computer Information				
	Federal Law No. 149-FZ of 27 July 2006 "On Information, Information Technologies, and Protection of Information" (with the latest amendments of 2 July 2021)				

establishment of a legislative structure that allows for cyber-security is also a crucial component. Every nation's governing body should enact basic criminal legislation to combat cybercrime to boost the level of trust and confidence that users have in cyberspace [37].

The Saudi Arabian Anti-Cyber Crime Law was finally approved in March 2007. (ACC). According to the ACCL, unauthorized access is defined as any person's deliberate computer access, internet sites, data management, and computer networks that are not permitted by the owner of such resources. This legislation provides both a definition of what it means to commit a crime online as well as the accompanying punishments for doing so. The Saudi ACCL has all of the essential qualities critical to safeguarding the network's integrity Despite this, there are still several areas in which the Saudi ACCL has room for improvement to become more successful [37] (Table 15).

Table 15. Categorization of Laws in Saudi Arabia

Law Type	Act Name	Introduce year	Laws Pros [23] [24] [25]	Laws Cons [23] [24] [25]	Global Ranking[25]
Electronic Transaction Laws	Electronic Transactions Law No. 18 of 2007	2007	To pursue violators, they adopt harsh legal procedures.	Their Technical Measurement is ineffective.	2
Data Security and Privacy Regulations	Personal Data Protection Law (PDPL)	2022	They have significant growth potential.		
Computer crime Statutes	Anti-Cybercrime Law 1428/2007[6]	2007	To tackle criminals, they adopt Cooperative Measures. They have effective organizational measures in place.		

2.16 South Africa

Particular cybercrime law has been enacted in South Africa, and it goes under the name of the Electronic Communications and Transaction Act [17], By Chapter 13 of this Act, the following behaviours are considered unlawful: The first clause of Section 86(1) makes it illegal to intercept or access information without authorization.

– Unauthorized willful interference with information that results in the information's change, ineffectiveness, or destruction is a violation of Section 86(2) of the Computer Fraud and Abuse Act.
– (Articles 86(3) and 86(4)): Avoiding security safeguards by any means, such.
– as advertising, spreading, or owning a gadget designed to do just that.
– An attack that results in a whole or partial denial of service is considered to violate Section 86(5).
– (Section 87): Theft, fraud, and counterfeiting that include the use of computers.
– Attempting any of the conduct listed above, as well as helping and abetting in any of the activities listed above, is a violation of Section 88 of the Criminal Code [17] (Table 16).

Table 16. Categorization of laws in South Africa

Law Type	Act Name	Introduce year	Laws Pros [23] [24] [25]	Laws Cons [23] [24] [25]	Global Ranking[25]
Electronic Transaction Laws	Electronic Communications and Transactions Act, updated in 2010[15]	2010	They have significant growth potential.	They have a less efficient Organizational Measurement.	59
Data Security and Privacy Regulations	Protection of Personal Information Act 4 of 2013	2013		Their Technical Measurement is ineffective.	
Computer crime Statutes	Electronic Transactions and Communications Act 2002[17]	2002		Cooperative Measures Are Weaker. They have a shaky judicial system for punishing offenders.	

2.17 Turkey

In October 2010, the Information and Communication Technologies Authority advised providers of telecommunications services to conform with the standards established by ISO 27001. In July 2014, the regulatory body established a new, stricter criterion for determining compliance with ISO 27001. (ICTA, 2014). The Telecommunications and Computer Security in the Communications Sector Act specifies the requirements for security countermeasures and information system attributes, as well as the external and internal audit mechanisms that must be implemented by operators [46].

The Banking Regulation and Supervision Agency have been responsible for the creation of several pieces of financial legislation. In January 2008, the BSRA published a legal announcement about the management of bank information security. The announcement includes a variety of measures, including Management of information security risks, management responsibility, internal audit, outsourcing regulations, function separation, and other issues (BRSA, 2007), (BRSA, 2010) [46]. Just one more piece of law lays forth the standards for independent external auditors to follow while conducting assessments of banks' information systems (Table 17).

Table 17. Categorization of laws in Turkey

Law Type	Act Name	Introduce year	Laws Pros [23] [24] [25]	Laws Cons [23] [24] [25]	Global Ranking[25]]
Electronic Transaction Laws	Law 5070/2004 Electronic signature	2004	To pursue violators, they adopt harsh legal procedures.	They have a less efficient Organizational Measurement.	11
Data Security and Privacy Regulations	Law on the Protection of Personal Data No. 6698, 2016[1]	2016	They have significant growth potential.		
Computer crime Statutes	Turkish Criminal Law	2004	To tackle criminals, they adopt Cooperative Measures. They took Technical Measurement.		

In February 2014, the Electronic Communications Law went through a round of revisions to reflect decisions taken by the cabinet in October 2012. (Turkish Cabinet, 2014) As a direct effect of these many adjustments:

- ECL was tasked with putting together the Cyber Resilience Council from the ground up. The leader of the Cyber Defense Commission is the Minister of Transport, Maritime Affairs, and the Cyber Security Interim president. For example, one task that fell under the council's purview was to provide final approval to a list of important infrastructure.
- An explanation of the Transportation Ministry, Communications Ministry and Maritime Affairs' cyber security responsibilities were provided. Identifying vital infrastructures, as well as their owners and the locations of such infrastructures, was one of the ministry's objectives.

2.18 United Kingdom

In the year 2000, the Electronic Communications Act was passed into law by the legislature of the United Kingdom. Encryption, encrypted communication services, and electronic signatures are some of the growing trends that were targeted by the act, which was passed to help with the monitoring and supervision of new trends in the eCommerce industry [8].

To ensure the legitimacy of electronic signatures and to regulate cryptographic services within the United Kingdom, a law was required to be developed and passed into law. The Electronic Communications Act of the United Kingdom is broken up into three distinct sections, each of which provides regulations and protections about a different facet of the subject matter that is detailed further below.

The First Section: Cryptographic Service Providers. E-commerce and the convenience of data storage are covered in Part 2. (Which is inclusive of eSignatures). The third section will include supplementary and other items (Table 18).

Table 18. Categorization of laws in United Kingdom

Law Type	Act Name	Introduce year	Laws Pros [23] [24] [25]	Laws Cons [23] [24] [25]	Global Ranking[25]
Electronic Transaction Laws	Electronic Communications Act 2000[16]	2000	To pursue violators, they adopt harsh legal procedures.	Their Technical Measurement is somewhere ineffective.	2
Data Security and Privacy Regulations	Data Protection Act 1998[12]	1998	They have significant growth potential.		
	Data Protection Act 2018[13]		To tackle criminals, they adopt Cooperative Measures.		
Computer crime Statutes	The Computer Misuse Act of 1990, as amended[9]	1990	They have effective organizational measures in place.		

Laws such as the United Kingdom Electronic Communications Act (2000) and the Electronic Signatures Ordinance of 2002 encourage and support robust e-Commerce activity for businesses while also improving the security and legitimacy of these forms of digital payments for customers [8].

2.19 United State of America

The United States of America was the world's first nation to pass legislation specifically addressing data privacy, which was known as "The Privacy Act of 1974." Information from a monitoring system can't be released without the explicit agreement of the individual in question, according to the Privacy Act. Unless the disclosure falls under one of twelve statutes about the subject material of the record. The relevance of revising laws governing cyber security is closely tied to digital change, cybercrime, and the investigation of cyber forensics. An integrated digital cyber legal system is required for a movement toward tech-centric smart cities and cyber-confident citizenship. Without such a system, the process of establishing the digital transformation and environment may become more disjointed. "Technology removes the need for, and indeed the ability to focus on specific, localized activity." This results in a new 2 The network is a type of social organization that is arranged in a physical domain. "Physical constraints, proximity, patterns, and scale are all important characteristics of verifiable wrongdoing. "Communication technologies liberate us from the constraints of the empirical world; we can communicate with anyone, from anywhere, in real-time." Technology removes the need for, and It is not required that the victim and the perpetrator be located near one another. "Because cybercrime is an unbounded crime, the victim and the perpetrator can be in different cities" [32]. "Cybercrime is a crime with no physical boundaries." (Table 19).

Table 19. Categorization of laws in United State

Law Type	Act Name	Introduce year	Laws Pros [23] [24] [25]	Laws Cons [23] [24] [25]	Global Ranking[25]
Electronic Transaction Laws	EElectronic Signatures in Global and National Commerce Act (E-SIGN), 15 U.S.C. 7001-7003	1996	To pursue violators, they adopt harsh legal procedures.		1
Data Security and Privacy Regulations	Privacy Act of 1974[12]	1974	They have significant growth potential.		
	Federal Trade Commission Act 15[22]		To tackle criminals, they adopt Cooperative Measures.		
Computer crime Statutes	Computer Fraud and Abuse Act 1986[7]	1986	They have effective organizational measures in place.		
	Title 18 – Crimes and Criminal Procedure		They took Technical Measurement.		

2.20   European Union

The Network and Information Security Agenda in 2001, the very first e-Privacy Guideline in 2002, the setup of ENISA in 2004, the Critical Information Infrastructure Information exchange in 2009, the Digital Ideology for Europe in 2010, and the EU Cybersecurity Strategy in 2013. All of these steps were taken by the European Commission. However, to what extent did it exert its influence? We have raised awareness between many elected figures, industry Chief executives, and the Computer Emergency Responders team in each of our 28 member countries. The majority of member states have already developed comprehensive national cybersecurity strategies. However, there is no comprehensive European Union policy document for network and data security. This system would need to include full event reporting (similar to what is done in the telecoms sector), as well as trustworthy communication about risks and attacks. Under NIS policy, which is designed to address these issues and is now the subject of negotiations between the European Council and the Parliament, which is currently under construction. The fact that cyber-security is widely regarded as a component of national security, and consequently comes within the purview of national sovereignty, continues to be a barrier to progress.

As a consequence of this, there is still a significant distance to go before Europe will have cyberspace that is both open and safe (Table 20).

Table 20. Categorization of laws in European Union

Law Type	Act Name	Introduce year	Laws Pros [23] [24] [25]	Laws Cons [23] [24] [25]	Global Ranking[25]
Electronic Transaction Laws	on electronic identification and trust services for electronic transactions in the internal market	2014	To pursue violators, they adopt harsh legal procedures.	They have a less efficient Organizational Measurement.	-
Data Security and Privacy Regulations	General Data Protection Regulation Act[35]	2016	They have significant growth potential.		
Computer crime Statutes	EU Cybersecurity Act	2019	To tackle criminals, they adopt Cooperative Measures. They took Technical Measurement.		

3 Conclusions

In this paper, We have analyzed the various laws of the G20 countries. We have identified their associated pros and cons and briefly summarized them. The article also presents a comparative study between them and suggests how the individual G20 country makes its decision by applying associated laws for a particular issue.

References

1. About legislation preparation procedures and principles regulation (2004). https://www.mev zuat.gov.tr
2. Act on the protection of personal information act no. 57 of (2003) (2003). https://www.cas. go.jp/jp/seisaku/hourei/data/APPI.pdf
3. An act to implement the council of Europe convention on cybercrime, and for other purposes (2001). http://www.comlaw.gov.au/. https://rm.coe.int/1680081561
4. Act to improve enforcement of the law in social networks (network enforcement act), 12 July 2017. https://www.bmj.de/SharedDocs
5. Advanced electronic signature law (2012). https://www.diputados.gob.mx/LeyesBiblio
6. Anti-cyber crime law (2007). https://wipolex-res.wipo.int/edocs/lexdocs/laws
7. Computer fraud and abuse act (2021). http://cio.doe.gov/Documents/CFA.HTM
8. Computer misuse act (1990). https://www.cps.gov.uk/legal-guidance/computer-misuseact
9. Computer misuse act 1990 (1998). https://www.legislation.gov.uk/ukpga/1990/18/contents
10. Crimes against public faith. https://www.brocardi.it/codice-penale/librosecondo/titolo-vii/
11. Criminal code act 1995 (1995). https://www.legislation.gov.au/Details/C2017C00235
12. Data protection act 1998 (1998). https://www.legislation.gov.uk/ukpga/1998/29/contents
13. Data protection act 2018 (2018). https://www.legislation.gov.uk/ukpga/2018/12/contents
14. Decision of the national people's congress on strengthening the network information protection, 28 December 2012. http://www.gov.cn/jrzg
15. e-government services (2001). https://www.eservices.gov.za/

16. Electronic communications act 2000 (2000). https://www.legislation.gov.uk/ukpga/2000
17. Electronic communications and transactions act 25 of 2002 (2002). https://www.gov.za/doc uments/electronic-communications-and-transactionsact
18. Electronic signature law of the people's republic of China (2004). http://www.npc.gov.cn/zgrdw/englishnpc/Law
19. Electronic transactions act 1999 (1999). https://www.legislation.gov.au/Details
20. Federal data protection act (bdsg) (2016). https://www.gesetze-im-internet.de
21. Federal law of the Russian federation (2017). https://cis-legislation.com
22. Federal trade commission act, 16 March 1914. https://www.ftc.gov/legal-library
23. Global cybersecurity index 2015 (2015). https://www.itu.int/en/ITU-D/Cybersecurity
24. Global cybersecurity index 2017 (2017). https://www.itu.int/en/ITU-D/Cybersecurity
25. Global cybersecurity index 2020 (2020). https://www.itu.int/en/ITU-D/Cybersecurity
26. International cybercrime research centre, simon fraser university. https://www.sfu.ca/iccrc.html
27. It act, 2000 (2000). https://www.meity.gov.in/content/information-technology-act-2000
28. Korean law information center (2009). https://www.law.go.kr
29. Law no. 2000-230 (2000). https://www.legifrance.gouv.fr
30. National people's congress standing committee decision concerning strengthening network information protection (2012). https://chinacopyrightandmedia.wordpress.com/2012/12/28/national-peoples-congress-standing-committee-decision-concerning-strengthening-network-information-protection/
31. On the security of the critical information infrastructure of the russian federation (2017). http://pravo.gov.ru/proxy/ips
32. Overview of the privacy act: 2020 edition (2020). https://www.justice.gov/opcl
33. Prescribed information for the description of a designated project regulations (2012). https://laws-lois.justice.gc.ca/pdf/SOR-2012-148.pdf
34. Provisional measure no. 2.200-2, of august 24, 2001 (2001). http://www.planalto.gov.br
35. Regulation (EU) 2016/679 of the European parliament (2016). http://data.europa.eu/eli/reg
36. The personal data protection bill, 2019. http://164.100.47.4/BillsTexts/LSBillTexts
37. Alshammari, T.S., Singh, H.P.: Preparedness of Saudi Arabia to defend against cyber crimes: an assessment with reference to anti-cyber crime law and GCI index. Arch. Bus. Res. **6**(12), 131–146 (2018)
38. Baylon, C.: Challenges at the intersection of cyber security and space security: country and international institution perspectives (2014)
39. Bolgov, R.: The UN and cybersecurity policy of Latin American countries. In: 2020 Seventh International Conference on eDemocracy and eGovernment (ICEDEG), pp. 259–263. IEEE (2020)
40. De Zan, T., Giacomello, G., Martino, L.: Italy's cyber security architecture and critical infrastructure. In: Routledge Companion to Global Cyber-Security Strategy, pp. 121–131. Routledge (2021)
41. Diniz, G., Muggah, R., Glenny, M.: Deconstructing cyber security in Brazil. Strategic Paper (2014)
42. Eom, Y.J., Ivanov, A.M.: A comparative analysis on cyber security law between republic of Korea and Russian federation. Publ. Inform. **1**(13), 69–79 (2020)
43. Huey, L., Ferguson, L.: Cyberpolicing in Canada: A Scoping Review, vol. 54. Sociology Publications (2022). https://ir.lib.uwo.ca/sociologypub/54
44. ITE, U.: The law of the republic of indonesia number 11 of 2008 concerning elec- tronic information and transactions (2008)
45. Kapila, P.: Cyber crimes and cyber laws in India: an overview. In: Contemporary Issues and Challenges in the Society, pp. 36–48. New Era International Imprint (2020)

46. Karabacak, B., Yildirim, S.O., Baykal, N.: Regulatory approaches for cyber security of critical infrastructures: the case of Turkey. Comput. Law Secur. Rev. **32**(3), 526–539 (2016)
47. Kavyn, S., Bratsuk, I., Lytvynenko, A.: Regulatory and legal enforcement of cyber security in countries of the European Union. The experience of Germany and France. Teise˙ **121**, 135–147 (2021)
48. Kshetri, N.: Cybersecurity in Brazil. In: The Quest to Cyber Superiority, pp. 195–209. Springer, Cham (2016). https://doi.org/10.1007/978-3-319-40554-4_12
49. Kshetri, N.: Cybersecurity in Russia. In: The Quest to Cyber Superiority, pp. 211–221. Springer, Cham (2016). https://doi.org/10.1007/978-3-319-40554-4_13
50. Rizal, M., Yani, Y.: Cybersecurity policy and its implementation in Indonesia. J. ASEAN Stud. **4**(1), 61–78 (2016)

Image Encryption Algorithm Based on Timeout, Pixel Transposition and Modified Fisher-Yates Shuffling

Sangeeta Sharma, Ankush Kumar[✉], Nishant singh Hada, Gaurav Choudhary, and Syed Mohd Kashif

NIT, Hamirpur, India
sanjsharma29@gmail.com, ankushk8030@gmail.com

Abstract. Social media has become an inseparable part of our lives which has increased the sharing of images across multiple platforms. To enhance the security, various image encryption algorithms are being used but there are still are a few areas that can be improved. First, the data transmission mostly includes the original image which can be secretly read by a middle man. Second, the sender loses control over the image after sharing. Third, generally, encryption keys are of fixed length and long which take up more memory & efforts in sharing them securely. Fourth, the key-space of algorithms is fixed, thus allowing an upper limit estimation to any brute force attack. In our work, we propose a timeout based symmetric key column-row transposition encryption algorithm for images providing the same level of security irrespective of the key size. The timeout feature allows the sender to specify a time until when the image can be decrypted by anyone. With the algorithm, we present an Android Library that implements this algorithm and provides ability to prevent unauthorized sharing of images in apps. To support other platforms as well, we present NPM & Python Package. Various performance measures were used to test the efficacy of the algorithm.

Keywords: Image encryption · SHA256 hashing · Fisher-yates shuffling · Android library

1 Introduction

We are now in a fast-growing technical world where social media has become an insep-arable part of our lives. The use of social networking platforms like Facebook, What-sApp, Instagram has taken over major day-time of various people everywhere. With this increase, there has been a tremendous gain in the content being shared across countries, states & cities in the form of images, videos, news [1] etc. Numbers of users on these platforms are in the scale of billions making them one of the most required technology in the market but with that also, one of the most vulnerable technology.

We have heard of various data thefts & security breaches over these platforms. Datum is one of the most important entities in the online world. Having information about what a person likes and dislikes is helping online marketplaces and companies to show exactly

© The Author(s), under exclusive license to Springer Nature Switzerland AG 2022
S. Rajagopal et al. (Eds.): ASCIS 2022, CCIS 1760, pp. 24–43, 2022.
https://doi.org/10.1007/978-3-031-23095-0_2

what the user wants. Amongst the content shared across these platforms, images & videos are most exposed. In this phase, new techniques and teams are being appointed to prevent data thefts, maintain privacy and increase security not only on social media platforms but over online platforms as well. To enhance privacy & security over platform encryption of the content is a widely known and accepted method. Social networking platforms like WhatsApp, Signal etc. have adopted encryption where data is encrypted and stored. It is being used to prevent data from being read or modified secretly.

We have various well-known encryption algorithms available like Data Encryption Standard with 56 bits & 64 bits key and block size respectively [3]. Another well-known algorithm is RSA, having a key size greater than 1024 bits and a block size of minimum 512 bits [4]. We have Advanced Encryption Standard (AES) which is faster than them having varying key sizes of 128, 192 or 256 bits and block size of 128 bits [5]. In terms of security, all are vulnerable to Brute Forced attacks. Further, DES and RSA are also vulnerable to differential cryptanalysis attack and Oracle attack respectively [2]. We can use these encryption algorithms on content like images directly, but this might be unwise for some reasons. First, images have some unique properties like high redundancy and correlation between pixels. Second, the size of images is hugely based on their dimension and quality, which makes the application of traditional encryption methods slow [6]. When talking with respect to social media platforms, we generally need almost real-time encryption and decryption to provide a better user interface to the users. So, the algorithms that are good for a particular type of data may not be suitable for another type of data. The well-known encryption algorithms mentioned above such as DES and AES were originally created not for multimedia data but for textual data [7, 8].

Due to the myriad use & sharing of digital images, researchers have worked on various types of algorithms for image encryption. Chaos-based image encryption is a widely used technique where we shuffle the positions of pixels and their intensities to encrypt an image [9–11, 13, 15]. Bit-plane based image encryption algorithm based on bit-plane decomposition and application of permutation and substitution steps on them [12, 16, 17]. CNN and DNA sequence operations-based Algorithms [14]. Image Encryption based on Transposition and Shuffling, where pixels positions are shuffled & transposed [18]. Farhan Musanna et al. [19] proposed a fractional-order chaos-based image encryption where various slices of equal size of an image are created, which are then shuffled using the 3-D chaotic map created with the help of Fisher-Yates algorithm. Abdelrahman Karawia [20] proposed a similar work based on 3D chaotic economic map and Fisher-Yates shuffling.

Quist-Aphetsi Kester [18] proposed an image encryption algorithm based on the individual pixel shuffling, where the red, green, blue pixel arrays are separated from the image, converted to 1D array, concatenated as a column matrix in the order of blue, green and red pixels, transposed and reshaped again to 1D array to output an encrypted image. The algorithm does not take any key as input and makes it simple to encrypt & decrypt, but not secure. Quist-Aphetsi Kester [26] proposed another image encryption algorithm but involving a key. Vike Maylana Putrie et al. [24] proposed a combination of Hill & Transposition cipher for the encryption of digital color images which improves the security of image sharing by combining these different cipher algorithms. Shrija

Somaraj et al. [27] proposed another encryption technique in which, the original and key image pixels are broken down to their RGB components and a cipher image is generated by the XORing and shuffling of the individual RGB components. There are various other image encryption works [21–23, 25] but, there are still some problems that need to be addressed.

First, to enhance the security & user experience, images are encrypted on the server-side, which prevents third parties to view the image and also makes the transmission very fast. But, the transmission includes the original image which can be covertly read by a middle man. Second, after sharing an image, the sender has no control over th e shared image. The recipient can share & save it without acknowledging the sender. Third, encryption keys are sometime of fixed length, too long to store or hard to remember in the case of manual encryption & decryption. Fourth, the key space of algorithms is very large but still fixed, thus giving an upper limit to any brute force attack. Fifth, various complex algorithms with better security take a long time to encryption & decrypt. In this paper, we propose a fast symmetric-key transposition encryption algorithm for images. The algorithm starts with a string key of any size containing any character and duration to fix a time until when the image can be decrypted by any user. The transposition keys to shuffle the rows and columns are created & shuffled individually using our modified version of Fisher-Yates shuffling algorithm. Our algorithm has both column and row transposition making it more secure and hard to break. The transposition is divided into several rounds depending dynamically on the dimension of the image. Each round takes in a SHA256 hashed key, which is generated by hashing the key used in previous round. This idea makes the key space of our algorithm large and dynamic. To demonstrate the physical implementation of our image encryption algorithm in Android mobile devices, an image viewing library is created. This library allows sender to encrypt the image on his device and transmit that over to the recipient through server. This process is different from existing process because the original image is not sent to the server for decryption. The network has the access to only the encrypted image and the image can be decrypted only at the recipient's side having the symmetric key. To prevent unauthorized sharing and saving of the image, the image is directly decrypted in the library instead of creating a decrypted copy and displaying that. If user tries to share the image, then the encrypted image will be shared.

The rest of the paper is organised as follows: Sect. 2 explains the process of encryption and decryption. Section 3 gives a brief discussion on the Android library & other implementations available of our algorithm. Section 4 contains the efficacy results of our algorithm based on various paraments. Section 5 addresses the conclusions we drew from the proposed work.

2   Proposed Work

The proposed timeout based symmetric key encryption algorithm is based on Fisher – Yates shuffling and SHA256 hashing to provide a safe encryption between the sender and the recipient. The proposed algorithm safeguards the image transmission over the network, and a new image displaying library for Android prevents the unauthorized forwarding and saving of the image. The timeout feature of the algorithm enables the sender to make the image decryptable only for a limited amount of time. To shuffle the positions of pixels in columns and rows on an image, an array-based key is used. This array-based key is generated from an initial string key. This string key has no defined size, can contain any number of characters and can be user defined or randomly generated. Allowing user defined string keys in our algorithm allows users to easily remember or share them. In our encryption algorithm randomly generated keys and user defined key, both provide similar level of encryption for all string lengths. The string key is hashed using SHA256 hashing algorithm which changes the key size to 256 bits (i.e., string of 64 hexadecimal character) providing larger key space and security. The proposed system comprises of three phases, which are key generation, encryption, and decryption.

2.1 Key Generation

In this phase, to encrypt an image we follow several steps to generate the key (referred to as transposition key in the further sections) represented as an array for the transposition of pixels. We start with a user defined or randomly generated string of any length and a time *duration* in milliseconds until when the image should be decryptable. The full process to generate the final transposition keys is listed below.

2.1.1 Modification of String Key

Instead of using *string-key* & *duration* as two separate components, we concatenate them as shown in Algo. 1. We divide the current system time in milliseconds (which can be easily fetched using any date & time library) by the *duration*. After the division, we take the maximum integer smaller or equal to the quotient (analogous to using floor function provided in various languages) as our *new-duration*. We concatenate this new *duration* to the original *string-key* to form a *new-string-key*.

> *Algo. 1*
> *string-key = "abcd"*
> *duration = 10000*
> *current-system-time = fetched using date & time librarynew-*
> *duration = floor(current-system-time / duration)*
> *new-string-key = string-key concatenated with new-duration*

2.1.2 Fisher-Yates Permutation Array Generation

Initially, Fisher-Yates Permutation array contains values between $[0, N − 1]$. Where N is a number specifying the maximum side length of the image. For example, to encrypt an image with dimensions 123×456, N will be 456. To generalize the algorithm for a set of images, it we can take a larger N, which will allow encryption of all the images with maximum side dimensions less than N. After creating the array, we shuffle the values using Fisher-Yates shuffling algorithm as shown in Algo. 2.

Algo. 2

procedure generate-fisher-yates-array(n)fisher-
*   yates-array = [0 ... n]*
*   for i = range(n-1, 0, -1) do*
*   j = generate random integer between 0 & i*
*   exchange   fisher-yates-array[j]   and   fisher-yates-*
*   array[i]*
*   end for*
*   return fisher-yates-arrayend*
procedure

2.1.3 Initialization of Transposition Keys

For an image defined as a 3-dimensional matrix with dimensions $N \times M \times 3$, where N is the number of rows, M is the number of columns and 3 defines RGB components. Each cell of this matrix contains an intensity value ranging from 0–255. For example, in an image represented by 3D matrix with name *img*, in *img[0][0][0]*, *img[0][0]*[1] & *img[0][0]*[2] the intensity of red, green & blue part of the first pixel will be stored respectively.

To proceed with the encryption, we need two shuffled matrices with length N & M and values between [0, N − 1] & [0, M − 1] in them. The array with size N (*row-key*) will help in the row transposition and array with size M (*column-key*) will help in the column transposition. We pass N & M in initialize-array-key procedure as shown in Algo. 3 to generate these matrices. The procedure uses the Fisher-Yates permutation array generated in Algo. 2 to shuffle and create these arrays. The algorithm to shuffle is shown in Algo. 3.

After the generation of *row-key* and *column-key*, the further shuffling occurs explained in Sect. 2.1.4. This shuffling is happening on first $N' \leq N$ and first $M' \leq M$ values (1-indexed), where N' & M' are the largest integer divisible by 16 and smaller or equal to N & M respectively.

```
Algo. 3
    procedure initialize-array-key(N, M)
            fisher-yates-array = generate-fisher-yates-array(max(N, M))row-key =
            []
            column-key = []
            for i in fisher-yates-arrayif i
                    < N do
                                    append i to row-key
                    end if
                    if i < M do
                                    append i to column-key
                    end if
            end for
            return row-key, column-keyend
```

2.1.4 Shuffling of Transposition Keys

We further shuffle our transposition keys (*row-key* & *column-key*) based on *new-string-key*. We hash the *new-string-key* using SHA256.

```
Algo. 4
procedure shuffle-key(column-key, M')
        counter = 0
for i in range(0, M', 16) do
        sub-sha-key       = sha-key[counter:counter+16]
        appended with "1A0B95C4D37286EF"
                temp-set = [] temp-
                index = 0
                for j = range(i, i + 16) do
                        while  sub-sha-key[temp-index]  in  temp-setdo
                                        increment temp-index by 1end while
                        append sub-sha-key[temp-index] to temp-setindex  =
                        convert  sub-sha-key[temp-index]
                        from base 16 to base10
                                swap column-key[j] & column-key[i+index]
                end for
                counter = counter + 16if
                counter = 64 then
                        counter = 0
                        sha-key = sha256(sha-key)
                end if
        end forend procedure
```

Hashing algorithm (can be easily hashed using various libraries) and create a string *sha-key* with length 64 containing character [0-9a-f] i.e., hexadecimal characters. Each *sha-key* is further divided into four *sub-sha-key* each having length equal to 16. Each *sub-sha-key* shuffle 16 consecutive values in the transposition keys. For every 64 consecutive values in transposition keys, old *sha-key* is hashed to generate a new *sha-key*.

Example: SHA256 Hashing of new-string-key
new-string-key = *"firstname.lastname@email.co-nameofuser-mobilenumber16061309"*
sha-key =
"d4fc3139bb76580869c5b30183afc7d9af7361b8444a26cd82171297573a3b66"

To shuffle, we modified the existing Fisher-Yates algorithm as shown in Algo. 4. The modified version of Fisher-Yates Algorithm uses the decimal values (0–15) of each hexadecimal character present in *sub-sha-key*, instead of using a randomly generated number to shuffle the indices. With this modification, we had to keep in mind that no character should repeat in *sub-sha-key* and no character should miss. To enable that each *sub-sha-key* is appended with "1a0b95c4d37286ef" and duplicate characters are removed starting from left.

Example: Duplicate Removal

sha-key =
"d4fc3139bb76580869c5b30183afc7d9af7361b8444a26cd82171297573a3b66"
sub-sha-key1 = *"d4fc3139bb765808"*
          = *remove-duplicates("d4fc3139bb765808" + "1a0b95c4d37286ef")*
          = *"d4fc319b76580abe"*

Correspondingly, we will generate another *sub-sha-key* as well. The whole process to generate *sha-key*, *sub-sha-key* & shuffling transposition keys is shown in Algo. 4. The shuffle-key procedure is called for *column-key* as well as *row-key* to shuffle the arrays individually. There is no relation between the shuffling of these two arrays so, we can run them on different threads as well to increase the performance.

2.2 Encryption Process

In Sec. 2.1.3 we initialized two transposition keys in the form of arrays and in Sec. 2.1.4 we shuffled the values in them depending on the *new-string-key*. After the key generation, we have another phase in our method that is encryption. Our algorithm has both column and row transposition as shown in Algo. 5.

We use the two transposition keys named *row-key* & *column-key* with size N & M and values between [0, N − 1] & [0, M − 1] respectively. The keys shuffle rows & columns as a whole. We perform the column transposition before row transposition. This fact means that the input for row-transposition is a column-transposed-image. In column transposition, we extract all the columns and using the *column-key* we assign them their new positions. The similar process is done in row transposition, where we extract all the rows and assign them new position using the *row-key*.

Algo. 5
procedure encrypt-transposition(image, column-key, row-key, N,M)
       cols = 0
       rows = 0
       column-transposed-image = empty N x M x 3 arrayrow-transposed-image = empty N x M x 3 array
     for i in column-key do
            for j in range(0, N) do
  column-transposed-image[j][cols][0]=
  image[j][i][0]
  column-transposed-image[j][cols][1]=
  image[j][i][1]
  column-transposed-image[j][cols][2]=
  image[j][i][2]
      end for
      cols = cols + 1
  end for
for i in row-key do
      for j in range(0, M) do
           row-transposed-image[rows][j][0] = column-transposed-image[i][j][0]
           row-transposed-image[rows][j][1] = column-transposed-image[i][j][1]
            row-transposed-image[rows][j][2] = column- transposed-image[i][j][2]
         end for
        rows = rows + 1
     end for
     return row-transposed-image
  end procedure

2.3 Decryption Process

To decrypt the image, we follow the similar process as mentioned in the above sections to generate the transposition-keys. After generating the keys, we perform the inverse of encryption as shown in Algo. 6. This fact means column-transposition follows row-transposition and the transposition-keys instead of specifying the new position of rows& columns, specify their original position.

Example: *Steps in Encryption & Decryption of a 4x4 Image*
let row-key & column-key = *[3, 0, 1, 2]*

In encryption,

1. *Column 0 in original image* →—— *will become* ——→   *Column 3 in semi-encrypted image*
2. *Column 1 in original image* →—— *will become* ——→   *Column 0 in semi-encrypted image*
3. *Column 2 in original image* →—— *will become* ——→   *Column 1 in semi-encrypted image*
4. *Column 3 in original image* →—— *will become* ——→   *Column 2 in semi-encrypted image*
5. *Row 0 in semi-encrypted image*   →—— *will become* ——→   *Row 3 in encrypted image*
6. *Row 1 in semi-encrypted image*   →—— *will become* ——→   *Row 0 in encrypted image*
7. *Row 2 in semi-encrypted image*   →—— *will become* ——→   *Row 1 in encrypted image*
8. *Row 3 in semi-encrypted image*   →—— *will become* ——→   *Row 2 in encrypted image*

In decryption,

1. *Row 3 in encrypted image*   →—— *will become* ——→   *Row 0 in semi-decrypted image*
2. *Row 0 in encrypted image*   →—— *will become* ——→   *Row 1 in semi-decrypted image*
3. *Row 1 in encrypted image*   →—— *will become* ——→   *Row 2 in semi-decrypted image*
4. *Row 2 in encrypted image*   →—— *will become* ——→   *Row 3 in semi-decrypted image*
5. *Column 3 in semi-decrypted image*   →—— *will become* ——→   *Column 0 in decrypted image*
6. *Column 0 in semi-decrypted image*   →—— *will become* ——→   *Column 1 in decrypted image*
7. *Column 1 in semi-decrypted image*   →—— *will become* ——→   *Column 2 in decrypted image*
8. *Column 2 in semi-decrypted image*   →—— *will become* ——→   *Column 3 in decrypted image*

Looking at the above example, we can see that decryption is the inverse of encryption. The positions that were changed in encryption are reverted back in decryption thus returning the original image matrix.

```
Algo. 6
procedure decrypt-transposition(image, column-key, row-key, N,M)
        rows = 0
        cols = 0
        row-inverse-transposed-image = empty N x M x 3 array column-inverse-
        transposed-image = empty N x M x 3 array
    for i in row-key do
                for j in range(0, M) do
                row-inverse-transposed-image[i][j][0]=
                image[rows][j][0]
                row-inverse-transposed-image[i][j][1] =
                image[rows][j][1]
                row-inverse-transposed-image[i][j][2]=
                image[rows][j][2]
        end for
        rows = rows + 1
    end for
for i in column-key do
        for j in range(0, N) do
column-inverse-transposed-image[j][i][0]row-inverse-transposed-image [j][cols][0]
column-inverse-transposed-image[j][i][1]row-inverse-transposed-image [j][cols][1]
column-inverse-transposed-image[j][i][2]row-inverse-transposed-image [j][cols][2]
        end for
        cols = cols + 1
end for
return column-inverse-transposed-image
end procedure
```

3 Library and Packages

We created an Android library, NPM Package & Python Package to allow easy access of our algorithm to where it is needed the most and make use of its full potential. To provide easy integration in the mobile application code without breaking any old functionality, we created an Android library which contains EnpixView class that extends the ImageView class provided by Android. By extending ImageView class, we made sure that all the methods in that class exist with our additional methods to provide on-device encryption & decryption.

Most mobile applications use ImageView Class to display an image. In our library we added new methods which take *image matrix*, *string-key* and *duration* as inputs to return an encrypted image or display a decrypted image. Users can transmit the encrypted image returned from the encryption method to the recipient through a method (for example, using backend APIs). After the image is received, with the use of this library, the encrypted image is decrypted and displayed on the recipient's side. No temporary or intermediate decrypted image is saved or created anywhere locally. If the recipient wishes to share or save the image, s/he can do that but the image accessible will be encrypted. The reason for this is the same as mentioned above that the decrypted image doesn't exist as any physical entity, instead it's freshly decrypted & displayed every time to maintain the privacy and support the timeout feature. This library will improve the security and privacy of images drastically over the various social media platforms and other platforms on mobile devices.

NPM & Python Package provide encryption and decryption functions which return encrypted and decrypted image respectively. The Android library can be easily implemented using Gradle Dependency. The NPM Package can be installed using *npm install enpix* command and using *pip install enpix* command for Python.

4 Performance Analysis and Results

In this section, we analyse our algorithm implemented on a system with 1.8 GHz Dual-Core Intel Core i5 processor, 8 GB RAM and Python 3.8. To test the efficacy of our proposed algorithm, we used various performance measures. For the experiments below, we have used "*stringkey16061309*" as our symmetric *new-string-key* (*string-key* concatenated with *new-duration*). The images used in the experiments are of 512×512 dimension and are shown in Fig. 1. The images were used from *Public- Domain Test Images for Homework and Projects* present at https://homepages.cae.wisc.edu/~ece533/ images/.

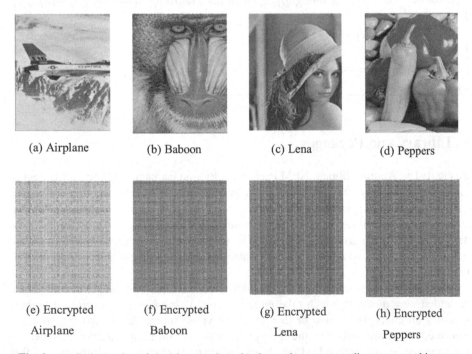

| (a) Airplane | (b) Baboon | (c) Lena | (d) Peppers |

| (e) Encrypted Airplane | (f) Encrypted Baboon | (g) Encrypted Lena | (h) Encrypted Peppers |

Fig. 1. (a–d) shows the original images & (e–h) shows the corresponding encrypted images

4.1 NPCR & UACI Test

These tests are performed to measure the differences between the original image and encrypted image. Net Pixel Change Ratio (NPCR) calculates the percentage of the number of pixels that differ in intensity values over the total number of pixels. Unified Average Change in Intensity (UACI) measures the percentage of the average difference in the intensities of the pixels to measure contrast in colour components. A higher value of NCPR & UCAI determines a better encryption algorithm [28–30].

NPCR & UCAI can be calculated using the following formulae:

$$NCPR(I1, I2) = \sum_{i,j} \frac{D(i,j)}{T} \times 100\%$$

$$UCAI(l1, l2) = \sum_{i,j} \frac{|I1(i,j) - I2(i,j)|}{F \cdot T} \times 100\%$$

$$D(i,j) = \begin{cases} 0, & if\ I1(i,j) = I2(i,j) \\ 1, & if\ I1(i,j) \neq I2(i,j) \end{cases}$$

In the formula above, I1 represents the original image, I2 represents the encrypted image, T represents the total pixels in the original image, F represents the maximum intensity pixel in the original image. The results are shown in Table 1. The Average NCPR & UCAI value achieved by our proposed algorithm over four images is found to be 99.0548 & 22.2374 respectively. These values show the high strength of encryption provided by the algorithm.

4.2 Mean Square Error (MSE)

Mean Square Error is used to calculate the error between the original and encrypted image i.e. quantify the difference in pixel intensities between images before and after encryption. MSE value is the square error between both the images. A higher value of MSE represents good shuffling of the pixels. We calculate MSE as shown in the formula below, where α represents the original image matrix and β represents the encrypted image. N and M are the number of rows and columns in the image respectively. The results are shown in Table 1.

$$MSE = \frac{1}{N \cdot M} \sum_{0}^{N-1} \sum_{0}^{M-1} \|\alpha(i,j) - \beta(i,j)\|^2$$

4.3 Root Mean Square Error (RMSE)

AS an addition to calculating mean square error between the original and encrypted image in Sec. 4.2, we calculated the Root Mean Square Error as well. Though MSE & RMSE share same units, RMSE can in some cases help readers to create clear distinctions based on its ability to penalize large errors more. The formula used to calculate RMSE is:

$$RMSE = \sqrt{\frac{1}{N \cdot M} \sum_{0}^{N-1} \sum_{0}^{M-1} \|\alpha(i,j) - \beta(i,j)\|^2}$$

In the RMSE formula, α, β, N & M represent the original image, encrypted image, number of rows and columns in the image respectively. The results are shown in Table 1.

4.4 Peak Signal to Noise Ratio (PSNR)

PSNR is the ratio between the power of the signal and the power of the noise. In this analysis, original image is referred as a signal and encrypted image is referred as noise. We calculated PSNR using the formula shown below:

$$PSNR = 20 \log_{10}(\frac{MAX_F}{\sqrt{MSE}})$$

where MAX is the maximum intensity value that exists in the original image [31]. The results are shown in Table 1. The average PSNR value returned by our algorithm over four images is 10.7642. The lower PSNR value determine better performance of the encryption algorithm. Thus, the returned PSNR value displays better distortion of the encrypted image.

4.5 Key Space Analysis

In cryptanalysis, Brute force attacks are a common type of attacks where all possible key combinations are tried to decrypt an encrypted method. Thus, a good encryption algorithm should have large key space so that brute force attacks become infeasible. We know various well-known algorithms like DES, RSA & AES which are vulnerable to brute-force attacks [2]. Key space depends on the key size, the smaller the key size smaller the key space. To analyse the key space of our proposed algorithm let us assume an image with dimensions 512 × 512. In Sect. 2.1.2, we talk about generating fisher-yates-array with size equal to the largest dimension of the image. This means we have 512! (! means factorial) possibilities to create the fisher-yates-array. In Sect. 2.1.4, we explain that *column-key* and *row-key* (initialization explained in Sect. 2.1.3) are divided into groups of 64 length which use 256 bit key (SHA256 hashed) to shuffle themselves i.e. (2^{256}) possibilities. So, for an image with 512 × 512 dimension, we will have 8 (512/64) groups of rows and 8 groups of columns. This means (2^{256})^8 possibilities to create the *row-key* & the *column-key*. Therefore, the final key space will be $512! \cdot (2^{256})^8$ which is able to resist any brute-force attack. But the key space is not limited to this figure, it grows and shrinks according to the image size. To generalize key space for an N × M dimension image.

4.6 Key Sensitivity Test

A good encryption should be highly key sensitive. This fact means that even with a very small change in the key the image should not decrypt or reveal the original image more or less. In our proposed algorithm, if a single bit in key changes, the image becomes non-decryptable. The results of this test are shown in Fig. 2 where only the first bit of *new-string-key* was changed and the encrypted image was tried to decrypt. The results show the high key sensitivity of our proposed algorithm, which makes the reconstruction of an image impossible if the key is not 100% correct.

4.7 Encryption Time

A good encryption algorithm should be secure but fast as well, even for high dimension images. Our proposed algorithm focuses on the quick encryption-decryption to provide real-time experience to the users and keeping in mind the limited processor & memory availability on mobile devices. Computational speed greatly depends on the types of processor, programming language and encryption techniques [31]. The encryption time results of the four images are shown in Table 2. The average encryption time for four images is 0.697675 s. This supports our claim to present a fast encryption algorithm. But this time can be reduced further by applying various parallel processing optimizations. These optimizations will be a part of our future work.

$$key\ space = \max(N, M)! \cdot (2^{256})^{\max(\frac{N}{64}, \frac{M}{64})}$$

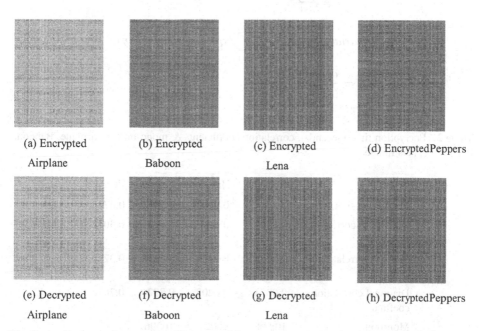

| (a) Encrypted Airplane | (b) Encrypted Baboon | (c) Encrypted Lena | (d) EncryptedPeppers |

| (e) Decrypted Airplane | (f) Decrypted Baboon | (g) Decrypted Lena | (h) DecryptedPeppers |

Fig. 2. (a–d) shows the encrypted images with correct key and (e-h) shows thecorresponding decrypted images with incorrect key

Table 1. NCPR, UCAI, MSE, RMSE & PSNR for Airplane, Baboon, Lena & Peppers Image

	Airplane	Baboon	Lena	Peppers
NCPR	98.4164	99.4549	99.2494	99.0985
UCAI	18.1846	24.6960	20.1233	25.9458
MSE	3793.3232	6152.7085	4283.8332	6434.0255
RMSE	61.59	78.4392	65.451	80.2124
PSNR	11.591	10.2401	11.8125	9.4101

4.8 Correlation Analysis

A good encryption algorithm should result into an image with no or zero correlation between pixels close to each other. Formulae given below were used to calculate the correlation coefficients in horizontal, vertical and diagonal directions for the encrypted image [31, 32]. x & y values in the formulae represent the adjacent pixels in the image. The results are shown in Table 2.

$$E(x) = \frac{1}{N} \sum_{i=1}^{N} x_i$$

$$D(x) = \frac{1}{N} \sum_{i=1}^{N} -E(x))^2$$

$$covariance(x, y) = \frac{1}{N} \sum_{i=1}^{N} (x_i - E(x))(y_i - E(y))$$

$$R_{xy} = \frac{covariance(x, y)}{\sqrt{D(x)}\sqrt{D(y)}}$$

Table 2. Encryption time (seconds), correlation coefficients & mono-bit for Airplane, Baboon, Lena & Peppers Image

	Airplane	Baboon	Lena	Peppers
Encryption time	0.7006	0.7388	0.6790	0.6723
Horizontal correlation coefficient	0.1505	0.1447	0.4094	0.3012
Vertical correlation coefficient	0.0959	0.2436	0.5158	0.3290
Diagonal correlation coefficient	0.0074	0.0202	0.3823	0.2638
Mono-bit	10838	9602	10296	9285

We can observe in Table 2 that the minimum horizontal, vertical and diagonal correlation coefficients is 0.1447, 0.0959 & 0.0074 respectively. These coefficients display a very less correlation between pixels of original and encrypted image. These coefficients can be reduced at a greater extent if we not only shuffle row & columns but also individual RGB intensities. But there is a trade-off between encryption time and correlation coefficients. Shuffling RBG intensities as well will bring down correlation but increase the encryption time. Thus, to present a fast algorithm we do not shuffle RGB intensities.

4.9 Mono-bit Test

In this test, we converted the encrypted image into binary bits and extracted the first 20,000 bits. In those 20,000 bits we calculated the number of times 1 appeared. The test is passed by the encrypted image if the frequency of 1 lies between 9000 and 11,000 in the extracted bits. The results are shown in Table 2. The purpose behind this test is to verify the randomness in the occurrence of 1s in a bit stream with defined size. The average 1s appeared in four encrypted images were 10005. This shows the randomness in the binary stream of the encrypted image.

4.10   Entropy Analysis

In this section we measure the randomness of the pixels in the encrypted image. We calculated the entropy of the Red, Green & Blue channels separately and the values are shown in Table 3. The resulting specifies the randomness and uncertainty in the pixel positions after encryption. We have 256 intensity values in a coloured image which can be represented using 8 bits. Thus, the ideal entropy should be 8 to be secured from the entropy attacks. The maximum entropy achieved is by Baboon image where values are closer to 8.

Table 3. Entropy of RGB channels for Airplane, Baboon, Lena & Peppers Image

	Airplane	Baboon	Lena	Peppers
Entropy red channel	6.717	7.7067	7.2531	7.3388
Entropy green channel	6.7990	7.4744	7.5940	7.4963
Entropy blue channel	6.2138	7.7522	6.9684	7.0583

4.11   Average Difference (AD) and Maximum Difference (MD)

We calculated the average difference between original & the encrypted image to analyse and estimate the dissimilarity between them. The formula used to calculate average difference is:

$$AD = \frac{1}{N \cdot M} \sum_{0}^{N-1} \sum_{0}^{M-1} |\alpha(i,j) - \beta(i,j)|$$

The maximum difference between the original image pixel intensity and encrypted image pixel intensity is calculated using the formula:

$$MD = Max(\sum_{0}^{N-1}\sum_{0}^{M-1} |\alpha(i,j) - \beta(i,j)|)$$

The higher value of Average Difference & Maximum Difference refers to poor quality of the image i.e. better encryption, with respect to an ideal image (original image). In formulae, α represents the original image matrix and β represents the encrypted image. N and M are the number of rows and columns in the image respectively. The results are shown in Table 4. The average AD & MD value over four images is 54.5832 & 235 respectively, which shows better shuffling and encryption of the image.

4.12 Structural Content (SC)

Structural Content value is used to find the resemblance between two images. We find SC value for the top-left, top-right, bottom-left and bottom-right segment of the original and encrypted image. The formula used to calculate structural content is:

$$SC_{top-left} = \frac{\sum_{0}^{N/2-1}\sum_{0}^{M/2-1} \alpha(i,j)^2}{\sum_{0}^{N/2-1}\sum_{0}^{M/2-1} \beta(i,j)^2}$$

$$SC_{top-right} = \frac{\sum_{0}^{N/2-1}\sum_{M/2}^{M-1} \alpha(i,j)^2}{\sum_{0}^{N/2-1}\sum_{M/2}^{M-1} \beta(i,j)^2}$$

$$SC_{bottom-left} = \frac{\sum_{N/2}^{N-1}\sum_{0}^{M/2-1} \alpha(i,j)^2}{\sum_{N/2}^{N-1}\sum_{0}^{M/2-1} \beta(i,j)^2}$$

$$SC_{bottom-right} = \frac{\sum_{N/2}^{N-1}\sum_{0}^{M/2-1} \alpha(i,j)^2}{\sum_{N/2}^{N-1}\sum_{M/2}^{M-1} \beta(i,j)^2}$$

In the formulae, α, β, N & M represent the original image, encrypted image, number of rows and columns in the image respectively. The results are shown in Table 4.

4.12.1 Normalized Absolute Error (NAE)

WE calculated the Normalized Absolute Error between the original and the encrypted image using the formula:

$$NAE = \frac{\sum_{0}^{N-1}\sum_{0}^{M-1} |\alpha(i,j) - \beta(i,j)|}{\sum_{0}^{N-1}\sum_{0}^{M-1} \alpha(i,j)}$$

In the formulae, α, β, N & M represent the original image, encrypted image, number of rows and columns in the image respectively. The results are shown in Table 4. The NAE values lie between [0–1] where 1 signifies low similarity and 0 signifies high similarity. Our algorithm does not shuffle RGB intensities, still is able to achieve NAE value close to 0.5.

Table 4. Average & maximum difference, structural content and NAE for Airplane, Baboon, Lena & Peppers Image

	Airplane	Baboon	Lena	Peppers
Average difference	42.5521	62.9747	51.3144	61.4916
Maximum difference	229	249	227	235
Structural content (top-left)	0.9991	0.9059	0.9696	1.0306
Structural content (top-right)	1.1039	1.0389	1.1723	1.1907
Structural content (bottom-left)	0.9184	1.1125	0.6992	0.9654
Structural content (bottom-right)	0.9798	0.9422	1.1662	0.8157
Normalized absolute error	0.234	0.498	0.4002	0.5558

5 Conclusion

In this paper, we proposed a new column-row transposition encryption algorithm for images based on timeout. The timeout feature restricts the recipient to decrypt the image after a specified amount of time. This will improve security & privacy over social media and various other image-sharing platforms. The algorithm displayed high strength & better performance by achieving ~99% NCPR value, ~11 dB PSNR value, high average & maximum difference, close to 0 correlation coefficients, ~0.7 s of encryption time and showed its random nature in mono-bit test and entropy analysis. The algorithm takes in variable-sized string key which provides the same level of security irrespective of its size and makes the key sharing process easier. The large key space makes the algorithm resistant to brute-force attacks and high key sensitivity restricts the decryption of an image even with a key having 1-bit change. We introduced our modified version of the Fisher-Yates Shuffling algorithm and used that with SHA256 Hashing to create transposition keys for the process. We also introduced an Android Library, NPM Package & Python Package to allow easy implementation of our algorithm on various platforms and restrict unauthorized sharing of images. For future work, we would want to extend the work and introduce parallel processing optimizations in the key generation process to reduce the encryption/decryption time and include RGB intensity shuffling to reduce correlation and other similarity parameter's values.

References

1. Nielsen, R.K., Schrøder, K.C.: The relative importance of social media for accessing, finding, and engaging with news. Digt. J. **2**(4), 472–489 (2014). https://doi.org/10.1080/21670811. 2013.872420
2. Chandel, G.S., Sharma, V., Singh, U.P.: Different image encryption techniques-survey and overview. Int. J. Adv. Res. Compu. Sci. Softw. Eng. **6**(8), (2016)
3. Coppersmith, D.: The data encryption standard (DES) and its strength against attacks. IBM J. Res. Dev. **38**(3), 243–250 (1994). https://doi.org/10.1147/rd.383.0243

4. Zhou, X., Tang, X.: Research and implementation of RSA algorithm for encryption and decryption. In: Proceedings of 2011 6th International Forum on Strategic Technology, pp. 1118–1121. Harbin, China (2011). https://doi.org/10.1109/IFOST.2011.6021216

5. Simon, H.: Advanced encryption standard (AES). Netw Secur. **2009**(12), 8–12 (2009). https://doi.org/10.1016/S1353-4858(10)70006-4

6. Prerna, M., Abhishek, S,: A Study of Encryption Algorithms AES, DES and RSA for Security. Global J. Comput. Sci. Technol. 13 (2013)

7. Li, X., Knipe, J., Cheng, H.: Image compression and encryption using tree structures. Pattern Recogn. Lett. **18**(11–13), 1253–1259 (1997). https://doi.org/10.1016/S0167-8655(97)000 99-8

8. Potdar, V., Chang, E.: Disguising text cryptography using image cryptography. In: Proceedings of the Fourth International Network Conference 2004 (INC2004), p. 361. Lulu. com (2004)

9. Mao, Y., Chen, G., Lian, S.: A novel fast image encryption scheme based on 3D chaotic baker maps. Int. J. Bifurcat. Chaos **14**(10), 3613–3624 (2004)

10. Nkandeu, Y.P.K., Tiedeu, A.: An image encryption algorithm based on substitution technique and chaos mixing. Multimed. Tools Appl. **78**(8), 10013–10034 (2018). https://doi.org/10.1007/s11042-018-6612-2

11. Guan, Z.-H., Huang, F., Guan, W.: Chaos-based image encryption algorithm. Phys. Lett. A **346**(1–3), 153–157 (2005). https://doi.org/10.1016/j.physleta.2005.08.006

12. Mozaffari, S.: Parallel image encryption with bitplane decomposition and genetic algorithm. Multimed. Tools Appl. **77**, 25799–25819 (2018). https://doi.org/10.1007/s11042-018-5817-8

13. Khan, M., Masood, F.: A novel chaotic image encryption technique based on multiple discrete dynamical maps. Multimed. Tools Appl. **78**(18), 26203–26222 (2019). https://doi.org/10.1007/s11042-019-07818-4

14. Norouzi, B., Mirzakuchaki, S.: An image encryption algorithm based on DNA sequence operations and cellular neural network. Multimed. Tools Appl. **76**(11), 13681–13701 (2016). https://doi.org/10.1007/s11042-016-3769-4

15. Xiong, Z., Wu, Y., Ye, C., Zhang, X., Xu, F.: Color image chaos encryption algorithm combining CRC and nine palace map. Multimed. Tools Appl. **78**(22), 31035–31055 (2019). https://doi.org/10.1007/s11042-018-7081-3

16. Zhou, Y., Cao, W., Philip Chen, C.L.: Image encryption using binary bitplane. Signal Process. **100**, 197–207 (2014). https://doi.org/10.1016/j.sigpro.2014.01.020

17. Tang, Z., Song, J., Zhang, X., Sun, R.: Multiple-image encryption with bit-plane decomposition and chaotic maps. Opt. Lasers Eng. **80**, 1–11 (2016). https://doi.org/10.1016/j.optlaseng.2015.12.004

18. Kester, Q.-A.: Image encryption based on the RGB PIXEL transposition and shuffling. Int. J. Comput. Netw. Inform. Secur. **5**(7), 43–50 (2013). https://doi.org/10.5815/ijcnis.2013.07.05

19. Musanna, F., Kumar, S.: A novel fractional order chaos-based image encryption using Fisher Yates algorithm and 3-D cat map. Multimed. Tools Appl. **78**(11), 14867–14895 (2018). https://doi.org/10.1007/s11042-018-6827-2

20. Karawia, A.: Image encryption based on Fisher-Yates shuffling and three dimensional chaotic economic map. IET Image Proc. **13**(12), 2086–2097 (2019). https://doi.org/10.1049/iet-ipr.2018.5142

21. Hazra, T.K., Bhattacharyya, S.: Image encryption by blockwise pixel shuffling using Modified Fisher Yates shuffle and pseudorandom permutations. In: 2016 IEEE 7th Annual Information Technology, Electronics and Mobile Communication Conference (IEMCON), Vancouver, BC, Canada, pp. 1–6 (2016). https://doi.org/10.1109/IEMCON.2016.7746312

22. Raghunandan, K.R., Nireshwalya, S.N., Sudhir, S., Bhat, M.S., Tanvi, H.M.: Securing media information using hybrid transposition using fisher yates algorithm and RSA public key algorithm using Pell's cubic equation. In: Chiplunkar, N.N., Fukao, T. (eds.) Advances in Artificial Intelligence and Data Engineering. AISC, vol. 1133, pp. 975–993. Springer, Singapore (2021). https://doi.org/10.1007/978-981-15-3514-7_73
23. Djamalilleil, A., Muslim, M., Salim, Y., Alwi, E.I., Azis, H., Herman: Modified transposition cipher algorithm for images encryption. In: 2018 2nd East Indonesia Conference on Computer and Information Technology (EIConCIT), pp. 1–4. Makassar, Indonesia (2018). https://doi.org/10.1109/EIConCIT.2018.8878326
24. Putrie, V.M., Sari, C.A., Setiadi, D.R.I.M., Rachmawanto, E.H.: Super encryption using transposition-hill cipher for digital color image. In: 2018 International Seminar on Research of Information Technology and Intelligent Systems (ISRITI), pp. 152–157. Yogyakarta, Indonesia (2018). https://doi.org/10.1109/ISRITI.2018.8864361
25. Andik, S., De Rosal, I.M.S.: Securing and hiding secret message in image using XOR transposition encryption and LSB method. J. Phys.: Conf. Ser. **1196**, 012039 (2019)
26. Kester, Q.: A hybrid cryptosystem based on vigenere cipher and columnar transposition cipher. Int. J. Adv. Technol. Eng. Res. **3**(1), 141–147 (2013)
27. Somaraj, S., Hussain, M.A.: A novel image encryption technique using RGB pixel displacement for color images. In: 2016 IEEE 6th International Conference on Advanced Computing (IACC), pp. 275–279. Bhimavaram, India (2016). https://doi.org/10.1109/IACC.2016.59
28. Wu, Y.: NPCR and UACI randomness tests for image encryption. Cyber J.: J. Sel. Areas Telecommun. (2011)
29. Malik, A., Gupta, S., Dhall, S.: Analysis of traditional and modern image encryption algorithms under realistic ambience. Multimed. Tools Appl. **79**(37–38), 27941–27993 (2020). https://doi.org/10.1007/s11042-020-09279-6
30. Gupta, M., Gupta, K.K., Shukla, P.K.: Session key based fast, secure and lightweight image encryption algorithm. Multimed. Tools Appl. **80**, 10391–10416 (2020). https://doi.org/10.1007/s11042-020-10116-z
31. Mohammad, O.F., Rahim, M., Zeebaree, S., Ahmed, F.: A survey and analysis of the image encryption methods. Int. J. Appl. Eng. Res. **12**, 13265–13280 (2017)
32. Senthilnathan, S.: Usefulness of correlation analysis. SSRN Electron. J. (2019). https://doi.org/10.2139/ssrn.3416918

EXAM: Explainable Models for Analyzing Malicious Android Applications

K. A. Asmitha, P. Vinod[(✉)], K. A. Rafidha Rehiman, Raman Prakash Verma,
Rajkishor Kumar, Surbhi Kumari, and Nishchaya Kumar

Department Computer Applications, Cochin University of Science and Technology, Kochi, India
asmitha@pg.cusat.ac.in, {vinod.p,rafidharehimanka}@cusat.ac.in

Abstract. The open source nature and high performance have made Android smartphones popular world wide. On the other hand, the ease of usage and popularity has prompted malware creation. The proposed method presents a lightweight solution capable of detecting unknown malware on Android smartphones based on static analysis of android.apk files. Here we extract three different kinds of features i.e. permissions, activities and receivers, in order to evaluate if individual features are effective in detecting malware. Experiments suggest that our proposed deep learnig detection method is able to identify Android malware with an overall classification accuracy of 97.35% using boolean representation of the feature vector table. Comparative analysis of individual features recommends that the deep learning model resulted in better detection rate with permission feature. We also performed obfuscation of selected malware.apk files and found that the detection rate of our trained model is about 100%. Moreover, we also show how explainability helps the analyst to assess different models.

Keywords: Android malware · Static analysis · Obfuscation · Explainable models · Deep learning

1 Introduction

Android is the most popular mobile operating system in the world with an 84 percent market share for smartphones. The open-source nature of Android applications and easiness of usage have led to an increase in the prevalence of security attacks. According to statistics, more than 50 million instances of malware and potentially unwanted apps for Android have been found [18]. Various commercial antivirus solutions, including McAfee, Avast, Kaspersky, BullGuard, Avira and Bitdefender were developed as a solution for the consequences of the threat. However, because they rely on the signatures of known malicious apps, they have a serious flaw that prevents them from detecting new malware. In order to safeguard users from evolving malware, the academic community has been emphasizing on designing effective methods for malware detection that employ machine learning or deep learning algorithm [1–3]. Many malware detection methods

© The Author(s), under exclusive license to Springer Nature Switzerland AG 2022
S. Rajagopal et al. (Eds.): ASCIS 2022, CCIS 1760, pp. 44–58, 2022.
https://doi.org/10.1007/978-3-031-23095-0_3

leveraging deep learning algorithms have recently been proposed. The researchers have addressed the malware detection that are based on a certain collection of attributes extracted from mobile applications in different approaches. The characteristics chosen for the proposed model may vary from static ones like commonly used APIs, permissions, and libraries to more action-related aspects like system call graphs. Nevertheless, these methods cannot provide the explanations of any kind of decision considered by the proposed model.

Machine learning algorithms create a predictive model to map features to classes through a training phase. However, biases might lead to inaccurate and unfair choices. The biggest drawback of black box method is that machine learning developers can't explain how the model came to a particular conclusion, especially when the model made a wrong decision. There comes the importance of Explainable Artificial Intelligence(XAI) and it is becoming a research topic in recent times [8]. XAI consists of techniques that helps the professionals to understand the results of their solutions by explaining the models.

This article suggests an obfuscation-resilient explainable method aimed at detecting Android malware, allowing security analysts to interpret and evaluate the predictions immediately. The main contributions are as follows:

- Propose a Deep learning based Android malware detection method using Permission, Activities and Receivers as features.
- Present an extensive research on several conventional machine learning models for Android malware detection.
- Analyze the effect of obfuscation on the effectiveness of the proposed approach.
- Demonstrate the attributes that our framework has learnt using explainable SHAP in order to assess how well it can distinguish between malware and benign.

The remaining sections of the article are arranged as follows: Sect. 2 presents the Related Works. The proposed method is introduced in Sect. 3. Section 4 details the experiments and test results. The conclusion and future work are covered in Sect. 5.

2   Related Works

Koli et al. [13] present a static analysis-based method for identifying malware on the Android operating system. It uses risky permission combinations and dubious API requests to train the SVM algorithm.

Abdulrahman et al. [9] proposed a new method based on deep learning for identifying malware applications that employ pseudo-dynamic analysis. The researchers instead developed an API call graph to represent the execution routes that malicious apps may follow during its entire duration. By comparing multiple methods and fine-tuning various network setup settings, they also focused on increasing network efficiency.

To identify Android malware, Suleiman et al. [10] devised a categorization technique based on parallel machine learning. Total 179 features were collected and separated into API calls, instructions and permissions. A parallel collection of heterogeneous classifiers, including Simple Naive Bayes, Logistic, RIDOR, PART, and Decision Tree, were used to create a composite classification model. PART surpassed all the other classifiers, achieving accuracy rates of 96%.

A lightweight machine learning-based system was proposed by Long et al. in [11] to distinguish between benign and malicious applications using both static and dynamic techniques. Additionally, he suggested a novel strategy for reducing the dimensionality of the features called PCA-RELIEF. By utilizing both their SVM model and the newly presented model to lower the dimensions, their study demonstrated a high degree of effectiveness in identifying malware and improving the detection rate.

Alhebsi, Mohamed Salem [12], proposed a technique to scan the application to identify malware using two types of features permissions and signature. They found that K-Nearest Neighbour(KNN) and Random Forest (RF) classifiers are effective in terms of detection rate.

The detailed review of the above papers shows enough space to enhance and construct new solutions for detecting Android malware employing explainable machine learning/deep learning models. Explainable models in Android malware detection are crucial as deep learning models are challenging to evaluate, since they cannot be broken down into simple, intuitive parts. Moreover, obfuscation-resiliency is needed as developers always use sophisticated obfuscations to conceal their dangerous activities.

The challenges mentioned above are addressed in our study by evaluating the model's resistance against obfuscation and generating model explanations. Additionally, our article compares and thoroughly examines the effectiveness of various conventional classification and deep learning techniques in identifying Android malware applications.

3 Proposed Method

In this section, we demonstrate our Android malware detection framework based on machine learning and deep learning models. We have extracted three prime features specifically-permissions, activities and receivers by disassembling.apk files using Androguard [4] tool. Experiments are conducted using boolean feature vector tables created individually for different feature category and prepared models using machine learning as well as deep learning. Figure 1 depicts the complete flow of our proposed system and we describe the different components in the following subsections.

3.1 Data Set Preparation

The research is based on 5000 malware.apk files gathered from Drebin dataset [7] and 7000 benign samples obtained from a variety of sources. Each benign.apk file examined using professional antivirus software to ensure that they were all trustworthy.

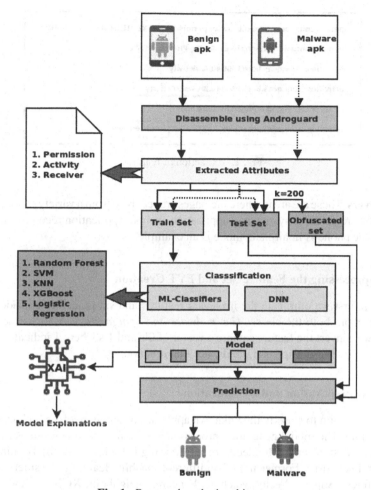

Fig. 1. Proposed method architecture

3.2 Feature Extraction

In the initial stage, the features are extracted from benign as well as malicious Android applications without execution. The disassembler tool called andro-guard gets the.apk files as input and an adroguard function called Analyze apk() which returns an object that has the capability to extract necessary features. The generation of model on each individual feature needs three different feature sets (Fig. 2):

1. **Permissions**: When a program wants to access sensitive user data or system functionalities, the authorisation is obtained through permissions. These are described statically in the AndroidManifest.XML file.
2. **Activities**: Activities are indeed the starting point for user interaction and launched to identify what should happen next when a user or another app launches an application. The activity names in the application are the features.

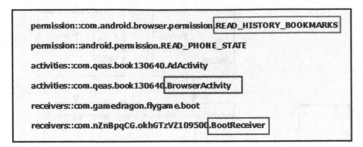

Fig. 2. Extraction of features

3. **Recievers**: These are areas where messages are received from a variety of sources and enable to register for system and application events. Application receives a message when the phone is in airplane mode is an example.

3.3 Pre-processing the Feature Set and FVT Creation

In this step, first we eliminate the irrelevant features and subsequently consider union of features from both the classes (*i.e. malware and benign files*). After extracting the features, we convert the feature set into a vector of 0's and 1's where 1 indicates that the feature is present in the app and 0 indicates that it is not.

3.4 Model Preparation and Classification

In this step, we aim to classify the unknown applications and it involves both training as well as testing. The model generation process using the feature vector tables generated in the previous step can be divided into: (a) Training ML classifiers (b) Training using deep neural networks. Former uses five different machine learning classifiers namely- Random forest, Support Vector Machine, K-nearest neighbour, XGBoost and Logistic Regression. Latter uses our own classifier for the classification The learned models will be used to predict the unseen samples.

3.5 Obfuscation of Samples

In our approach, we further tried to inspect the impact of obfuscation by generating obfuscated samples using the advanced obfuscator for Android app called *Obfuscapk* [14]. It will decompile the original input apk file and give an obfuscated app having same functionality as output. For obfuscating the samples, we have used four types of process called (1) Call indirection: It alters the control-flow graph (CFG) without compromising the semantics of the function. (2) Re-build: Rearrange the bytecode without altering its meaning but maintaining the app's original behavior (3) New alignment: The output is a restructured application with an improved file structure for Android device compatibility (4) New signature: Re-sign phase is the final step after applying obfuscation since Android mandates that all APKs be digitally signed with certificates or updated.

3.6 Interpretation of Results Using SHAP

Explainable AI (XAI) is a developing area of study in machine learning with the goal of enabling people to comprehend, believe in, and efficiently manage the next-AI solutions [5, 6]. The majority of XAI techniques created in recent times aim to describe supervised machine learning models. The SHAP [6] technique is a unified strategy that attempts to describe the output data using shapely values to determine the respective contributions of various coalition members. In order to develop effective solutions, the explanation for the result is particularly crucial in malware detection. In this investigation, we employ the SHAP technique that is especially well-suited for explaining machine learning models.

4 Experiments and Results

The investigations are performed on a computer with Ubuntu 21.10 as OS, Intel core i9 CPU and 32 GB RAM. The extensive experimentation involves two parts (1) Prepared models using the real samples considering individual features and (2) Models are tested against obfuscated samples.

4.1 Evaluation Measures

The confusion matrix which summarises the classifier's prediction outcomes was used for empirical evaluation of its performance and effectiveness. In order to forecast unknown samples, many assessment measures such as accuracy, precision, recall, and F-measure are calculated.

$$Accuracy = \frac{TP + TN}{TP + TN + FP + FN} \tag{1}$$

$$Precision = \frac{TP}{TP + FP} \tag{2}$$

$$Recall = \frac{TP}{TP + FN} \tag{3}$$

$$F - measeure = 2 * \frac{P * R}{P + R} \tag{4}$$

Here, the malicious app that has been identified as malicious is referred to as TP, and the malicious app that has not been detected as malicious is referred to as TN. The Benign app that has been designated as benign iteself is FN and FP denotes the number of benign app's that have been misclassified as malicous.

4.2 Research Questions

The following five major research questions are addressed in this paper:

RQ1: How effective our android malware detection framework in detecting malicious apps?

RQ2 Whether the model prepared is resilient against obfuscation?
RQ3: Can proposed method interpret the classification results?
RQ4: Which type of permissions, activities, recievers are used more?

***RQ1*: Our proposed Android malware detection framework is effective enough in detection of malicious apps?** First, we carry out tests to see whether our proposed method is capable of categorising basic Android malware. Both deep learning and conventional machine learning classifiers have been used in our experiments. We first use the dataset to train the classifiers, test and finally,assess the results. The classifications in both trials are based on features from permissions, activities, and receivers categories. A feature's presence or absence is recorded (i.e. Boolean features) to create the classification models.

Conventional Approach: From Table 1 we can observe that, RF classifier is getting highest F-measure of 0.97 for permissions. Receivers category of features also have highest F-measure of 0.90 with RF classifier. From Table 4, it is evident that the model is classifying samples with an F-measure of 0.95 when RF is used. The above observations shows that the model designed using permissions features is performing well with highest F-measure when Random Forest classifier is used. An app's functionality is dependent on the rights (permissions) it requests, and all malicious applications require some permissions that are different from those required by benign.apk files.

Table 1. Evaluation measures for permissions

Classifiers	Accuracy	Recall	F-measure	Precision
RF	97.04	97	**97**	97
SVM	88.42	78.53	90.5	94.12
XGBoost	87.86	97.59	86.0	84.03
KNN	82.55	90.04	80.5	77.26
LR	88.47	98.42	89.2	84.30

Deep Learning: From the Table 3, it is clear that using activities and Recievers we were able to classify the samples with 0.85%, 0.88% F-measure respectively with a 100% Detection Rate. Moreover, our deep learning technique has highest F-measure of 0.973% and successfully categorized Android malware with 100% detection rate using permissions as features. The results demonstrate that deep learning techniques have improved model performance and outperform those of conventional machine learning classifiers.

Summary of RQ1: *Our proposed deep learning approach classifies more accurately than conventional approach. However, both studies produced outstanding results, making the models based on permissions look promising for detecting Android malware.*

Table 2. Evaluation measures for recievers

Classifiers	Accuracy	Recall	F-measure	Precision
RF	90	90	**90**	92
SVM	85.95	87.53	87.82	88.13
XGBoost	82.36	84.40	84.72	85.05
KNN	83.94	84.38	85.89	87.47
LR	85.60	86.93	87.49	88.06

Table 3. Performance measures for deep learning model

Classifiers	Activity		Permissions		Receivers	
	F-Measure	DR	F-Measure	DR	F-Measure	DR
DNN	85.86	100	97.35	100	88.21	100

Table 4. Evaluation measures for activities

Classifiers	Accuracy	Recall	F-measure	Precision
RF	95.34	95	**95**	95
SVM	88.42	97.59	89	84.03
XGBoost	82.55	99.04	80.50	77.26
KNN	87.86	97.59	89.00	84.03
LR	88.47	98.42	89.2	84.30

RQ2: Whether the model prepared is resilient against obfuscation? Next, we evaluate the effectiveness of our proposed strategy in classifying Android malware that has been obfuscated using Obfuscapk, which obfuscates Android apps automatically. Specifically, we use 80% samples from the dataset to train the model. Then, select 200 samples correctly predicted as malware from the test set and use them for obfuscation. Table 5 demonstrates the evaluation results after obfuscation. RF classifier can correctly classify the obfuscated samples with a detection rate of 100% using permissions features. Using Activities, Receivers can also classify obfuscated samples with 88.5%, 86.6% detection rates, respectively. On comparing Table 1, we noticed that the proposed model outperforms with obfuscated samples when permissions are used as features. When Activities are used, all the obfuscated samples can correctly classify with an average true positive rate of 88.5% using RF. Therefore the effectiveness is marginally reduced.

Summary of RQ2: *When permissions are used as features, even if the samples are obfuscated, the samples are correctly classified with high detection accuracy. Additionally, obfuscation has seriously affected the detection rate of obfuscated samples when other types of features are used. Utilizing deep learning on permissions may increase the detection rate and robustness of the model.*

Table 5. Detetction rate of obfuscated samples

Classifiers	Detection rate		
	Permissions	Activities	Recievers
Random Forest	**100**	88.5	86.6
SVM	96.01	80.51	79.20
KNN	96.75	80.51	79.87
XGboost	96.00	75.97	68.83
LR	96.00	79.87	77.92

RQ3: Can proposed method interpret the classification results? Since Random Forest is performing well in terms of true positive rate in all the feature categories, we decided to generate visual explanations to interpret our classification results. Security analysts can use these interpretations to better comprehend the reasons behind a malware samples classification. Specifically, we use SHAP summary plots to display the importance and effects of the features. Each point on the summary plot represents a feature's Shapley value for the prediction. Red indicates a feature's value is higher whereas blue denotes features with a lesser value. Based on the distribution of the red and blue dots, we may generalize the directionality influence of the features. a request to the external storage-Fig. 3 reveals that the permission called read_phone_state have a greater and a positive impact in prediction of a malware. The features such as read_sms and send_sms are positively correlated with prediction but the permission called access_network_state is negatively correlated with prediction.

The Fig. 4 shows that the messageReceiver is positively correlated with prediction but HireBaseInstanceIdReceiver has a negative impact on prediction. From the Fig. 5, it is clear that the Adactivity and MainActivity is negatively contributing to the prediction. Since deep learning on permissions outperforms all other methods, we construct the SHAP summary plot (Refer Fig. 6). The Send_Sms permission have a high and positive impact on predicting malware and low impact when it is having a low value. Similarly, Read_Phone_State also have a negative correlation with the class malware.

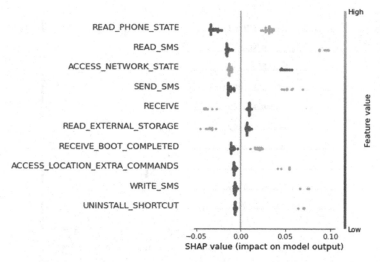

Fig. 3. Summary plot of Random Forest classifier using SHAP

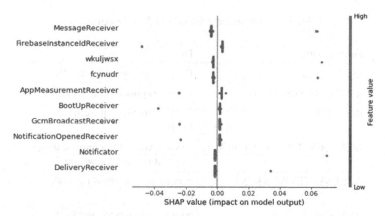

Fig. 4. SHAP summary plot of Random Forest classifier for Receivers

Summary of RQ3: The proposed method uses a graphical tool called SHAP to interpret the findings of the malware categorization. Since it provides information about the contribution of each feature in predicting malware, we can even distinguish the malware from benign files directly through the summary plots (Table 6).

RQ4: Which type of permissions, activities, recievers are used more? The features with high absolute Shapley values are the most prominent ones and are arranged in the order of importance. The SHAP feature importance for the deep learning model is shown in the Fig. 7. Send_sms, Read_phone_state, Recieve, Read_External_Storage, Access_network_State, Read_Sms are the most prominent permissions. We can observe from the results that the malware always captures personal data and writes it into newly

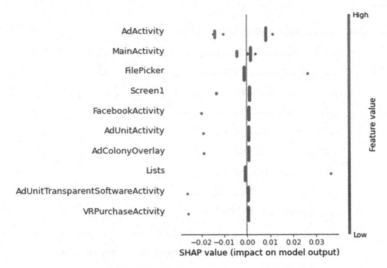

Fig. 5. SHAP summary plot of activities

Table 6. The prominent features and its descriptions

Feature name	Descriptions
SEND_SMS	Enables an app to send SMS
READ_PHONE_STATE	Accesses phone state read-only
RECEIVE	Obtain information from the Internet
READ_EXTERNAL_STORAGE	Authorization for a request to the external storage for writing
ACCESS_NETWORK_STATE	Permission to access network data
READ_SMS	App permission to read SMS

generated files. Then, these files are uploaded to the network or kept on other external storage systems and can be misused to discover the victim's location or to distinguish between the actual system and sandboxes. This can be considered as a suspicious behavior and qualifies it as malware.

Summary of RQ4: The findings show that the explanation technique (SHAP) is capable of evaluating the model as well as assisting us in learning about the most prevalent and harmful features for malware classification.

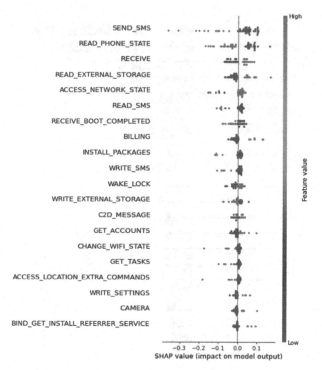

Fig. 6. SHAP summary plot for deep learning using permissions

4.3 Comparison with State-of-the-Art Approaches

Table 7 presents the comparison of the proposed scheme to other state-of-the-art techniques in terms of F1 sore reported in [15–17] which is tested on DREBIN dataset. Our detection scheme accurately classifies the samples with an F1 of 97.35% using explainable deep neural network. Also, the obfuscated samples are detected using Random Forest classifier with 100% detection rate.

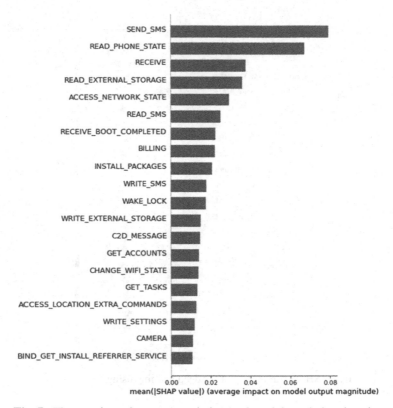

Fig. 7. The prominent features (permissions) selected through deep learning

Table 7. Comparative analysis

No.	Author	Remarks	Explainable model	Obfuscation
1	Masum et.al. [15]	Droid-NNet, a neural network-based framework with a L^2 regularization approach, early stopping criterion, and the mini-batch gradient descent method, is used to train the Droid-NNet. Obtained F1 score of 0.98	✗	✗
2	Sharma et.al. [16]	Hybrid technique based on Deep learning and Binary Particle Swarm Optimization (BPSO) Obtained an F1 score of 92.39% for DREBIN dataset	✗	✗

(continued)

Table 7. (*continued*)

No.	Author	Remarks	Explainable model	Obfuscation
	Shiqi et.al. [17]	The deep residual LSTM-based sequence model known as MalResLSTM is then used to identify and categorize Android malware. Using static features obtained an F1 score of 0.92%	✗	✗
	Proposed method	Obtained an F-measure of 0.973 using Deep learning Achieved 100% detection rate for obfuscated samples	✓	✓

5 Conclusion

This research presents an explainable deep learning model based on static features using SHAP to detect Android malware. The proposed system is helpful for the primary classification of malicious samples. Additionally, classic machine learning and deep learning techniques are used to select the most effective model for identifying Android malware. Evaluation results reveal that the deep learning model outperforms all conventional machine learning algorithms with an F-measure of 0.973 and a detection rate of 100%. Furthermore, we have examined the effect of obfuscation on the model's efficacy, and the proposed method can categorize all obfuscated malware samples with a 100% detection rate. Such a finding implies that our model is resistant to obfuscation.

Future of this work extends to combine static and dynamic features for ensuring greater accuracy. Additionally, it is necessary to test different obfuscation techniques in combination. Future assessments of the effects of adversarial attacks can also be estimated using explainable techniques.

References

1. Karbab, E.B., Debbabi, M., Derhab, A., Mouheb, D.: Android malware detection using deep learning on API method sequences. Comput. Sci. arXiv:1712.08996v1 (2017)
2. Kim, T., Kang, B., Rho, M., Sezer, S., Im, E.G.: A multimodal deep learning method for android malware detection using various features. IEEE Trans. Inform. Forensics Secur. **14**(3), 733–788 (2018)
3. Hou, S., Saas, A., Chen, L., Ye, Y.: Deep4MalDroid: a deep learning framework for android malware detection based on linux kernel system call graphs. In: IEEE/WIC/ACM International Conference on Web Intelligence Workshops (WIW), pp. 104–111 (2016)
4. Androguard: http://code.google.com/p/androguard/ (2019). v3.3.5
5. Gunning, D.: In: Defense Advanced Research Projects Agency (DARPA), nd Web 2. Explainable artificial intelligence (xai) (2017)

6. Scott, M.L., Su-In, L.: A unified approach to interpreting model predictions. In Proceedings of the 31st International Conference on Neural Information Processing Systems (NIPS'17), pp. 4768–4777. Curran Associates Inc., Red Hook, NY, USA (2017)
7. Arp, D., Spreitzenbarth, M., Hübner, M., Gascon, H., Rieck, K.D.: Effective and explainable detection of android malware in your pocket. In: Proceedings of the 21st annual network distributed system security symposium (NDSS). The Internet Society (2014)
8. Arrieta, A.B., et al.: Explainable Artificial Intelligence (XAI): Concepts, taxonomies, opportunities and challenges toward responsible AI. Inform. Fusion **58**, 82–115 (2020)
9. Pektaş, A., Acarman, T.: Deep learning for effective android malware detection using API call graph embeddings. Soft Comput. **24**(2), 1027–1043 (2019). https://doi.org/10.1007/s00 500-019-03940-5
10. Yerima, S.Y., Sezer, S., Muttik, I.: Android malware detection using parallel machine learning classifiers. In: 2014 Eighth International Conference on Next Generation Mobile Apps, Services and Technologies, pp. 37–42. IEEE (2014)
11. Wen, L., Yu, H.: An android malware detection system based on machine learning. In: AIP Conference Proceedings, vol. 1864. AIP Publishing LLC (2017)
12. Alhebsi, M.S.: Android Malware Detection using Machine Learning Techniques. Thesis. Rochester Institute of Technology (2022)
13. Koli. J.D.: RanDroid: android malware detection using random machine learning classifiers. In: International Conference on Technologies for Smart City Energy Security and Power (ICSESP) IEEE (2018)
14. Aonzo, S., Georgiu, G.C., Verderame, L., Merlo, A.: Obfuscapk: an open-source black-box obfuscation tool for android apps. SoftwareX **11**, 100403 (2020)
15. Masum, M., Shahriar, H.: Droid-NNet: Deep learning neural network for android malware detection. In: 2019 IEEE International Conference on Big Data (Big Data). IEEE (2019)
16. Sharma, R.M., Agrawal, C.P.: A BPSO and deep learning based hybrid approach for android feature selection and malware detection. In: 2022 IEEE 11th International Conference on Communication Systems and Network Technologies (CSNT). IEEE (2022)
17. Shiqi, L., et al.: Android malicious code classification using deep belief network. KSII Trans. Internet Inform. Syst. **12**(1), 454–475 (2018)
18. https://www.mcafee.com/content/dam/global/infographics/McAfeeMobileThreatReport 2021.pdf

Data Encryption Approach Using Hybrid Cryptography and Steganography with Combination of Block Ciphers

Het Shah, Parita Oza$^{(\boxtimes)}$, and Smita Agrawal$^{(\boxtimes)}$

Institute of Technology, Nirma University, Ahmedabad, Gujarat, India
{Parita.prajapati,smita.agrawal}@nirmauni.ac.in

Abstract. Information security has been one of the prominent fields due to the concerns regarding it, for the past few decades. Any loopholes in these may lead to dire consequences depending upon the importance of the message being transmitted. Thus there have emerged many techniques for this purpose, one such is crypto steganography which has been implemented in this paper, our algorithm uses a combination of Advanced Encryption Standard (AES) and columnar block ciphers to encrypt message and embedding it into the image using 1-Least Significant Bit (1-LSB) method and the reverse is done to get the data back at the other end. Hence this algorithm adds another layer of security with strong encryption techniques while maintaining the structure of the image. There is low distortion in the image with Mean Squared Error (MSE) as 0.028, Peak Signal-to-Noise Ratio (PSNR) as 63.719 and Structural Similarity Index (SSIM) values as 0.999 for png image and 0.044, 61.728, 0.999 respectively for bmp image.

Keywords: Steganography · Cryptography · Cryptosteganography · Block cipher · AES

1 Introduction

Computer security is said to be the art and science of protecting the assets of computers from unauthorized activities and their consequences. This is done by one of two ways i.e. preventing these actions from happening or by detecting them first or by recovering from them. Along with this, security aims to protect computer data, hardware and software, other related physical devices and elements they control, and communications networks from conscious abuse by these unauthorized groups i.e. done by accessing or controlling these assets [1].

The primary objectives of computer security are to hide the information from unauthorized parties i.e. confidentiality, to safeguard information from being altered by unauthorized groups i.e. integrity and lastly to make information readily available and accessible to authorized parties i.e. availability, this is the CIA triad of computer security [2]. In order to overcome this problem of security of information, many ways have been proposed in the literature of the domain, under information encryption i.e. cryptography

S. Rajagopal et al. (Eds.): ASCIS 2022, CCIS 1760, pp. 59–69, 2022.
https://doi.org/10.1007/978-3-031-23095-0_4

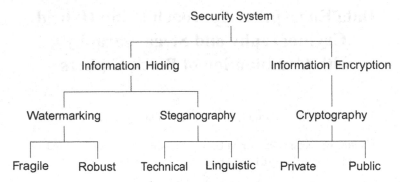

Fig. 1. Basic security system classification [5]

and information hiding i.e. steganography or watermarking. Figure 1 shows the pictorial representation of classification of security system.

Cryptography - The word cryptography finds its meaning from two different Greek words, 'Kryptos' meaning 'secret' and 'Graphein' meaning 'write', thus cryptography can be translated as secret write or language [3]. It is the art of converting plaint text into cipher text using encryption techniques and viceversa. One of the main problems with cryptography is privacy concerns as in an insecure channel any unauthorized party can extract information from the communication [4] (see Fig. 2).

Steganography - The word steganography finds its meaning from two different Greek words, 'Steganos' meaning 'covered or hidden' and 'Graphein' meaning 'write or writting', thus steganography can be translated as covered writing [5]. The main aim of steganography is to camouflage the information in some sort digital media, usually an image, in a way that doesn't allow unauthorized entities to detect the existence of this

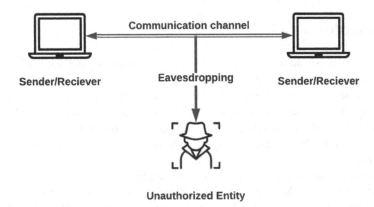

Fig. 2. Pictorial depicting flaw in encryption system [6]

secret information. This is done through steganographic techniques which allow disguising the fact that there are messages which are being transmitted between the sender and the receiver [6]. Figure 3 shows classification of steganography techniques.

1.1 Research Contribution

Both cryptography and steganography have loopholes individually as mentioned above, which can be exploited by the attackers, so in order to provide a solution to this problem, in this paper we have adopted a combinational model of cryptography and steganography, we have implemented a combination of columnar and AES for text encryption and 1-bit LSB insertion for image encryption.

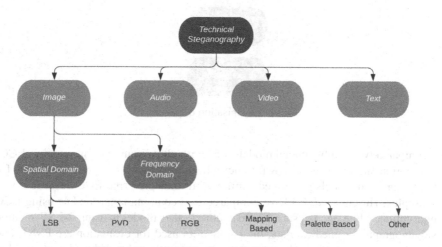

Fig. 3. Classification of technical steganography [7]

1.2 Paper Organisation

The overall structure of the paper is as follows. Section 2 reviews the related works in the domain of cryptography and steganography along with the trends of this domain as observed in the past few years. Section 3 provides information on the proposed methodology and details of the work carried out. Finally, the paper ends with results and discussion in Sect. 4, followed by a conclusion in Sect. 5. Figure 4 presents the organisation of the paper.

2 Related Work in the Domain

Cryptography is very prominent field and a lot of research has been done in this domain, we have gone through lots of surveys and papers that have been published in reputed journals in the last few years and tried to summarize them below. Hureib *et al.* [8]

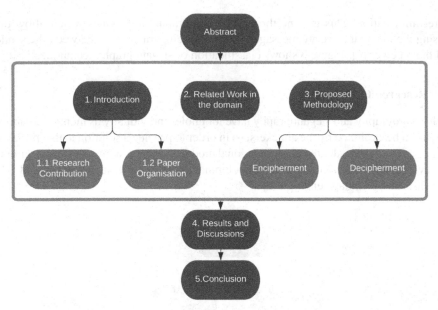

Fig. 4. Organisation of paper

have compared two combinational models, one with elliptic curve cryptography (ECC) for encryption and other with RSA for encryption, along with LSB steganography for medical data, both models performed similarly but they preferred ECC because it was less complex. Hureib *et al.* [9] have compared two combinational models using ECC for encryption, while one is using 1-LSB method other model is using 2-LSB method for steganography on medical data, the parameters used for evaluation are PSNR and capacity i.e. ratio of total data bits to total bits in image, they also deduced a relationship between the steganography techniques and the parameters. Biswas *et al.* [10] proposed a hybrid cryptography model using LSB steganography, AES for encryption, key is encrypted using Rivest Shamir Adleman encryption (RSA) and used hashing techniques too, they focused on encryption to improve the security of model but the model is incompatible with post-processing procedures as it would lead to alteration of pixel values. Alsaffar *et al.* [11] have proposed a different approach to hybrid cryptography, they used encryption techniques based on Deoxyribonucleic acid (DNA) and AES to embed information in color images using LSB steganography. Hassoon *et al.* [12] have proposed a hybrid model which uses blowfish algorithm for getting a key which is XORed with plaintext to get encrypted text, then hiding positions are chosen using edge detection and bat algorithms, and then LSB is used to embed data into the image. Wai *et al.* [13] provides a comparative study of LSB, MSB and a new hybrid steganography(NHB) technique, the NHB works on last two bits of pixel, the new technique proved to be more secure but it inherits all the faults of the bit substitution techniques. Saravanan *et al.* [14] have proposed a novel technique for transmission of images, in which image is converted to audio signal and then transmitted thus making it hard for attackers to know what content is being transmitted. Jassim *et al.* [15] have proposed a combination model which uses RSA for encryption and LSB for steganography, they have added functionality of cross-checking receivers MAC address. Abbas *et al.* [16] have proposed a model with a combinational encryption technique involving RSA and AES while using LSB for steganography, for improving security in cloud based data. Patel *et al.* [17] have used a different encryption known as homomorphic which applies operations on cipher text rather than plain text. Oza *et al.* [18] have proposed a new encryption technique based on Rubik's cube principle for image encryption based on the pixel values. Shah *et al.* [19] have discussed and compared the various types of security mechanism in information security, ranging from watermarking to crypto steganography etc. Sharma *et al.* [20] have proposed a hybrid model which uses a different approach, involving CNN architecture with adam optimizer for hiding data into the image.

3 Proposed Methodology

Both the combinational encryption technique and 1-LSB method are applied on the cover image ie coloured input image of any dimensions to generate stego image at the sender side and then the same is applied to get the text on the receiver side. Figure 5 depicts the whole process of encoding at the sender side while Fig. 6 depicts the whole process of decoding at the receiver's end to recover the hidden message. For encoding and embedding process as in Algorithm 1, a 16-Byte KEY is randomly generated and KEYCOL is extracted from this. KEYCOL and Plaintext are used to get Ciphertext1 using Columnar encryption and then this passed to AES encryption with KEY to generate Ciphertext. Finally this ciphertext is embedded in image using 1-LSB method. And reverse is done for decoding and extracting process as described in Algorithm 2.

Algorithm 1: Encoding and Embedding process

Input   : Plaintext (Message) and CoverImage
Output: StegoImage
1 Generate a 16 Byte random KEY
2 Use Key Extractor to generate KEYCOL for Columnar function

$$KEYCOL = EXTRACT\_KEY(KEY)$$

3 Apply Columnar encryption on Plaintext using KEYCOL to get Ciphertext1

$$Ciphertext1 = ENCRYPT_{\text{COLUMNAR}}(Plaintext, KEYCOL)$$

4 Apply AES encryption on Ciphertext1 using KEY to get Ciphertext2

$$Ciphertext2 = ENCRYPT_{\text{AES}}(Ciphertext1, KEY)$$

5 Get StegoImage by 1-LSB embedding using Ciphertext2 and CoverImage

$$StegoImage = ENCODE_{\text{LSB}}(Ciphertext2, CoverImage)$$

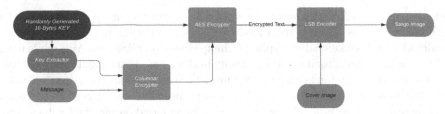

Fig. 5. Encoding process

4 Results and Discussions

We applied the proposed model of security on two image types naming png and bmp, the following methodology has been applied on random images and below we have displayed some examples of the same. We present the results of a sample image in Figs. 7 and 8 respectively, we analysed images with respect to their histogram. The visual quality measuring metrics used for evaluation are MSE, PSNR and SSIM [21]. MSE is used to calculate the difference between each pixel, PSNR gives the quality of image compared to another and SSIM compares the images based on their structure.

Algorithm 2: Decoding and Extracting process

Input : StegoImage and KEY
Output: Plaintext (Message)
1 Get Ciphertext by 1-LSB extracting on StegoImage

$$Ciphertext = DECODE_{\text{LSB}}(StegoImage)$$

2 Apply AES decryption on Ciphertext using KEY to get Plaintext1

$$Plaintext1 = DECRYPT_{\text{AES}}(Ciphertext, KEY)$$

3 Use Key Extractor to generate KEYCOL for Columnar function

$$KEYCOL = EXTRACT\_KEY(KEY)$$

4 Apply Columnar decryption on Plaintext1 using KEYCOL to get Plaintext

$$Plaintext = DECRYPT_{\text{COLUMNAR}}(Plaintext1, KEYCOL)$$

The ideal value for MSE should be low, for PSNR it should be high and lastly for SSIM it should be close to one for a good quality stego image. For png image of width 1200 px and height 675 px we're getting values as 0.028, 63.719 and (0.999, 0.999) for MSE, PSNR and SSIM respectively which suggests that the difference between the pixels is very less and image quality as well as the structure of original image is maintained. For bmp image of width 600 px and height 400 px we're getting values as 0.044, 61.728 and (0.999, 0.999) for MSE, PSNR and SSIM respectively, hence it can be inferred from Table 1, that the structure of image is very similar to original image and the difference is very marginal. Both the images had been given the same message as

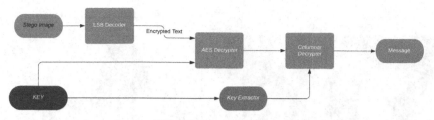

Fig. 6. Decoding process

input. From Figs. 7 and 8, it can be seen that, the histogram of cover image and stego image are almost identical. Table 2 shows comparision of the proposed methodology with others. Our model performs better than others because of difference in approach.

Table 1: Results of the proposed methodology

Image Type	Details	Input	Output	Comparision metrics		
				MSE	PSNR	SSIM
PNG	Width: 1200 Height: 675 Channel: 3	Cover image	Stego image	0.028	63.719	0.999
BMP	Width: 600 Height: 400 Channel: 3	Cover image	Stego image	0.044	61.728	0.999

Table 2. Comparision of methods for similar size png image

Method	MSE	PSNR
[13]	0.63	50.11
[22]	–	62.5332
Proposed methodology	0.028	63.719

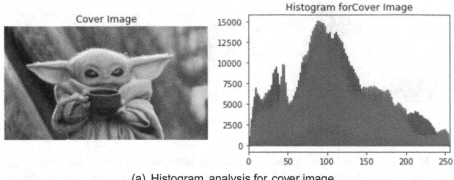

(a) Histogram analysis for cover image

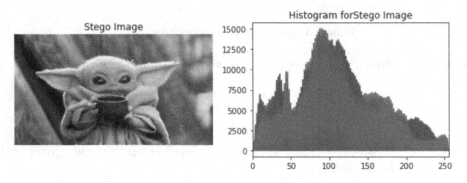

(b) Histogram analysis for Stego image

Fig. 7. Performance of model on PNG image.

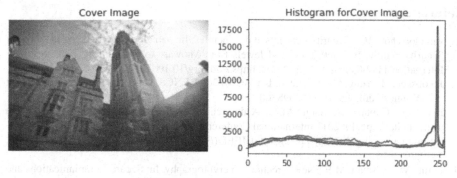

(a) Histogram analysis for cover image

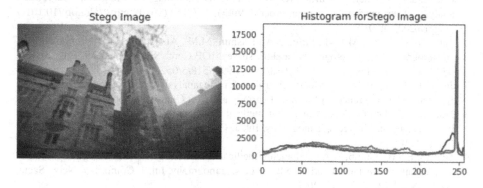

(b) Histogram analysis for Stego image

Fig. 8. Performance of model on BMP image.

5   Conclusion

Cryptosteganography have been applied to generate the stego image in this paper, here we used a combination of columnar and AES encryption techniques for encrypting the message which gives the model additional security as deciphering it becomes harder and trickier compared to when only one of them is used. The information is encrypted before embedding and hidden in image so unauthorized entity would consider it a simple image and thus improves the security. As shown in the results section there is almost no loss of the image quality and structure, so it is visually very hard to distinguish between an image generated by the model and the original one. The message was successfully decoded from the stego image too. Thus the model proves to be resistant to attacks by malicious parties. Some of the recent works in the field of steganography and cryptography have been focused on use of generative adverarial network (GAN) and convolutional neural network (CNN) techniques. Despite all this, the model inherits its predecessor's limitation, as 1-LSB method is implemented, i.e. it is not fit for post processing on the generated image as it would lead to alteration of pixel values and thus loss of information.

References

1. van Oorschot, P.C.: Security concepts and principles. In: van Oorschot, P.C. (ed.) Computer Security and the Internet: Tools and Jewels from Malware to Bitcoin, pp. 1–28. Springer International Publishing, Cham (2021). https://doi.org/10.1007/978-3-030-83411-1_1
2. Jakobsson, M., Yung, M., Zhou, J. (eds.): ACNS 2004. LNCS, vol. 3089. Springer, Heidelberg (2004). https://doi.org/10.1007/b98360
3. Biswas, C., Gupta, U.D., Haque, M.M.: A hierarchical key derivative symmetric key algorithm using digital logic. In: 2017 International Conference on Electrical, Computer and Communication Engineering (ECCE), pp. 604–609. IEEE (Feb 2017). https://doi.org/10.1109/ECACE.2017.7912976
4. Diffie, W., Hellman, M.E.: New directions in cryptography. In: Secure Communications and Asymmetric Cryptosystems, pp. 143–180. Routledge (2019)
5. Cheddad, A., Condell, J., Curran, K., Kevitt, P.M.: Digital image steganography: survey and analysis of current methods. Signal Process. **90**(3), 727–752 (2010). https://doi.org/10.1016/j.sigpro.2009.08.010
6. Taha, M.S., Rahim, M.S.M., Lafta, S.A., Hashim, M.M., Alzuabidi, H.M.: Combination of steganography and cryptography: a short survey. IOP Conf. Ser.: Mater. Sci. Eng. **518**(5), 052003 (2019). https://doi.org/10.1088/1757-899X/518/5/052003
7. Jung, K.H.: A study on machine learning for steganalysis. In: Proceedings of the 3rd International Conference on Machine Learning and Soft Computing, pp. 12–15 (Jan 2019)
8. Hureib, E.S., Gutub, A.A.: Enhancing medical data security via combining elliptic curve cryptography and image steganography. Int. J. Comput. Sci. Netw. Secur. (IJCSNS) **20**(8), 1–8 (2020)
9. Hureib, E.S.B., Gutub, A.A.: Enhancing medical data security via combining elliptic curve cryptography with 1-LSB and 2-LSB image steganography. Int. J. Comp. Sci. Netw. Secur. (IJCSNS) **20**(12), 232–241 (2020)
10. Biswas, C., Gupta, U.D., Haque, M.M.: An efficient algorithm for confidentiality, integrity and authentication using hybrid cryptography and steganography. In: 2019 International Conference on Electrical, Computer and Communication Engineering (ECCE), pp. 1–5. IEEE (Feb 2019)
11. Alsaffar, Q.S., Mohaisen, H.N., Almashhdini, F.N.: An encryption based on DNA and AES algorithms for hiding a compressed text in colored Image. IOP Conf. Ser.: Mater. Sci. Eng. **1058**(1), 012048 (2021). https://doi.org/10.1088/1757-899X/1058/1/012048
12. Hassoon, N.H., Ali, R.A., Abed, H.N., Alkhazraji, A.A.J.: Multilevel hiding text security using hybrid technique steganography and cryptography. Int. J. Eng. Technol. **7**(4), 3674–3677 (2018)
13. Wai, Y.Y., Myat, E.E.: Comparison of LSB, MSB and New Hybrid (NHB) of steganography in digital image. Int. J. Eng. Trends Appl. **5**(4), 16–19 (2018)
14. Saravanan, M., Priya, A.: An algorithm for security enhancement in image transmission using steganography. Journal of the Institute of Electronics and Computer **1**(1), 1–8 (2019)
15. Jassim, K.N., et al.: Hybrid cryptography and steganography method to embed encrypted text message within image. J. Phys. Conf. Ser. **1339**(1), 012061 (2019). https://doi.org/10.1088/1742-6596/1339/1/012061
16. Abbas, M.S., Mahdi, S.S., Hussien, S.A.: Security improvement of cloud data using hybrid cryptography and steganography. In: 2020 International Conference on Computer Science and Software Engineering (CSASE), pp. 123–127. IEEE (Apr 2020)
17. Patel, N., Oza, P., Agrawal, S.: Homomorphic cryptography and its applications in various domains. In: Bhattacharyya, S., Hassanien, A.E., Gupta, D., Khanna, A., Pan, I. (eds.) International Conference on Innovative Computing and Communications. LNNS, vol. 55, pp. 269–278. Springer, Singapore (2019). https://doi.org/10.1007/978-981-13-2324-9_27

18. Oza, P., Kathrecha, V., Malvi, P.: Encryption algorithm using rubik's cube principle for secure transmission of multimedia files. In: Third International Conference on Multidisciplinary Research and Practice IJRSI, vol. 4, pp. 239–243 (2016)
19. Shah, Y., Joshi, S., Oza, P., Agrawal, S.: An insight of information security: a skeleton. Int. J. Recent Technol. Eng. (IJRTE) **8**(3), 2600–2605 (2019). https://doi.org/10.35940/ijrte.C4922. 098319
20. Sharma, K., Aggarwal, A., Singhania, T., Gupta, D., Khanna, A.: Hiding data in images using cryptography and deep neural network. arXiv preprint arXiv:1912.10413 (2019)
21. Wang, Z., Bovik, A.C., Sheikh, H.R., Simoncelli, E.P.: Image quality assessment: from error visibility to structural similarity. IEEE Trans. Image Process. **13**(4), 600–612 (2004)
22. Al-Afandy, K.A., Faragallah, O.S., ELmhalawy, A., El-Rabaie, E.S.M., El-Banby, G.M.: High security data hiding using image cropping and LSB least significant bit steganography. In: 2016 4th IEEE International Colloquium on Information Science and Technology (CiSt), pp. 400–404. IEEE (Oct 2016)

Mitigation and Prevention Methods for Distributed Denial-of-Service Attacks on Network Servers

Kwitee D. Gaylah[1(✉)] and Ravirajsinh S. Vaghela[2]

[1] Cyber Security, Marwadi University, Gujarat, India
kwiteed.gaylah.115593@marwadiuniversity.ac.in
[2] Marwadi University, Gujarat, India

Abstract. Present-day Different network-based attacks increased rapidly as internet-based communication increased. Recent DDoS attacks noticed throughout the Ukrainian government, defense, and banking websites. DDoS attacks become a major threat because the different vectors of malicious attacks increased this year with different motivations. This paper shows a cutting-edge overview of DDoS attacks, defense strategies, and migration methods. This article gives a systematic analysis of DDoS attacks that include the classification of different sorts of DDoS attacks and their mitigation and preventative methods. This research study examined well-known preventative and mitigation approaches. Additionally, it provided an overview of various attack kinds, filtering strategies, and attack detection approaches. It outlined the salient aspects of the attacks as well as the benefits and drawbacks of various forms of defense.

Keywords: Denial-of-service · Autonomous System (AS) · Botnet · Distributed denial-of-service · Load balancing · Log analysis · Filtering

1 Introduction

Distributed denial-of-service (DDoS) attacks, one of the numerous forms of illegal activities that take place online, can overwhelm even the biggest servers with too many requests, causing them to crash. Figure 1 represents a DDoS attack.

Current conflicts between Russia and Ukraine, which accounted for a major portion of all DDoS-related news in these nations in mid-January, had a big impact on the DDoS trend in 2022 [35]. The Internet sector, followed by cryptocurrency and later retail was the second most targeted. On March 1st, 2022, a DDoS attack on Kyiv Mayor Vitali Klitschko's website, and several Ukrainian ministries' websites were hacked [17]. The Ukrainian Ministry of Defence's website, the online services of Oschadbank and Privat Bank, as well as the hosting company Mirohost, were all subject to DDoS attacks in the middle of February [29]. Customers of Privat Banks reported receiving phone SMS messages regarding inoperable ATMs around the same time, which appeared to be sent to cause panic. On the 2 of February, a new DDoS attack consumed Ukrainian government

The original version of this chapter was revised: the 30th reference line has been updated. The correction to this chapter is available at https://doi.org/10.1007/978-3-031-23095-0_21

S. Rajagopal et al. (Eds.): ASCIS 2022, CCIS 1760, pp. 70–82, 2022.
https://doi.org/10.1007/978-3-031-23095-0_5

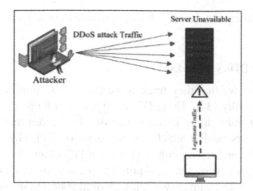

Fig. 1. DDoS attack

resources, and in late February and early March, the State Special Communications Service of Ukraine reported a mass of ongoing attacks [17].

DDoS attacks have grown in scale and regularity over the past few years. According to Kaspersky's Securelist blog, a percent of all recorded DDoS attacks in Q1 2022 occurred in the US. China and Germany, which were affected by 9.96% and 4.85% of recorded attacks during the same period, were closely behind it [36] (Fig. 2).

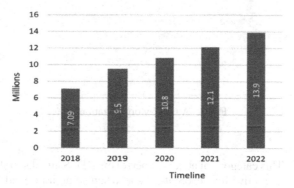

Fig. 2. DDoS attack trends

2 Proposed Survey

The Internet's architecture offers users the best-effort, packet-switched services. This leads to resource sharing amongst several users. As a result, one user's actions could interfere with another user's ability to access the services [21]. DDoS attack often seeks to obstruct authenticated users' access to services by depleting the system's resources. DDoS attack packets typically lack any glaring characteristics that would allow people to tell the difference between the bad stream from legitimate ones.

This paper shows a cutting-edge overview of DDoS attacks, defense strategies, and migration methods. This article gives a systematic analysis of DDoS attacks that include the classification of different sorts of DDoS attacks and their mitigation and preventative methods.

2.1 Motivation for DDoS Attacks

Check Point study shows that they track more than 1000 significant, diverse DDoS attacks every day globally [35]. These DDoS attacks can be directed at anyone, from an individual user at home to an entire government. The desire for financial gain is one of the main drivers behind attacks on these users [37]. However, pornographic or gambling websites can be tempting targets for a DDoS attack. Additionally, DDoS attacks frequently target governments and political organizations. DDoS attacks can also target financial markets and gaming websites, as demonstrated in Fig. 3.

In Cloudflare Lab quarterly report, we observe that most manufacturing, business services, and gaming are most affected by DDoS attacks [38].

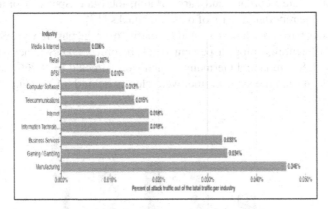

Fig. 3. Attack by organizations

- *Show of power:* This category of attackers performs DDoS attacks to show their skills.
- *Revenge:* Another motive for DDoS attacks is when some irate (and less technically proficient) individuals carry them out as revenge for perceived oppression.
- *Cyberwarfare:* This is another crucial attack motive that puts its targets in danger and has a big negative economic impact. An attack of this kind is often carried out by a few well-trained members of a military or terrorist organization.
- *Financial benefit:* This category of DDoS attacks is thought to be the most dangerous, they aim to earn some financial benefit from the hacks.

2.2 Attack Strategies and Phases

Figure 4 shows the DDoS attack's composition. A victim or target machine, numerous control masters, slaves, agents, and an attacker make up the components of a DDoS attack [13].

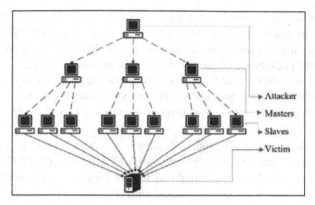

Fig. 4. DDoS attack components

- *Phase one:* The hacker acquires a good number of infected machines during the early phase. These infected devices are referred to as the masters because they direct other compromised machines into the attacking army [16].
- *Phase two:* The second step starts if enough devices have been enlisted in a compromised army. The term for this hacker army is a botnet. The attacker prepares for the attack by sending all essential information to the master armies in the second phase. The master armies then send the information to all slave armies.
- *Phase three:* In the last stage, the army of the attacker launches and executes attacks [33].

2.3 Attack Methods

Understanding DDoS attack classification methods are essential for comprehending DDoS attack studies. This study's goal is to investigate each attack taxonomy and give a complete, straightforward classification scheme. Figure 5 presents a classification scheme.

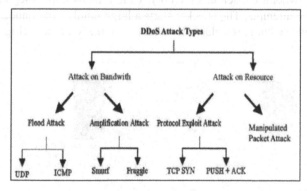

Fig. 5. Attack methods

- *Resource Depletion Attacks:* These attacks' purpose is to overload or crashes the system's significant resources, including memory, sockets, and CPU [9]. Initially, the attacker makes use of certain protocols along the application, transport, and network levels. Spoofed packets are employed as a second method of attack.
- *Protocol Exploit Attacks:* The weaknesses in the various network layer protocols are used by known protocol-based attacks. This attack causes the victim to use all of its memory while carrying out various memory-demanding tasks [22, 23].

Flood Attack. An example of resource depletion is a flood attack, in which a victim is attacked using the application layer protocol HTTP [19]. The HTTP GET and HTTP POST requests are specifically manipulated in this form of attack while a server or particular application is being communicated with (Fig. 6).

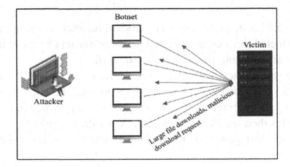

Fig. 6. Flood attack

TCP SYN Hack. The client sends an SYN packet to a server in three-way handshaking to start the handshaking. The server responds by delivering an SYN+ ACK packet. Finally, the client sends back the final ACK packet which completes the handshake and establishes the TCP connection [7]. By taking advantage of this functionality, the attacker can overwhelm the server's memory, which finally causes legitimate users to refuse connection attempts. The attacker starts a large number of connections but does not finish the handshaking procedure, flooding the victim's memory (Fig. 7).

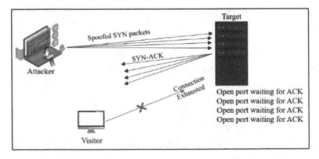

Fig. 7. TCP SYN attack

DNS Amplification Attack. The goal of the most prevalent cyberattacks in the world is the network bandwidth of the victim. In this instance, the goal of the attacker is to leverage a DNS's weak points to scale up an intrusion significantly [3]. This exploit is also an illustration of a reflection attack that floods a victim with a large number of UDP packets by using several open recursive DNS servers [3, 25, 33] (Fig. 8).

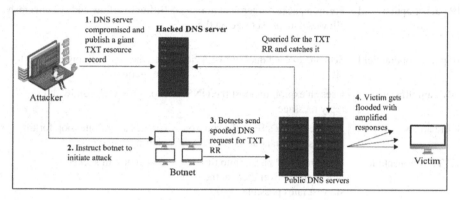

Fig. 8. DNS amplification attack

Infrastructure Attack. The purpose of this attack is to seriously harm essential components of the Internet. As a result, it also targets the resources (memory, CPU) of the targeted system in addition to the network bandwidth [14]. Infrastructural attacks, for instance, target the DNS, particularly the root. A botnet sends standard UDP requests to the DNS server throughout a DNS flooding attack [2]. But because there are so many of them, the system becomes overwhelmed, and eventually, all of the resources are used up.

Zero-day Attack. Using some undiscovered security flaws or vulnerabilities, a zero-day attack takes place on day 0 [27, 34]. A "zero-day" is the first day after an attack when the system's vulnerabilities are discovered. For exposing zero-day vulnerabilities, many private software businesses or security organizations offer incentives and prizes [15] (Table 1).

Table 1. DDoS attacks summary

Attack Type	Description	Impact
HTTP flood	Exploits HTTP POST and GET request	Deplete all server resources
DNS flooding	Uses an exploit to boost the DNS response message	Flood network bandwidth

(*continued*)

Table 1. (*continued*)

Attack Type	Description	Impact
TCP SYN attack	Exploits the three-way handshaking of TCP	Deplete all server resources
ICMP flood	Exploits ICMP request	Flood network bandwidth
IP packet option field	Forms a packet larger than the allowed data packet size on the server	Buffer overflow and system crash
IP packet option field	Sets one to each quality-of-service bit	Inundates processing ability of the victim
DNS amplification	Uses an exploit to boost the DNS reply message	Flood network bandwidth
Land attack	Use the victim's IP as the source and destination address	Creates an infinite loop for the victim
HTTP fragmentation	Split an HTTP packet into tiny pieces and deliver them at the slowest rates possible	Consumes all sockets
Slow read	Reads the response as slowly as possible	Consumes all connections in the connection table
Slowlories	Opens the HTTP connection for the longest feasible time	Consumes all sockets
R.U.D. Y	Exploits the form submission field by sending data with the smallest packet size possible	Consumes all the connections
UDP flood	Sends a significant volume of UDP packets to a target's chosen or random port	Consumes network bandwidth

3   Prevention Methods

The best defensive strategy against DDoS attacks is to prevent them from happening (Fig. 9).

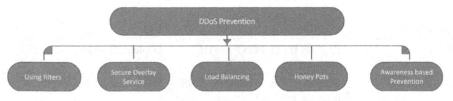

Fig. 9. DDoS prevention

3.1 Prevention Using Filters

Filtering strategies primarily shield a victim from attacks and keep an offender from being an unwitting victim. In essence, all filtering methods are used on the routers to guarantee that only authorized traffic can enter a system. This section will discuss several filtering strategies.

Route-based Packet Filtering. Route-based Packet Filtering uses routing information to evaluate whether a packet will reach a route [26]. An IP packet with a source address that differs from a set range of addresses is rejected by the core routers since it seems faked to the router [4].

According to Kihong Park and Heejo Lee's research, route-based packet filtering occurs on two timescales: packet forwarding based on table lookup at the fast time, and filter table update the slow one. As a result, its forwarding/discard function can be executed nearly at line speed subject to general processing overhead. That is, the core filtering function itself is not subject to a DoS attack [26].

Access Control Lists (ACL). This method can only be used for a brief period of historical time because it requires a lot of computing power. Markus et al. provided a fresh approach to reducing DDoS attacks based on collected information in their research. Instead of trying to identify DDoS attacks, the system aims to automatically create filter rules for IP firewalls. By doing so, the server will be able to continue serving legitimate users even when it is being heavily attacked by Denial-of-Service Attacks. [12].

Ingress Filtering. Egress filtering is the idea of firewalling traffic that originates on a local network but is going to a distant network. Like most other comparable for-profit and open-source solutions, pfSense includes a LAN rule that permits all traffic from the LAN to the Internet. However, this is not a good approach. Since most people anticipate it, it has been the de facto default in most firewall implementations. The common belief is that anything on the internal network is "trustworthy," so why bother screening?[10] RFC 226768's definition of ingress filtering permits network traffic that corresponds to a present range of the network's domain prefix to enter [30]. As a result, if an attacker uses a spoof IP address that does not match the prefix, the routers will disregard it. These filtering algorithms guarantee protection from a sizable number of DDoS attacks that employ faked IP [11].

Source Address Validity Enforcement Protocol (SAVE). The previously described RPF protocol has been improved with the SAVE protocol. It mandates that all destination routers linked to a source receive messages containing the most recent source information from the routers [20]. Each router then utilizes its forwarding table, which has been updated with the most recent data, to filter packets according to RPF's techniques.

Hop-count Filtering. This method doesn't ensure complete detection, but it can reject the majority of the spoof IP packets that make up the attack flow. The HCF Mechanism uses the IP header information, which is difficult to fabricate, to distinguish between faked and genuine packets [8]. To stop an attack, the filter discards packets that it recognizes as being part of a flow of faked packets.

History-based Filtering. To distinguish between legitimate traffic and malicious traffic, an efficient method (history-based IP filtering (HIF)) was proposed [24]. This method examines several DDoS attack features as well as regular traffic to extract traits that reveal information about the DDoS attack's occurrence. An attack is anything that deviates from the regular traffic profile.

3.2 Secure Overlay

The aim behind this method is to build an overlay network over the main IP network [32]. This overlay network serves as the gateway for outside networks to connect to the secured network. It is expected that safety can be attained if a network utilizes a distributed firewall or hides its IP addresses [18, 31].

3.3 Honeypots

An intriguing DDoS protection method is a honeypot. A honeypot is a network-attached system that hackers use to identify and research the tactics and types of attacks they utilize [9, 33]. On the internet, it serves as a potential target and alerts the defenders to any unauthorized attempts to access the information system. The actual system is thus kept secure [39]. The problem with this approach is skilled attackers can quickly recognize it because it can be distinguished from production systems [21].

3.4 Load Balancing

Dividing network traffic among several servers is known as load balancing. It ensures that a single server will not be overloaded. Load balancing increases the responsiveness of an application by distributing the work evenly (Fig. 10).

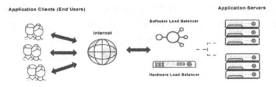

Fig. 10. Load balancing

3.5 Additional Security Patches

To prevent the system from being compromised by DDoS attacks, it is important to update software security patches regularly. The following are additional strategies to mitigate DDoS attacks.

Changing IP Addresses. Using this strategy, the computer system switches its IP address to a different one. Since the previous one could potentially be the target of DDoS attacks. However, there are other administrative costs associated with this. This strategy is effective as long as the attacker is not knowledgeable of the new IP address

Disabling Unusual Services. This is a DDoS defense technique. DDoS attacks could happen to some services, like character generator and UDP echo. By blocking these services, a system can be shielded from some DDoS attacks. Telnet and SSH remote access options to network servers should be disabled (Table 2).

Table 2. DDoS prevention using filters

Filter method	Description	Source of action
Route-based packet filtering	Uses a routing table to determine whether a packet arriving at a route is valid to the source and destination addresses	Main router
Access Control Lists (ACL)	Use a set of rules to specify which systems or users are permitted or denied access to a specific item or system resource	Main router
Ingress filtering	Uses a predetermined range of domain prefixes to filter traffic	Edge router for the victim's network
Source Address Validity Enforcement Protocol	Prevents delivery of packets based on source and destination addresses	Every inbound router
Hop-count filtering	Operates based on a packet's hop counts	The router at the victim's location
History-based filtering	The history of the normal traffic is used to determine malicious traffic	The router at the victim's location
Martian address filtering	Blocks the transmission of packets with IPs from the unallocated range of IP addresses	Every inbound router
Packet-score	A statistical technique that evaluates the profile values of each packet to award it a score	The router at the victim's location
Path identifier–based filtering	Works according to the attacker's known route	The router at the victim's location
SAVE	Makes the routers transmit messages with updated source addresses to all of the destination routers	Main router

4 DDoS Mitigation Methods

This section is crucial for defending against numerous DDoS attacks. However, despite new attack signatures and updates, DDoS attacks continue to pose a concern. As a result, there are numerous research efforts taking place in the area of DDoS mitigation, which is the next step of defense.

4.1 Detection of DDoS Attacks

It is fairly simple to detect an attack because it significantly reduces service or system performance. Sometimes a response necessitates tracing the origin of the attack, while other times it necessitates spotting the malevolent activity.

Signature-based Detection. To distinguish between legitimate traffic and malicious traffic, signature-based detection methods use known DDoS attacks to determine the attack signatures [24]. As a result, they are effective in identifying known DDoS attacks. But these detection systems fail to pick up on any variations in currently occurring attacks. This section of the paper will discuss some well-known signature-based detection mechanisms.

Log Analysis. Because they offer real-time information and statistics about your web traffic, log analysis tools are helpful software solutions for DDoS monitoring and detection. Spikes in activity suggestive of a DDoS attack can be found using tools like SolarWinds Loggly, and Splunk for instance [28]. To do this, Loggly uses an anomaly-detection program that scans servers for an excessive quantity of 503 errors.

Spectral Analysis. The methods described here use spectrum analysis to separate attack flow from regular traffic. For instance, attack flow is identified using the packets' power spectral density detection based on anomalies [1]. Attacks with new signatures and freshly discovered attacks can both be handled by anomaly -based detection mechanisms [6].

SNORT. SNORT is a highly popular tool for detecting network intrusions. It is a simple rule-based tool for detecting a variety of attacks and probes [5]. It has coupled anomaly-based security with signature-based detection to broaden the scope of attacks it can identify. However, because SNORT relies on precise pattern matching, it may cause a bottleneck in the system's performance due to the high volume of traffic and Internet speed.

5 Conclusion

Based on their successes and failures, this study examined well-known preventative and mitigation approaches for DDoS attacks. Additionally, it provided an overview of various attack kinds, filtering strategies, and attack detection approaches. It outlined the benefits and drawbacks of various forms of DDoS defense strategies. However, further research is necessary to fight new and undiscovered attacks with new signatures.

References

1. Agrawal, N., Tapaswi, S.: Low rate cloud DDoS attack defense method based on power spectral density analysis. Inf. Process. Lett. **138**, 44–50 (2018). https://doi.org/10.1016/j.ipl. 2018.06.001
2. Alonso, R., Monroy, R., Trejo, L.A.: Mining IP to domain name interactions to detect DNS flood attacks on recursive DNS servers. Sensors (Switzerland) **16**(8), 1311 (2016). https:// doi.org/10.3390/s16081311
3. Anagnostopoulos, M., Kambourakis, G., Kopanos, P., Louloudakis, G., Gritzalis, S.: DNS amplification attack revisited. Comput. Secur. **39**, 475–485 (2013). https://doi.org/10.1016/j. cose.2013.10.001
4. Armbruster, B., Smith, J.C., Park, K.: A packet filter placement problem with application to defense against spoofed denial of service attacks. Eur. J. Oper. Res. **176**(2), 1283–1292 (2007). https://doi.org/10.1016/j.ejor.2005.09.031
5. Badotra, S., Panda, S.N.: SNORT based early DDoS detection system using Opendaylight and open networking operating system in software defined networking. Clust. Comput. **24**(1), 501–513 (2020). https://doi.org/10.1007/s10586-020-03133-y
6. Chen, Y., Hwang, K.: Collaborative detection and filtering of shrew DDoS attacks using spectral analysis. J. Parallel Distrib. Comput. **66**(9), 1137–1151 (2006). https://doi.org/10. 1016/j.jpdc.2006.04.007
7. Deng, Y., et al.: Resource provisioning for mitigating edge DDoS attacks in MEC-Enabled SDVN. IEEE Internet Things J. **9**(23), 24264–24280 (2022). https://doi.org/10.1109/JIOT. 2022.3189975
8. Devi, G.U.: Detection of DDoS attack using optimized hop count filtering technique. Indian J. Sci. Technol. **8**(26), 1–6 (2015). https://doi.org/10.17485/ijst/2015/v8i26/83981
9. Erhan, D., Anarim, E.: Hybrid DDoS detection framework using matching pursuit algorithm. IEEE Access **8**, 118912–118923 (2020). https://doi.org/10.1109/ACCESS.2020.3005781
10. Baker, F., Savola, P.: Ingress Filtering for Multihomed Networks. RFC 3704 (2004)
11. Ferguson, P., Senie, D.: Network ingress filtering: defeating denial of service attacks which employ IP source address spoofing. In: Request for Comments (2000)
12. Goldstein, M., Lampert, C., Reif, M., Stahl, A., Breuel, T.: Bayes optimal DDoS mitigation by adaptive history-based IP filtering. In: Proceedings - 7th International Conference on Networking. ICN 2008 (2008)
13. Gupta, B.B., Chaudhary, P., Chang, X., Nedjah, N.: Smart defense against distributed Denial of service attack in IoT networks using supervised learning classifiers. Comput. Electr. Eng. **98**, 107726 (2022). https://doi.org/10.1016/j.compeleceng.2022.107726
14. Hasan, D., Hussin, M., Abdullah, A.: Effective amplification mitigation and spoofing detection during DNS flooding attacks on internet. J. Eng. Appl. Sci. **12**(3), 475–480 (2017). https:// doi.org/10.3923/jeasci.2017.475.480
15. Hindy, H., Atkinson, R., Tachtatzis, C., Colin, J.N., Bayne, E., Bellekens, X.: Utilising deep learning techniques for effective zero-day attack detection. Electronics (Switzerland) **9**(10), 1684 (2020). https://doi.org/10.3390/electronics9101684
16. Huang, K., Yang, L.X., Yang, X., Xiang, Y., Tang, Y.Y.: A low-cost distributed denial-of-service attack architecture. IEEE Access **8**, 42111–42119 (2020). https://doi.org/10.1109/ ACCESS.2020.2977112
17. Husák, M., Laštovička, M., Plesník, T.: Handling internet activism during the Russian invasion of ukraine: a campus network perspective. Digital Threats: Research and Practice (2022). https://doi.org/10.1145/3534566
18. Keromytis, A.D., Misra, V., Rubenstein, D.: SOS: Secure overlay services. In: Computer Communication Review (2002)

19. Kshirsagar, D., Kumar, S.: An ontology approach for proactive detection of HTTP flood DoS attack. Int. J. Syst. Assur. Eng. Manag. (2021). https://doi.org/10.1007/s13198-021-01170-3
20. Li, J., Mirkovic, J., Ehrenkranz, T., Wang, M., Reiher, P., Zhang, L.: Learning the valid incoming direction of IP packets. Comput. Netw. **52**(2), 399–417 (2008). https://doi.org/10.1016/j.comnet.2007.09.024
21. Mahjabin, T., Xiao, Y., Sun, G., Jiang, W.: A survey of distributed denial-of-service attack, prevention, and mitigation techniques. Int. J. Distrib. Sens. Netw. **13** (2017). https://doi.org/10.1177/1550147717741463
22. Manickam, S., et al.: Labelled dataset on distributed denial-of-service (DDoS) attacks based on internet control message protocol version 6 (ICMPv6). Wirel. Commun. Mob. Comput. **2022** (2022). https://doi.org/10.1155/2022/8060333
23. Manso, P., Moura, J., Serrão, C.: SDN-based intrusion detection system for early detection and mitigation of DDoS attacks. Information (Switzerland) **10**(3), 106 (2019). https://doi.org/10.3390/info10030106
24. Obaidat, M.S. (ed.): ICETE 2016. CCIS, vol. 764. Springer, Cham (2017). https://doi.org/10.1007/978-3-319-67876-4
25. Nuiaa, R.R., Manickam, S., Alsaeedi, A.H.: Distributed reflection denial of service attack: a critical review. Int. J. Electr. Comput. Eng. (IJECE) **11**(6), 5327 (2021). https://doi.org/10.11591/ijece.v11i6.pp5327-5341
26. Park, K., Lee, H.: On the effectiveness of route-based packet filtering for distributed DoS attack prevention in power-law internets * (2001)
27. Parrend, P., Navarro, J., Guigou, F., Deruyver, A., Collet, P.: Foundations and applications of artificial intelligence for zero-day and multi-step attack detection. EURASIP J. Inf. Secur. **2018**(1), 1–21 (2018). https://doi.org/10.1186/s13635-018-0074-y
28. Rodrigues, K., Luo, Y., Yuan, D.: CLP: Efficient and scalable search on compressed text logs. In: Proceedings of the 15th USENIX Symposium on Operating Systems Design and Implementation. OSDI 2021 (2021)
29. Serpanos, D., Komninos, T.: The cyberwarfare in Ukraine. Computer (Long Beach Calif) **55**, 88–91 (2022). https://doi.org/10.1109/MC.2022.3170644
30. Tandon, R.: A Survey of distributed denial of service attacks and defenses (2020). https://arxiv.org/abs/2008.01345
31. Wang, X., Chellappan, S., Boyer, P., Xuan, D.: On the effectiveness of secure overlay forwarding systems under intelligent distributed DoS attacks. IEEE Trans. Parallel Distrib. Syst. **17**(7), 619–632 (2006). https://doi.org/10.1109/TPDS.2006.93
32. Yang, X., Yu, Y.: DDoS attacks defense mechanism based on secure routing alliance. Int. J. Performability Eng. **14**, 515–520 (2018). https://doi.org/10.23940/ijpe.18.03.p12.512520
33. Zhang, C.: Impact of defending strategy decision on DDoS attack. Complexity **2021**(2), 1–11 (2021). https://doi.org/10.1155/2021/6694383
34. Zoppi, T., Ceccarelli, A., Bondavalli, A.: Unsupervised algorithms to detect zero-day attacks: strategy and application. IEEE Access **9** (2021). https://doi.org/10.1109/ACCESS.2021.3090957
35. CYBER AT TACK TRENDS Check Point's 2022 Mid-Year Report
36. kaspersky.de APT trends report Q1 2022 GReAT
37. DDoS attack trends for Q1 2021
38. Network-Layer DDoS Attack Trends for Q4'20
39. Five Best Practices for Mitigating DDoS Attacks How to defend against rapidly evolving Distributed Denial-of-Service threats and address vulnerabilities at every layer

A Machine Learning Framework for Automatic Detection of Malware

Syed Shabbeer Ahmad[1], Atheequllah Khan[1], Pankaj Kawadkar[2], Imtiyaz Khan[1] (ID),
Mummadi Upendra Kumar[1]([⊠]) (ID), and D. Shravani[3] (ID)

[1] Department of CSE, MJCET, OU, Hyderabad, India
{shabbeer.ahmad,atheequllah.khan,imtiyaz.khan,
upendra.kumar}@mjcollege.ac.in
[2] Department of CSE, SSSUTMS, Sehore, India
[3] Department of CSE, Stanley College of Engineering and Technology for Women, OU,
Hyderabad, India
drdasarishravani@stanley.edu.in

Abstract. Cyberspace is every expanding with inclusion of diversified networks
and systems. With the emerging technologies such as Internet of Things (IoT) and
distributed computing, there is seamless integration of heterogeneous applications
with interoperability. This has brought unprecedented use cases and applications in
various domains. Unfortunately, there is every growing threat to cyberspace due
to different kinds of malicious programs termed as malware. Since adversaries
are developing various kinds of malware, its detection has become a challenging task. Of late, machine learning (ML) techniques are widely used to solve
problems in real world applications. Plenty of supervised learning methods came
into existence. The objective of this paper is to explore and evaluate different
ML models with empirical study. In this paper, we proposed a ML framework
for analysing performance of different prediction models. An algorithm known
as Machine Learning based Automatic Malware Detection (ML-AMD) is proposed. This algorithm is used to realize the framework with supervised learning.
This empirical study has resulted in knowledge about ML models such as Decision
Tree (DT), Logistic Regression (LR), Random Forest (RF), Multilayer Perceptron
(MLP) and Gradient Boosting (GB). Random Forest model has exhibited highest
accuracy with 97.96%. The research outcomes in this paper help in triggering
further investigations towards automatic detection of malware.

Keywords: Malware detection · Machine learning · Decision tree · Logistic
regression · Random forest · Multilayer perceptron · Gradient boosting

1 Introduction

Malware is the malicious software that is created with bad intentions. It is often used
to spread unwanted software that causes damage to systems. Adversaries are making
business out of it and there are many incidents of it in the recent past. The term malware
refers to software that damages devices, steals data, and causes chaos. There are many

S. Rajagopal et al. (Eds.): ASCIS 2022, CCIS 1760, pp. 83–95, 2022.
https://doi.org/10.1007/978-3-031-23095-0_6

types of malware—viruses, Trojans, spyware, ransomware, and more. With the availability of malware instances and signatures, it became easier to identify known malware. Machine learning domain provides required AI enabled techniques that can be exploited for malware detection. With the recent advancements in ML, it is possible to achieve near real time detection of malware [1]. It is observed from existing methods that there are many advantages of using ML techniques. The advantages include prediction accuracy, ability to use supervised learning samples and so on.

ML models are widely used for detection of malware with supervised learning. Such models are explored in [1, 5, 8–11, 14] and [15]. Gibert *et al.* [1] proposed a dep learning model for malware classification. It is made up of multiple models for efficient predictions. Karbab *et al.* [5] proposed a data-driven malware detection approach using ML techniques. They used behaviour analysis reports for their empirical study. Mahindru *et al.* [8] proposed a methodology for automatic Android malware detection using ML techniques. Hosseinzadeh *et al.* [9] proposed ML approaches that can be used for prediction of given disease. Chin *et al.* [10] also focused on DGA based machine learning models for malware detection. Chen *et al.* [11] used malware detection approach for Android malware using ML techniques. Masum *et al.* proposed a deep learning model for Android malware detection. The model is known as Droid-NNet. Usman *et al.* [14] focused on building an intelligent system for malware detection and that is associated with digital forensics. Singh *et al.* [15] used ML techniques to detect malware in executable files. From the review of literature, it is ascertained that machine learning models are very useful for creating artificial intelligence (AI) needed to detect malware automatically. There are many ML models available. However, it is important to analyse each model for its modus operandi and performance for making choices for building a real malware detection model. Our contributions in this paper are as follows.

1. We proposed a ML based framework for automatic detection of malware by exploiting many detection models using supervised learning.
2. An algorithm known as Machine Learning based Automatic Malware Detection (ML-AMD) is proposed to realize the framework.
3. We built a prototype for evaluation of the framework and the underlying models.
4. We have made performance analysis of the ML models that has resulted in various insights and capabilities of the models.

The remainder of the paper is structured as follows. Section 2 focused on the review of literature covering different ML models for malware detection. Section 3 presents the proposed methodology for automatic detection of malware. Section 4 presents experimental results while Sect. 5 concludes our work and bestows directions for future work.

2   Literature Review

This section review literature on existing methods for detection of malware. Gibert *et al.* [1] proposed a dep learning model for malware classification. It is made up of multiple models for efficient predictions. Li *et al.* [2] proposed a malware detection model based on Domain Generation Algorithm (DGA). It is based on machine learning techniques. Pei *et al.* [3] proposed a deep learning framework known as AMalNet based on CNN for malware detection. Karbab *et al.* [4] focused on Android malware detection by defining an automated framework using deep learning methods. Karbab *et al.* [5] proposed a data-driven malware detection approach using ML techniques. They used behaviour analysis reports for their empirical study. Wu [6] focused on a systematic study of malware detection methods based on deep learning. Jangam [7] explored deep learning, stacking and transfer learning methods for prediction purposes. Mahindru *et al.* [8] proposed a methodology for automatic Android malware detection using ML techniques. Hosseinzadeh *et al.* [9] proposed ML approaches that can be used for prediction of given disease. Chin *et al.* [10] also focused on DGA based machine learning models for malware detection. Chen *et al.* [11] used malware detection approach for Android malware using ML techniques. Masum *et al.* proposed a deep learning model for Android malware detection. The model is known as Droid-NNet.

Xiao *et al.* [13] defined a model based on deep learning behaviour graphs for malware detection. Usman *et al.* [14] focused on building an intelligent system for malware detection and that is associated with digital forensics. Singh *et al.* [15] used ML techniques to detect malware in executable files. Zhang *et al.* [16] focused on feature exploration using deep learning towards classification of Android malware. Alzaylaee *et al.* [17] proposed a deep learning framework known as DL-Droid for Android malware detection for real devices. Akarsh *et al.* [18] used deep learning and visualized the detection of malware and the classification results. Dib *et al.* [19] proposed multi-dimensional deep learning framework for malware classification in IoT environment. Kim *et al.* [20] focused on extraction of features along with multi-modal deep learning in order to achieve Android malware detection performance. Pektaş *et al.* [21] used opcode sequences and deep learning to detect Android malware. Gohari *et al.* [22] used network traffic based deep learning for Android malware detection and classification. Bawazeer et al. [25] exploited hardware performance counters to detect malware using ML models. Kambar et al. [26] investigated on several kinds of existing methods used to detect mobile malware.

From the review of literature, it is ascertained that machine learning models are very useful for creating artificial intelligence (AI) needed to detect malware automatically. There are many ML models available. However, it is important to analyse each model for its modus operandi and performance for making choices for building a real malware detection model.

3 Proposed Framework

We proposed a ML framework for automatic detection of malware. The framework, as presented in Fig. 1, takes malware dataset [27] and uses it for training and testing with 80:20 ratio in the form of pre-processing. The training dataset is subjected to learning a classifier. Different classifiers are exploited for malware detection. Logistic Regression, Decision Tree, Random Forest, MLP and Gradient Boosting are the prediction models used in the framework. After completion of training process, the ML models gain required intelligence to form a malware detection system which takes testing data and performs malware detection process resulting in classification of malware samples discriminated from genuine instances.

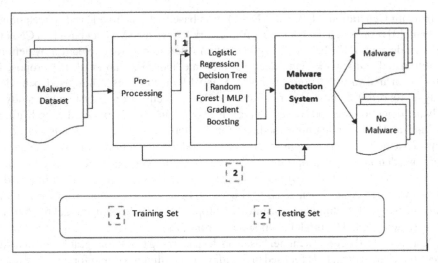

Fig. 1. ML framework for automatic malware detection

Logistic Regression is a statistical model which models a binary dependent variable by using a logistic function. It is also known as sigmoid function which is as given in Eq. 1.

$$F(x) = \frac{1}{1 + e^{-x}} = \frac{e^x}{e^x + 1} \tag{1}$$

This function helps the model to obtain values required by binary classification. If p(x), an unbounded linear function, is assumed as linear function, probability is denoted by p which ranges from 0 to 1. To solve the problem, let log p(x) is a linear function and log p(x)/(1−p(x)) is expressed as in Eq. 2.

$$\mathrm{Log}\frac{p(x)}{1 - p(x)} = \alpha_0 + \alpha.x \tag{2}$$

Once the problem of p(x) is solved, it can be expressed as in Eq. 3.

$$P(x) = \frac{e^{\alpha_0 + \alpha}}{e^{\alpha_0 + \alpha} + 1} \tag{3}$$

In order to make logistic regression as a linear function there is need for a threshold which is set to 0.5 and rate of misclassification is minimized.

Decision Tree is another algorithm used in the proposed framework. It models given data in the form of a tree so as to converge into useful decisions. In order words, it solves given problem with tree representation of data. It makes use of two important measures known as entropy and Gini index. Entropy is computed as in Eq. 4.

$$\mathrm{Entropy} = -\sum_{i=1}^{n} p_i * \log(p_i) \tag{4}$$

Gini index is another measuring for knowing inequality. It results in a value between 0 and 1. Lowest value indicates homogenous elements while higher value indicates heterogeneous elements indicating maximum inequality. This measure reflects sum of the square of probabilities associated with each class. It is computed as in Eq. 5.

$$\text{Gini index} = 1 - \sum_{i=1}^{n} p_i^2 \tag{5}$$

Random Forest is another popular ML technique. It makes use of many decision trees internally. It gets predictions of all trees and make a final decision. Multilayer perceptron, on the other hand, is an Artificial Neural Network (ANN) variant. It has input layer, output layer and at least one hidden layer. Its important computations are as in Eq. 6 and Eq. 7.

$$h^1 = step\left(z^1\right) = step\left(w^1.x + b^1\right) \tag{6}$$

$$y = step\left(z^2\right) = step\left(w^2.h^1 + b^2\right) \tag{7}$$

Any ANN is generally trained in batches. Each input value in the batch is a vector denoted as X. From the available m instances, k instances are derived as in Eq. 8.

$$x_1 = \begin{pmatrix} x_{1,1} \\ \ldots \ldots \\ x_{1,n} \end{pmatrix}, \ldots\ldots\ldots, x_k = \begin{pmatrix} x_{k,1} \\ \ldots \ldots \\ x_{k,n} \end{pmatrix} \tag{8}$$

Then the k instances are combined as in Eq. 9.

$$X = \begin{pmatrix} x_1^T \\ \ldots \ldots \\ x_k^T \end{pmatrix} = \begin{pmatrix} x_{1,1} \ldots \ldots \ldots x_{1,n} \\ \ldots \ldots \ldots \\ x_{k,1},\ldots\ldots\ldots x_{k,n} \end{pmatrix} \tag{9}$$

Provided this, the computation of y is changed to the expression in Eq. 10.

$$y = step(z) = step(X.W + b) \tag{10}$$

X is an input with shape (k,n) where number of input values is denoted as n while k denotes number of instances. W is nothing but a matrix with shape (n, u).

Gradient boosting is another algorithm used in the empirical study. Here new trees are built with significant difference. It has ensemble concept in machine learning which tries to reduce bias. The model is built as expressed in Eq. 11.

$$f_0(x) = argminA_\gamma L\left(y, \hat{\gamma}\right) \tag{11}$$

where $f_0(x)$ is the model to be built, gamma is the predicted value while y denotes actual value. Loss function is denoted as L. Now an improved model, expressed in Eq. 12, is used where residual is computed.

$$f_1(x) = f_0(x) + h_1(x) \tag{12}$$

The above process is repeated for several times. The general form of expression to be carried out at each iteration is as in Eq. 13.

$$f_m(x) = f_{m-1}(x) + h_m(x) \tag{13}$$

It is the general form for boosting algorithm. It is meant for classification of malware test samples in this paper. It exploits ensemble approach in order to have improved performance. In the framework shown in Fig. 1, different ML models are used in pipeline and the performance of the models is evaluated.

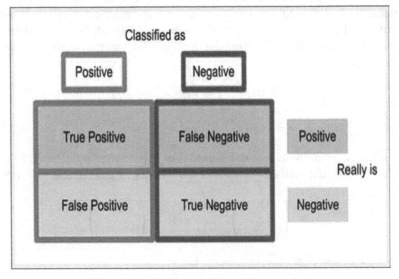

Fig. 2. Confusion matrix to evaluate models

As presented in Fig. 2, confusion matrix is used to derive many metrics for performance evaluation. The metrics are as in Table 1.

Table 1. Performance metrics used for evaluation

Metric	Formula	Value range	Best value
Precision (p)	$\frac{TP}{TP+FP}$	[0; 1]	1
Recall (r)	$\frac{TP}{TP+FN}$	[0; 1]	1
Accuracy	$\frac{TP+TN}{TP+TN+FP+FN}$	[0; 1]	1
F1-Score	$2 * \frac{(p*r)}{(p+r)}$	[0; 1]	1

Each measure has its value range between 0 and 1 indicating least and highest performance in prediction. An algorithm known as Machine Learning based Automatic Malware Detection (ML-AMD) is proposed to realize the framework.

Algorithm: Machine Learning based Automatic Malware Detection (ML-AMD)

Inputs: D (dataset), M (ML models)
Output: Predictions P

1. Start
2. Initialize map R for results
3. $(T1, T2) \leftarrow$ PreProcess(D)
4. $F \leftarrow$ FeatureExtraction($T1$)
5. For each model m in M
6.   Train the model m using F
7.   results $\leftarrow$ FitTheModel(m, T2)
8.   Update R with the model and results
9. End For
10. For each r in R
11. Print results
12. End For
13. End

Algorithm 1. Machine Learning based Automatic Malware Detection (ML-AMD)

As presented in Algorithm 1, it takes given malware dataset and set of ML models as inputs. Then it performs pre-processing of the dataset. It follows supervised learning approach to train each model present in the pipeline. Prior to training process, it has provision for feature extraction to get useful features. Each model is trained with the training set and then test set is used to perform prediction process.

4 Experimental Results

This section presents results of experiments. Each model is evaluated and their ability to discriminate between genuine and malware instances is recorded. Then different metrics are used to evaluate their performance. The performance of different ML models in detection of malware is evaluated in this section.

Table 2. Performance of different prediction models

Prediction model	TP	TN	FP	FN
Logistic regression	640	1400	13	70
Decision tree	680	1400	15	37
Random forest	670	1400	9	34
MLP	670	1400	23	35
Gradient Boosting Classifier	660	1400	7	48

As presented in Table 2, the malware prediction models along with their prediction values in terms of TP, TN, FP and FN are provided. Based on these values, different metrics are computed. For instance, the computation of performance metrics for Logistic Regression is given below. Computations are made as per equations given in Table 1.

$$Precision = 640/640 + 13 = 0.98$$

$$Recall = 640/640 + 70 = 0.90$$

$$F1 - Score = 2 \times 0.98 * 0.90/0.98 + 0.90 = 0.94$$

$$Accuracy = 640 + 1400/640 + 1400 + 13 + 70 = 0.96$$

In this fashion, each model's performance computed and the results are shown in Table 3.

Table 3. Malware detection performance comparison

Malware detection model	Performance (%)			
	Precision	Recall	F1-Score	Accuracy
Logistic regression	0.98	0.90	0.94	0.96
Decision tree	0.98	0.95	0.97	0.9777
Random forest	0.99	0.95	0.97	**0.9796**
MLP	0.97	0.95	0.96	0.97248
Gradient boosting	0.99	0.93	0.96	0.9739

Each model is evaluated with performance metrics reflecting the capabilities of the prediction models in malware detection.

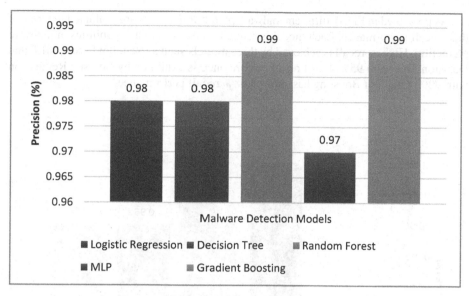

Fig. 3. Precision comparison

As presented in Fig. 3, different malware prediction models are evaluated in terms of their precision performance. Each model is found to have different capabilities in malware prediction. Highest precision is achieved by two models such as Random Forest and Gradient Boosting with 99%. Least precision performance is exhibited by MLP with 97%. Logistic Regression and Decision Tree showed 98%.

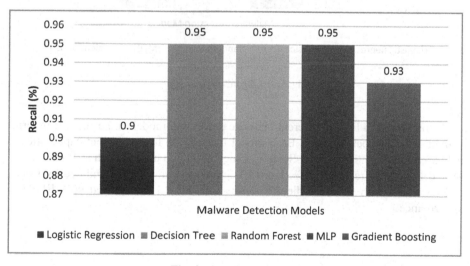

Fig. 4. Recall comparison

As presented in Fig. 4, different malware prediction models are evaluated in terms of their recall performance. Each model is found to have different capabilities in malware prediction. Highest recall is achieved by three models such as Random Forest, MLP and Decision Tree with 95%. Least recall performance is exhibited by Logistic Regression with 90%. Gradient Boosting has showed 98% recall performance.

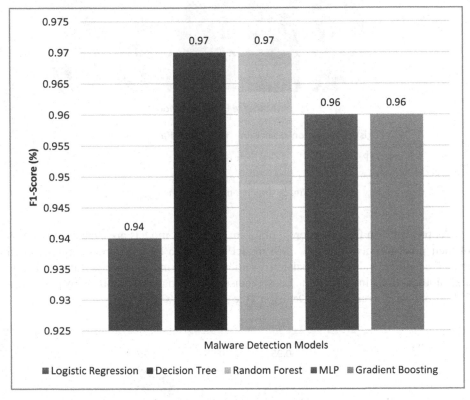

Fig. 5. F1-Score comparison

As presented in Fig. 5, different malware prediction models are evaluated in terms of their F1-Score performance. Each model is found to have different capabilities in malware prediction. Highest F1-Score is achieved by two models such as Random Forest and Decision Tree with 97%. Least F1-Score performance is exhibited by Logistic Regression with 94%. Gradient Boosting and MLP have showed 96% F1-Score performance.

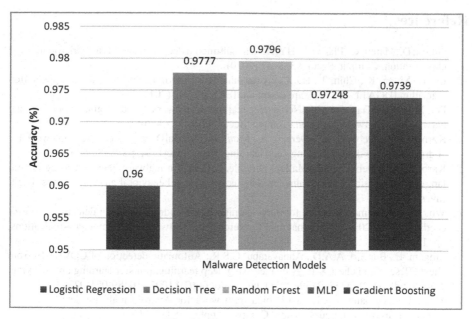

Fig. 6. Accuracy comparison

As presented in Fig. 6, different malware prediction models are evaluated in terms of their accuracy. Each model is found to have different capabilities in malware prediction. Highest accuracy is achieved by Random Forest with 97.96%. Least accuracy is exhibited by Logistic Regression with 96%. Gradient Boosting showed 97.39% accuracy while MLP showed 97.24% accuracy.

5 Conclusion and Future Work

In this paper, we proposed a ML framework for analysing performance of different prediction models. This empirical study has resulted in knowledge about ML models such as Decision Tree (DT), Logistic Regression (LR), Random Forest (RF), Multilayer Perceptron (MLP) and Gradient Boosting (GB). An algorithm known as Machine Learning based Automatic Malware Detection (ML-AMD) is proposed. This algorithm is used to realize the framework with supervised learning. It exploits a pipeline of aforementioned ML models to evaluate their performance in malware detection. Out experimental results revealed the utility of various ML models. Performance of different models are evaluated in terms of precision, recall, F1-Score and accuracy. Random Forest model has exhibited highest accuracy with 97.96%. The research outcomes in this paper help in triggering further investigations towards automatic detection of malware. In future, we explore deep learning models for malware detection as they have the capacity to have in-depth learning of features from data leading to improved prediction performance.

References

1. Gibert, D., Mateu, C., Planes, J.: HYDRA: a multimodal deep learning framework for malware classification. Comput. Secur. **95**, 1–47 (2020)
2. Li, Y., Xiong, K., Chin, T., Hu, C.: A machine learning framework for domain generation algorithm (DGA)-based malware detection. IEEE Access (2019)
3. Pei, X., Yu, L., Tian, S.: AMalNet: a deep learning framework based on graph convolutional networks for malware detection. Comput. Secur. **93**, 1–21 (2020)
4. Karbab, E.B., Debbabi, M., Derhab, A., Mouheb, D.: MalDozer: automatic framework for android malware detection using deep learning. Digit. Invest. **24**, pS48–S59 (2018)
5. Karbab, E.B., Debbabi, M.: MalDy: portable, data-driven malware detection using natural language processing and machine learning techniques on behavioral analysis reports. Digit. Invest. **28**, pS77–S87 (2019)
6. Wu, H.: A systematical study for deep learning based android malware detection. In: Proceedings of the 2020 9th International Conference on Software and Computer Applications, pp. 1–6 (2020)
7. Jangam, E., Barreto, A.A.D., Annavarapu, C.S.R.: Automatic detection of COVID-19 from chest CT scan and chest X-Rays images using deep learning, transfer learning and stacking. Appl. Intell. **52**(2), 2243–2259 (2021). https://doi.org/10.1007/s10489-021-02393-4
8. Mahindru, A., Sangal, A.L.: MLDroidâ framework for Android malware detection using machine learning techniques. Neural Comput. Appl., 1–58 (2020)
9. Sara, H.K., Peyman, H.K., Wesolowskic, M.J., Schneidera, K.A., Detersa, R.: Automatic detection of coronavirus disease (COVID-19) in X-ray and CT images: a machine learning based approach. Biocybern. Biomed. Eng., 1–13 (2021)
10. Chin, T., Xiong, K., Hu, C., Li, Y.: A machine learning framework for studying domain generation algorithm (DGA)-based malware. Secur. Priv. Commun. Netw., 433–448 (2018)
11. Chen, X., et al.: Android HIV: a study of repackaging malware for evading machine-learning detection. IEEE Trans. Inf. Forens. Secur., 1–15 (2019)
12. Masum, M., Shahriar, H.: IEEE 2019 IEEE International Conference on Big Data (Big Data), Los Angeles, CA, USA, 9–12 December 2019, pp. 5789–5793 (2019)
13. Xiao, F., Lin, Z., Sun, Y., Ma, Y.: Malware detection based on deep learning of behavior graphs. Math. Probl. Eng. **2019**, 1–10 (2019)
14. Usman, N., Usman, S., Khan, F., Jan, M.A., Sajid, A., Alazab, M., Watters, P.: Intelligent dynamic malware detection using machine learning in ip reputation for forensics data analytics. Future Gener. Comput. Syst., 1–18 (2021)
15. Singh, J., Singh, J.: A survey on machine learning-based malware detection in executable files. J. Syst. Arch., 1–24 (2020)
16. Zhang, N., Tan, Y., Yang, C., Li, Y.: Deep learning feature exploration for Android malware detection. Appl. Soft Comput., 1–7 (2021)
17. Alzaylaee, M.K., Yerima, S.Y., Sezer, S.: DL-droid: deep learning based android malware detection using real devices. Comput. Secur., 1–28 (2019)
18. Akarsh, S., Simran, K., Poornachandran, P., Menon, V.K., Soman, K.P.: IEEE 2019 5th International Conference on Advanced Computing & Communication Systems (ICACCS) - Coimbatore, India, 15–16 March 2019, pp. 1059–1063 (2019)
19. Dib, M., Torabi, S., Bou-Harb, E., Assi, C.: A multi-dimensional deep learning framework for IoT malware classification and family attribution. IEEE Trans. Netw. Serv. Manag. **18**(2), 1165–1177 (2021)
20. Kim, T.G., Kang, B.J., Rho, M., Sezer, S., Im, E.G.: A multimodal deep learning method for android malware detection using various features. IEEE Trans. Inf. Forens. Secur., 1–16 (2018)

21. Pektaş, A., Acarman, T.: Deep LEARNING to detect android malware via opcode sequences. Neurocomputing, 1–21 (2019)
22. Gohari, M., Hashemi, S., Abdi, L.: Android malware detection and classification based on network traffic using deep learning. In: 2021 7th International Conference on Web Research (ICWR), pp. 1–7 (2021)
23. Chandrashekar, G., Sahin, F.: A survey on feature selection methods. Comput. Electr. Eng. **40**(1), 16–28 (2014). https://doi.org/10.1016/j.compeleceng.2013.11.024
24. Karunakaran, V., Rajasekar, V., Joseph, S.I.T.: Exploring a filter and wrapper feature selection techniques in machine learning. In: Smys, S., Tavares, J.M.R.S., Bestak, R., Shi, F. (eds.) Computational Vision and Bio-Inspired Computing. AISC, vol. 1318, pp. 497–506. Springer, Singapore (2021). https://doi.org/10.1007/978-981-33-6862-0_40
25. Bawazeer, O., Helmy, T., Al-Hadhrami, S.: Malware detection using machine learning algorithms based on hardware performance counters: analysis and simulation. J. Phys: Conf. Ser. **1962**, 012010 (2021). https://doi.org/10.1088/1742-6596/1962/1/012010
26. Kambar, M.E.Z.N., Esmaeilzadeh, A., Kim, Y., Taghva, K.: A survey on mobile malware detection methods using machine learning. In: 2022 IEEE 12th Annual Computing and Communication Workshop and Conference (CCWC), pp. 0215–0221 (2022). https://doi.org/10.1109/CCWC54503.2022.9720753
27. Malware Exploratory Dataset. https://www.kaggle.com/code/lucaslba/malware-exploratory/data

DNNdroid: Android Malware Detection Framework Based on Federated Learning and Edge Computing

Arvind Mahindru[1][(⊠)] [iD] and Himani Arora[2]

[1] Department of Computer Science and Applications, DAV University,
Jalandhar, India
er.arvindmahindru@gmail.com
[2] Department of Mathematics, Guru Nanak Dev University, Amritsar, India

Abstract. The fact that apps are available for free via Android's official store has helped the platform become more popular. The functionality of Android apps is reliant on permissions. Due to these permissions, cyber-criminals developed malware-infected apps for smartphone users. The main fault lies in the permission model of Android. To address this issue, a framework entitled "DNNdroid" is proposed that work on the principle of federated learning. Information related to newly installed apps is stored on the user's device only and this information is not revealed to the developer. In the meantime, input from all the users is collected simultaneously to train the model with a federated learning process, so that a better classification model is developed. The main challenge in this is that a user is not able to identify whether an app is malware-infected or not. The experiment result reveals that the cloud server has an F1 score of 97.8% having a recall rate of client than 0.95 false positive rates using 1,00,000 unique Android apps with 500 plus users and 50 rounds of the federation. Further, an experiment is performed by using frameworks available in the literature and different anti-virus scanners.

Keywords: Android apps · Smartphones · Machine learning · Deep neural network · Security

1 Introduction

According to the global data report[1], Android has captured 71.54% market share. The main reason for its popularity is the availability of free apps in its official play store. Cybercriminals are taking advantage of this and developing malware-infected apps on a daily basis for smartphone users. In the literature [5, 16–18], researchers and academicians proposed different malware detection frameworks that work on machine learning techniques and achieved success too. Often, developing an accurate malware detection model with classification machine learning algorithms is dependent upon the extensive collection of datasets. But it has

---

[1] https://gs.statcounter.com/os-market-share/mobile/worldwide.

© The Author(s), under exclusive license to Springer Nature Switzerland AG 2022
S. Rajagopal et al. (Eds.): ASCIS 2022, CCIS 1760, pp. 96–107, 2022.
https://doi.org/10.1007/978-3-031-23095-0_7

a limitation, it affects the privacy of smartphone users [23]. To address these issues, there is a need for decentralized entry information which also respects the user's privacy and will not expose to third parties too.

In the literature [14, 19], academicians and researchers proposed three different machine learning solutions for malware detection i.e., client-based, cloud-based, and hybrid (combination of cloud-based and client-based) techniques. In the client-based approach, collected data is protected due to the machine learning model being developed locally on the host computer but the process is time-consuming and has the highest value of false positives. In the cloud-based approach, this process is reversed of it. It is developed by using a large set of features and reveals which app is installed by the users too. Last, in the hybrid model, Android apps that are malware-infected are sent to the cloud for further analysis. This type of solution has a high number of false positives and reveals users' private data to the cloud.

In identifying malware from Android devices, machine learning algorithms are without a doubt incredibly effective. But, to develop effective malware detection model, a large amount of information is required. In the literature [25], it was observed that large amount of features are available at the central place for training and testing the model. Addition to it, it has seen that developed model memorize and disclose information related to the dataset. To address this issue, we consider the key question that is to be answer in this study, i.e. *How can we create a decentralized, privacy-preserving classifier for Android malware?*

In this study, we proposed DNNdroid - a model that is based on classification techniques and uses the principle of federated learning and respecting the user's privacy. The proposed model collects the features from the user's smartphone without prior knowledge that an app was installed from its official play store or any other promised repositories. The proposed framework reduces the dependency of users on cloud-based technique and also benefit them in term of privacy.

In the literature [1, 2, 6, 12, 21], state-of-the-art federated learning techniques were discussed by researchers and academicians. In which, smartphone users test their data locally by using a supervised machine learning algorithm and the resultant performance is updated to the cloud for the betterment of the model. Our proposed model enhances the existing work by incorporating the principle of deep learning at the time of training the model. Further, we evaluate our proposed model by using 1,00,000 unique Android apps out of which 75,000 are benign and 25,000 are malware-infected apps with 500 plus users and 108 rounds of the federation. Additionally, we contrasted our approach with pre-existing frameworks found in the literature and several anti-virus scanners sold today.

The novel and unique contributions of this study are as under:

- To the best of our knowledge, this is the first research paper, which trained with the help of dynamic features of Android apps and prevent the users privacy too.
- In this study, we also demonstrate the effectiveness of our proposed model against malware-infected apps.

The rest of the paper is organized as follows. In Sect. 2, we discuss the related work done in the field of Android malware detection using federated learning. Section 3, described the collection of datasets from different promised repositories. The machine learning technique implemented in our proposed framework is discussed in Sect. 4. Section 5 describes the architecture of our proposed framework. Evaluating the proposed framework is discussed in Sect. 6. In Sect. 7, we compare our proposed framework with the existing framework and the distinct anti-virus available in the market. The experimental finding is discussed in Sect. 7. Section 8 discusses the conclusion and the future scope of this study.

2   Related Work

Hsu et al. [9] proposed a malware detection for Android named as privacy-preserving federated learning (PPFL). The proposed model is trained by using SVM as a base classifier. They developed their model by trained them using static analysis. Experiment result reveals that proposed model achieved higher detection rate as compared to decentralized models. Empirical results also reveals that if number of clients increases the accuracy is also increases. Gálvez et al. [6] proposed a malware detection model named as LiM that work on the principles of semi-supervised machine learning technique and federated learning. Experiment was performed on 50,000 Android apps having 200 users and 50 rounds of federation. Taheri et al. [26] proposed malware detection model entitled FEd-IIoT for detecting malware in IIoT. The results of the experiment corroborate the high accuracy rates of our attack and defence algorithms and demonstrate how the A3GAN defensive strategy protects the robustness of data privacy for Android mobile users and is around 8% more accurate than current state-of-the-art solutions.

3   Datasets

In this study, we collect Android application packages (.apk) from Google play store[2], AppChina[3], Android[4] and Mumayi[5]. Malware-infected apps were collected from AndroMalShare[6] and Malgenomeproject [29]. Table 1 represent the collected Android apps.

Feature Dataset. Extraction of features are done as per the study [15]. 1844 distinct features are extracted from collected Android apps. Features play an important role to train the classification model. In the literature [11,20], different feature selection techniques were proposed by researchers and academics. In this work, we implement chi-square test to select significant features that helps to train the model.

---

[2] https://play.google.com/store?hl=en.
[3] http://m.appchina.com/.
[4] https://android.d.cn/.
[5] http://www.mumayi.com/.
[6] http://sanddroid.xjtu.edu.cn:8080/.

Table 1. Collected Android apps.

Category	Normal	Trojan	Backdoor	Worms	Botnet	Spyware
Books and reference	12205	100	16	52	120	150
Business	1308	110	120	130	22	14
Casual	11271	3250	79	66	160	130
Communication	1414	2500	50	420	33	23
Entertainment	1222	5000	500	400	102	40
Health and fitness	1551	98	85	25	120	160
Lifestyle	10650	135	150	150	195	190
News and magazines	1064	500	42	500	200	22
Social	2159	100	240	300	450	112
Weather	11841	2	200	300	200	10

4   Machine Learning Technique

Deep Neural Network (DNN) is implemented to train the model in cloud-based architecture i.e., base learner in our study. In the literature, authors proposed two distinct methods to develop model using DNN i.e., Deep Belief Networks (DBN) and Convolutional neural networks (CNN). In the current study, we decide to build our deep learning model using DBN architecture. The deep learning method's architecture is shown in Fig. 1. It consists of two stages: supervised back propagation in the first and unsupervised pre-training in the second. Restricted Boltzmann Machines (RBM) and a deep neural network are used to train the model in the initial stages of model construction. The model is built

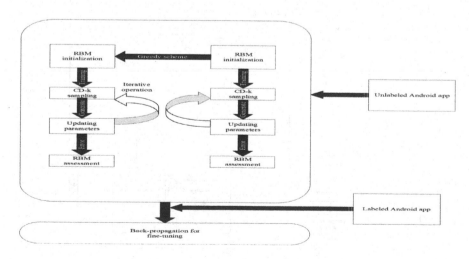

Fig. 1. Architecture of deep neural network.

using an iterative procedure in the training phase using unlabeled Android apps. Pre-trained DBN is adjusted using labelled Android apps in a supervised way during the back-propagation step. An Android app is used in both stages of the training process for a model created using the deep learning technique.

5   Proposed Framework Architecture

Federated learning is implemented based on a decentralized approach to training the model. Clients implement the process locally and the outcome is shared with the service provider. The main success of federated learning is dependent upon the labeled dataset which can be used to train the model. But it has one limitation, smartphone users do not know what to label malicious or benign. To overcome this issue, in our study we implement supervised learning at the cloud-based structure i.e., labeled dataset, and unsupervised learning at the client-based structure i.e., unlabelled dataset.

In the proposed framework, the federation of learning has happened in the cloud database and the client estimates the unlabeled dataset at the time of testing. In addition, this cloud server collects all the data from clients and aggregates them, and presents the weight. Figure 2 demonstrates the architecture of the proposed work. The following steps are taken to train and evaluate the model.

1. **Server Side:** First of all, labeled data is given to the server to train it as a base classifier and send unlabeled data to assess the weight from it.
2. **Client Side:** Client receive baseline classifier and base learner.
3. **Weight Gain:** Client gained the estimated weights from installed apps.

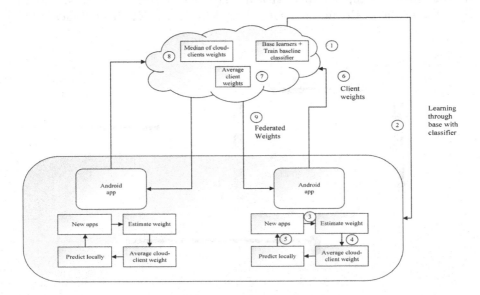

Fig. 2. Proposed framework i.e., DNNDroid.

4. **Calculate Estimate Weight:** Client calculates the average weight.
5. **Predict at the Client Side:** Client classifies the installed apps.
6. **Complete the process:** Client computes the aggregate weight and uploads them to the cloud for further processing.
7. **Aggregate at the cloud:** Cloud collects all the weight and averages them.
8. **Median client-cloud weight:** At last the median weight of both client and cloud are computed and used for further processing.

6 Evaluation of Proposed Framework

To evaluate the proposed framework, we set up a server with 500 users iterating over 100 different federation rounds. The client model is run parallelly on Intel Core i7 machine having 16 GB RAM. In this study, we consider two different parameters to evaluate our proposed model i.e., Accuracy and F-measure. Table 2 shows the confusion matrix for determining if an app is malware-infected or benign.

Table 2. Confusion matrix consider in this study. (.*apk*)

	Benign	Malware
Benign	Benign->Benign (TP)	Benign->Malware (FP)
Malware	Malware->Benign (FN)	Malware->Malware (TN)

Following terminology are used in this study for evaluate the proposed framework.

- Recall: Recall measures the number of precise class predictions generated from all of the positive examples in the dataset.

$$Recall = \frac{a}{a + c}, \qquad (1)$$

where $a = N_{Malware \to Malware}$,
$b = N_{Benign \to Malware}$,
$c = N_{Malware \to Benign}$

- Precision: Precision is the percentage of predicted members of a positive class that really belong to that class.

$$Precision = \frac{a}{a + b}. \qquad (2)$$

Accuracy: Accuracy is computed as mentioned in [14]:

$$Accuracy = \frac{a+d}{N_{classes}}, \tag{3}$$

where $N_{classes} = a + b + c + d$,
$d = N_{Benign \rightarrow Benign}$

F-measure: F-measure is computed as mentioned in [14]:

$$F - measure = \frac{2 * Recall * Precision}{Recall + Precision}$$
$$= \frac{2 * a}{2 * a + b + c} \tag{4}$$

Table 3 shows the calculated value of accuracy and F-measure using above mentioned equations features selected by using chi-square analysis. From empirical study, it can be observed that by using 300 unique features we gain the optimal value in terms of detection rate. Figure 3, demonstrate the computed value of the F-measure and False positive rate having 40 round of federation.

Table 3. Calculated Accuracy and F-measure by using first 50, 100, 150, 200 and 300 features having 50 rounds of federation learning.

ID	Accuracy					F-measure				
	50	100	150	200	300	50	100	150	200	300
C1	**81.4**	80.0	**81.4**	80.6	**81.4**	**0.8**	0.73	**0.8**	0.72	**0.8**
C2	82.4	83	83.4	81.9	**93.8**	0.77	0.79	0.82	0.83	**0.94**
C3	82.4	83	83.4	83	**94.9**	0.82	0.81	0.82	0.83	**0.94**
C4	80.4	83	83.4	83.8	**93.8**	0.83	0.80	0.81	0.82	**0.93**
C5	80.4	82	83.4	84.8	**94.9**	0.82	0.83	0.83	0.82	**0.94**
C6	83.4	84	83.4	84.8	**95.2**	0.83	0.84	0.82	0.84	**0.95**
C7	80.4	83	83.4	83.8	**93.8**	0.83	0.80	0.81	0.82	**0.93**
C8	83.4	82	84.4	83	**94**	0.73	0.75	0.80	0.82	**0.94**
C9	80.4	83	83.4	83.8	**93.8**	0.83	0.80	0.81	0.82	**0.93**
C10	80.4	83	83.4	83.8	**93.8**	0.83	0.80	0.81	0.82	**0.93**

Based on Table 3 and Fig. 3, we are having the following observations:

- It can be inferred that how an optimal number of features are required to train the model.
- It can reveal that increasing the value of the federated learning model it is a directly paid impact on the detection rate of malware-infected apps.
- By increasing the value of the federated model, it can also be paid to impact the value of the false positive rate.

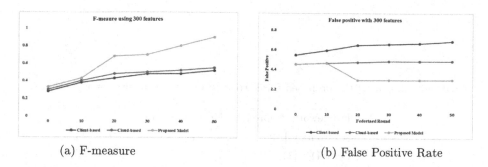

(a) F-measure   (b) False Positive Rate

Fig. 3. F-measure and False positive rate after federation round.

7 Comparison of Proposed Framework

In this study, we select two different methods to validate our proposed work which are described below:

7.1 Comparison on the Basis of Framework Available in the Literature

To examine whether our proposed framework is equivalent to a previously developed framework or not, we compare our proposed framework with ten distinct previously developed frameworks available in the literature. To perform this, we consider Drebin dataset [3] in our study. Table 4 shows the result of our empirical analysis.

7.2 Comparison of the Proposed Framework with Different Anti-virus Scanners

In this study, we evaluate the available free antivirus scanners on the market with our suggested framework for detecting malware. In this study, the Drebin dataset is used to provide empirical results. Table 5 compares various antivirus scanners using the structure we've suggested.

8 Experimental Findings

Based on the experimental outcomes, the following are the experimental findings of this research article.

- Tables 4 and 5 provide evidence that the suggested framework is capable of identifying malware in real-world apps.
- Based on empirical findings, it can be concluded that the suggested methodology can identify malware-infected apps more quickly than other anti-virus scanners on the market.

Table 4. Comparing the proposed framework to existing frameworks or methods.

Framework/Approach	Detection rate
Andromaly [24]	78.9%
DroidDet [31]	76.3%
AndroSimilar [5]	78.2%
Aurasium [28]	79.1%
Andrubis [13]	82.5%
TaintDroid [4]	88.9%
Paranoid Android [22]	89.9%
MalDozer [10]	80.5%
HinDroid [8]	86.3%
HEMD [30]	87.9%
MalInsight [7]	90.2%
Wei Wang [27]	93.8%
Proposed framework	96.3%

Table 5. Comparative analysis using various antivirus scanners.

Name of the anti-virus	Detection rate (in %)	Speed to detect malware in sec
Ikarus	81.68	68
McAfee	82.9	38
AVG	91.2	30
ESET NOD32	93.9	29
Proposed framework	98.5	12

9   Conclusion

Based on empirical studies, it can be concluded that our suggested framework has an accuracy of 98.7% and can identify malware-infected apps with 500 unique attributes and 40 different federation rounds. Additionally, experimental results show that our suggested framework is more accurate than other anti-virus scanners and proposed frameworks in the literature. Further, the work will be extended by implementing distinct feature selection approaches and soft computing techniques.

References

1. Alyamani, H.J.: Cyber security for federated learning environment using AI technique. Expert Syst. e13080 (2022)
2. Arisdakessian, S., Wahab, O.A., Mourad, A., Otrok, H., Guizani, M.: A survey on IoT intrusion detection: federated learning, game theory, social psychology and explainable AI as future directions. IEEE Internet Things J. (2022). https://doi.org/10.1109/JIOT.2022.3203249
3. Arp, D., Spreitzenbarth, M., Hubner, M., Gascon, H., Rieck, K., Siemens, C.: Drebin: effective and explainable detection of android malware in your pocket. In: NDSS, vol. 14, pp. 23–26 (2014)
4. Enck, W., et al.: TaintDroid: an information-flow tracking system for realtime privacy monitoring on smartphones. ACM Trans. Comput. Syst. (TOCS) 32(2), 1–29 (2014)
5. Faruki, P., Ganmoor, V., Laxmi, V., Gaur, M.S., Bharmal, A.: AndroSimilar: robust statistical feature signature for android malware detection. In: Proceedings of the 6th International Conference on Security of Information and Networks, pp. 152–159 (2013)
6. Gálvez, R., Moonsamy, V., Diaz, C.: Less is more: a privacy-respecting android malware classifier using federated learning. arXiv preprint arXiv:2007.08319 (2020)
7. Han, W., Xue, J., Wang, Y., Liu, Z., Kong, Z.: MalInsight: a systematic profiling based malware detection framework. J. Netw. Comput. Appl. 125, 236–250 (2019)
8. Hou, S., Ye, Y., Song, Y., Abdulhayoglu, M.: HinDroid: an intelligent android malware detection system based on structured heterogeneous information network. In: Proceedings of the 23rd ACM SIGKDD International Conference on Knowledge Discovery and Data Mining, pp. 1507–1515 (2017)
9. Hsu, R.H., et al.: A privacy-preserving federated learning system for android malware detection based on edge computing. In: 2020 15th Asia Joint Conference on Information Security (AsiaJCIS), pp. 128–136. IEEE (2020)
10. Karbab, E.B., Debbabi, M., Derhab, A., Mouheb, D.: MalDozer: automatic framework for android malware detection using deep learning. Digital Invest. 24, S48–S59 (2018)
11. Kumar, L., Misra, S., Rath, S.K.: An empirical analysis of the effectiveness of software metrics and fault prediction model for identifying faulty classes. Comput. Stand. Interfaces 53, 1–32 (2017)
12. Lin, K.Y., Huang, W.R.: Using federated learning on malware classification. In: 2020 22nd International Conference on Advanced Communication Technology (ICACT), pp. 585–589. IEEE (2020)

13. Lindorfer, M., Neugschwandtner, M., Weichselbaum, L., Fratantonio, Y., Veen, V.V.D., Platzer, C.: ANDRUBIS-1,000,000 apps later: a view on current android malware behaviors. In: 2014 Third International Workshop on Building Analysis Datasets and Gathering Experience Returns for Security (BADGERS), pp. 3–17. IEEE (2014)
14. Mahindru, A., Sangal, A.: MLDroid-framework for android malware detection using machine learning techniques. Neural Comput. Appl. **33**, 5183–5240 (2020)
15. Mahindru, A., Sangal, A.: PARUDroid: validation of android malware detection dataset. J. Cybersecurity Inf. Manage. **3**(02), 42–52 (2020)
16. Mahindru, A., Sangal, A.L.: PerbDroid: effective malware detection model developed using machine learning classification techniques. In: Singh, J., Bilgaiyan, S., Mishra, B.S.P., Dehuri, S. (eds.) A Journey Towards Bio-inspired Techniques in Software Engineering. ISRL, vol. 185, pp. 103–139. Springer, Cham (2020). https://doi.org/10.1007/978-3-030-40928-9_7
17. Mahindru, A., Sangal, A.L.: SOMDROID: android malware detection by artificial neural network trained using unsupervised learning. Evol. Intell. **15**(1), 407–437 (2020)
18. Mahindru, A., Sangal, A.: HybriDroid: an empirical analysis on effective malware detection model developed using ensemble methods. J. Supercomput. **77**(8), 8209–8251 (2021)
19. Mariconti, E., Onwuzurike, L., Andriotis, P., Cristofaro, E.D., Ross, G., Stringhini, G.: MamaDroid: detecting android malware by building Markov chains of behavioral models. arXiv preprint arXiv:1612.04433 (2016)
20. Martín, A., Menéndez, H.D., Camacho, D.: MOCDroid: multi-objective evolutionary classifier for android malware detection. Soft Comput. **21**(24), 7405–7415 (2017)
21. Pei, X., Deng, X., Tian, S., Zhang, L., Xue, K.: A knowledge transfer-based semi-supervised federated learning for IoT malware detection. IEEE Trans. Dependable Secure Comput. **21**, 7405–7415 (2022)
22. Portokalidis, G., Homburg, P., Anagnostakis, K., Bos, H.: Paranoid android: versatile protection for smartphones. In: Proceedings of the 26th Annual Computer Security Applications Conference, pp. 347–356 (2010)
23. Saracino, A., Sgandurra, D., Dini, G., Martinelli, F.: MADAM: effective and efficient behavior-based android malware detection and prevention. IEEE Trans. Dependable Secure Comput. **15**(1), 83–97 (2016)
24. Shabtai, A., Kanonov, U., Elovici, Y., Glezer, C., Weiss, Y.: "Andromaly": a behavioral malware detection framework for android devices. J. Intell. Inf. Syst. **38**(1), 161–190 (2012)
25. Song, C., Ristenpart, T., Shmatikov, V.: Machine learning models that remember too much. In: Proceedings of the 2017 ACM SIGSAC Conference on Computer and Communications Security, pp. 587–601 (2017)
26. Taheri, R., Shojafar, M., Alazab, M., Tafazolli, R.: FED-IIoT: a robust federated malware detection architecture in industrial IoT. IEEE Trans. Ind. Inf. **17**(12), 8442–8452 (2020)
27. Wang, W., Zhao, M., Wang, J.: Effective android malware detection with a hybrid model based on deep autoencoder and convolutional neural network. J. Ambient Intell. Humanized Comput. **10**(8), 3035–3043 (2019)
28. Xu, R., Saidi, H., Anderson, R.: Aurasium: practical policy enforcement for android applications. In: Presented as part of the 21st USENIX Security Symposium USENIX Security 2012, pp. 539–552 (2012)

29. Zhou, Y., Jiang, X.: Dissecting android malware: characterization and evolution. In: 2012 IEEE Symposium on Security and Privacy, pp. 95–109. IEEE (2012)

30. Zhu, H.J., Jiang, T.H., Ma, B., You, Z.H., Shi, W.L., Cheng, L.: HEMD: a highly efficient random forest-based malware detection framework for android. Neural Comput. Appl. **30**(11), 3353–3361 (2018)

31. Zhu, H.J., You, Z.H., Zhu, Z.X., Shi, W.L., Chen, X., Cheng, L.: DroidDet: effective and robust detection of android malware using static analysis along with rotation forest model. Neurocomputing **272**, 638–646 (2018)

An Improved Symmetric Key Encryption Method Using Randomized Matrix Generation

Karan Padhiyar, Divyang Chauhan, Riya Solanki, and Debabrata swain[✉]

Department of CSE, Pandit Deendayal Energy University, Gandhinagar, India
{Karan.pmtcs21,Divyang.cmtcs21,riya.smtcs21}@sot.pdpu.ac.in

Abstract. Currently, digital data security has appeared as the largest challenge before the society. This concern has become more serious due to the data movement through the unsecured wireless medium. The text format data are mostly targeted by different attackers because of its usage in various finance and other sectors. Different advanced approaches were proposed for securing text data but security concern still remains. In the proposed method a symmetric key cryptographic algorithm is developed for securing the text data. The encryption and decryption key is generated through a set of matrix operations. The Key is generated by the multiplication of random matrices followed by a determinant operation of the same transposed and conversed matrix. The performance of the proposed method is compared with a few existing algorithms using throughput expressed in kilobytes per second. The result analysis has shown that the proposed work with both variations performed well compared to all other discussed algorithms.

Keywords: AES · DES · BLOWFISH · Matrix multiplication

1 Introduction

In the digital world, information security and systems refer to protecting data in terms of availability, confidentiality, and integrity of data. Availability represents features of systems information that can be accessed and utilized on a basis of the specified and desired pattern, as well as when asked in an acceptable manner and according to the system's proper standards. Confidentiality refers to the no-changes, loss of data or authorized users can only disclose the data and information. The guarantee that the information is reliable and correct is known as integrity. It has grown increasingly prone to data exploitation as information systems have gotten more integrated. Here, Cryptographical techniques can be the solution. A cryptographic algorithm is a system that can change data from its original readable form to an encrypted version that prevents fraudsters from accessing the original data. On the other side, Decrypting is the process of turning unrecognizable text back to its original pattern. With the use of certain keys, encryption and decryption are feasible. To protect the data and confidentiality of data we use Cryptography encryption methods. Every encryption technique is designed to make decoding as complicated as possible without the usage of the encryption key.

© The Author(s), under exclusive license to Springer Nature Switzerland AG 2022
S. Rajagopal et al. (Eds.): ASCIS 2022, CCIS 1760, pp. 108–117, 2022.
https://doi.org/10.1007/978-3-031-23095-0_8

In the symmetric key cryptography approach, we use the same or single key to perform Encryption and decryption on both sides known as a private key or secret key. Symmetric key cryptographic calculations are isolated into two parts based on the input information: square ciphers and stream ciphers. In square cipher-based frameworks, information is scrambled on a fixed-length bunch of bits called a square, while, in-stream cipher-based frameworks, information is being prepared on a stream of bits [1]. Many methods for encryption with the same key have been developed, each involving various conceptions of cryptographic and temporal complexity other than the concept of processing capabilities during run time. The main purpose of our proposed system is to take a lower total time to execute while retaining the system's complexity. Complex mathematical processes are performed to keep the system's complexity [2].

When compared to asymmetric key methods, the Symmetric Encryption Algorithm is quicker. Because the encryption process is simpler, these algorithms are substantially quicker than asymmetric algorithms in terms of computing. In addition, the Symmetric approach uses less memory than the Asymmetric algorithm [3].

Our Contribution. An effective approach based on symmetric cryptography is established in this suggested system, and its performance is shown based on its required execution time for different sizes of message files.

2   Types of Encryption Technique

Asymmetric cryptographic techniques, symmetric cryptographic techniques, and hash functions are the three most common forms of cryptographic techniques. In the symmetric cryptography technique, we use the same key encryption and decryption of data. Symmetric encryption Some examples include the DES, AES, Blowfish, Carlisle Adams, and Stafford Tavares (CAST) algorithm, SAFER, and IDEA [4].

2.1   AES

AES is a symmetric block cipher technique that encrypts and decrypts using the same key. Joan Daemen and Vincent Rijmen, two Belgian cryptographers [5], invented AES as a variation of the Rijndael block cipher. It is also an iterative cipher since the original input block and key are transformed numerous times before the output is produced. The AES standard specifies that only 128-bit blocks can be accepted, with key sizes of 128, 192, and 256 specified to have the following features: Efficiency in software and hardware, To resist all known attacks, Simplicity in design, and Speed. Ibtihal Mohamed A. Fadul et al. [6] advocated using two secret keys to improve the security of AES. To boost the security strength, the second key is used in encryption and decryption on both sides. Reena Mehla et al. [7] suggested their work to improve the shift row transformation and key expansion of the algorithm to make it more resistant to assaults. Their suggested approach speeds up the picture of encryption and outperforms AES. Faisal Riaz et al. [8] worked together to improve AES by utilizing the DES. They updated the AES algorithm by replacing the Mix Columns phase with the Permutation step. The suggested approach may be used to encrypt both text and images. Aparna V S et al. [9] proposed the AES technique for secure data transfer. The whole algorithm is coded using MATLAB software. Sumira Hameed et al. [8] also worked on improving AES by utilizing the DES algorithm. Instead of utilizing the Mix Columns step, they updated the AES by employing the Permutation phase. The suggested approach may be used to encrypt both text and graphics. In [10], the author introduced a new approach to AES named revised AES (AES-R). They conclude that AES-R can be the option of the AES because its performance is closed to the traditional AES. Because AES' algorithm is strong and employs longer key sizes, it is safer than DES and 3DES. This method also allows for speedier encryption, making it ideal for applications like firewalls and routers that demand either low idleness or high output. Despite the fact that this technology is powerful and has several uses, this method was found vulnerable by using a side-channel attack [11].

2.2 DES

The DES is the most extensively used for encryption technologies since the 1970s [12]. It is a symmetric block encryption technique. Whereas some older applications and systems are still employing DES encryption, despite the fact that DES is now considered insecure for to the short key size used in DES encryption, which can be easily broken by today's current computer platforms. In [13], Ramya G et al. enhanced the DES algorithm's performance by expanding the key length to 128 bits, as opposed to the suggested technique, which inserts keys fully independently.

When this method was created [11], it was a well-designed block cipher that was frequently used. However, this technique was subject to brute force assaults, as it could be cracked via an exhaustive key search. As a result, this method was replaced by AES, a considerably more powerful and efficient algorithm. The KE-DES [14] is an improved version of the DES algorithm developed in this study. A new KD function uses to provide improved data security and efficacy in textual data encryption.

2.3 Blowfish

In 1993 [15], Blowfish was first produced. Blowfish is a symmetric block cipher with a variable key length that is 64 bits long. The algorithm is divided into two sections: a key expansion section and a data encryption section. [16], a comprehensive evaluation was done by the cryptography methods like AES, DES, 3DES, RSA, and Blowfish. Which they stated that the blowfish algorithm is strongest for guessing attacks.

3   Proposed Technique

The suggested Random key generation technology is based on the calculating complexity of the random matrix multiplication and determinant of the same size large matrices to generate a set of keys by using the Matrices Transpose function.

The algorithm goes through each character of the input text and generates an encrypted message only once at a time. The algorithm goes till the entire text encryption is generated as shown in Fig. 1.

Flow Chart of Proposed Method:

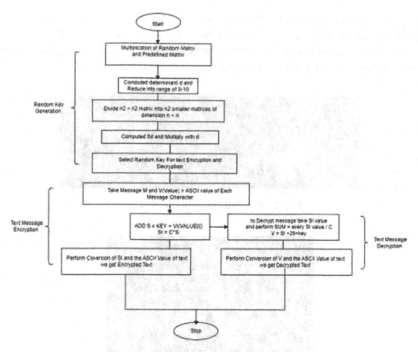

Fig. 1. Flow chart of proposed method

3.1 Random Key Generation Algorithm

1. The First step Generate a 9×9 or $n^2 \times n^2$ random Matrix.
2. Create a predefined matrix size of $n^2 \times n^2$.
3. Compute Multiplication between the generated random matrix and a predefined matrix size of $n^2 \times n^2$.
4. Perform a Matrix Transpose operation of Multiplication matrix.
5. Calculate the determinant d of the matrix generated in the previous step.
6. Reassign it to d in the rand between 0–10.
7. Create a smaller matrix n x n from transpose matrix $n^2 \times n^2$.
8. Compute Determinants of all smaller matrix
9. Perform Multiplication of d with all smaller matrix determinants.
10. Reduce the determinant number in the range of 0–99.
11. Select any Random key from the random numbers, selected primary key we can use for encryption and decryption operations.
12. Reduce the key to the range of 0–10 to generate a multiplication factor k.

The algorithm creates random key generation and it is very complex and hard to perform message decode operations and generate the key by a third person. This algorithm generates every time different matrix, different key and also different encryption for the same message every time as shown in Fig. 2, 3 and 4. Because the method of computing keys requires randomization and sophisticated matrix computations, the adversary will not be able to get the right key in the time allotted. The technique becomes exceedingly complex and impossible to obtain the key within the entire time provided by internet services since many matrix transformations are necessary and the key generation is random. As a result, this method will be considered safe for its intended use.

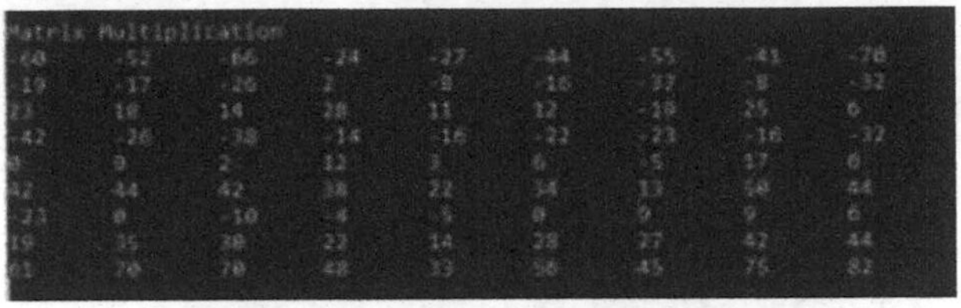

Fig. 2. Random matrix multiplication

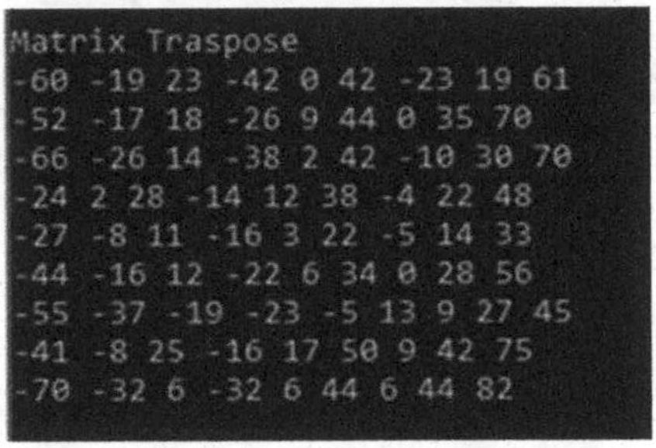

Fig. 3. Perform transpose operation of matrix

Fig. 4. Selecting a random key for encryption and decryption operations

3.2 Text Message Encryption Algorithm

1. Take text message M for encryption.
2. For every text message character equivalent ASCII value will be denoted as V(Value).
3. Compute Sum S for every ASCII value in the message characters ADD S = KEY + Vi(VALUE[i])
4. Using the previous step calculation we can obtain SI value for every value of the Sum, SI = C * S

   here C is the multiplicative factor computed while generating key
5. For encryption of text messages we can perform the conversion between the value of SI and the ASCII value of text message characters. By performing this conversion our text message is encrypted and it is ready for message communication as shown in Fig. 5.

Encrypted message:vóⱪöíÉůỳ¥ûûûồ¿ÓôⱪÍÔôô¥ůÔt¥Æí¿fúỳ¥ⱪÓÉ¥ÓÓsôÆí¿fúỳ¥ⱪÓⱫÉôóôÔⱪ¥ÓůÉ¥ÔⱪÉỳ−y¥ûÔ|Éúíỳⱸᵖᵖᵖᵖᵖ

Fig. 5. Text encryption

3.3 Text Message Decryption Algorithm

1. For decryption of the encrypted text let's take the Si value to be the encrypted message.
2. To find Sum for every SI value by performing a division between every SI value / C (Multiplicative factor).
3. To get the value of V, compute the subtraction of the key from the S value.
4. To obtain the decryption message to perform a Conversion of every value of V to the equivalent value of ASCII character. The generated characters are our decrypted messages as shown in Fig. 6.

Decoded Message: Generating Key for Text Encryption and Decryption based on Scrambling Matrix!!!!

Fig. 6. Text decryption

4 Matrix Operations

4.1 Matrix Determinant

Let, $I = n * n$ matrix

$$I = \begin{pmatrix} i11 & i12 & \dots & i1n \\ i21 & i22 & \dots & i2n \\ \dots & \dots & \dots & \dots \\ \dots & \dots & \dots & \dots \\ in1 & in2 & \dots & inn \end{pmatrix}$$

formula for the determinant of $F(I) = \sum sgn(\sigma) \prod_{i=1}^{n} i$ where $\sigma \in sn$.

4.2 Matrix Multiplication

$$X = \begin{bmatrix} a11 & a12 & \dots & a1n \\ a21 & a22 & \dots & a2n \\ \dots & \dots & \dots & \dots \\ \dots & \dots & \dots & \dots \\ an1 & an2 & \dots & ann \end{bmatrix} \quad Y = \begin{bmatrix} b11 & b12 & \dots & b1n \\ b21 & b22 & \dots & b2n \\ \dots & \dots & \dots & \dots \\ \dots & \dots & \dots & \dots \\ bn1 & bn2 & \dots & bnn \end{bmatrix} \quad Z = \begin{pmatrix} c11 & c12 & \dots & c1n \\ c21 & c22 & \dots & c2n \\ \dots & \dots & \dots & \dots \\ \dots & \dots & \dots & \dots \\ cn1 & cn2 & \dots & cnn \end{pmatrix}$$

where X is $n \times n$ matrices and Y is $n \times n$ matrices and the result matrices Z is XY.
Such that $C_{ij} = a_{i1}b_{1j} + \dots + a_{in}b_{nj} = \sum_{k=1}^{m} a_{ik}b_{kj}$, for $i = 1$ to n and $j = 1$ to n.

4.3 Matrix Transpose Operation

Transpose of a Matrix can be defined as "A given Matrix which is transform in the form of all rows into columns and vice-versa.

If $A = [a_{mn}]_{p \times q}$, Then $A' = [a_{nm}]_{q \times p}$

$$A = \begin{bmatrix} a11 \ a12 \ a13 \\ a21 \ a22 \ a23 \\ a31 \ a32 \ a33 \end{bmatrix} A^T = \begin{bmatrix} a11 \ a21 \ a31 \\ a12 \ a22 \ a32 \\ a13 \ a23 \ a33 \end{bmatrix}$$

5 Performance Analysis

5.1 Implementation of System

The implementation of proposed algorithm (in C programming language) is performed on a machine that supports the following specifications machine processor with 8 GB RAM Windows 11, 64-bit @ 2.2 GHz Intel i5 10th Generation and to Performing program we use DEV C++ IDE software tool (C Programming Language).

5.2 Text Encryption Algorithms Performance Analysis

When we compute the execution time, throughput, and how much storage is required for execution. of traditional encryption algorithms like BLOWFISH, DES, and AES by using these measurements we can calculate performance analysis. To calculate Throughput perform division between the file size in bytes and the execution time in seconds. High throughput means higher performance because it is required less power consumption.

5.3 Analysis of Complexity for Random Key Generation

In the proposed random key generation algorithm, every step has n number of computations. so, the total time complexity we can say that O(n) of the Random key generation.

5.4 Analysis of Execution Time

In the proposed algorithm computational run time required for first text message encryption and then successfully decoding a specified size text file. In comparison of proposed algorithm and existing algorithms like BLOWFISH, AES and DES using throughput parameter and execution time for algorithm. The comparison is of those system performed using different size of text files which is shows on the Table 1 with their run time. By comparing proposed algorithm is very efficient then the existing algorithm: AES, DES, BLOWFISH are encrypted.

5.5   Analysis of Throughput

Table 1. Analysis of execution time

Comparison between existing algorithms and proposed algorithm					
Input file size	Existing algorithms			Matrix operations	
	DES	AES	BLOWFISH	Converse of matrix	Transpose of matrix
20 KB	2	4	2	7	6.5
40 KB	5	8	4	10.6	9.5
150 KB	20	30	16	12.8	10.2
250 KB	30	44	24	13.4	11.1
Total consummation time	57	86	46	43.8	37.3
Average consummation time	14.25	21.5	11.5	10.95	9.325

Consumption of Power analyze by using throughput. Unit of throughput is Kilobytes per Second (Table 2).

Table 2. Throughput analysis

Algorithms	Throughput (KB/sec)
DES	8.07
AES	5.34
BLOWFISH	10
Converse of matrix	10.5
Transpose of matrix	12.3

Throughput is a ratio of total KB data that has been give as an input divided by total time in second required to compute and execute the code.

Throughput = Total Consummation Time/Total Time Taken For Execution

If Throughput is High than we can say that our algorithm is efficient that other algorithms.

6   Conclusion

From the throughput, we can see that the matrix transpose has the highest throughput, so we can say that the proposed encryption algorithm is much more efficient than other encryption algorithms. This paper represents a new Symmetric key encryption algorithm to encrypt and decrypt data in form of files. This algorithm works on two matrix-based operation that is used to encrypt and decrypt the text from the files. Here we can see that average computation time for BLOWFISH, Converse of matrix and Transpose of matrix are same so in conclusion we can say that all three techniques can be used to encrypt and decrypt data efficiently.

References

1. Alenezi, M., Alabdulrazzaq, H., Mohammad, N.: Symmetric encryption algorithms: review and evaluation study. Int. J. Commun. Netw. Inf. **12** (2020)
2. Mante, P., Harsh, R., Swain, D., Deshpande, D.: A symmetrical encryption technique for text encryption using randomized matrix based key generation **10**(100) (2020)
3. Panda, M., Nag, A.: Plain text encryption using AES, DES, and SALSA20 by java-based bouncy castle API on windows and Linux. In: IEEE 2015 Second International Conference on Advances in Computing and Communication Engineering (ICACCE), Dehradun, India (2015.5.1–2015.5.2), pp. 541–548 (2015). https://doi.org/10.1109/ICACCE.2015.130
4. Dixit, P., Gupta, A.K., Trivedi, M.C., Yadav, V.K.: Traditional and hybrid encryption techniques: a survey. In: Perez, G.M., Mishra, K.K., Tiwari, S., Trivedi, M.C. (eds.) Networking Communication and Data Knowledge Engineering. LNDECT, vol. 4, pp. 239–248. Springer, Singapore (2018). https://doi.org/10.1007/978-981-10-4600-1_22
5. Daemen, J., Rijmen, V.: "AES Proposal: Rijndael" (PDF). National Institute of Standards and Technology. p. 1. Archived (PDF) from the original on 5 March 2013, 9 March 2003. Accessed 21 Feb 2013
6. Fadul, I.M.A., Ahmed, T.M.H.: Enhanced security of Rijndael algorithm using two secret keys. Int. J. Secur. Appl. **7**(4), 127–134 (2013)
7. Mehla, R., Kaur, H.: Different reviews and variants of advance encryption standard. Int. J. Sci. Res. (IJSR), 1895–1896 (2012). ISSN (Online): 2319-7064 Impact Factor (2012):3.358
8. Hameed, S., Riaz, F., Moghal, R., Akhtar, G., Ahmed, A., Dar, A.G.: Modified advanced encryption standard for text and images. Comput. Sci. J. **1**(3), 120–129 (2011)
9. Aparna, V.S., Rajan, A., Jairaj, I., Nandita, B., Madhusoodanan, P., Remya, A.A.S.: Implementation of AES algorithm on text and image using MATLAB. In: IEEE 2019 3rd International Conference on Trends in Electronics and Informatics (ICOEI), Tirunelveli, India, (2019.4.23–2019.4.25), pp. 1279–1283 (2019). https://doi.org/10.1109/ICOEI.2019.8862703
10. Thinn, A.A., Thwin, M.M.S.: Modification of AES algorithm by using second key and modified subbytes operation for text encryption. In: Alfred, R., Lim, Y., Ibrahim, A., Anthony, P. (eds.) Computational Science and Technology. LNEE, vol. 481, pp. 435–444. Springer, Singapore (2019). https://doi.org/10.1007/978-981-13-2622-6_42
11. Mante, P.G., Oswal, H.R., Swain, D., Deshpande, D.: A symmetrical encryption technique for text encryption using randomized matrix based key generation. In: Borah, S., Emilia Balas, V., Polkowski, Z. (eds.) Advances in Data Science and Management. LNDECT, vol. 37, pp. 137–148. Springer, Singapore (2020). https://doi.org/10.1007/978-981-15-0978-0_13
12. Hamza, A., Kumar, B.: A review paper on DES, AES, RSA encryption standards. In: 2020 9th International Conference System Modeling and Advancement in Research Trends (SMART) (2020). https://doi.org/10.1109/smart50582.2020.9336800
13. Bansal, D.R., Thakur, P.: Improved key generation algorithm in data encryption standard (DES) (2016)
14. Reyad, O., Mansour, H.M., Heshmat, M., Zanaty, E.A.: Key-based enhancement of data encryption standard for text security. In: 2021 National Computing Colleges Conference (NCCC) (2021). https://doi.org/10.1109/nccc49330.2021.9428818

15. Mandal, P.C.: Superiority of blowfish algorithm. Int. J. Adv. Res. Comput. Sci. Softw. Eng. **2**(9) (2012). ISSN 2277 128X
16. Patil, P., Narayankar, P., Narayan, D.G., Meena S.M.: A comprehensive evaluation of cryptographic algorithms: DES, 3DES, AES, RSA, and Blowfish. Procedia Comput. Sci. **78** (2016)

Performance Analyses of Black Hole Attack in AODV Routing Protocol in Vanet Using NS3

Dhananjay Yadav[1]([✉]) [iD] and Nirbhay K. Chaubey[2] [iD]

[1] Gujarat Technological University, Ahmedabad, Gujarat, India
Yadavdhananjay1@gmail.com
[2] Ganpat University, Mehsana, Gujarat, India

Abstract. VANET(Vehicclar ad hoc network) is an extension to MANET(Mobile Ad Hoc Network) that is mainly used for providing communications between different vehicles in the network. It is an emerging technology which will play a major role in furnishing intelligent transportation system. Vehicles become able to pass messages to each other, send alert message in case of accidents and inform other vehicles about traffic situation on road. Vanet has high advantage for safety and security of people in network but due to high mobility of vehicle and frequent topology changes creates numerous security issues also. Besides various security issues, one of the main security issues in VANET is the Black Hole Attack (BHA) in which attacker, at the time of routing impose itself that it has shortest route for communication and hence legitimate nodes starts communicating with that attacker node. Now the attacker node can drop the packet or pass the packet to other malicious node. In this research paper the performance in vehicular network is compared at time of black hole attack and without attack in AODV routing Protocol. Simulation has been carried out using NS3 and the result shows that packet delivery ratio decreases with less throughput in case of attack.

Keywords: Vanet · Security · Black Hole Attack (BHA) · AODV · Packet delivery ratio

1 Introduction

Vehicular Ad Hoc Network provides communication among vehicles on road. The vehicular communication can be categorized in to three types [1] as vehicle to vehicle communication in which a vehicle communicates with another vehicle and vehicle to infrastructure communication in which vehicle communicates with Road Side Unit (RSU). A device named On Board Unit (OBU) helps in furnishing communication between vehicle to vehicle communications. The communication is totally wireless and uses Dedicated Short Range Communication (DSRC) protocol [2] for communication in vanet. The US FCC has allocated 75 MHz bandwidth which is currently use by IEEE 802.11P standard [3].

Vanet routing protocols can be classified into (a) Topology Based Routing Protocol and (b) Position Based Routing protocol [4]. Topology based routing protocol uses source

S. Rajagopal et al. (Eds.): ASCIS 2022, CCIS 1760, pp. 118–127, 2022.
https://doi.org/10.1007/978-3-031-23095-0_9

to destination information by constantly checking into routing table. The position based routing works on the information about position of nodes in the routing process [5].

Topology based routing protocol are divided into reactive routing and proactive routing protocols [6]. In Reactive routing protocols source request a route to destination. DSR, AODV and TORA are many exemplifications of reactive routing protocols. In Proactive routing protocols information about all routes are maintained in a table whether that route are required or not at that particular time. The main exemplifications of proactive routing protocols include OLSR and FSR.

AODV (Ad Hoc on Demand Distance Vector routing protocol) is the most frequently used and also the most prone to security attacks in vanet [7].

In this research paper we have simulated the vanet network and Black Hole Attack using NS3 network Simulator and compared the performance of vanet network in AODV routing protocol with and without the Black Hole attack. The analyses report shows that packet delivery ratio(pdr) and throughput decreases in case of black hole attack.

The rest of the paper is structured as follows. In section-1 we have discussed AODV routing protocol and Black Hole attack (BHA), section-2 covers literature survey, section-3 covers simulation setup and result analyses and at last section-4 covers the conclusion and future work.

1.1 AODV Routing Protocol

AODV routing protocol is the most frequently used routing protocol in vanet. It is a reactive routing protocol in which routes are discovered on demand. It means when a node has some message for communication with another node it perform route discovery. The route discovery can be performed in two ways.

1.Route Request (RREQ): During RREQ Source node broadcast RREQ packet to its neighbour. The neighbour nodes admit this RREQ packet and check its routing table to match the destination address. If destination address found then it send RREP packet to source else it again broadcast to its nearest neighbour [8].

2.Route Reply (RREP): During RREP When any node after RREQ found destination address in its routing table, it replies with RREP packet to source in same direction from where RREQ packet comes.

The Fig. 1 shows the route discovery and route reply in AODV routing protocol in vanet.

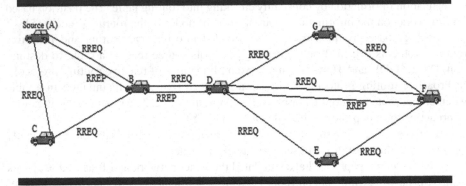

Fig. 1. AODV routing protocol

The Fig. 1 shows that the source node broadcast RREQ packet to its neighbour B and C. The nodes B and C check its routing table and again broadcast this RREQ to its neighbour after not finding the destination address. The process is repeated till the destination address not found. When destination address matched it send RREP packet to source following the same route from which RREQ packet arrives. So in Fig. 1 the route A-B-D-F will be chosen for communication.

1.2 Black Hole Attack

In this attack, attacker node sends a false RREP message to source by imposing that it has the smallest route to destination and communication starts through this malicious node [9]. Now the attacker node can prevent the packet from reaching to the right destination by dropping the packet or send to another malignant node. The working of BHA is shown in Fig. 2.

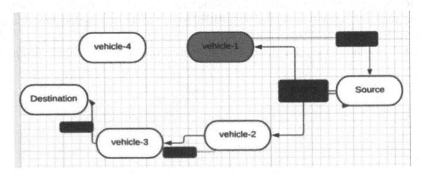

Fig. 2. Structure of black hole attack

The source node broadcast RREQ packet to its neighbour. Vehicle-2 is legitimate and after finding no destination address in its routing table it further broadcast the RREQ packet. When vehicle-3 finds destination address in its routing table, it reply with RREP message. B ut as from Fig. 1, it is clear that vehicle-1 has no route for destination but still it reply with false RREP packet to destination. Because vehicle-1 has less hope count and replied first so a route is established between source and vehicle-1.

BHA can be classified into two types as [10].

1. Single BHA: In single BHA only one attacker node is present to perform the attack.
2. Collaborative BHA: In collaborative attack multiple nodes collaboratively perform the attack.

Our research work shows that packet delivery ratio and throughput decreases due to BHA. In coming section we have elaborate the effects of BHA in vanet.

1.3 Literature Survey

The authors in [11] discussed the security threats to AODV routing protocol. The main attacks to AODV routing protocol are Denial of service attack, Impersonation Attack, Sybil attack etc. The research paper also surveyed some researches about the detection techniques of BHA.

Authors in [12] explain the various security issues in vanet and give a comparative study of Black hole and Gray hole attack. They concluded that BHA causes more packet drop compared to Gray hole attack.

The authors in this research paper [13] detected the BHA by measuring the deviation in end to end delay and throughput with attack and without attack. The observed value of throughput and end to end delay with and without attack are different.

In this research paper [14] authors measure the performance of network in AODV, BHAODV, FHAODV and WHAODV. There result show that PDR value decreases rapidly in BHAODV, FHAODV and WHAODV. It is also shown that it has higher end to end delay as compared to other protocols.

The authors in [15] detected the BHA by dividing the nodes into different clusters. Each cluster has a cluster head and nodes communicate only through the cluster head. Some check point nodes are taken to monitor the packet drop ratio and if observed the PDR less then threshold then it is considered as attack. This approach increases the network overhead by making clusters, cluster head and some check point nodes. Authors in paper [16] proposed a machine learning approach to detect the BHA in vanet. They have first simulated the BHA using NS2 simulator and then applied the one class support vector machine algorithm to classify the black hole behavior of vehicles.

Authors in [17] uses multipath technique to detect and prevent BHA in Mobile ADHoc Network. In this approach communication is done through a cluster head. A data message and ctrl message are send through different paths. The sink nodes compares the message to check whether the message is tempered or not and then a alarm is raised in case of BHA.

Authors in [18] detected and prevented the BHA in three phases. First, in connectivity phase a connection for communication between vehicles is established. Second in detection phase attack is detected by calculating the threshold value of all destination sequence numbers and then comparing the new destination sequence number with threshold value and at last in prevention phase the attack is prevented by first sending a message with false destination address. If reply received then it is an attack.

Authors in [19] review various papers published for detection of BHA in MANET and concluded that computation and storage overhead, routing and end to end delay is the major drawbacks of recent researches.

1.4 Simulation Set-Up

We have used NS3 for simulating the BHA in vanet. The BHA is generated in AODV routing protocol by taking varying number of vehicles which range from 30 to 150 and data rate is 250 kbps. The following table shows the simulation environment that we have used in our experiment to generate the BHA.

Table 1. Simulation parameters

Parameters	Values
Simulator	NS 3.25
Routing Protocol	AODV
Data Rate	250kbps
Mobility Model	Constant Position Mobility Model
Channel Type	Wireless
Number of Nodes	30,50,70,100,130,150
Packet Size	1040 bytes
Malicious Node	3
Traffic Type	Constant Bit Rate(CBR)
Simulation Time	100 s

The parameter given in Table 1 is used for simulation of BHA using NS3.25 network simulator [20].

1.5 Result Analyses

The network performance can be measured using Packet Delivery ratio (PDR) and Throughput. The PDR can be calculated by dividing the total packets received and the total packets transmitted [21]. The experimental result show that packet delivery ratio decreases with BHA. The Fig. 3 shows PDR without attack and Fig. 4 shows PDR with attack.

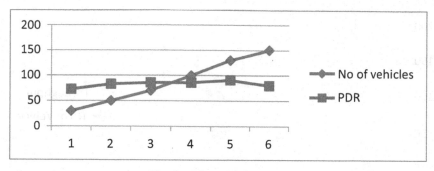

Fig. 3. (PDR without attack)

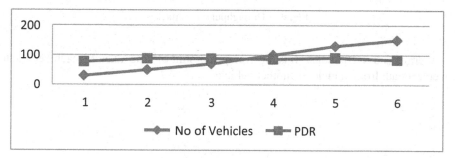

Fig. 4. (PDR with attack)

Throughput: It is calculated by dividing the total number of packets delivered to the total simulation time. The increasing throughput value indicates high performance.

Throughput = (Total delivered packets*packet size*8)/total simulation time

The Fig. 5 shows the throughput without attack and Fig. 6 shows throughput with attack (Fig. 7 and Fig. 8).

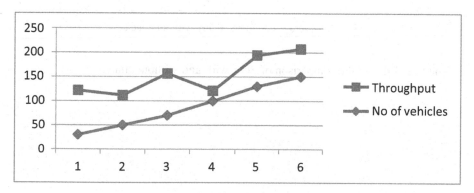

Fig. 5. (Throughput without attack)

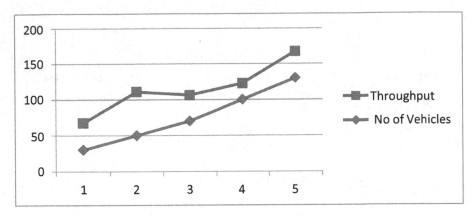

Fig. 6. (Throughput with attack)

Average end to end delay: It is the average amount of time taken by each vehicle to traverse a path from vehicle to another vehicle.

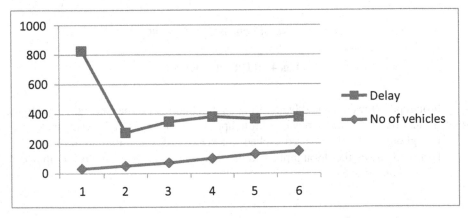

Fig. 7. (Average end to end delay without attack)

The Fig. 9 shows the comparison of PDR with and without attack.

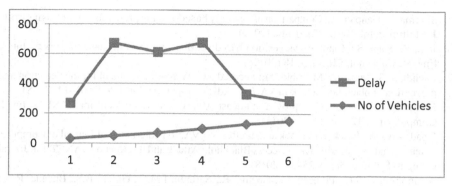

Fig. 8. (Average End to End Delay with attack)

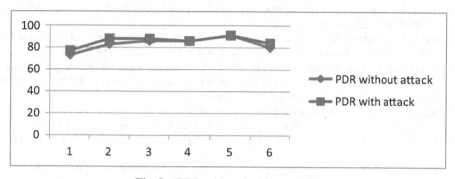

Fig. 9. (PDR with and without attack)

1.6 Conclusion

Simulation results show that packet drop ratio decreases with less throughput at time of BHA. This is due to the high packet drop from the malicious vehicle. Some researches has been done to detect and prevent BHA in vanet but still there is requirement for more researches to improve the detection and prevention methods.In future we will do some research to prevent this attack in vanet.

References

1. Chaubey, N.K., Yadav, D.: A Taxonomy of Sybil Attacks in Vehicular Ad-Hoc Network (VANET). In: Rao, R., Jain, V., Kaiwartya, O., Singh, N. (eds.) IoT and Cloud Computing Advancements in Vehicular Ad-Hoc Networks, pp. 174–190. IGI Global (2020). https://doi.org/10.4018/978-1-7998-2570-8.ch009
2. Perry, F., Raboy, K., Leslie, E., Huang, Z., Van Duren, D.: Dedicated Short-Range Communications Roadside Unit Specifications, vol. FHWA-JPO-1. p. 142 (2017)
3. Schoch, E., Kargl, F., Weber, M., Leinmüller, T.: Communication patterns in VANETs. IEEE Commun. Mag. **46**(11), 119–125 (2008)
4. Yasser, A., Zorkany, M., Abdel Kader, N.: VANET routing protocol for V2V implementation: A suitable solution for developing countries. Cogent Eng. **4**(1), 1–26 (2017)

5. Sharma, V., Ganpati, A.: Comparison of topology based-routing protocols in wireless network. J. Multimed. Inf. Syst. **6**(2), 61–66 (2019)
6. Jain, S., Sahu, S.: Topology vs position based routing protocols in manet: a survey. Int. J. Eng. Res. Technol. **51**(14), 9–18 (2012)
7. Lachdhaf, S., Mazouzi, M., Abid, M.: Secured AODV routing protocol for the detection and prevention of black hole attack in VANET. Adv. Comput. An Int. J. **9**(1), 01–14 (2018)
8. Kaur, M., Virk, A.K.: An improved multicast AODV routing protocol for VANETs. Int. J. Comput. Appl. **121**(6), 14–23 (2015)
9. Upadhyaya, A.: Blackhole Attack and its effect on VANET International Journal of Computer Sciences and Engineering Open Access Blackhole Attack and its effect on VANET. Int. Journl Comput. Sci. Eng. **5**(11), 25–32 (2018)
10. Arvindakshan, S.R., Praneeth, S., Gogula, R., Sainath, I.M.S., Girish, B.S., Badana, R.A.: Review on Black Hole Attack Identifier using Vanet Communication in Vehicle. open Access Int J. Sci. Eng. **6**(8), 77–83 (2021)
11. Tayal, S., Gupta, V.: A survey of attacks on monitoring schemes. Int. J. Innov. Res. Sci. Eng. Technol. **2**(6), 2280–2285 (2013)
12. Rathod, A., Patel, P.S.: A survey on black hole & gray hole attacks detection scheme for vehicular Ad-Hoc network. Int. Res. J. Eng. Technol. **4**(11), 1508–1511 (2017)
13. Cherkaoui, B., Beni-hssane, A., Erritali, M.: Variable control chart for detecting black hole attack in vehicular ad-hoc networks. J. Ambient. Intell. Humaniz. Comput. **11**(11), 5129–5138 (2020). https://doi.org/10.1007/s12652-020-01825-2
14. Kumar, A., Sinha, M.: Design and development of new framework for detection and mitigation of wormhole and black hole attacks in VANET. J. Stat. Manag. Syst. **22**(4), 753–761 (2019)
15. Rashmi, Seehra, A.: A novel approach for preventing black-hole attack in MANETs. Int. J. Ambient Syst. Appl. **2**(3), 01–09 (2014)
16. Kyaw, N.A.N.Z., Aye, T.: A mechanism to classify the black hole behavior of vehicles in VANET using one class SVM. Int. J. Electr. Electron. Data Commun. **6**(9), 61–64 (2018)
17. Ramachandran, D., et al.: A Low-Latency and High-Throughput Multipath Technique to Overcome Black Hole Attack in Mobile Ad Hoc Network (MTBD). Hindway Security and Communication Networks, Vol-2022, pp. 13, 25 (August 2022)
18. Malik, A., Zahid Khan, M., Faisal, M., Khan, F., Seo, J.-T.: An Efficient Dynamic Solution for the Detection and Prevention of Black Hole Attack in VANETs. Sensors **2022**(5) (2022). https://doi.org/10.3390/s22051897
19. Kaur, P., Kaur, K.: A Review on various Single and Collaborative Black Hole Detection Schemes in Manet. International Journal of Engineering Trends and Technology (IJETT), V48(7), 363–367 (June 2017)

20. Tahiliani, M., Satare, S.: Black Hole Attack Simulation NS3 (2014). [Online]. Available: http://mohittahiliani.blogspot.com/2014/12/ns-3-blackhole-attack-simulation-inns-3.htrnl. Accessed: 12 May 2022
21. Malik, S., Sahu, P.K.: A comparative study on routing protocols for VANETs. Heliyon (E1sevier) **5**(8), 1–9 (2019)

Comparative Analysis of Several Approaches of Encoding Audio Files

Lakhichand Khushal Patil[✉] and Kalpesh A. Popat

Faculty of Computer Applications, Marwadi University, Rajkot, Gujarat, India
lakhichand.patil@fergusson.edu,
Kalpesh.popat@marwadieducation.edu.in

Abstract. The use of cryptography is essential to ensure confidential communication across networks. Concerns about the safety of digital data as a result of its fast expansion has increased the need for the development of more sophisticated methods of cryptography. Cryptography is a procedure that rearranges and replaces content inside the information in order to scramble it, making it unintelligible to anybody other than the person who is capable of deciphering it. This becomes cryptography a sort of information security. This process is known as encoding. Cryptanalysis, sometimes known as "breaking the code," refers to the process of deciphering a communication even when the decipherer has no idea how the information was encrypted in the first place. The use of encryption is no longer restricted to just textual information. There are algorithms for a variety of data types, including images, audio, and video, amongst others. A few of the criteria that are considered while evaluating cryptographic algorithms are throughput, speed, CPU time, battery power consumption, and memory requirements. In this work, an investigation into many commonly used algorithms like as RC6, RC4, ThreeFish, Twofish, Blowfish, AES, 3DES, and DES is carried out on the aforementioned parameters in order to locate the most effective solution. This work's objective is to provide a comprehensive introduction to a few of the already – present cryptographic approaches and their respective work quality for a wide variety of data types, with a particular emphasis on audio file encryption.

Keywords: Cryptography · Security · Encryption · Decryption · Ciphers · Cryptanalysis · Cryptographic algorithm · Audio file encryption

1 Introduction

It is impossible to deny the importance of networks, their effects, or their existence in the digital environment of the present day. Because of the pervasive use of digital data in applications that are used in everyday life and the importance of those data, there is an urgent need for innovative and efficient ways to protect those data. Because of the rapid advancements made in the internet and computer technologies, the safety of data

---

Research Supervisor

© The Author(s), under exclusive license to Springer Nature Switzerland AG 2022
S. Rajagopal et al. (Eds.): ASCIS 2022, CCIS 1760, pp. 128–143, 2022.
https://doi.org/10.1007/978-3-031-23095-0_10

has become the single most critical element in the fields of information technology and communication.

The terms "information security" and "computer security" are often used interchangeably. Information security refers to the methods, rules, and tactics that are utilized to protect and secure sensitive information and computer systems. Through a series of mathematical and logical transformations, cryptography renders the data incomprehensible to anyone on the outside. In this scenario, the adversary is given permission to find out, intercept, and change messages in spite of having the ability to breach specific guidelines understood by a cryptosystem. People will have only been exposed to text data for a couple of decades at most. Therefore, the focus was solely on the process of encrypting and decrypting text data. However, because more people are using the internet and collecting multimedia data, there is an increasing demand for the protection of multimedia data.

Today, audio encryption is more necessary than ever to facilitate the propagation of encrypted voice communication for real-time applications among parties such as of the intelligence bureau, voice talk among officials, officials of the CBI, defence, and other agencies, etc. for top-secret communication. Similar hackers or individuals having harmful intentions wouldn't be possible to decipher similar communication with the use of audio encryption, which will help to ensure the safety of the nation [5].

In today's sophisticated security systems, cryptography has emerged as an essential component for ensuring the confidentiality of data transmissions. Because of the widespread utility of multimedia data, like audio files in their many formats, it has become of the utmost importance to ensure that this data is securely sent while maintaining its quality. The message which should be transmitted while still being safeguarded is referred to as the plaintext. Encryption refers to the process of using a key or combination of keys to scramble the plaintext so that it cannot be read. The ciphertext is what is produced once the encryption procedure is complete. Decryption refers to the process of converting ciphertext back into its original plaintext form. The term "cryptosystem" refers to any system that is capable of both encryption and decryption. Kirchhoff put forth a security principle that should serve as the basis for any and all cryptosystems' security measures. The confidentiality rather than the encryption algorithm, of the encryption/decryption key, should be the determining factor criteria determining how secure an encryption system is, according to the Kirchhoff [9].

The purpose of this document is to give a description of the various methods that are utilized when audio is encrypted. It illustrates the viability of a range of approaches for a selection of applications that are very different from one another. The organization of the paper can be summarized as follows: Sect. 2 presents an overview of cryptography, including its many subfields, subtypes, and ideas. Section 3 discusses some applications of cryptography. In Sect. 3, a concise introduction is provided to some of the most widely used algorithms in cryptography. In Sect. 4, we evaluate the effectiveness of various encryption methods, taking into account both the context of the data and the type of data being protected. In Sect. 5, the limits of currently used methods are outlined, and suggestions for upcoming method advancements are provided. The writers present their conclusion in Sect. 6 of the text.

2 Overview of Cryptography

Cryptography is the study of how to keep sensitive information secure. The origin of the word can be traced back to the Greek words kryptos, which means "hidden," as well as graphia, which means "writing or study."

Cryptography is a physical process that rearranges and replaces content inside the information in order to scramble it, making it unintelligible to anybody other than the person who is competent of deciphering it. This becomes cryptography a sort of information security. Encoding is the name given to this process. Putting it another way, a particular message is changed from its original form into a safe message, which is also referred to as ciphertext, through the application of particular replacement techniques. The goal of this process is to render the input message unreadable to anyone while it is being transmitted. The message can only be deciphered by the person who was intended to receive it. Because of the exponential growth of data transmission over the internet, the security of this medium has become a major concern. The objective is to raise the price of gathering information to a point where it is more than the value of the data on its own, given that no cryptographic technique can be guaranteed to be completely secure.

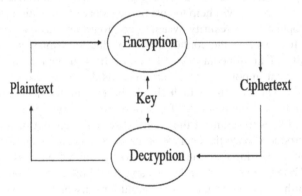

Fig. 1. Representation of cryptography

3 Aims of Cryptography

The following are the four goals that contemporary cryptography focuses on:

1) The information cannot be comprehended by anybody other than those who are authorized to use it in the manner for which it was intended.
2) Integrity refers to the fact that the information cannot be changed while it is being stored or sent from the sender to the intended recipient having the change not being discovered.
3) Non-repudiation: The originator of the information or the person who sent it cannot subsequently deny having certain intents when it came to the creation of the information or the sending of the data.

4) Authentication: Both transmitters, as well as the receiver, are able to verify the identity of the other party, as well as the origin and destination of the information.

3.1 The Many Forms that Cryptography Can Take

The following are the three distinct dimensions that can be used to divide cryptographic systems:

1. The categories of procedures that are utilized in the process of converting plaintext to ciphertext:

    a) Substitution: The mapping process transforms every element of the plaintext as a similar element.
    b) Transposition: This step involves rearranging the elements of the plaintext.
        In either of these two approaches, the operation being performed must be reversible, which means that no information should be lost in the process.

2. The number of keys used:

    a) Symmetric: Sender and receiver utilize the same key; also known as conventional encryption, private encryption, secret key encryption, or single key encryption.
    b) Asymmetric encryption, also known as two-key or public-key encryption. Both the sender and the receiver will need to use a different key.

3. The procedure that is followed when processing plaintext:

    a) Block Ciphers: Ciphers that works by processing to generate an output block, each individual input block only one at an instance.
    b) Stream Ciphers: These perform continuous processing of input items, one element at a time.
        The symmetric algorithms RC6, RC4, ThreeFish, Twofish, Blowfish, AES, 3DES, and DES are among the most popular and commonly used algorithms. Elliptic Curve Cryptosystem (ECC) and Rivest-Shamir-Adelman (RSA) are two of the most popular asymmetric key algorithms that are currently in use.

4 Cryptographic Algorithms at a Glance

4.1 DES

The Data Encryption Standard (DES) is a block cipher that is based on a slight modification of the Feistel structure [1, 2, 9]. The National Institute of Standards and Technology (NIST) published it in 1977 as FIPS PUB 46 (Federal Information Processing Standards), which was followed by the widespread adoption and use for a higher time like twenty years. The plaintext is handled in 64-bit chunks during processing. The length of the key is 56 bits, and it is broken into 16 subkeys so that it may be processed in 16 rounds. Each subkey is utilized just once during each round. The process of decryption is identical to the process of encryption; the ciphertext serves as the input to DES, and the sub-keys Ki are utilized in the opposite sequence, moving from K16 to K1 in the last round, in the initial round. Because there are 256, which is equivalent to 7.2 × 1016 potential keys, a brute-force attack is impracticable when using a key that has 56 bits.

But the Data Encryption Standard (DES) was shown to be insecure once and for all in July 1998, when the EFF98 (Electronic Frontier Foundation) revealed that they have cracked a DES encryption utilizing a "DES Cracker" designed specifically for that purpose.

4.2 3DES

In 1985, the ANSI standard X9.17 was the first time that Triple DES (3DES) was standardized for use in the context of financial applications. In 1999, with the publication of FIPS PUB 46-3, it was adopted as a part of the Data Encryption Standard. It is the symmetric block cipher that has been authorized by FIPS. Because it uses a plaintext of 64 bits and a key length of 168 bits, a brute force attack is difficult to launch against it. It uses three keys in conjunction with three separate runs of the DES algorithm and works as an Encrypt-Decrypt-Encrypt sequence. Its cryptanalysis-resistant 168- bit key length makes it difficult to crack. The software that uses it is also somewhat slow, it doesn't enable effective software codes, and it is slower than DES since it uses three times as many rounds.

4.3 AES

Since 3DES and DES are not promising options for long-term security, the National Institute of Standards and Technology (NIST) issued a request for submissions in 1997 for a new Advanced Encryption Standard [1, 2, 9]. NIST chose Rijndael as the proposed algorithm for the Advanced Encryption Standard (AES) from among the 15 algorithms that were accepted after the first phase of the proposal process. In the second round, five algorithms were shortlisted. The block length of an AES encryption is 128 bits, while the key length can be any of 128, 192, or 256 bits in length. It is not a Feistel Structure but rather an iterative process.

4.4 Blowfish

Bruce Schneier developed the keyed block cipher known as Blowfish [1, 2, 9] in 1993. Since then, it has found widespread application in a variety of different cryptographic devices. It has a positive impact on the performance of the software. Blowfish has a block size of 64 bits, and the key length can be anything to 448 bits from 32 bits in length. The key length can also be arbitrary. The algorithm is made up of dual distinct functional components: a data encryption component and a key expansion component. Both of these components are necessary for the algorithm to perform its intended function. During the process of key expansion, a key that has a maximum of 448 bits will be divided into several subkey arrays, and the total size of these arrays will be 4168 bytes. In order to encrypt the data, a sizable array of key -dependent S-Boxes is utilized and a 16-round Feistel structure is also utilized during the process.

Applications in which the key does not change frequently, such as a communications link or automatic file encryption, are ideal candidates for this method. When it is implemented on 32-bit microprocessors that have substantial data caches, it is significantly faster than the majority of encryption techniques.

4.5 RC4

Ron Rivest created the stream cipher known as RC4 [11] in 1987 specifically for use by RSA Security. The formal designation for this cipher is "Rivest Cipher 4." It is a stream cipher that utilizes byte-oriented operations and has a configurable key size. When it comes to processing in real-time, stream ciphers are more effective. A random permutation serves as the foundation for this technique. The length of the cipher's period is longer than 10 100. It takes anywhere from eight to sixteen machine operations to produce a single byte of output. It is straightforward to understand and not complicated at all. RSA Security maintained RC4's use as a closely guarded commercial secret. However, the RC4 algorithm was made public on the internet in September of 1994 when it was put to the Cipher punks anonymous remailers list. The technique is easily implementable in both hardware and software, and it can do so efficiently.

4.6 Twofish

The algorithm known as Twofish [19] was developed by counterpane Internet Security. It is an excellent choice for use in both large microprocessors and the microprocessors found in smart cards. The NIST's design criteria for AES were taken into consideration throughout the development of Twofish. The Feistel network serves as the foundation for it. To be more specific, with key lengths of 128 bits, 192 bits, as well as 256 bits, they are a symmetric block cipher. The cipher's bit length is 128. It functions correctly on the Intel Pentium Pro as well as on other software and hardware platforms. It is possible to implementable on a broad number of platforms and applications, and it offers flexible design features such as accepting additional key lengths.

4.7 ThreeFish

Niels Ferguson and a few other individuals came up with the idea for the Threefish block cipher. They created them with the goals of maximizing their speed, security, ease of use, and adaptability [21]. Threefish is a large block cipher that may be modified. The initialization of vectors is accomplished by the use of tweak. There are three different block sizes that are defined for it: 256 bits, 512 bits, and 1024 bits. The block size determines the size of the key, which is also equal to the block size; however, the tweak value is always 128 bits. In order to achieve non-linearity and, hence, high levels of security, Threefish makes use of XOR and modulus addition rather than S-boxes. Because it operates on words that are 64 bits in size, it is also appropriate for use in software and hardware implementations, in particular those designed for 64-bit platforms.

5 Background and Related Works

All different kinds of cryptographic techniques are broken down and examined so that the work of audio encryption can take precedence. In the modern workplace, both the type of media and whether it is wired or wireless are significant concerns. In the process of examining all of the algorithms, the demand for computer resources such as battery power, memory, and CPU time is of the biggest concern. Although considerations such as throughput, speed, and security are significant. In a wireless context, these resources are severely restricted. When comparing symmetric and asymmetric encryption algorithms, it is possible to see that public key encryption relies on mathematical functions, requires a lot of computing power, and is neither highly effective for use on small mobile devices [17]. Due to the large number of computations required, asymmetric encryption methods are nearly one thousand times more time-consuming than symmetric encryption methods.

Again, block ciphers and stream ciphers are essential components of symmetric ciphers and play a vital role. A block cipher, on the other hand, can only process one block of data at a time, whereas a stream cipher can process the input components in a continuous stream, one element at a time, unlike a block cipher, which only processes one block at a time. Block cipher will give a satisfactory result whilst also encrypting an offline file and delivering it across networks; however, a stream cipher is going to be a smarter choice for encrypting real-time data on a continuous basis on a network. This is because block cipher is designed to encrypt data that is already stored. Stream ciphers are used when encrypting real-time data. All of the algorithms that were covered in the part before this one are symmetric block ciphers. This is because the focus of the current work is on recorded audio files.

Researchers in the paper [10, 17] have already evaluated by comparing the prevalent encryption algorithms such as RC6, RC4, ThreeFish, Twofish, Blowfish, AES, 3DES, and DES on characteristics such as CPU clock cycles, CPU process time, Encryption time, and power consumption had come to the conclusion that DES was the most efficient algorithm and have arrived to the conclusion that the performance of Blowfish is superior to that of all other algorithms, including RC6. AES offers superior performance as compared to DES, 3DES, and RC2 respectively. Even with the introduction of new data formats like audio and video files, Blowfish has maintained its position as the industry leader. Increasing the size of the key enhances security, but it also clearly increases the amount of time and power that is consumed.

DES and AES were compared by researchers in a publication [1] about the avalanche effect, memory requirements, and the amount of time required for encryption. AES is a superior solution in situations where less memory is needed, in addition to providing faster encryption. Applications in the financial sector are where DES shines the brightest. It is helpful for objects which is a function of a game as well as anything which is part of the monetary transaction to use AES as it is a better alternative to employ while encrypting messages that are delivered between objects via chat channels.

In practical cases, speed and performance are of key relevance. In light of the aforementioned considerations, the research presented in paper [2] compares the data encryption algorithms Blowfish, 3DES, AES, and DES on a variety of data block sizes as well as hardware and software platforms. As a result, Blowfish emerged as the algorithm with the highest level of performance in terms of protection against unauthorized attacks. Experiments have shown that 3DES has a throughput that is almost one-third that of DES, which means that DES is three times quicker than 3DES.

It is possible to utilize Blowfish for a variety of purposes, including packet encryption, Network security, Random Bit Generation, and Bulk encryption due to the fact that it is the algorithm with the smallest key size that also offers the highest level of security. In spite of the given benefits, it still has a weak key problem that has to be fixed as well as investigated further.

The superiority of symmetric algorithms over asymmetric algorithms was reaffirmed by researchers in a work titled [11], which can be found here. They examined AES and RC4 on a variety of metrics including throughput, CPU process time, memory use, encryption/decryption time, and variation in key size. Compared to AES, RC4 was found to be significantly faster while using significantly less energy. Large amounts of data can be encrypted using the RC4 algorithm.

5.1 Related Research and Development on Audio Encryption

Researchers wrote in an article [8] that all encryption methods can be broken down into three major categories, such as a strategy that combines compression and encryption, selective encryption, and complete encryption. With the size of audio files in mind, these researchers wrote that all encryption methods can be broken down into these categories. [8]

Complete encryption is the standard method for achieving content confidentiality. This method encrypts the entire file with the assistance of conventional ciphers such as RSA, RC$, 3DES, AES, or DES. Because of this, the processing, as well as computing complexity, is significantly increased. In order to lessen the computational burden placed on the user's end by real-time applications, the selective encryption method encrypts only certain sections of a multimedia file. The most difficult part of using this strategy is deciding which pieces of information are vital enough to encrypt. The combined compression encryption method performs both the process of compressing data as well as the process of encrypting it in a single step.

The authors of the paper [8] decided to use a comprehensive encryption technique for real-time multimedia data, including video, audio, and image, communication applications, as a result of the research that they conducted. This was done in order to protect the data. A full binary tree is used to carry out the substitution, while a two -dimensional array is used to carry out the linear diffusion. The results of the trial demonstrate that the method is successful, but with a somewhat longer start-up time. The researchers are attempting to have their findings implemented in embedded and mobile apps.

The term "biography cryptography" was coined by researchers in a work that was referenced [3]. They have used the AES method as the foundation for the encryption, and the secret key has been derived from the iris characteristics. MATLAB is used to convert the audio signals that are being recorded in real time into binary form. The iris image is used to decrypt the secret key, which is 128 bits long. To ensure a higher level of protection, the key that possesses a greater degree of unpredictability is chosen.

Researchers have presented a new higher dimensional chaotic system for audio encryption in their study [7], which states that variables are to be considered as encryption keys in order to ensure the safe transmission of audio signals. This new system was developed in order to combat previous methods of audio encryption that were either too simple or too complex. This method is suitable for the encryption of large amounts of data, including audio, image, and video files. The algorithm possesses the characteristics of being sensitive to the beginning condition, having a high key space, maintaining pixel distribution uniformity, and not breaking when subjected to a known or chosen plaintext assault. In addition, the algorithm is able to maintain pixel distribution uniformity. This algorithm has excellent key sensitivity, which means that a modification of just a single bit in the secret key will lead in an entirely new piece of audio that has been encrypted. This should be the case because this algorithm is sensitive to changes in the key.

The researchers that wrote the paper [9] analyzed how long it took to process audio and video data using DES, AES, and Blowfish and compared the three algorithms. They have determined that AES is the superior solution. Researchers have utilized the RSA encryption approach on the lower frequency bands in their study [4] because they realized that not all frequency areas participate in communication in the same proportions. The objective is to differentiate between essential audio information and other audio information that is not as relevant so that selective encryption can be carried out on the basis of this differentiation. They have proposed that in the future, encryption may be made more effective by using either a modified version of RSA or an enhanced version of DES.

On audio files, researchers have looked at complete AES, Total DES, and selective AES and discussed their findings in paper [14, 22]. For the algorithms that have been presented thus far, the time consumption and SNR values, which stand for signal-to-noise ratio, have been determined. When it comes to encryption and decryption, audio files that are larger in size require more time. After the audio file has been compressed, a selective encryption algorithm is then applied to it. They had arrived at the conclusion, after much deliberation, that selective encryption was superior to full encryption in terms of performance.

An effective method for encrypting data is proposed by researchers in Paper [13]. This method is based on transposition and substitution ciphers. Audio encryption that is reversible and lossless in both directions is still a pipe dream. The use of cryptography in online applications presents a significant number of exciting opportunities.

In the research described in the paper [14], the quantization of the audio data was done using the AES approach. This step came before Huffman's entropy coding process. The results of the experiments show that the AES encryption method provides an exceptionally high level of security against cryptographic assaults.

Because the encryption method has been deployed to the entirety of the audio data in this scenario, it is now significantly harder for a user who is not permitted to view the audio data. The use of the AES encryption method results in an increase in the level of cryptographic protection afforded to the MP3 audio information. There is a very limited amount of conversation surrounding mp4 audio data.

The dissemination of compressed audio in a secure manner while maintaining its original quality was the primary focus of the research presented in the article [6]. Using stream ciphers that are created using a modular division circuit and LFSR allows for selective encryption to be performed. The process of encrypting the audio data involves XORing the key with the data. LFSR is used in order to obtain the key (Linear Feedback Shift Register). The method that has been proposed has a lower level of complexity when it comes to the underlying hardware, and it is able to withstand many forms of attacks, including known plaintext attacks and ciphertext-only attacks. The technique involves ideal for encrypting audio files in the MP3 format as well as a variety of other audio formats for use in commercial and confidential applications respectively.

In their recent publication [12], the researchers recommended for the Selective encryption technique rather than the Full encryption strategy. They have especially in comparison a few of the established selective encryption methods to full encryption and have come to the realization that full encryption algorithms are slow, whereas selective encryption techniques save time, speed, overhead, and computational power. After examining a few of the contemporary selective encryption algorithms in conjunction with complete encryption, they arrived at this result.

Block cipher techniques, such as DES, AES, and public key systems, have been mentioned by researchers in a work titled [16] as not being suitable for use with real-time audio data due to the complexity and slower performance of these algorithms. Researchers have developed a selective audio encryption technology that has lower implementation costs and is compliant with industry standards through the course of their study.

Here LFSR-based keystream generators are used in the encoding process for audio data. A shorter key stream is formed from the longer key stream that was generated from the updated ASG. This is done so that the longer key stream can be utilized as the different key streams for the various frames of audio data. The suggested approach is safe from any known attacks based on plaintext and is compatible with all audio coding standards.

In the research work referred to as [15], the authors propose a selective encryption strategy that uses a unique approach. The RSA encryption technique is used to encrypt part of the power spectrum of an audio wav file in this research. The Fast Fourier Transform is used to convert an audio signal in the time domain into a signal in the transform domain, which is the frequency domain. A signal can be segmented into many frequency areas, each of which has its own magnitude and phase value when transformed using a transform domain. After that, an encryption approach is utilized on the low frequencies, which are characterized by higher magnitude values.

Even if the method might be considered a good answer in terms of cryptanalysis assaults, it still requires significant work to determine which parts of an audio sample are relevant and which parts are not important in a dynamic manner.

The researchers conducted an analysis of the Twofish and AES algorithms on performance and security on varied sizes of RAMs for a variety of data kinds, and they published their findings in the publication [19]. It was shown that AES has a stress distribution that is less than 2, thus renders it vulnerable to assaults employing cryptanalysis. These attacks can be prevented by adopting a stronger encryption algorithm. In order to get AES up to the same level of security as Twofish, which requires 24 rounds, the algorithm's performance must be decreased.

It was discovered that AES is a quicker algorithm than Twofish for encrypting text and images; nevertheless, if RAM is increased, Twofish becomes a faster algorithm than AES. Twofish provides superior performance for sound encryption, and its speed improves along with the amount of RAM available to it.

In 2007, the creator of Blowfish suggested that Twofish might be a better alternative to Blowfish. In the most recent work, researchers developed modified Blowfish, which is a symmetric block cipher that takes various length keys ranging from 32 bits to 448 bits. These findings were published in paper number [18]. For the same plaintext that is supplied into the improved method, a different ciphertext will be generated each time, and the process will take up less time and produce more throughputs. The researchers are open to continuing their work with modified Blowfish for applications involving images, audio, and video.

The Blowfish technique was utilized by researchers in paper [24] to encrypt a picture using file formats such as TIF,.bmp, PNG, and jpg. They came to the conclusion that the Blowfish encryption cannot be cracked until an attacker tries 28r+1 different permutations, where r is a random number, the number of times something occurs. The level of protection provided by the method can be improved by increasing the total number of iterations. Table 1 gives the differences between various encryption algorithms and Table 2 gives the Performance metrics of various encryption algorithms.

Table 1. Differences between various encryption algorithms

Factors	Block size	Cipher Type	Security
DES	64 Bits	Block Cipher	Inadequate
3DES	64 Bits	Block Cipher	Inadequate
RC2	64 Bits	Block Cipher	Vulnerable
RC4	Byte Oriented	Stream Cipher	Weak Security
RC6	128 Bits	Symmetric Algorithm	Vulnerable
Blowfish	64 Bits	Symmetric Block Cipher	Less Secure

Table 2. Performance metrics of various encryption algorithms

Factors	DES	3DES	RC2	RC4	RC6	AES	BLOWFISH
Key size	56 bits	168 bits	8–128 bits	40–128 bits	128.192 or 256 bits	128, 192 or 256 bits	32–448 bits
Block size	64 bits	64 bits	64 bits	Byte oriented	128 bits	128, 192, or 256 bits	64 bits
Cipher type	Block cipher	Block cipher	Block cipher	Stream cipher	Symmetric block cipher	Symmetric block cipher	Symmetric block cipher
Keys	Private keys	Private keys	Single key	Single key	Single key	Secret key (shared)	Private key
Attacks	Vulnerable to differential, and linear attacks	Vulnerable to differential, Bruite force attacks	Vulnerable to differential, Bruite force Attacks	Vulnerable to Bruite force attacks	Vulnerable to differential, Bruite force attacks	Strong against differential, Bruite, Linear Force Attacks	Vulnerable to differential, Bruite force attacks
Security	Proven Inadequate	Inadequate	Vulnerable	Weak security	Vulnerable	Considered most secure	Less secure

6 Recent Works on Audio Encryption

The field of cryptography makes extensive use of chaos due to its pseudo-randomness, sensitivity to beginning values, and other properties. Encryption algorithms for multimedia information that make use of chaos theory are becoming increasingly popular in today's world and have produced positive outcomes. As an illustration, Yahi et al. [20] developed an Enhanced chaotic map that was influenced by the cubic map.

They conducted an analysis of the dynamic behaviour of this system and found that its picture encryption capabilities were satisfactory. Midoun et al. came up with the idea for the 1-DFCS, and they used it to generate the keystream that was necessary for the cryptosystem [21]. The vast majority of one-dimensional chaotic systems only have one parameter, and the parameter space in the chaotic state is discontinuous. As a consequence, the parameter space available to cryptosystems is rather limited. In addition, the trajectory of some one-dimensional systems can be anticipated, as stated in Reference [22, 23].

It has been found that images are the most easily understood kind of information conveyed through the use of multimedia [25–28]. Nevertheless, the importance of audio information cannot be overstated in the vast majority of cases. For instance, using the infrasound waves that are generated by the aurora, one might be able to investigate the laws that govern auroral activity [29–31]. There is a pressing need to find a solution to the difficulty of ensuring the secure transmission of this audio information via the internet. The researchers Gnanajeyaraman et al. created a chaotic lookup table and used it to encrypt audio using the blockchain model. The algorithm is challenging to develop and suffers from a wide variety of drawbacks [32]. A Chen Memristor chaotic system was proposed by Dai and colleagues. They evaluated the dynamic nature of it, and then used this technique to encrypt audio. Scrambling and diffusion were treated as two different operations within the encryption mechanism. The encryption method produces a satisfactory result; nevertheless, the key space of the cryptosystem is limited (there are only three initial keys), making it simple to break the algorithm through the use of brute force attacks [33]. The DNA encoding technology was used to the process of audio encryption by El et al. [34] and Abdelfatah [35]. However, despite the fact that this technology makes the algorithm more secure, it is extremely inefficient. The DNA encoding and decoding processes are utilized in the audio encryption technique that Wang and Su devised [36]. This algorithm makes use of PWLCM for the generation of the keystream. PWLCM contains only one control parameter, and in order to generate the keystream, numerous instances of PWLCM need to be used, despite the fact that the experimental findings are positive. In addition, the scrambling and diffusion separation encryption technique that was presented by Feistel [37] is thought to have some vulnerabilities in terms of data protection. The ciphertext attack method that made use of an influence network was the one that Solak et al. decided to use in order to break this independent scrambling and diffusion structure [38].

After that, Xie et al. pointed out the flaws that were present in Sorak's technique, and they enhanced the attack algorithm [39]. A similar issue exists in Naskar et al. novel's audio encryption technique, which requires repeated applications of a logistic map in order to generate a keystream [40]. This is due to the fact that Naskar et al. algorithm's employs DNA Encoding in addition to the logistic map.

7 Limitations

After looking at a number of different research articles, it was discovered that there are two distinct categories into which all audio encryption methods fall: full encryption and partial encryption. During the process of comparing full and partial encryption, it was discovered that partial encryption incurs a greater amount of overhead than full encryption does. As part of this overhead, it is necessary to identify which audio data is vital and which is not, encrypt the vital audio data, combine it with the unnecessary audio data, and then finally send it through a communication network. The same efforts need to be made at the receiving end in order to separate encrypted data from unencrypted data. In the final step, the data that has been encrypted must have the vital audio information extracted from it. The algorithm becomes increasingly complicated and difficult to grasp as a result. The decision of whether to employ a prerecorded audio clip or audio captured in real-time is another factor that requires careful study. The comparison of encryption time is given in Table 3.

Table 3. Comparison of encryption time

Encryption time comparison.

Algorithms	Sizes	Encryption time (s)	Speed (s/KB)
AEA-NCS	430 KB	0.2318	0.0005
KK [29]	544 KB	1.3240	0.0024
DXS [33]	260 KB	0.6364	0.0024
ARI [35]	984 KB	198.26	0.2014
WS [36]	123 KB	14.6000	0.0370
NPN [45]	304 KB	58.6300	0.1928
NBC [46]	439 KB	1.1760	0.0026

8 Conclusion

The study that has been given here suggests that there is sufficient room for further investigation into this topic. Therefore, we need to come up with a new algorithm that is capable of providing full encryption while at the same time being less difficult, having in terms of CPU time, a great energy efficiency rating, and a fast transmission speed. In addition to this, it is taking into consideration the development of bidirectional functional original audio based on time and speed, with less noise and a better security key in the original encrypted audio. This is being done in this manner since it is now being considered. As a consequence of this, the primary focus of our work is on the development and deployment of an altogether fresh algorithm for audio encryption that is based on the criteria that were stated earlier.

References

1. Mondal, A.K., Prakash, C., Tiwari, A.: Performance evaluation of cryptographic algorithms: DES and AES. In: IEEEStudents' Conference on Electrical, Electronics and Computer Science (2011)
2. Verma, O.P., Agarwal, R., Dafouti, D., Tyagi, S.: Performance analysis of data encryption algorithms. IEEE (2011)
3. Asok, S.B., Karthigaikumar, P., Sandhya, R., Jarold, K.N., Siva Mangai, N.M.: A secure cryptographic scheme for audio signals. In: International Conference on communication and Signal Processing, 3–5 Apr 2013, India
4. Sharma, S., Sharma, L.K.H.: Encryption of an audio file on lower frequency band for secure communication. Int. J. Comput. Sci. Softw. Eng. 3(7) (2013)
5. Gandhi, R.A., Gosai, A.M.: Steganography – a Sin qua non for disguised communication. Int. J. Innov. Res. Adv. Eng. 1(8) (2014)s
6. James, S.P., George, S.N., Deepthi, P.P.: Secure selective encryption of compressed audio. In: International Conference on Microelectronics, Communication and Renewable Energy, IEEE (2013)
7. Ganesh Babu, S., Ilango, P.: Higher Dimensional Chaos for Audio Encryption. IEEE (2013)
8. Radha Aathithan, N., Venkatesulu, M.: A complete binary tree structure block cipher for real-time multimedia. In: Science and Information Conference, London, UK, 7–9 Oct 2013
9. Pavithra, S., Ramadevi, E.: Throughput analysis of symmetric algorithms. Int. J. Adv. Netw. Appl. 4(2), 1574–1577 (2012)

10. Salama1, D., Kader, H.A., Hadhoud, M.: Evaluating the performance of symmetric encryption algorithms. Int. J. Netw. Secur. **10**(3), 213–219 (2010)
11. Singhal, N., Raina, J.P.S.: Comparative analysis of AES and RC4 algorithms for better utilization. Int. J. Comput. Trends Technol. **1**(3), 259–263 (2011)
12. Sharma, S., Pateriya, P.K.: A study on different approaches of selective encryption technique. Int. J. Comput. Sci. Commun. Netw. **2**(6), 658–662 (2016)
13. Al-qdah, M., Hui, L.Y.: Simple encryption/decryption application. Int. J. Comput. Sci. Secur. **1**(1), 33–40 (2022)
14. Gadanayak, B., Pradhan, C.: Encryption on MP3 compression. MES J. Technol. Manag. **2**(1), 86–89 (2011)
15. Sharma, S., Sharma, H., Kumar, L.: Power spectrum encryption and decryption of an audio file. Int. J. Res. Comput. Sci. **1** (2013)
16. James, S.P., George, S.N., Deepthi, P.P.: An audio encryption technique based on LFSR based alternating step generator. In: IEEE Connect (2014)
17. Salama1, D., Kader, H.A., Hadhoud, M.M.: Evaluating the effects of symmetric cryptography algorithms on power consumption for different data types. Int. J. Netw. Secur. **11**(2), 78–87 (2010)
18. Kumar, R., Saini, B., Kumar, S.: A novel approach to blowfish encryption algorithm. Int. J. Adv. Found. Res. Sci. Eng. **1**(2) (2014)
19. Rizvi, S.A.M., Hussain, S.Z., Wadhwa, N.: Performance analysis of AES and twofish encryption schemes. In: International Conference on Communication Systems and Network Technologies (2011)
20. Yahi, A., Bekkouche, T., Daachi, M.E.H., et al.: A color image encryption scheme based on 1D cubic map. Optik **249**, 168290 (2022)
21. Midoun, M.A., Wang, X., Talhaoui, M.Z.: A sensitive dynamic mutual encryption system based on a new 1D chaotic map. Opt. Lasers Eng. **139**, 106485 (2021)
22. Li, C., Lin, D., Lü, J., et al.: Cryptanalyzing an image encryption algorithm based on autoblocking and electrocardiography. IEEE Multimedia **25**(4), 46–56 (2018)
23. Zareai, D., Balafar, M., Derakhshi, M.R.F.: A new grayscale image encryption algorithm composed of logistic mapping, Arnold cat, and image blocking. Multimedia Tools Appl. **80**(12), 18317–18344 (2021)
24. Cao, W., Mao, Y., Zhou, Y.: Designing a 2D infinite collapse map for image encryption. Sig. Process **171**, 107457 (2020)
25. Chai, X., Fu, X., Gan, Z., et al.: A color image cryptosystem based on dynamic DNA encryption and chaos. Signal Process **155**, 44–62 (2019)
26. Gao, X., Mou, J., Xiong, L., et al.: A fast and efficient multiple images encryption based on single -channel encryption and chaotic system. Nonlinear Dynam. **108**(1), 613–636 (2022)
27. Zhou, S., Wang, X., Wang, M., et al.: Simple colour image cryptosystem with very high level of security. Chaos Solitons Fractals **141**, 110225 (2020)
28. Wang, M., Wang, X., Wang, C., et al.: Spatiotemporal chaos in cross coupled map lattice with dynamic coupling coefficient and its application in bit-level color image encryption. Chaos Solitons Fractals **139**, 110028 (2020)
29. Kordov, K.: A novel audio encryption algorithm with permutation-substitution architecture. Electronics **8**(5), 530 (2019)
30. Lima, J.B., da Silva Neto, E.F.: Audio encryption based on the cosine number transform. Multimedia Tools Appl. **75**(14), 8403–8418 (2015). https://doi.org/10.1007/s11042-015-2755-6
31. Parvees, M.Y.M., Samath, J.A., Bose, B.P.: Audio encryption–a chaos-based data byte scrambling technique. Int. J. Appl. Syst. Stud. **8**(1), 51–75 (2018)
32. Gnanajeyaraman R, Prasadh K.: Audio encryption using higher dimensional chaotic map. Int. J. Recent Trends Eng. **1**(2), 103 (2009)

33. Dai, W., Xu, X., Song, X., et al.: Audio encryption algorithm based on Chen Memristor chaotic system. Symmetry 14(1), 17 (2021)
34. El Hanouti, I., El Fadili, H.: Security analysis of an audio data encryption scheme based on key chaining and DNA encoding. Multimedia Tools Appl. 80(8), 12077–12099 (2021)
35. Abdelfatah, R.I.: Audio encryption scheme using self-adaptive bit scrambling and two multi chaotic-based dynamic DNA computations. IEEE Access 8, 69894–69907 (2020)
36. Wang, X., Su, Y.: An audio encryption algorithm based on DNA coding and chaotic system. IEEE Access 8, 9260–9270 (2019)
37. Feistel, H.: Cryptography and computer privacy. Sci. Am. 228(5), 15–23 (1973)
38. Solak, E., Cokal, C., Yildiz, O.T., et al.: Cryptanalysis of Fridrich's chaotic image encryption. Int. J. Bifurcation Chaos 20(05), 1405–1413 (2010)
39. Xie, E.Y., Li, C., Yu, S., et al.: On the cryptanalysis of Fridrich's chaotic image encryption scheme. Signal Process 132, 150–154 (2017)
40. Naskar, P.K., Paul, S., Nandy, D., et al.: DNA encoding and channel shuffling for secured encryption of audio data. Multimedia Tools Appl. 78(17), 25019–25042 (2019)

A Secure Mechanism for Safeguarding Cloud Infrastructure

Khare Pratyush, Vivek Kumar Prasad(✉), Rachana Mehta, and Madhuri Bhavsar

Department of CSE, Nirma University, Ahmedabad, India
{20bce519,vivek.prasad,rachana.mehta,
madhuri.bhavsar}@nirmauni.ac.in

Abstract. Security is frequently viewed as the largest impediment to a cloud-based approach, but in actuality, it can be the majorenabler. Cloud security guarantees that your information and apps are easily accessible to authorized users. In this paper, we shall be putting forward, the cloud ecosystem's security concerns. The most crucial concerns for the popularity of cloud computing services are privacy and security. Here we try to depict a study of data that is hosted on the cloud and the issues in its security. The study will examine the particular data protection practices used globally to offer optimum data security while reducing threats and risks. Although many apps benefit by having access to data on the cloud, but doing so poses concerns since it makes data accessible to apps that could already contain security flaws. Analog to this, data may be at risk if a guest OS operates on top of the hypervisor, without consideration for dependability of the guest OS, resulting in a flaw in security. The paper ends with a case study where the request has been classified as safe or malicious. If the malicious request is identified, then these requests are to be discarded so that the cloud remains safe. The classification has been conducted using Machine Learning and Deep Learning concepts and an accuracy of 85% has been achieved.

Keywords: Threats · Risks · Data security · Data protection

1 Introduction

Cloud computing has fundamentally changed how end users access computers as well as other IT resources in the contemporary technological era. But yet computing based on cloud system is a new term which has not yet been widely accepted. Among the various definitions available, "A network solution for providing inexpensive, reliable, easy and simple access to IT resources" is one of the most basic definition. Cloud Computing provides IT access that is low-cost, dependable, as well as straightforward. Cloud is service focused rather than application oriented [8].

Cloud Computing's nature not only reduces the timeframe needed to execute a task, but it also minimizes the amount of infrastructure and ownership costs, and also provides end-user flexibility and enhanced efficiency. The latest web-based computer network, cloud computing, provides users with simple and adaptable resources to access or use

S. Rajagopal et al. (Eds.): ASCIS 2022, CCIS 1760, pp. 144–158, 2022.
https://doi.org/10.1007/978-3-031-23095-0_11

various cloud apps. Without explicit user's active control, cloud computing is the availability of computer network services, primarily for storing data and computing power [9].

Research on cloud computing is now being extensively used in both academia and business. Cloud computing benefits users as well as cloud service providers (CSPs). The difficulties with security that come with cloud computing have been extensively researched and we try to propose solutions to those limitations. In a cloud environment information may be shared throughout different businesses, which is an advantage of Cloud Computing. However with greater conveniences, comes great responsibility of safeguarding that shared data so that it is not misused by any illegitimate user or an attacker [10].

As and when one decides to use the services of cloud to store data, a crucial decision has to be formed as to employ a 3rd- party cloud service provider or develop one's own personal business cloud. Data pertaining to national security or highly secretive upcoming product information, for instance, is often too delicate to be kept on a public cloud. Data pertaining such information can be exceedingly sensitive, and moreover exposing it to the public cloud can have catastrophic effects. On such cases, it is strongly advised to store data in an organization's personal internal cloud. This approach can promote data security by enforcing on-premises data usage regulations. Furthermore, many businesses lack the expertise to apply all necessary layers of security to critical data, therefore total data security and privacy are still not guaranteed [11].

In order to safeguard and secure information stored in the cloud, this study examines data security strategies that are employed worldwide. It examines potential hazards to cloud data as well as the precautions taken by different service providers in order to ensure its security.

The remaining work is structured as hereunder. A survey of the literature in Sect. 2 provides an overview of earlier studies in this area. We try to look at the several different types of cloud computing security in Sect. 3. The dangers to data in the cloud are discussed in Sect. 4. Section 5 looks at some of the most effective security techniques used for data security around the globe. This is followed by Sect. 6, which presents the major security challenges that are posed upon cloud infrastructure. Section 7 shows how we can use Encryption in order to provide Security to the data. A Case Study on Cloud Security Model is presented in Sect. 8. The paper's last section, the conclusion, offers an overview of the whole body of research.

2 Literature Review

We utilized a variety of sources in order to gain an insight over the principles of cloud computing and also on how we can securely store data over there. A literature review is included in this part to set the stage for examining various data security challenges.

J. Shrinivas talked about how consumers are concerned about shifting their data to the cloud. He asserts that security concerns are the main causes why big businesses are still hesitant to migrate their data on to the cloud. The authors did an excellent job of analyzing security issues in data and privacy preservation challenges in the cloud. Additionally, he also discusses some viable remedies for these problems [1].

M. A. Vouk, on the other hand, designed a standard for protecting cloud data while it is in motion. A starting point of encryption has been considered for data security during transfer. Additional encryption is necessary for trustworthy security, but it greatly lengthens the latency. The benchmark they utilized in their investigation finds an equilibrium between security and encryption overhead [2].

By giving the end user power over their data, P. S. Wooley investigates the privacy concern in an effort to inspire confidence. He examines numerous attacks based on cloud, and also proposes ways to combat them [3].

V. Kavitha and S. Subashini offer a cloud computing data protection paradigm which is based on architecture of the cloud. They have also developed tools to add to the effort in developing a prototype for security of data in Cloud Computing [5].

An efficient method for implementing security policies in web services was put out by Ranchal and Bhargava. This method can preserve user privacy, provide data owners control over data disclosure decisions, and lower the danger of unauthorized access [6].

According to a study by Martin, consumers pay greater concern to privacy, but it doesn't provide them the capacity to regulate their online-experience. That evaluated how important privacy expectations violations are in relation to consumer website trust [7].

Several dangers in the cloud environment have been thoroughly analyzed and studied in [22, 23]. According to current trends, machine learning techniques are being used to advance cloud and network security, as mentioned in [24].

To improve cloud security, Support Vector Machine (SVM)-based classifiers are used in [25, 26]. Cloud abnormalities were found using a different machine learning classifier that is frequently employed to increase cloud security in [27, 28].

3   Types of Security in Cloud Computing

A set of security measures known as cloud security, often referred to as Cloud Security, is intended to safeguard the architecture, applications, and data stored in the cloud. The different sorts of Security Models have been depicted in Fig. 1.

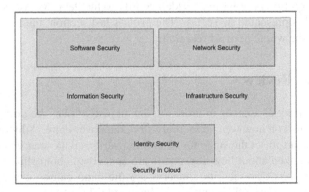

Fig. 1. Different types of security in cloud

3.1 Information Security

No matter if the data is encoded, moved, processed, or deposited, maintaining a set of business policies that will secure data resources is necessary for information protection [13].

3.2 Identity Security

It is referred to be the privacy and professional approach that "allows the authenticating users to obtain the resources at the proper moment and for the excellent aims" [14]. While preserving the confidentiality and security of data and programs, it enhances access to certified users.

3.3 Network Security

An important computing necessity is network security. It entails taking protective hardware and software measures to guard against unauthorized users, breakups, revisions, violations, degradation, or inappropriate dissemination of the existing networking infrastructure, thereby providing a stable platform for machines, clients, and services to carry out their essential tasks in a secure setting [15]. Web systems in particular may be influenced by network level issues, which fundamentally reduce capacity and lengthen device delay.

3.4 Software Security

Security concerns for software should be established as a procedure of security analysis, starting with the concept of the program and continuing through the design and execution procedures. To provide the highest level of software security, each of these procedures depends on the others [16]. Although the complexity of software development efforts varies greatly, they always require security assurance.

3.5 Infrastructure Security

It is very vital for an enterprise to be able to verify that the infrastructure is secure in order to do business. It's important to keep things separate [17].

4 Security Concerns in Cloud

Cloud-computing and its data are related with a number of dangers and security issues. However, this research will focus on virtualization, multitenancy and public cloud storage, of which, all are connected to cloud-computing's data security. The areas pertaining to Cloud Security are showcased in Fig. 2.

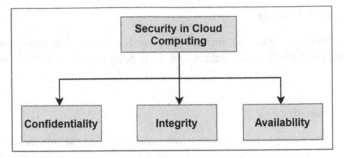

Fig. 2. CIA appendix in cloud

4.1 Virtualization

Virtualization is a technique for copying the image of a completely operational operating system to some another operating system. A specific component known as a hypervisor is essential in order to execute a guest operating-system as a virtual- machine in a host operating-system [18]. The architecture of Virtual Machines is shown in Fig. 3.

Virtualization is the primary technology that has altered how cloud computing data centers operate. Multiple copies of VMs may be created over the same physical infrastructure, which improves resource utilization and boosts return over Investment. Matter of concern in this case is the breach of the hypervisor itself. A weak hypervisor can end up becoming the primary target. The entire system and the data are at danger if a hypervisor is compromised [12].

The de-allocation and assignment of resources is another danger associated with virtualization. If the data of a particular VM is directed to the memory and not destructed before memory is allocated to some other VM, there are high chances that the data will

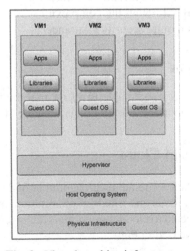

Fig. 3. Virtual machine infrastructure

be visible to new VM that has been allocated the same memory which is not ideal at all [19].

Improved and enhanced planning for virtualization's usage is a solution to the challenges listed above. Before de-allocating resources, care should be taken in their use and data must be properly validated.

A virtualized infrastructure or environment is protected by a combination of policies, practices, and procedures known as virtualization security. It examines security concerns that affect the elements of a virtualized system and solutions for mitigating or preventing them. A wide range of techniques are included in the broad notion of virtualization security, which may be used to assess, deploy, monitor, and manage security inside a virtualized infrastructure or environment. Virtualization security involves procedures like granular implementation of security processes and controls at each virtual machine, protecting virtual networks, virtual computers, and other virtual appliances from threats and flaws that the underlying physical equipment may have revealed and ensuring that each virtual machine is within your control and responsibility.

4.2 Public-Cloud Storage

Public clouds are affordable, incredibly adaptable, and infrastructure ready. However, there are significant problems when it comes to sensitive data. Normally, clouds use centralized storage, which makes them an easy victim [20].

Resources for storage are complex systems which combine software as well as hardware solutions, and in the public cloud, even a little compromise would result in data breach. For particularly sensitive data, it is usually advisable to have a private cloud if possible to eliminate such hazards.

4.3 Multitenancy

The greatest threats to cloud's data is shared access, commonly known as multitenancy. Multitenancy in cloud-computing refers to shared hosting, where server resources are distributed among various clients. It is the opposite of single tenancy, which occurs when a computer system or software instance has just one end user or set of users [21].

Multitenancy is posing problem to the clients as if there are issues with any of the client, it will impact the others in the same pool too. It is so because the other clients will be vulnerable to attacks as they are using shared server resources.

By thoroughly confirming individuals' identities before providing anyone access to the data, these issues may be avoided.

4.4 Identity and Access Management (IAM)

IAM relates to the user accounts' accessibility privileges. Managing user account authentication and authorization also applies here. Access controls are essential for preventing users, both good and bad, from accessing and jeopardizing systems and sensitive data. IAM encompasses techniques like password management and multi- factor authentication, among others.

5 Security of Data in Cloud-Computing

Data security is much more than only encryption of data in Cloud. Data security requirements are differing in all the three cloud service models. The Architecture of Cloud is depicted in Fig. 4.

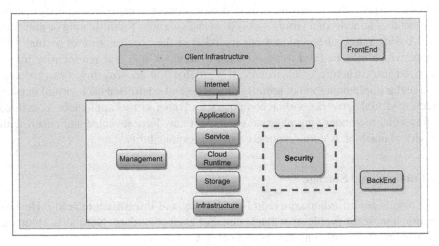

Fig. 4. Cloud system architecture

Cloud's data can be categorized in several ways. The type of data protection techniques, processes and procedures determines data confidentiality and integrity. The most important issue is data exposure in the two states stated below.

Types of Data in Cloud:
A. Data at Rest
Data at rest or data on cloud is the data which can be easily accessed with the help of internet. This shall include both – backed up data as well as the live-data. It contains everything, including the database for the program, log files, system configuration files, backups, and archives.

B. Data in Motion
In general, moving data pertains to information that enters and exits the cloud every now and then. This is information that the program is actively accessing and using. It could involve the transfer of data between two separate apps or services, or even between clients and servers or other parts of the same application.

Because the later must travel from one area to another, data-in-transit is often much vulnerable when compared to prior. There are several ways that intermediate software might monitor data and, occasionally, change it as it moves toward its target. One of the best methods for securing data in transit is encryption. Both kinds of data can be identified in Fig. 5.

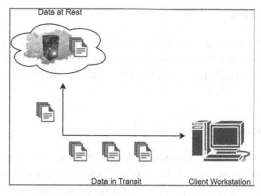

Fig. 5. Data-at-rest and data-in-transit

6 Major Security Challenges

There is no question that using the cloud instead of more established on premise systems has the ability to increase security. The term "potential" is crucial here. Businesses may not always benefit from increased protection when they go to the cloud, despite the fact that it might be more secure. The following are the primary obstacles to overcome:

6.1 Internal Attacks

The design of cloud computing networks might occasionally put customers' security and privacy at risk. Despite the fact that it occurs infrequently, this risk is extremely difficult to manage. For instance, admins and managers may occasionally act as nefarious agents, endangering the security of customers who utilize cloud computing services.. This type of attack is also known as Insider Attack in Security paradigm. Types of Internal Attacks are showcased in Fig. 6.

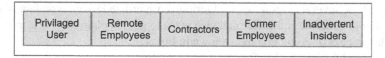

Fig. 6. Internal attacks

6.2 Partial/Incomplete Data Deletion

It is very critical to erase all the data from the cloud when there is no need of it or the client has asked to do so. If the data is not deleted precisely and the same resources are allocated to some other user, then there is a high probability of information leakage. This makes it more difficult for customers to sign up for cloud computing services.

6.3 Interception of Data

When compared to traditional computing, cloud computing divides and distributes data while it is in transit. Because of the weakness and fragility of computing technologies, attacks like reply assaults, 3rd party attacks and spoofing-snipping attacks offers agreater hazard.

6.4 Failure of Isolation

The pooling of resources that occurs as a result of cloud computing's multi-tenancy is a problematic quality in and of itself. For a business, not having separate storage might be deadly. The use and adoption of cloud-based services are considered as being significantly hampered by additional concerns regarding guest hop attacks and their effects.

7 Using Encryption for Data Protection

Encryption is the method of converting plain text into encrypted text using an algorithm in order to make sure that private information is unreadable by unauthorized users. Encrypted data often looks as a long list of random letters and numbers. Once information has been encoded, using the proper encryption key is the only method to decode it and regain access to it.

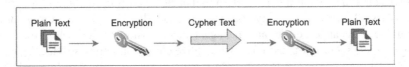

Fig. 7. Cryptography process

These days, several cryptographic algorithms are utilized to encrypt data. We use a key in order to generate cipher text and vice versa to get the plain text back in its actual form. The process of cryptography is shown in Fig. 7.

Cryptography typically has four basic applications:

7.1 Block-Cipher

Block cypher is an encryption technique that generates a cipher text of the same size as the input, say b bits, using a set input size of b bits. The dissemination of a block cypher is high. Because symbols cannot readily be inserted in the midst of a block, it is also quite challenging for an attacker to insert them without being noticed.

This technique ensures that similar blocks of text in a message are not encrypted in the same way. The cypher text from the preceding encrypted block is often used to encrypt the next block in the sequence. Block Cipher Algorithm is depicted in Fig. 8.

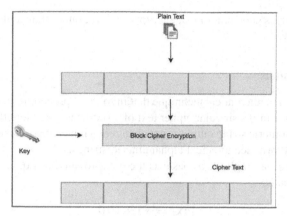

Fig. 8. Block cipher

7.2 Stream Ciphers

A stream cypher is an encryption method that converts plain text into codes that is unintelligible to anybody without the right key by working byte by byte. The same key is used to encrypt and decode messages with stream cyphers since they are linear.

Stream cyphers often operate more quickly than block cyphers due to their minimal hardware complexity. However, if not handled appropriately, this strategy might lead to major security issues. Figure 9 clearly shows the representation of Stream Cipher.

Stream cyphers are dependent on:

Plaintext: A message that you want to encrypt must already exist.

Keystreams: The plaintext characters are replaced with a set of random characters. There may be symbols, characters, or numbers among them.

Cipher text: The message that has been encrypted.

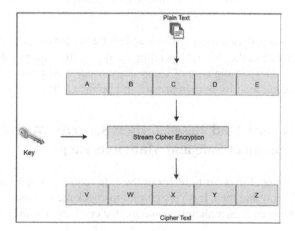

Fig. 9. Stream cipher

Stream cypher, as shown in Fig. 9, encrypts each bit rather than a block of text using an encryption key.

7.3 Hash Functions

Hash Function is a mathematical technique that involves a procedure that turns plaintext material of any size into a singular cipher text of a predetermined length. Generally, the size of the alphanumeric string output is not changed. This method makes guarantee that no two words will produce identical alphanumeric strings.

This hash function might be as basic as the one provided in Eq. (1) or also it might be quite sophisticated.

$$F(x) = x \bmod 20 \tag{1}$$

The method of hash function cryptography is depicted in Fig. 10.

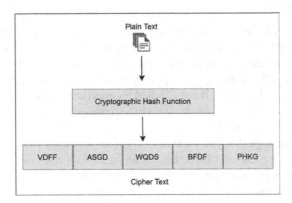

Fig. 10. Hash function mechanism

To protect data security, all of the methods and strategies covered above are frequently utilized to protect data in the cloud. Depending on the circumstance, various tactics are applied differently. Despite the type of technology used, it is highly recommended to safeguard information security both in private and public clouds.

8 Case Study on Cloud Based Cyber Security Model for Identification of Safe and Malicious Request

We try to depict a model in order to filter out the safe requests that might go in and out of the cloud every now and then. It is very crucial to check the requests as there is a high probability that it can contain malicious contents that can harm the integrity of the cloud data system.

The Table 1 shows the parameters of the data that has been used to implement the Case Study.

Table 1. Parameters of dataset

Parameter	Meaning
Base URL	URL of Application
Title of Person	Person's Title. Ex. Mr/Mrs
Name	Name of the Person
Body of Data	Message/Content
Host	Website Host
User-Agent	Request Header
Content-Type	Type - json/html etc
User's Session ID	Unique ID
Content Length	Length of Data
User Role	Role of Person
Protocol	Type of Protocol used. Ex. HTTP
IP Address	IP Address of User
isSafe	Added Parameter to mark a request as Safe/Unsafe

Models Used for filtration of data:

1. Exploratory Data Analysis (EDA) for Pre Processing of Data
   It is a strategy for data analysis that uses visual methods. With the use of statistical summaries and graphical depiction, it is used to identify patterns, trends, and also to verify presumptions (Fig. 11).

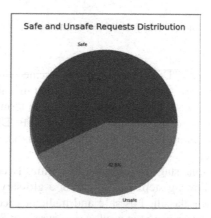

Fig. 11. Actual data distribution for safe and unsafe data

2. Bag-of-Words Model
   Natural language processing employs the text modelling technique known as "bag of words." To explain it formally, it is a method for extraction of features from text data. This approach makes it simple and flexible to extract traits from documents.
   Confusion Matrix for the above model is depicted in Table 2.

Table 2. Confusion matrix for bag of words model

49	32
0	119

Results of the model:

Table 3. Result obtained for Bag of Words Model

	Precision	Recall	F1 score	Support
0	1	0.6	0.75	81
1	0.79	1	0.88	119
Accuracy			0.84	200
Macro Average	0.89	0.8	0.82	200
Weighted Average	0.87	0.84	0.83	200

   We could achieve an Accuracy of 84% for the above model and it is showcased in Table 3.

3. TF-IDF Technique
   Term Frequency - Inverse Document Frequency scale is used to assess a word's uniqueness. Sentences are transformed into vectors (after tokenization, stemming, and lemmatization). The semantic significance of the term is not provided by the Bag of Words approach in this situation; instead, the TF-IDF is used.
   We achieved an accuracy of 84% with this method too.

4. Deep Learning Model
   Tokenization is the initial stage in text data modelling. To create tokens, the corpus is tokenized. The following step is to construct a glossary using the below-listed tokens. These are then classified as safe and malicious requests. To achieve this, Tensor Flow's tokenization has been used. An Accuracy of 84.5% could be achieved using this model which is depicted in Fig. 12.

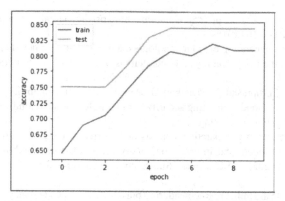

Fig. 12. Accuracy of deep learning tokenization model

9 Conclusion

The trend for improved cloud data storage techniques is surely intensifying as cloud computing is increasingly used for data storage. If data stored in the cloud is not properly safeguarded, it may be at danger. The hazards and security threats to data in the cloud were explored in this study. Also, an overview of three categories of security problems was discussed. The hazards that the hypervisor poses are examined when it comes to virtualization.

Multitenancy and risks associated with public clouds have also been addressed. One of the primary subjects of the article was data security, including its difficulties and solutions in cloud computing. It has been looked at how to encrypt data in the cloud using efficient methods and data at various stages.

The study examined block, stream, and hash ciphers—all of which are used to encrypt data in the cloud, whether it is at rest or in transit. An overview of Hash Functions is also provided discussing its functionalities and usage. Finally, a Case Study on Cloud based Cyber Security Model for Identification of Safe and Malicious Request has been presented which applies different models to filter the request and an accuracy of 85% has been achieved for the same.

References

1. Srinivas, J., Reddy, K., Qyser, A.: Cloud computing basics. Build Infrastruct. Cloud Secur. **1**(2011), 3–22 (2014)
2. Vouk, M.A.: Cloud computing - issues, research and implementations. In: Proceedings of the International Conference on Information Technologies Interfaces, ITI, pp. 31–40 (2008)
3. Wooley, P.S.: Identifying cloud computing security risks. Contin. Educ. **1277** (2011)
4. Alharthi, A., Yahya, F., Walters, R.J., Wills, G.B.: An Overview of Cloud Services Adoption Challenges in Higher Education Institutions (2015)
5. Subashini, S., Kavitha, V.: A survey on security issues in service delivery models of cloud computing. J. Netw. Comput. Appl. **34**(1), 1–11 (2011)
6. Ranchal, R., Bhargava, B.: Epics: A framework for enforcing security policies in composite Web services. IEEE Trans. Services Comput. **12**(3), 12–22(2019)

7. Martin, K.: The penalty for privacy violations: how privacy violations impact trust online. J. Bus. Res. **82**, 103–116 (2018)
8. Ali, T.: The next generation cloud technologies: a review on distributed cloud, fog and edge computing and their opportunities and challenges. Res. Berg Rev. Sci. Technol. **1**(1), 1–15 (2021)
9. Ramesh, N.P., Guruprasad, N., Dankan Gowda, V.: A high-availability and integrity layer for cloud storage, cloud computing security: from single to multi-clouds. J. Phys. Conf. Ser. **1921**(1) (2021). (IOP Publishing)
10. Abhishek, S., et al.: A comparative analysis of security issues & vulnerabilities of leading cloud service providers and in-house university cloud platform for hosting e-educational applications. In: 2021 IEEE Mysore Sub Section International Conference (MysuruCon). IEEE (2021)
11. Tawalbeh, L.A., Saldamli, G.: Reconsidering big data security and privacy in cloud and mobile cloud systems. J. King Saud Univ. Comput. Inform. Sci. **33.7**, 810–819 (2021)
12. Bhardwaj, A., Krishna, C.R.: Virtualization in cloud computing: moving from hypervisor to containerization—a survey. Arab. J. Sci. Eng. **46**, 8585–8601 (2021)
13. Ali, O.: Assessing information security risks in the cloud: a case study of Australian local government authorities. Gov. Inf. Q. **37**(1), 101419 (2020)
14. Identity, I., Anand, P.M.R., Bhaskar, V.: Identity and access management in cloud environment: mechanisms and challenges. Eng. Sci. Technol. Int. J. **21.4**, 574–588 (2018)
15. Wu, H., et al.: Network security for virtual machine in cloud omputing. In: 5th International Conference on Computer Sciences and Convergence Information Technology. IEEE (2010)
16. Gururaj, R., Iftikhar, M., Khan, F.A.: A comprehensive survey on security in cloud computing. Procedia Comput. Sci. **110**, 465–472 (2017)
17. Hassan, R.: Data and infrastructure security auditing in cloud computing environments. Int. J. Inform. Manage. **34.3**, 364–368 (2014)
18. Hanan, S., et al.: Cloud computing virtualization of resources allocation for distributed systems. J. Appl. Sci. Technol. Trends **1.3**, 98–105 (2020)
19. Theodor, B., et al.: Digital transformation of manufacturing through cloud services and resource virtualization. Comput. Indust. **108**,150–162 (2019)
20. Xue, Y., et al.: An attribute-based controlled collaborative access control scheme for public cloud storage. IEEE Trans. Inform. Forens. Secur. **14.11**, 2927–2942 (2019)
21. Ru, J., et al.: A systematic review of scheduling approaches on multi-tenancy cloud platforms. Inform. Softw. Technol. **132**, 106478 (2021)
22. Kandukuri, B., Paturi, V., Rakshit, A.: Cloud security issues. In: International Conference on Services Computing, pp. 517–520. IEEE (2009)
23. Almulla, S., Yeun, C.: Cloud computing security management. In: 2nd International Conference on ICESMA, pp 1–7. IEEE (2010)
24. Palivela, H., Chawande, N., Wani, A.: Development of server in cloud computing to solve issues related to security and backup. In: IEEE CCIS, pp 158–163 (2011)
25. Laura, A., Moro, R.: Support vector machines (SVM) as a technique for solvency analysis. DIW Berlin discussion paper (2008)
26. Zhang, X., Zhao, Y.: Application of support vector machine to reliability analysis of engine systems. Telkomnika **11**(7), 3352–3560 (2013)
27. Haykin, S.: Neural Networks: A Comprehensive Foundation, 2nd edn. Prentice Hall, Englewood Cliffs, NJ (2009)
28. Michalski, R., Carbonell, J., Mitchell, T.: Machine Learning: An Artificial Intelligence Approach. Springer, Berlin (2013)

Phishing URLs Detection Using Machine Learning

Wend-Benedo Simeon Zongo$^{(\boxtimes)}$, Boukary Kabore, and Ravirajsinh Sajubha Vaghela

Marwadi University, Rajkot, India
{zongowend-benedosimeon.114273,
kaboreboukarykaboretiga.114984}@marwadiuniversity.ac.in,
Ravirajsinh.vaghela@marwadieducation.edu.in

Abstract. Nowadays, internet user numbers are growing steadily, covering online services, and goods transactions. This growth can lead to the theft of users' private information for malicious purposes. Phishing is one technique that can cause users to be redirected to sites with malicious content and steal all of their information. The main purpose of phishing is to steal user identities such as online credentials, bank transaction details, etc. As technology advances, the mechanism of phishing attacks begins to take place, so to prevent it from happening, some mechanism anti-phishing is used to detect phishing links or URLs Machine learning is the most solutions tools against phishing offensive, and with its algorithms, we can rank all content and determine whether it is phishing or not. We tested cross-validation as well as the correlation between features. Using Logistic Regression, we determined the importance of the features. Finally, we tested the Multinomial Naïve Baye classifier. We found that the Logistic Regression classifier had better accuracy for the best accuracy.

Keywords: Phishing · Domain name · Machine learning · URL · Classification models

1 Introduction

Internet services have brought immense changes to people's lives styles. Most online services are designed to connect users to membership systems and individual users must register and log in to receive these personalized services. For this reason, people must provide their personal information when entertaining this convenient and efficient service in a secure network. The environment, transmission, and storage of information are protected by network security technology. In addition, many cybercriminals use different methods to attack and steal personal information such as the case of phishing attacks.

Phishing is a technique used by most criminals via social digging of information and technical loopholes to steal consumers' secret information [1]. It is also a well-known, computer-based social engineering technique. Attackers are using disguised email addresses as a weapon to target large corporations to steal sensitive data. According

S. Rajagopal et al. (Eds.): ASCIS 2022, CCIS 1760, pp. 159–167, 2022.
https://doi.org/10.1007/978-3-031-23095-0_12

to some reports, as CISCO, in 2021, approximately 90% of data was breached due to phishing. Spear phishing is the most widely used type of phishing attack, comprising 65% of all phishing attacks. Studies carried out by Tessian in 2021 reveal that employees receive an average of 14 malicious emails per year. Cybercriminals use email scams because that way is simple, functional, and free. So, they encrypt all your email address information and send you emails in the name of a legitimate or original source.

To reduce this scourge which is a real threat to companies and individuals, approaches such as the anti-phishing extension for chrome and automatic detection of phishing links based on machine learning have been proposed. Anti-phishing chrome extension analyses all visited links to identify fake or right links related to their content [2]. Machine learning uses some algorithms to automatically analyzes and detects phishing URL with malicious content [3, 5, 6].

Machine learning is the ability of a computer to learn without being explicitly programmed [13]. Machine learning algorithms allow a system to automatically and repetitively learn from big data to predict or classify outcomes. The accuracy of predictions is determined through the quality and quantity of data. The learning process allows the machine to adjust over time to better adapt to the data, which improves performance. Consequently, an effective and efficient phishing detection approach is important to tackle the problem of phishing attacks [4]. This paper outlines different classification models of machine learning for phishing link detection such as logistic regression, decision trees, and natural language processing. Our work will be divided into 3 main parts to better analyze our document. As follow, Sect. 1: determine something related to the work. Section 2: Evoque our research methodology. Section 3: determine the results funds and analyze the best algorithms used.

2 Related Work

2.1 Literature Review

Phishing attack nowadays is increasing day by day. Since 2020 APWG was observing between 68 000 and 94 000 phishing attacks per month. But this number has tripled, APWG reported 316 747 unique phishing Web sites attacks in December 2021 which was the highest monthly total in APWG's reporting history during the period [8]. APWG recorded 1,025,968 total phishing attacks in Q1 2022. APWG counted 384,291 attacks in March 2022.

Regarding this report, in recent years, many documents and articles have been published demonstrating some methodologies and strategies to detect phishing domains or URLs. Many of them use a machine learning algorithm to detect malicious URLs. Classification model techniques are the better learning capabilities from cyber data [9] (Fig. 1).

Fig. 1. APWG report in 2022

It mainly presents a machine learning-based approach to detect phishing websites in real-time, considering hybrid features based on URLs and hyperlinks to achieve high accuracy without relying on third-party systems.

Yadav, N., and Panda. [10] presented a mixed-selection model that combined both contents- and behavior-based methods to help identify the attacker using email headers. Manish Jain, Kanishk Rattan, Divya Sharma, Kriti Goel, and Nidhi Gupta have proposed a framework for detecting phishing sites using machine learning algorithms such as Naive Bayes Classifier, Random Forest, and Support Vector Machine. Among all these algorithms, Random Forest gives the most accuracy and this framework uses address bases, domains and HTML JS features to detect the legitimacy of the website.[11]

Suleiman Y. Yerima and Mohammed K. Alzaylae proposed a framework for detecting phishing websites using a deep learning approach [11]. They used the CNN (Convolutional Neural Network) model to achieve high accuracy. They used only the URL-based feature to detect the phishing site, it has 30 URL attributes. This approach has a better score than any other approach.

Weiwei Zhuang, Qingshan Jiang, and Tengke Xiong proposed an intelligent anti-phishing strategy model for phishing site detection [11]. It uses a heuristic URL detection module. It has a categorization module. It categorizes phishing as a bank, lottery, etc. It uses a hierarchical clustering algorithm for phishing categorization. Rishikesh Mahajan and Irfan Siddavatam developed a phishing site detection system using machine learning algorithms such as decision trees, random forest, and support vector machine, where random forest gave the best accuracy [11].

2.2 URLs Descriptions

URL Description

A URL (Uniform Resource Locator) is a unique address in a computer network, which allows to index of a data source. This data source or address can be an HTML page, an image, a document, etc... Each URL has a set structure [12].

http://www.yourbank.in:80/Upload?key=values&keys=value#otherContent
Structure and description of URLs

> **Scheme**: HTTP or HTTPS. It represents the protocol
> **Authority:** www. yourbank.in:80. It represents part of the domain name and port number which the protocol is able to use
> **Resource Path: /Upload/.** It mentions files directories
> **Parameters- Parameters:** Key=values&keys=value. Pieces of information in a query string of a URL

Phishing URL

Attackers, usually change the subdomain name and path of the URL.

Example: http://yourbank.in.account.yourbanks.it/ users
Structure:

> Protocol: Http
> Domain Name: yourbanks.it
> > Subdomain item 1: yourbanks.in
> > Subdomain item2: account
> Path: users

Additionally, Attackers use Cybersquatting and Typo squatting techniques to tempt users. Example: facebook.com, they change one or many letters from the main, meaning the phishing link can be facebool.com.

3   Research Methodology

This section revolves around the different processes and methodologies used to achieve the result (Fig. 2).

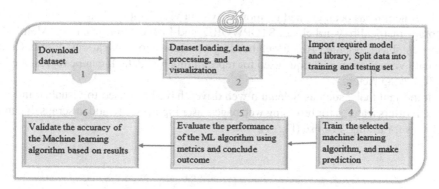

Fig. 2. Research methodology

Step 1: Dataset download
Dataset has been downloaded from Kaggle (Kaggle.com), a website containing many machine- learning datasets. The dataset is named "phishing_site_urls.csv", and has 549346 entries and 2 columns. The prediction column is the Label which has 2 categories.

Bad: URLs contain malicious elements and these sites are phishing websites
Good: URLs don't contain malicious elements these sites are good websites

Step 2: Dataset loading and processing
Panda's library has been imported to load the dataset. The method *read_csv()* is used to create the Data Frame from the CSV file (dataset). Methods such as *IsNull()*, and *sum()* have been used for dataset processing. Indeed *IsNull().sum()* counts all null values of each column. We used the *value_count()* method on the label column to find the number of good and bad URLs. As a result, we found 392924 for good and 156422 for bad. Seaborn from matplotlib is used to visualize the data of the target column (Label).

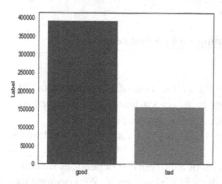

Fig. 3. Dataset visualisation based on label categories

Count Vectorizer and tokenizer are used to prepare the predictive columns. We imported Regex Tokenizer and Snowball Stemmer functions from the *nltk* library. *Regex Tokenizer* through regular expressions splits a string into substrings and allows special characters to be removed from the URL using the Tokenize method. As for *Snowball Stemmer*, it reduces the words of the URL to their base root. We have created columns for tokenizing named "text tokenized" text and snowball text named" text_stemmed". After we have combined both into a single column named "text_send" (Fig. 3).

A function has been created to allow easy data visualization. This function uses as a library matplotlib, word cloud, STOPWORD, and Image color generator. Matplotlib provides object- oriented API for embedding plot info into applications. Words Cloud is a data visualization technique used for representing text data. It can be represented in the following picture.

Important tools, such as Selenium web driver, have been used to visualize internal links. It offers features for browsing web pages, user input, etc. To add, it scraps dynamic websites for testing. For use (Fig. 4):

Fig. 4. Word Cloud data visualisation

Download chromedriver.exe corresponding to the same version of your navigation. Set up the Chrome driver by creating a list of URLs.

List all links to the created list Create an empty list that will append all links containing each website.

Use the Beautiful Soup library to extract only hyperlinks that are relevant to Google: links only with ' <'a'> ' tags with href attributes.

Step 3: Model library, splitting data into training and testing sets
Some libraries are imported for data predictions:

Count vectorizer is a python library that allows the conversion of a collection of text documents to a matrix of token counts. It comes from sci-kit-learn. The *fit transform* method is called to transform all text that we tokenized and stemmed.

Train test split allows splitting the dataset into train and test data. This function is imported from the sci-kit-learn library.

Logistic Regression is used to predict the likelihood of a categorical dependent variable. In other words, the logistic regression model predicts P(Y=1) given X. We appealed the Naive Bayes multinomial classifier to predict the tags of the text of our label with the greatest chance. It is well known for discrete feature classification such as spam filtering, sentiment analysis, and text Classification. *Classification report and accuracy score* are used to give all reports about metric as recall, f1 score, prediction, etc...

Confusion metric is used to give all info of actual prediction.

Step 4: Train the selected machine learning algorithm, and make a prediction
Function train_test_split() is used for data training and testing. The column Label is used as a Y value for prediction. For the x value, we used the fit transform method from the count vectorizer library to transform all text that has been tokenized of text_sent columns. The x value is named *"feature"*.

4 Result and Analysis

4.1 Result

The results prediction of our two algorithms (Logistic Regression and Multinomial Naïve Baye) are returned in the below table (Table 1).

Table 1. Evaluation of algorithms score

Algorithm	Function	Result percent
Logistic regression	Testing accuracy (score)	96%
	Training accuracy	97%
Multinomial Naïve Bayes	Testing accuracy (score)	95%
	Training accuracy	96%

Based on preview results we see that logistic regression gives a better prediction of 96%.

4.2 Analysis

The pipeline is used with Logistic Regression to analyze the model of classification. We use the *make pipeline* function to combine all processor techniques for predicting URLs real. We graph file a database named "phishing. Pkl" for testing with other links. The output predicts the stat of URLs (Fig. 5).

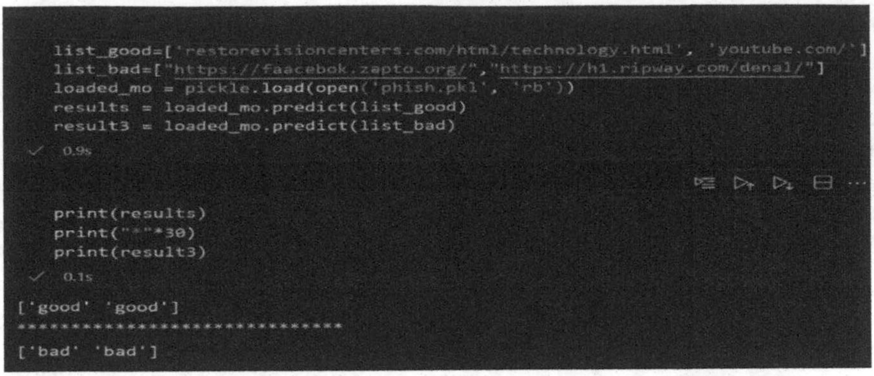

```
list_good=['restorevisioncenters.com/html/technology.html', 'youtube.com/']
list_bad=["https://faacebok.zapto.org/","https://h1.ripway.com/denal/"]
loaded_mo = pickle.load(open('phish.pkl', 'rb'))
results = loaded_mo.predict(list_good)
result3 = loaded_mo.predict(list_bad)
   0.9s

print(results)
print("*"*30)
print(result3)
   0.1s
['good' 'good']
******************************
['bad' 'bad']
```

Fig. 5. Data prediction using graph file.

5   Conclusion

This paper presents a mechanism used to detect phishing URLs. We have managed to use machine learning as a more powerful tool to solve this problem. Two machine learning algorithms were used to predict the data. Among them, Logistic Regression gives a better score of about 96%. This classification model is used to predict URLs outside the dataset. The results predict the status of the website. As a perspective, we will link the algorithms to a browser for visibility of the prediction results.

References

1. Hong, J., Kim, T., Liu, J., Park, N., Kim, S.-W.: Phishing URL detection with lexical features and blacklisted domains. In: Jajodia, S., Cybenko, G., Subrahmanian, V.S., Swarup, V., Wang, C., Wellman, M. (eds.) Adaptive autonomous secure cyber systems, pp. 253–267. Springer, Cham (2020). https://doi.org/10.1007/978-3-030-33432-1_12
2. Sharma, H., Meenakshi, E., Bhatia, S.K.: A comparative analysis and awareness survey of phishing detection tools. In: Proceedings of the 2017 2nd IEEE International Conference on Recent Trends in Electronics, Information and Communication Technology (RTEICT), pp. 1437–1442. IEEE (2017)
3. Dutta, A.K.: Detecting phishing websites using machine learning techniques. PLoS ONE 16(10), e0258361 (2021)
4. Assegie, T.A.: K-nearest neighbor based URL identification model for phishing attack detection. Indian J. Artif. Intell. Neural Networking (IJAINN) (2021)
5. Homayoun, S., Hageman, K., Afzal-Houshmand, S., Jensen, C.D., Pedersen, J.M.: Detecting ambiguous phishing certificates using machine learning. In: Proceedings of the 2022 International Conference on Information Networking (ICOIN), pp. 1–6. IEEE (2022)
6. Rather, D., Mann, S.: Detection of E-mail phishing attacks–using machine learning and deep learning. Int. J. Comput. Appl. 183, 1–7 (2022)
7. Butt, U.A., Amin, R., Aldabbas, H., Mohan, S., Alouffi, B., Ahmadian, A.: Cloud-based email phishing attack using machine and deep learning algorithms. Complex Intell. Syst., 1–28 (2022)
8. APWG: Phishing activity trends report, 1st quarter 2022, June 2022

9. Das Guptta, S., Shahriar, K.T., Alqahtani, H., Alsalman, D., Sarker, I.H.: Modeling hybrid feature-based phishing websites detection using machine learning techniques. Ann. Data Sci. **1874**, 1–26 (2022). https://doi.org/10.1007/s40745-022-00379-8

10. Yadav, N., Panda, S.P.: Feature selection for email phishing detection using machine learning. In: Khanna, A., Gupta, D., Bhattacharyya, S., Hassanien, A.E., Anand, S., Jaiswal, A. (eds.) International Conference on Innovative Computing and Communications. AISC, vol. 1388, pp. 365–378. Springer, Singapore (2022). https://doi.org/10.1007/978-981-16-2597-8_31

11. Kureel, V.K., Maurya, S., Shaikh, A., Tiwari, S., Nagmote, S.: Phishing website detection using machine learning, 7421. Journal homepage: www.ijrpr.com. ISSN: 2582

12. Chaudhari, M.S.S., Gujar, S.N. and Jummani, F., Detection of phishing web as an attack: a comprehensive analysis of machine learning algorithms on phishing dataset (2022)

13. Ott, M.A.: Bias in, bias out: ethical considerations for the application of machine learning in pediatrics. J. Pediatrics (2022). https://www.kaggle.com/datasets/taruntiwarihp/phishing-site-urls, GitHub link: https://github.com/phishing-ml/phishing-ml

Android Malware Detection with Classification Based on Hybrid Analysis and N-gram Feature Extraction

Eslavath Ravi[1(✉)] and Mummadi Upendra Kumar[2]

[1] Department of Computer Science and Engineering, Osmania University, Hyderabad, Telangana, India
eslavathravi@gmail.com
[2] Department of Computer Science and Artificial Intelligence, Muffakham Jah College of Engineering and Technology, Hyderabad, Telangana, India
upendra.kumar@mjcollege.ac.in

Abstract. Mobile devices will have the potential to expose to various cyber-attacks with the explosive growth of mobile networks. Unknown malware may proliferate dramatically in areas where existing security software is incapable of detecting it. As a result, it is critical to propose a new malware detection classification method. In this paper, an n-gram hybrid analysis-based approach is used to extract all n-gram byte codes from training samples, as well as the most relevant attributes, which are planned to be selected. The test samples are determined to check whether they are malware or benign and thus malware samples are classified and detected using a convolution neural network (CNN) classifier.

Keywords: Android malware · Convolution neural network classifier · Hybrid analysis · Malware detection · Mobile malware · N-gram

1 Introduction

With the development of mobile and smart gadgets, particularly when connected to the internet, cyberinfrastructure is expanding quickly [1]. Cyber threats have been growing exponentially while the world is becoming increasingly digital. This situation is not so different in India. According to CERT-In, India faced 11.5 million cyber-attack incidents during the year 2021. These incidents cover threats to the critical infrastructure of India such as airlines, banking systems, financial institutions, power communications, and railways. Such attacks are also becoming common even in the corporate sector by facing data breaches to proprietary data, thus showing the importance of cyber security in government and business operations [2]. Cyber-attacks are carried out with malicious intent in order to exploit a vulnerability or weakness in an individual's or organization's system. The intent of these attacks could be to steal, alter, destroy, or gain access to unauthorized information, content, or asset of such an organization. Different types of cyber-attacks include Malware attacks, Network security attacks, social engineering attacks, and Wireless security attacks [3]. For example, one of the recent major data

S. Rajagopal et al. (Eds.): ASCIS 2022, CCIS 1760, pp. 168–184, 2022.
https://doi.org/10.1007/978-3-031-23095-0_13

breach examples is the Saudi Aramco $50 Million Data breach [4]. According to Sonic wall's Cyber Threat Report (2019), about 22% increase in malware attacks and IoT attacks enhanced by about 217.5% were observed during the year 2018 [1]. Chander, N.et al. [58] proposed Metaheuristic feature selection with deep learning enabled cascaded recurrent neural network for anomaly detection in Industrial IoT Environment. Kumar, M.U. et al. [59] proposed Dependable Solutions Design by Agile Modeled Layered Security Architectures. Shravani, D. et al. [60] proposed Designing Dependable Web Services Security Architecture Solutions. Krishna Prasad, A.V. et al. [61] proposed Designing Dependable Business Intelligence Solutions Using Agile Web Services Mining Architectures, Mahalakshmi et al. [62] proposed Automatic Water Level Detection Using IoT.

1.1   Average Cost of a Data Breach

The average cost of a data breach to companies worldwide is about $3.8 million. An organization takes about an average of 6–7 months to identify data breaches. The following table provides the global average cost of a data breach in US million dollars during the year 2014–2019 [6] (Chart 1 and Table 1).

Table 1. Average cost of data breach to companies worldwide

Year	2014	2015	2016	2017	2018	2019
Average cost of data breach	3.5	3.79	4.00	3.62	3.86	3.92

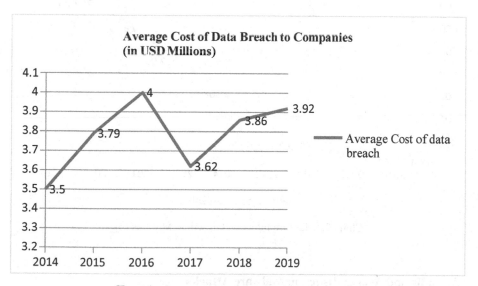

Chart 1. Average cost of data breach to companies

1.2 Growth Rate of Malware Infections

According to Kaspersky, the software security provider company, a data breach is basically exposing or providing unauthorized access to confidential or sensitive, or protected information (Kaspersky). Malware or malicious software is a software piece of code that is written with the intent to damage devices, and harm data, devices, and people. Different types of malware include Adware, Computer viruses, File-Less malware, Ransomware Trojan, Spyware, or Hybrid attacks [5]. With the advent of Artificial Intelligence (AI) and Machine Learning (ML) technologies, recent malware attacks have been becoming more sophisticated. The following chart provides the total malware infection growth rate in millions during 2009–2018 [6] (Chart 2 and Table 2).

Table 2. Growth rate of total malware infections in millions during 2009–2018 [6]

Year	2009	2010	2011	2012	2013	2014	2015	2016	2017	2018
Malware infection growth Rate	12.4	29.97	48.17	82.62	165.81	308.96	452.93	580.40	702.06	812.67

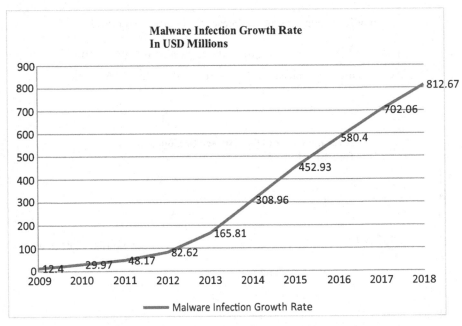

Chart 2. Malware Infection Growth in Millions [6]

1.3 India and Asia Statistics on Malware Attacks

According to Business Standard News, India is among the top 3 most affected nations by cyber-attacks in Asia in the year 2021, with two others being Japan and Australia. These top three cyber-attacks are: (i) Server access attacks (20%); (ii) Ransomware (11%) and (iii) Data theft (10%) (Chart 3, Tables 3 and 4).

Table 3. Top 10 Industries that are affected/attacked by malware in India (Data Source: Malhotra 2022)

Si no.	Indian industries Being attacked by Malware
1	Education & Research
2	Health Care
3	Utilities
4	Government/Military
5	Insurance/Legal
6	ISPs
7	Manufacturing
8	Finance/Banking
9	Transportation
10	Software Vendor

Table 4. Industry-wise share of malware attacks in percent in Asia (Data Source: Business Standard News, Feb 24, 2022)

Si. no.	Industry	Percent
1	Finance & Insurance	30
2	Manufacturing	29
3	Professional & Business Services	13
4	Transportation	10
5	Others	18

So, assessment of vulnerability or identifying security vulnerabilities such as detecting malware in systems is becoming an essential part of a holistic security program [7].

Android is the most widely used mobile operating system (OS). The market share of Mobile Android OS was 72.2% followed by Apple iOS at 26.99% and the rest such as Samsung, Kai OS, and others are 0.81% [8] (Chart 4).

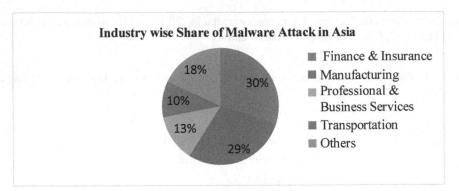

Chart 3. Industry-wise share of malware attack in Asia (Data Source: Business Standard News 2022)

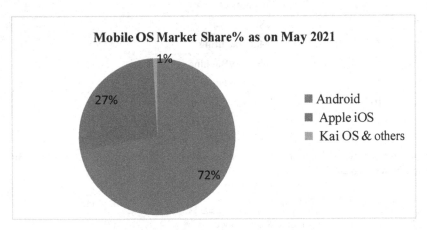

Chart 4. Mobile OS market share % as on May 2021 [8]

1.4 Trends in the Number of Attacks

In the year 2021, Kaspresky, one of the cyber security software developing companies has noted a decline in the frequency of assaults against mobile users [9] (Chart 5).

1.5 Users Attacked by Malware

It is now widely acknowledged that Android OS has dominated the market for smartphones and has emerged as the most widely used and desired mobile operating system. However, there is also an increase in security risks for Android applications. For instance, in 2017 there were more than three million new malware samples found that targeted the Android OS [10]. Though the trends show that the number of threats has been in declining trend, but new kinds of new malware may evolve too with novel approaches of development activities taking place in the information and communication technologies field. Therefore, mobile applications should be designed to detect malicious activities

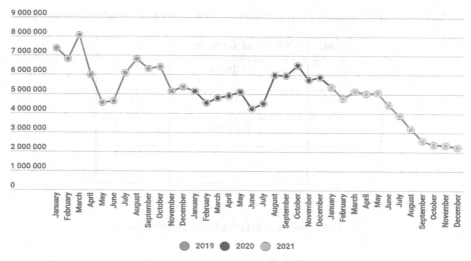

Chart 5. No of attacks on Mobile users [9]

towards protecting the important digital assets of the stakeholder activities. It helps automatically detecting malware and help naïve users in detecting and thus protecting malware [11] (Charts 6, 7, 8 and Tables 5, 6).

Table 5. Top 10 nations by the percentage of users targeted by mobile malware that used Kasparcsky Mobile Technologies [9]

Si. no	Country	%
1	Iran	40.22
2	China	28.86
3	Saudi Arabia	27.99
4	Algeria	24.49
5	**India**	**20.91**
6	Iraq	19.65
7	Yemen	19.26
8	Oman	17.89
9	Kuwait	17.30
10	Morocco	17.09

Table 6. Attack frequency by type of software used (as per Kasperesky Technologies)

Si. No.	Type of software	%
1.	Malware	80.69
2.	Adware	16.92
3.	Riskware	2.38
		100.00

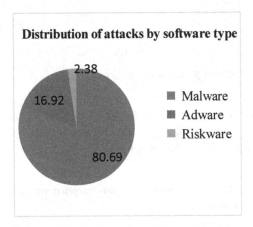

Chart 6. Distribution of attacks by software type

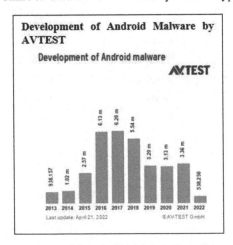

Chart 7. Development of Android Malware (Data Source: AVTEST)

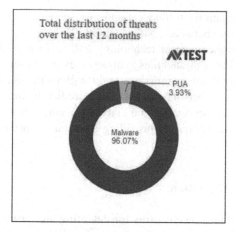

Chart 8. Total Distribution of threats over last 12 months (Data Source: AVTEST)

2 Research Objective/Problem Statement

Based on the above content, The existence of malware is considered a serious threat that makes cyber security more vulnerable. To prevent the release of sensitive data, malware must be recognized or detected and removed from the compromised system. Even though several security solutions are available right now in terms of Antivirus, Secure Socket Layer (SSL) certificate encryption, Firewall protection, etc. more defensive mechanisms are required to be developed. To do that first the malicious activities are required to be detected/identified so that mitigation can be well planned. Out of many available pre-classified malware detection techniques such as permission-based, signature-based, behavior-based, statistical-based, API calls, heuristic techniques, and anomaly-based [12], the scope of this paper is restricted to adopt deep learning and hybrid strategies to conduct N-gram opcode analysis in order to detect malware on Android mobiles.

3 Challenges in Malware Detection

Real-time malware detection is still becoming a challenge, in spite of a number of malware detection methods that have evolved. Even though the process of malware detection can be accomplished using (i) dictionary based-detection approach and (ii) Role-based or signature-based detection methods, comparatively signature or dictionary-based detection is known to be more effective for malware detection [13]. Ideally, perfect detection is impossible. Because a perfect detection method must produce True Positive and True Negative at 100% as well as False Positive and False Negative as 0% where true positive and false positive complement each other and so the true negative and true false negative. Despite having malware detection engines available in the market such as AutoShun, PhishLabs, Kaspersky, StopBadware, Sophos & Netcraft etc., malware detection is a problem in which researchers try to solve it using enormous types of methods. Each type of method has its own weakness and which may be attempted to improve later. On the other hand, malware, writers keep improving their malware code to confuse the analysts and try to play cat and mouse game. It is a vicious circle that keeps working on fighting between good and evil [14].

Along with the advancement of technology anti-malware software is receiving a massive number of malware-pirated files to undergo examination. The hackers' mafia is using these methods to entice them into systems through vulnerable databases. Therefore, it is highly necessary to use prediction methods to predict the malware at an early stage to avoid further loss [15]. However, if the malware occurrence is new, signature-based methods may become ineffective in providing an accurate prediction of zero attacks [16].

4 Theoretical Framework

Malware detection includes mechanisms for detecting and protecting against viruses, worms, Trojan horses, spyware, and other forms of malicious code [17]. Malware detection technologies that are monitored automatically or identification of malicious code are possible with different components of computer infrastructure such as servers, gateways, user workstations, and mobile devices [18]. Robust security systems are important to prevent and mitigate the harmful effects of security attacks and deep learning models can solve them because they can learn feature representations from raw, non-processed data [19].

Applications of Machine Learning are one of the fastest-growing fields of cyber security [20]. To counteract malicious cyber-attacks, several machine learning and deep learning algorithms have been used to predict malware detection [21]. A lot of companies are moving forward in adopting automatically detecting of malware with the help of applying Artificial Intelligence techniques and algorithms [22].

5 Hypothesis Declaration

H_{01} = Deep Learning algorithms such as convolution neural network algorithm-based N-gram approach under hybrid analysis provides better accuracy than another machine learning-based algorithmic approaches.

6 Methodology

Identification and removal of modern malware are becoming vital for operating the organization norms [23]. Protective mechanisms are increasingly becoming futile due to the use of techniques such as code obfuscation, polymorphism, and metamorphism used by attackers to reinforce the resilience of malware, the research work done by [24] used a dynamic analysis approach. So, in this paper, another method for malware detection that uses N-grams in deep learning with a hybrid analysis technique is considered to extract indicators of compromise (IoC) for malicious content, and are required to be analyzed using N-grams [24]. Indicators of Compromise (IoCs) provide evidence of an attack and aid in determining the type of attack and its source. Automated and predictive solutions use IoCs to quickly connect cyber security incidents to known threat profiles [25].

7 Approach

The approach to detect android malware is intended to achieve by combining the use of static and dynamic techniques (hybrid analysis technique) [26]. While static analysis analyses the source apk file of an android application and identifies cyber risks without the use of a mobile device or emulator, dynamic analysis runs the apk file in a virtual emulator environment and analyses it to detect malicious activities [27]. Earlier analysis approach followed controlling and monitoring malicious code either by executing and controlling the process through a debugger interface or by using a virtual machine (sandboxing environment approach) [28]. In this paper, adopting sandbox environment approach is planned to be adopted. The virtual machine (sandbox environment processing) approach is advantageous in that the underlying system is isolated from the malware's effects and can continue monitoring the program's execution approach [29].

8 Outline of the Work Proposed

8.1 Process for the Proposed Scheme of Work

(i) (a) Collect the samples and (b) Use classification algorithms to classify the samples into benign and malware.
(ii) Conduct Hybrid Analysis
(iii) By using hybrid analysis, extract the features from executables.
(iv) Create N-grams for both benign and malicious samples with $n = (1, 6)$ (v) Select features using the feature reduction technique
(v) Generate N-gram models using selected and preferred algorithms that can give better accuracy
(vi) To determine sensitivity and accuracy, test samples are created and validated against each N-gram model and True Positive Ratio, False Negative Ratio, and True Negative Ratio and False Positive Ratio.

A pictorial depiction of the process has been shown in Fig. 1.

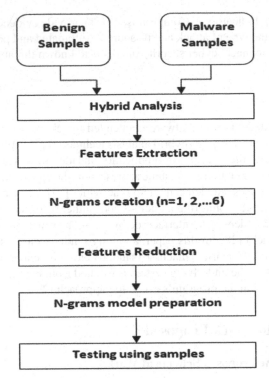

Fig. 1. Proposed scheme of work (Adapted Source: Ali, Shiaeles, Bendiab & Ghita 2020)

The conceptual background for each of the process steps is explained below:

8.1.1   Collection and Classification of Benign and Malware Samples

In this step, the threat data set is collected and the treat data set is classified for detecting different types of threats such as Benign, Trojan Virus, Worm, Rootkit, Backdoor, Flooder and Exploit [30]. Malware detection is performed in a sandbox environment in runtime to provide a safer environment to execute malware without infecting the whole system [31]. Data is gathered from open sources like publicly accessible global threat databases and data sets like known malware signatures, closed sources like forprofit cyber security research feeds and hacker resources, log data from IT systems under protection, and interviews with experts on attacks or attackers [25]. Applications are separated from essential system resources and other programs by sandboxing [32]. Any individual software or app that is present on the system is less impactful thanks to sandboxing [20]. For example, Cuckoo is one of the most popular sandbox environments for malware analysis. For conducting android-based malware detection using dynamic analysis only, Cuckoodroid tool can be adopted [27]. Cukoo performs malware analysis services for free. These submitted files are not shared publicly or privately unless it is specified to do so [33]. Many sandboxes environments demand big data analytics kind of environment capabilities such as Hadoop implementation to enable the system's deployment on a cluster that is largely reliable and testable [34].

Existing cyber security point solutions like Firewalls, Data Loss Prevention (DLP) tools, and traditional Security Information and Event Management (SIEM) technology do not provide actionable context about risks they may detect [35]. The main disadvantage of these conventional technologies is to focus on events and deliver a flood of information and alerts [36]. So Gurucul's Unified Security and Risk Analytics kind of platform automates the context gathering with historical information about users, entities, and accounts to significantly improve the speed of threat investigations and provide resolutions. It analyses the user behavior across automated security workflows including insider threats, data ex-filtration, account compromise, privileged access abuse, cloud security access, zero exploits, malware, and IoT threats [36].

8.1.2 Hybrid Analysis

The ability to undertake both static and dynamic analysis simultaneously is referred to as hybrid analysis [37]. Static analysis is carried out either by disassembling the binary files or analyzing at the source code level, without running the program (for example, opcode sequences, and control flow graphs) [38]. The APK file will be examined by static analysis, along with user permissions and suspicious code and in order to examine the behavior of an application, dynamic analysis runs a suspicious APK file on an emulator [39]. Permission extraction uses static analysis [40]. The Boolean feature vector is constructed for each APK [41]. APK files are extracted using an APK tool and converted into XML-based readable format [42]. Dynamic analysis is performed by executing the program in a virtual environment. An API-CFG model, for example, is created in dynamic analysis by extracting a set of program API calls and combining them with control flow graphs [43]. The API calls in this case can be used with N-gram techniques [44]. To identify whether a section of code is identical to that of specific malware, API call sequences and opcode sequences are employed (Citation required). Malware detection uses API sequences. Frequency analysis of API call sequences is used to analyze [44]. However, compared to static or dynamic analysis approaches, the HDM analyzer can offer greater overall accuracy and time complexity [44] as most decision points about the existence of malware are predicted using statistical data obtained from dynamic analysis [45].

8.1.3 Features Extraction

Contemporary mobile devices are smarter. They contain sensitive data such as credit card or debit card information such as account number, username, password etc. Therefore, Android mobile phones are becoming an ideal target for malware and malicious apps [46]. Before extracting the features, features are selected to remove noise and irrelevant data from threat data sets to lead to obtaining more accurate results using machine learning algorithms [47]. The method of feature extraction for identifying rogue executables is planned to consist of some of the following features: N-gram (1…6), permissions, signatures, API function calls, binary executables, and executable headers. An effective feature of unknown malware is API call sequence [45].

N-grams, which are regarded as a feature, is retrieved from portable executables of benign and malicious samples. Raw byte patterns are used to extract N-grams in the range of 1 to 6 [48]. One of the classifier algorithms like SVM or Random Forest is being developed to detect malicious executables with greater accuracy and a lower false positive rate and is selected to be trained for classifying benign and malware [49]. But in this research paper, the adoption of the Convolution Neural Network method is planned to be adapted to classify benign and malware groups of executables to compare the accuracy with other supervised learning algorithms such as SVM and Random Forest algorithms-based [50] accuracy obtained. As a part of the triangulation approach of validation, it is planned to conduct analysis and measure the model accuracy based on permissions and API calls [51] as one set of features and based on binary opcode and frequency opcode as another set of features and are compared for finding better model accuracy [52].

8.1.4 N-gram Creation

N-gram is a continuous sequence of 'N' words or tokens; where 'N' is a discrete number that can range from 1 to infinity. Unigram means sequence of one word e.g. "onion" when two words are combined like "onion flavored" then it is a 2-g or bigram, similarly three-word combination "onion flavored snack" is a 3-g or trigram, etc. so on and so forth. N-gram ranking means, it is the frequency of those terms that are appearing in a body of text (e.g. a book or tweet, etc.). N-gram ranking is a Natural Language Processing technique [53]. Term Frequency – The Inverse Document Frequency (TF-IDF) technique can be used for information retrieval to represent the importance of a word or a phrase in each document [54]. While in the static analysis, a permission-based feature is used for classification [55], the N-gram approach can be used to create malware signatures [56]. Using the N-grams technique, one may extract text and code snippets from a large piece of malware that must be run in a controlled environment. In order to train and test the classifier, signatures of this executable code are constructed. In a controlled environment, malware sample data sets are run to determine the Indicators of Compromise (IoC) via dynamic analysis [24].

8.1.5 Features Reduction

Once the Indicators of Compromise (IoC), also called technical indicators are obtained, they become input to perform feature reduction tasks and data scaling. Improving the performance requires a significant understanding of the impact of feature reduction on the quality of prediction as well as identifying which issues of data source selection and preprocessing. This can be accomplished by Auto-Encoders and Restricted Boltzmann Machines than using linear methods [57].

8.1.6 N-grams Model Preparation

This method involves transferring the malware data flow into a text file, which may then contain several domains. The text may have a sizable number of words in each domain. Each sentence in the text is a byte of flow material. The processing of the malware data flow is proposed using a convolution neural network model. There will be two stages to the model. In the first stage, word representation with domain composition is used to create continuous domain vectors, which are then used to describe data flow. The features for flow-level malware detection are then based on these data flow representations. Each flow has a related label with which the algorithm training is associated [56].

8.1.7 Testing Using Samples

Additionally, hypothesis testing will be carried out on Ubuntu, with 64GB of RAM and one GPU card being recommended. The Tensor flow and Python scripting languages are used by Keras to build, train, and test the machine learning and deep learning models. It is intended to check the compatibility of the most recent versions throughout the implementation phase. The suggested ratio for training, validation, and test data are 6:1:1. The training data are used to train the model. The test data are used to calculate the model performance [56].

9   Conclusion

Malware is one of the critical security threats. It propagates autonomously through vulnerabilities. Detection of malware is important to protect mobile from infections as well as from a compromised mobile system. In order to accurately detect malware, a suggestion is made to identify malware on Android mobile devices via text processing and extracting data flow load. As an initial effort, secondary data from Github/Kaggle is planned to be used to conduct a hybrid analysis. It uses the CNN model for classifying secondary threat data sets using Python coding and Python's deep learning algorithm libraries.

10   Further Research

A multi-filter CNN model is planned to be employed to generate the text and transferred it into domain representation and flow representation. Then, these data flow representations are utilized as characteristics for malware detection. Each flow has a matching label with which the training of the algorithm is related. The validity of test samples is checked against each N-gram model and confusion matrix. From the confusion matrix the model sensitivity and accuracy or calculated.

References

1. Madan, S., Sofat, S., Bansal, D.: Tools and Techniques for collection and analysis of Internet-of-Things malware: a systematic state-of-art review. J. King Saud Univ. Comput. Inform. Sci. (In Press), KSU, Riyadh, KSA (2022)
2. Akter, S., Uddin, M.R., Sajib, S., et al.: Reconceptualizing cybersecurity awareness capability in the data-driven digital economy. Ann. Oper. Res. (2022). https://doi.org/10.1007/s10479-022-04844_8

3. Özer, B.M., Tepecik, A.: Cybersecurity, computer networks phishing, malware, ransomware, and social engineering anti-piracy reviews. In: 2021 3rd International Congress on Human-Computer Interaction, Optimization and Robotic Applications (HORA). IEEE (2021)

4. El Yattioui, M.B., El Yattioui, Y.: Saudi Arabia and security in the Middle East: New challenges and opportunities. Handbook of Regional Conflict Resolution Initiatives in the Global South, pp. 43–58 (2022)

5. Jasmeet, K.: Taxonomy of malware: virus, worms and trojan. Int. J. Res. Anal Rev **6.1**, 192–196 (2019)

6. Fabrício, C., et al.: Fast & Furious: on the modelling of malware detection as an evolving data stream. Expert Syst. Appl. **212**, 118590 (2023)

7. Ranganath, V.-P., Mitra, J.: Are free android app security analysis tools effective in detecting known vulnerabilities? Empirical Softw. Eng. **25**(1), 178–219 (2020)

8. Janaka, S., Kalutarage, H., Al-Kadri, M.O.: Android mobile malware detection using machine learning: a systematic review. Electronics **10.13**, 1606 (2021)

9. Shishkova, T., Kivva A.: Mobile malware evolution 2021 (2022). https://securelist.com/mob ile-malware-evolution-2021/105876/. Accessed on 22 April 2022

10. Asma, R., et al.: A survey of malware detection in Android apps: Recommendations and perspectives for future research. Comput. Sci. Rev. **39**, 100358 (2021)

11. Md Jobair Hossain, F., et al.: Malware detection and prevention using artificial intelligence techniques. In: 2021 IEEE International Conference on Big Data (Big Data). IEEE (2021)

12. Muchammad, N., et al.: Malware detection: issues and challenges. J. Phys. Conf. Ser. **1807**(1) (2021). (IOP Publishing)

13. Mohammad, A., Alsmadi, I., Alazab, M.: The malware detection challenge of accuracy. In: 2016 2nd International Conference on Open Source Software Computing (OSSCOM). IEEE (2016)

14. Muhammad Najmi Ahmad, Z., Maarof, M.A., Zainal, A.: Challenges in high accuracy of malware detection. In: 2012 IEEE Control and System Graduate Research Colloquium. IEEE (2012)

15. Mukherjee, S., Das, T., Patra R.: Malware attacks prediction system. A Bachelor degree Project Report, School of Computer science, p. 751024 KIIT, Bhubneswar (2020)

16. Sharma, S., Rama Krishna, C., Sahay, S.K.: Detection of advanced malware by machine learning techniques. In: Ray, K., Sharma, T., Rawat, S., Saini, R., Bandyopadhyay, A. (eds.) Soft Computing: Theories and Applications. AISC, vol. 742. Springer, Singapore (2019). https://doi.org/10.1007/978-981-13-0589-4_31

17. Cheerala, R., Kaur, G.: A Comprehensive study on malware detection and prevention techniques used by anti-virus. In: 2021 2nd International Conference on Intelligent Engineering and Management (ICIEM). IEEE (2021)

18. Stephen, D.G., Philpott, D.R.: Thinking About Risk (2013)

19. Marín, G., Caasas, P., Capdehourat, G.: DeepMAL - Deep Learning Models for Malware Traffic Detection and Classification. In: Haber, P., Lampoltshammer, T., Mayr, M., Plankensteiner, K. (eds.) Data Science – Analytics and Applications. Springer, Wiesbaden (2021). https://doi.org/10.1007/978-3-658-32182-6_16

20. Rajeshkumar, K., Dhanasekaran, S., Vasudevan, V.: Applications of machine learning algorithms for HDFS big data security. In: 2022 International Conference on Computer Communication and Informatics (ICCCI). IEEE (2022)

21. Geetha, R., Thilagam, T.: A review on the effectiveness of machine learning and deep learning algorithms for cyber security. Arch. Comput. Meth. Eng. **28**(4), 2861–2879 (2021)

22. Mark, S.: Applied Machine Learning for Cybersecurity in Spam Filtering and Malware Detection. East Carolina University (2020)

23. Gibert, D., Mateu, C., Planes, J.: The rise of machine learning for de - tection and classification of malware: research developments, trends and challenges. J. Netw. Comput. Appl. **153**, 102526 (2020)
24. Ali, M., et al. "MALGRA: machine learning and N-gram malware feature extraction and detection system. Electronics **9.11**, 1777 (2020)
25. Imperva: what is Threat Intelligence, [Available at] (1) New Messages! (imperva.com)
26. Ankita, K.: Static and dynamic analysis for android malware detection (2016)
27. Hossain, S., Talukder, M.A., Islam, M.S.: An exploratory analysis of mobile security tools (2019)
28. Lin, C.-H., Pao, H.-K., Liao, J.-W.: Efficient dynamic malware analysis using virtual time control mechanics. Comput. Secur. **73**, 359–373 (2018)
29. Alan, M., Legg, P.: Investigating anti-evasion malware triggers using automated sandbox reconfiguration techniques. J. Cybersecur. Privacy **1.1**, 19–39 (2020)
30. Shalaginov, A., Dyrkolbotn, G.O., Alazab, M.: Review of the malware categorization in the era of changing cybethreats landscape: common approaches, challenges and future needs. In: Stamp, M., Alazab, M., Shalaginov, A. (eds.) Malware Analysis Using Artificial Intelligence and Deep Learning. Springer, Cham (2021). https://doi.org/10.1007/978-3-030-62582-5_3
31. Bruce, N., et al.: Cross-method-based analysis and classification of malicious behavior by api calls extraction. Appl. Sci. **9.2**, 239 (2019)
32. Mail, M.A.F., Ab Razak, M.F., Ab Rahman, M.: Malware detection system using cloud sandbox, machine learning. Int. J. Softw. Eng. Comput. Syst. **8.2**, 25–32 (2022)
33. Chris, S., Smith, J.: Applied Network Security Monitoring: Collection, Detection, and Analysis (2013)
34. John, P., et al.: Threat Forecasting: Leveraging Big Data for Predictive Analysis (2016)
35. Georgeta, C.: Detecting insider threats using Security Information and Event Management (SIEM). University of Applied Sciences Technikum Wien. shorturl. at/dtzOT (2018)
36. Laufer, E.: Automate Gurucul Behaviour Analytics Threat Detection and Response Workflows (2021). https://gurucul.com/news/automate-gurucul-behavior-analytics-threat-detection-and-response-workflows
37. Rami, S., Omar, K., Ariffin, K.A.: A survey on malware analysis techniques: static, dynamic, hybrid and memory analysis. Int. J. Adv. Sci. Eng. Inf. Technol **8.4–2**, 1662–1671(2018)
38. Saed, A., Debbabi, M., Wang, L.: A survey of binary code fingerprinting approaches: taxonomy, methodologies, and features. ACM Comput. Surv. **55.1**, 1–41 (2022)
39. Yunus, Y.K.B.M., Ngah, S.B.: Review of hybrid analysis technique for malware detection. In: IOP Conference Series: Materials Science and Engineering, vol. 769. no. 1. IOP Publishing (2020)
40. Ya, P., et al.: A systematic literature review of android malware detection using static analysis. IEEE Access **8**, 116363–116379 (2020)
41. Roni, M., et al.: Decompiled APK based malicious code classification. Future Gener. Comput. Syst. **110**,. 135–147 (2020)
42. Dhanya, K.A., Gireesh Kumar, T.: Efficient android malware scanner using hybrid analysis. (2019)
43. Ma, Z., et al.: A combination method for android malware detection based on control flow graphs and machine learning algorithms. IEEE Access **7**, 21235–21245 (2019)
44. Anusha, D., et al.: A comparison of static, dynamic, and hybrid analysis for malware detection. J. Comput. Virol. Hack. Techn. **13**, 1–12 (2015)
45. Mojtaba, E., et al.: HDM-Analyser: a hybrid analysis approach based on data mining techniques for malware detection. J. Comput. Virol. Hack. Techn. **9**, 77–93 (2013)
46. Aminuddin, N.I., Abdullah, Z.: Android trojan detection based on dynamic analysis. Adv. Comput. Intell. Syst. **1.1** (2019)

47. Myat, S.M., Kyaw, M.T.: Feature Extraction using Hybrid Analysis for Android Malware Detection Framework (2019)
48. Sachin, J., Meena, Y.K..: Byte Level n–Gram Analysis for Malware Detection (2011)
49. Masud, M.M. et al.: A scalable multi -level feature extraction technique to detect malicious executables. Inform. Syst. Front. **10**, 33–45 (2008)
50. Liu, T.Y., et al.: Convolution neural network with batch normalization and inception-residual modules for Android malware classification. Sci. Rep. **12.1**, 1–17 (2022)
51. Akanksha, S., Dash, S.K.: Mining API Calls and Permissions for Android Malware Detection. CANS (2014)
52. Boojoong, K., et al.: "N-gram opcode analysis for android malware detection. Int. J. Cyber Situat. Aware. **1**, 231–255 (2016)
53. Mahmood, Y.-A., et al.: Mutual Information and Feature Importance Gradient Boosting: automatic byte n-gram feature reranking for Android malware detection. Softw. Pract. Exper. **51.7**, 1518–1539 (2021)
54. Ravinder, A., et al.: The impact of features extraction on the sentiment analysis. Procedia Comput. Sci. **152**, 341–348 (2019)
55. Juliza, M.J., et al.: A static analysis approach for Android permission-based malware detection systems. PloS one **16.9**, e0257968 (2021)
56. Huiwen, B., et al.: N-gram, semantic-based neural network for mobile malware network traffic detection. Security and Communication Networks 2021 (2021)
57. Luigi, T., et al.: On Feature Reduction using Deep Learning for Trend Prediction in Finance. ArXiv:abs/1704.03205 (2017)
58. Chander, N., Upendra Kumar, M.: Metaheuristic feature selection with deep learning enabled cascaded recurrent neural network for anomaly detection in Industrial Internet of Things environment. Cluster Comput (2022). https://doi.org/10.1007/s10586-022-03719-8
59. Kumar, M.U., et al.: Lecture Notes of the Institute for Computer Sciences, Social Informatics and Telecommunications Engineering, 2012, vol. 84. Springer, Berlin, Heidelberg (2012)
60. Shravani, D., Suresh Varma, P., Padmaja Rani, B., Upendra Kumar, M., Krishna Prasad, A.V.: Designing dependable web services security architecture solutions. In: Wyld, D.C., Wozniak, M., Chaki, N., Meghanathan, N., Nagamalai, D. (eds.) CNSA 2011. CCIS, vol. 196, pp. 140–149. Springer, Heidelberg (2011). https://doi.org/10.1007/978-3-642-22540-6_14
61. Krishna Prasad, A. V., Ramakrishna, S., Padmaja Rani, B., Upendra Kumar, M., Shravani, D.: Designing dependable business intelligence solutions using agile web services mining architectures. In: Das, V.V., Thomas, G., Lumban Gaol, F. (eds.) AIM 2011. CCIS, vol. 147, pp. 301–304. Springer, Heidelberg (2011). https://doi.org/10.1007/978-3-642-20573-6_51
62. Mahalakshmi, C.V.S.S., Mridula, B., Shravani, D.: Automatic water level detection using IoT. In: Satapathy, S., Raju, K., Shyamala, K., Krishna, D., Favorskaya, M. (eds.) Advances in Decision Sciences, Image Processing, Security and Computer Vision. LAIS, vol. 4. Springer, Cham (2020). https://doi.org/10.1007/978-3-030-24318-0_76

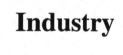

Industry

Image Processing and Deep Neural Networks for Face Mask Detection

Mrunali Mahesh Wakarekar and Uma Gurav[✉]

Computer Science and Engineering, KIT College of Engineering Kolhapur, Kolhapur, India
gurav.uma@kitcoek.in

Abstract. The proper use of a mask is crucial for lowering COVID 19 and transmission. According to the research, transmission is completely decreased when the mask is used appropriately. Factors like sunlight and several items can affect how appropriatel y applied face masks are classified and detected. Cotton masks, sponge masks, scarves, and other options greatly lessen the effect of personal protection in such circumstances. The research suggests a novel modified formula for classifying masks into three categories—a proper mask, a no mask, and an erroneous mask—using deep learning and machine learning. First, we provide a brand-new face mask classification and detection algorithm that combines deep learning, the viola Jones method, and Efficient-Yolov3 Wearing a mask, not wearing a mask, or wearing the wrong mask are the three options. On the dataset with or without mask pictures, the suggested system outperforms and is more accurate when compared to existing techniques. The results of experiments and analysis are also based on the classification knowledge set. In comparison to the present methodology's categorization accuracy of 84%, the anticipated formula boosted it to 97%.

Keywords: Image processing · Deep neural network · Mask detection · Mask classification · Yolo V3 Model

1 Introduction

Coronavirus illness 2019 suddenly became in 2019 and seriously affected all over the world. As per the report on 26 March 2021, COVID-19 has infected over one hundred twenty million people. One and each of the transmission routes of COVID-19 are through droplets or nasal discharges. However, no people are getting infected due to Coronavirus throughout the world.

An infected person has coughs or sneezes that are infectious and can be worse in jam-panicked places. As we all know that for covid19 no any treatments are currently available. Infections are restricted through hindrance ways. Studies have shown that carrying masks can cut back the prospect of coronavirus transmission, which means taking masks is presently one of the effective hindrance ways.

As per the report of World Health Organization (WHO), properly wearing a mask is by correctly adjusting the mask to cover the mouth, nose, and chin. If person is not

S. Rajagopal et al. (Eds.): ASCIS 2022, CCIS 1760, pp. 187–200, 2022.
https://doi.org/10.1007/978-3-031-23095-0_14

wear the mask correctly then the protection is too much reduced and it is highly risky. At present in the current system, security guards organized publically area or places to cue people to wear masks. But this not only exposes to the guards to the air which will contain the virus but jointly lands up in overcrowding at the entrances due to its unskillfulness. Therefore, a fast and effective methodology is needed to affect matters.

Computer vision is an associate degree knowledge domain scientific field that involves computers gaining advanced understanding from digital pictures or videos. Ancient vision tasks embrace the image process, image classification, object detection, and Image Recognition. Object discovers version will detect mask instances of visual objects of a particular categ ory within the pictures. Consequently, mask classification and detection has become a significant pc vital work to assist worldwide society.

2 Literature Review

The author's work developed face mask detection and classification with the help of YOLO V4 algorithm. This algorithm has a deep learning method to detect the object correctly. In this system device is installed in real-time application to avoid the spreading of COVID-19 in the public areas [1].

Face mask classification and detection using machine learning: this is one of the approaches to minimize the risk of Coronavirus spread. It is the approach for avoiding corona virus with detecting masks. The invented method effectively handles obstruction in great conditions by utilization of detectors with single and two stage detectors. The approach achieves the speed of detection and high accuracy [2].

This is one of the real-time implementation of Al-based face mask classification and detection with two person's social distancing measuring system for COVID-19 prevention. This embedded system can be used in a variety of environments, including public places, corporate settings, streets, shopping malls, and examination centers, where precision and accuracy are highly desirable. This application will boost the system development process in lot of developing countries [3].

Face masks detection and classification using machine learning. It is real-time software for detecting face masks [4].

The method uses the ML technique with the high accuracy. This System can be used for a variety of application. Many community facility providers will ask their customers and display the notice boards to worn the mask correctly for avail or get their services. This system continuously helps the immensely to the community health care system [5] (Table 1)

Table 1. Comparative analysis of existing system

No.	Title	Concept	Dataset	Algorithm	Advantages	Limitation
1.	The Detection of Face Masks for avoiding the Increase in At Politeknik, COVID-19 Little Batam	Through the use of the YOLO V4 algorithm, this work established the face mask detection. Deep learning techniques are used in the YOLO V4 algorithm to accurately recognise objects	FDDB dataset	Deep Neural Network Known as YOLO V4	The use of a mask can be accurately determined using an algorithm	The device cannot be detected thermally in this article. Device installation is required near the crowd
2.	Deep learning face mask identification as a method to lessen the danger of Coronavirus spread	In order to stop the Coronavirus from spreading across the community, a deep learning-based method for spotting masks over faces in public spaces is provided in this study. The suggested method employs an ensemble of single and two stage detectors at the pre-processing level to effectively handle occlusions in dense environments	MAFA is a facemask-focused dataset with a total of 25,876 pictures	CNN	uses a group of single stage and two stage detectors to effectively manage occlusions in dense environments	Only image and low-quality video surveillance are used for this work. Future plans include detecting face masks and using the landmarks on the face for biometric identification

(continued)

Table 1. (*continued*)

No.	Title	Concept	Dataset	Algorithm	Advantages	Limitation
3.	Real time Face mask detection using machine learning	Any working environment Where accuracy and precision are strongly wanted to perform the goal, such as a public space, station, a shopping mall, or a testing facility, can employ this embedded vision-based application	It is a balanced dataset with a total of 3835 photos and two categories, faces with masks (1919 images) and without masks (1916 images), with a mean height and width of 283.68 and 278.77, respectively. There are two categories	ResNet -50, VGG-16, and VGG-19 are CNN models (Dense Net, Inception onV3, Mobile Net, Mobile NetV2, and	helps achieve excellent accuracy and significantly increases detecting speed	No drone technology that can take pictures in public settings and identify masks may be used for this task. helps achieve excellent accuracy and significantly increases Detecting speed
4.	Face Mask Detection System Using AI	Real-time software is used to find face masks	FDDD Dataset	CNN	The results of the experimental analysis demonstrate that the proposed approach may be successfully used to identify face mask violations	This work hasn't been Evaluated with actual IOT devices

(*continued*)

Table 1. (*continued*)

No.	Title	Concept	Dataset	Algorithm	Advantages	Limitation
5.	Face Mask recognition using CNN model	The strategy has produced reasonably high accuracy using simple ML tools and techniques. There are numerous applications for it. A mask may soon be required to wear, given the Covid-19 problem. To use the services of several public service providers, clients must correctly wear masks. The implemented model will make a significant contribution to the public health care system	Face dataset	CNN MODEL	To accurately detect the presence of masks without leading to overfitting, investigate optimized values ofparameters using the Sequential Convolutional NeuralNetwork model	This study did not evaluate whether surgical masks or N95 masks are virus-prone or not

3 Proposed System

3.1 Machine Learning Approach

Machine learning methods unit of measurement trained on datasets, and a model is created for analysis.

Based on the model's accuracy, the machine learning technique is suitable. The three methods in machine learning algorithms' unit of measurement expert system, learning without attendance, and reinforcement learning. As a part of supervised learning, the model is trained victimization tagged data that contains every input and result. Unsupervised learning methods do not use employment data or tags; Instead, it. It finds the hidden structures or patterns from unlabeled data.

3.2 Supervised Learning

Supervised learning desires a well-labeled dataset to educate. Supervised learning is of two types regression and classification. In this System, classification techniques facilitate hunting out the acceptable class labels, which can predict whether the Mask is present or not or not worn properly. A machine learning model uses the labeled information to educate, classify the images and predict the mask status.

3.3 Unsupervised Learning

Unsupervised ways are supported by machine learning. The necessity of labeled datasets isn't needed in unsupervised learning. Image analysis was once done using unsupervised learning.

3.4 Viola Jones algorithm

This algorithm of face identification was developed by Paul Viola, and Michael Jones. Author invents set of rules for the object- popularity framework that lets in the detection of image features.

This algorithm has four main steps, which are as follows:

1. The Selection of Haar like Features
2. Integrating Image
3. Taking part in AdaBoost training
4. Cascaded classifiers

This system is supposed to be a sculptural model. Tensor flow, Keras, and OpenCV are explicitly used in Python libraries. The model we plan to use is the MobileNetV2 of a convolutional neural network. A plan of action for MobileNetV2 is described in the model. Machine learning is victimization some pre-trained model to educate your gift model and procure the prediction that saves time and makes victimization work the assorted models straightforwardly. An image dataset with three classes is used to train the model: with and no mask, wearing no mask, and wearing an improper mask.mproper masks

(i) The train dataset is used to train the model.
(ii) Model Deployment

Using high-specified libraries, a system model is developed in this paper. The model is tested under different conditions and different parameters. Firstly, we have a tendency to feed the dataset into the model and then we have a tendency to run a tutorial that trains the model based on the given dataset, then we need to run a detection program that activates in the video stream and captures frames continuously from the video stream using an academic degree anchor box model object detection technique.

The MobileNetV2 classifier classifies the images as mask, improper mask and without mask. If person is wearing or not wearing the mask then box is displayed on the face. For the no mask red box is displayed

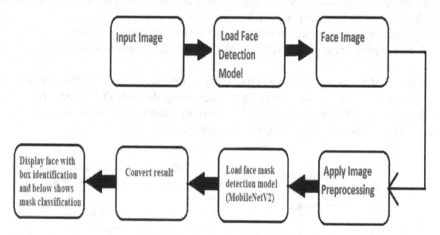

Fig. 1. System architecture

Figure 1 shows the proposed model architecture. In this first user select image from the selected Image, we grab the face image using the Haar Cascade classifier. From the face image, we apply image processing on the Image and apply the MobileNETV2. Classifier mask detection model and display result.

Figure 2 displays the working flow. Firstly preprocessing is done then we extract the feature from the Image. Finally, with the training set, we classify the Image with the database and display the Image.

The Objective of the System

1. To identify various applications used to detect User Faces by Image or Video Surveillance.
2. To Finding Mask is Present or not on Image or video surveillance using Machine Learning technique, applying YOLO, i.e., object detection algorithm and convolution neural network algorithm.

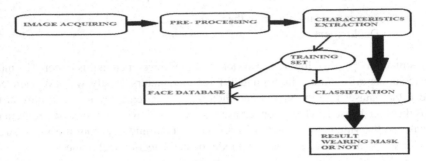

Fig. 2. Flow of work

3. To recognize the correctly wearing of the Mask and calculate the accuracy of the Mask to ensure how properly the Mask is worn.
4. To generate a message/alarm to wear a mask if Mask is not present.
5. To develop the most effective facemask detection and classification system.

In this System, using the Image Processing technique, first, detect the face from the input image and then see the object on the face using the YOLOV3 model [10]. Then our deep neural network MobileNETV2 Classifier model predicts the result of Mask, without Mask, and incorrect Mask with percentage (Fig. 3).

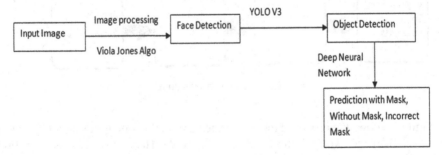

Fig. 3. Block diagram of system

4 Mathematical Formulation

When the system is training, it compares the default face with bounding boxes with different sizes and aspect ratios with the ground truth boxes for each pixel generated value, and for selecting the best matching box; this paper uses the Intersection over Union (IoU) method. We evaluate and calculate our predicted box based on the actual ground conditions. Increasing IoU values determine the accuracy of the prediction; the highest value of IoU determines the most accurate value.

The equation and picture description of IoU are given as follows:

$$\text{IoU}(B1,B2) = \frac{B1 \cap B2}{B1 \cup B2} = B1 > B2 \;\&\&\; B1 < 100\%$$

Fig. 4. Intersection points of facial mode

Dataset Used

The Face Mask Dataset With
Mask: - 690 images Without
Mask: - 685 images Incorrect
Mask: - 701 images
In total 2076 images are contained in the dataset.

https://www.kaggle.com/spandanpatnaik09/face-mask-detectormask-not-mask-incorrect-mask

The categories of mask are wearing of mask (Correct-mask) and without masks (NO mask), and unqualified Mask (Incorrect Mask) (Table 2).

Table 2. Sample image annotation data

Thing	Crate
Face	381,207,618,561
Face_mask	156,141,393,418

1. Using the experiments folder to create and load image dataset for training and testing

   - Training Dataset: A dataset that is used for training
   - A testing dataset:- This dataset is used for testing the accuracy of the system model. It is also called as validation dataset.

2. Model Training
3. Image Visualization

5   Results and Discussion

1. Detection with Mask

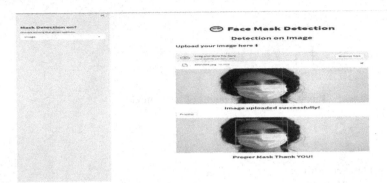

Fig. 5. With mask detection image

Figure 5 displays the user interface for the website in that users have options for choosing the file. When the user selects the file image preview displays in the image box and when the user clicks on the process button mask detection process starts in Fig. 4 displays the detection of the Mask

2. Detection without Mask

Fig. 6. Without mask detection image

In Fig. 6 displays user has not worn the Mask. This indication is done by a red line with accuracy in percentage.

3. Detection of improper wearing of mask

In Fig. 7 Displays, the user has not worn the Mask properly with its percentage of accuracy of the Mask.

Fig. 7. Improper wearing of mask

4. Model Summary

The following figure shows the model of how many parameters are used for each layer distribution of parameter and output shape (Fig. 8).

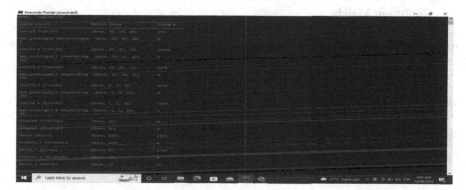

Fig. 8. Model summary

5. Prediction Result from Model

Fig. 9. Prediction Result from model

The Fig. 9 shows the prediction result from the model.

6. Training Loss & Accuracy

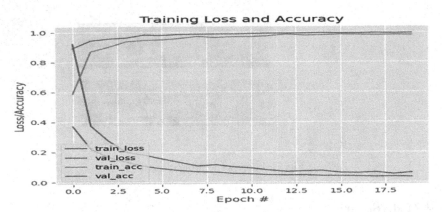

Fig. 10. Training loss & accuracy

Figure 10 shows the accuracy with respect to the training loss curve plot.

7. Confusion Matrix

In order to compare actual values with predicted values, a confusion matrix is used. We can use it to calculate the performance of our system. The tables are used to represent the data.

A Confusion Matrix for a binary classification problem looks like this

Precision: Therefore, it measures how many positive classes were correctly predicted by the model, and how many were actually realize. The formula below can be used to calculate it.

$$\text{Precision} = \frac{\text{TP}}{Tp + FP}$$

Recall: The number of total positive classes correctly predicted by the system model. The recall must be as high as possible.

$$\text{Recall} = \frac{\text{TP}}{Tp + FN}$$

The Fig. 11. Shows the confusion matrix of the model with mask and without the Mask and Incorrect Mask. The model gives 98% accuracy for face mask detection after training.

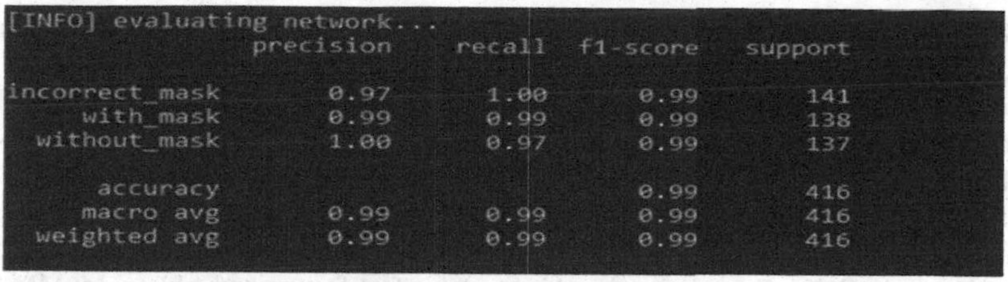

```
[INFO] evaluating network...
                 precision    recall   f1-score    support

incorrect_mask      0.97       1.00      0.99        141
    with_mask       0.99       0.99      0.99        138
 without_mask       1.00       0.97      0.99        137

     accuracy                            0.99        416
    macro avg       0.99       0.99      0.99        416
 weighted avg       0.99       0.99      0.99        416
```

Fig. 11. Confusion matrix

8. Comparative Analysis of Detection
(See Table 3)

Table 3. Comparative analysis of mask detection

SR NO	Number of images testing	With mask(Accuracy)	Without mask (Accuracy)	Improper mask (Accuracy)
1	40	98%	–	–
2	16	–	95%	–
3	15	–	–	92%

6 Conclusion

A face mask detector is proposed in this research, which can assist with public health-care. Mobile Net is a mild spine that can take care of each excessive and occasional processing workload. Deep Learning is used to undertake weights from a related job, face Mask detection that is found out on a huge dataset, to extract extra-strong features on a public face masks dataset. The advised technique yields cutting-edge results. It also can be utilized in college department stores and universities. This approach has been implemented in Image and video surveillance. We have three approaches for the Mask Category: with mask, without mask, and improper mask. The accuracy is expressed as a percentage

References

1. Howard, A.G., Zhu, M., Chen, B., et al.: Applied convolutional neural networks to mobile vision applications using mobile nets (2017)
2. Wang, W., Li, Y., Zou, T., Wang, X., You, J., Luo, Y.: Dense-mobile net models for image classification. Mobile Inform. Syst. **2020** (2020)
3. Venkateswarlu, I.B., Kakarla, J., Prakash, S.: Face mask detection using Mobile Nets and Global Pooling Blocks. In: IEEE 4th Conference on Information and Communication Technology (CICT) (2020)

4. M. S. Ejaz and M. R. Islam, " Convolutional neural networks for masked face recognition," 2019 International Conference on Sustainable Technologies for Industry 4.0(STI)

5. Li, C., Cao, J., Zhang, X.: A robust deep learning method for detecting face masks. In: Proceedings of the 2nd International Conference on Artificial Intelligence and Advanced Manufacturing (2020)

6. Chiang, D.: Detect faces and determine whether people are wearing Mask (2020). https://git hub.com/AIZOOTech/FaceMaskDetection

7. Jia, Y., et al.: Caffe: Convolutional architecture for fast feature embedding. In: MM 2014 - Proceedings of the 2014 ACM Conference on Multimedia (2014). https://doi.org/10.1145/2647868.2654889

8. Eigen, D., Sermanet, P., Zhang, X., Mathieu, M., Fergus, R., Lancun, Y.: OverFeat: Integrated Recognition, Localization, and Detection (2014)

9. Erhan, D., Szegedy, C., Toshev, A., Anguelov, D.: Scalable object detection by deep neural networks. In: Proceedings of the IEEE Conference on Computer Vision and Pattern Recognition (2014)

10. You only look once: Unified, realtime object detection. In: Proceedings of the IEEE Computer Society Conference on Computer Vision and Pattern Recognition, vol. 2016-Decem, pp. 779–788 (2016)

An Analysis of Lightweight Cryptographic Algorithms for IoT-Applications

Jigneshkumar A. Chauhan[1], Ankitkumar R. Patel[1(✉)], Satyen Parikh[1], and Nilesh Modi[2]

[1] AMPICS, Ganpat University, Kherva, India
jignesh.the.mca@gmail.com, ankit_kansa@yahoo.com,
satyen.parikh@ganpatuniversity.ac.in
[2] Dr. Babasaheb Ambedkar Open University, Ahmedabad, India
drnileshmodi@gmail.com

Abstract. With the arrival of advanced technologies, IoT has enabled the connection of many devices that can collect huge amounts of data. IoT security requirements are therefore supreme. Cryptography is used to secure the confidentiality, data integrity, authentication and control access to networks. To provide a complete overview of this field, we have compared some existing algorithms based on hardware and software performance and expectations of different attacks. We also discussed the requirement and direction of novel research in lightweight cryptography to improve security and performance. This paper presents the performance comparison of their memory, latency & throughput, Area (GE), Key & Block size and other parameters of hardware and software efficient LWC algorithm. Primarily for lightweight block ciphers and further shows new research directions for developing new algorithms with the performance, security, and cost characteristics.

Keywords: Internet of Things (IoT) · Lightweight cryptography (LWC) · Block ciphers · Stream ciphers

1 Introduction

Lightweight cryptography is a new word that refers to a type of encryption that secures data more effectively while using less resources and consuming less power. They gather data from the real domain and transmit it thru the internet. Similarly, lightweight cryptographic algorithms are two types one is symmetric cryptography and second is asymmetric cryptography. Lightweight symmetric block cyphers are commonly used in persistent assuming. Block and Stream Ciphers are examples of symmetric cyphers. They are designed to be used with devices, and there are no strict requirements to be categorized as lightweight. Each lightweight cryptography architect must deal with three distinct aspects: security, cost, and performance. Implementing the three key design goals of security and performance, cost and performance, or security and cost all at once is extremely difficult, although improving just one of them is simple [1]. A rare creator

S. Rajagopal et al. (Eds.): ASCIS 2022, CCIS 1760, pp. 201–216, 2022.
https://doi.org/10.1007/978-3-031-23095-0_15

reasoned that both Asymmetric cyphers [1] are computationally more demanding in and programming. As per ISO/IEC it is necessary that the design be created with 1000–2000 GE. This research compares lightweight algorithms implemented on software tools and different hardware. The improved results of a specific algorithm are distinct from changes to the application or platform. LWA are frequently used in IoT innovation to increase model security while consuming the least amount of memory and power. This paper discusses how lightweight block cyphers, stream cyphers, and even hash functions should be classified based on their performance on a platform.

2 Introduction of IoT

Many academicians and IT professionals have specified different meanings of IoT based on their work experience, but in general, IoT is a network of associated things, each with a separated id, capable of collecting and swapping data via or without person interference [40].

"Machine-to-machine communication" (M2M) [3] refers to the process of linking smart gadgets or objects. It can assist you in making intelligent judgments by enhancing efficiency, benefit usage, and process efficiency. Ubiquitous computing [4, 5] has now become a reality, thanks to help in difficult sectors such as WSN, computer calculations, automated diagnostics, and so on, thanks to the powerful and fast Internet speed. The goal of the Internet of Things is to ensure that all types of communication are available at all times and in all places [6]. Despite the fact that there are fewer issues such as customer safety and security, retention, communication, efficiency, performance, and legal rights, the features and services supplied by the IoT error are superior. There are a few building blocks in embedded technology: Internet gates, sensors/actuators, big data and cloud/server framework, and eventually end users. The image below shows the design of the "Internet of Things" (IoT) (Fig. 1).

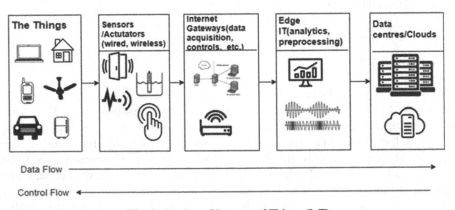

Fig. 1. Design of Internet of Things (IoT)

3   Software and Hardware Performance Metrics

Based on the physical characteristics and performance of the LWC algorithm, the following software and hardware requirements can be defined:

1) MEMORY REQUIREMENTS
RAM is used to store medium values for usage on computers, while ROM is used to store system(algorithm) and fixed data, such as S-box (for some conditions), algorithm keys and so on [6] it measure in KB.

2) GATE AREA
GE is the amount of physical space necessary to run/implement an algorithm on a board/circuit, measured in square metres. For FPGA, this area may be set using logical blocks, and for ASIC, it can be specified using GE (2 input-NAND Gate= 1GE) [6]. In an affordable RFID tag, 200 to 2000 GE are typically assigned for security reasons [4].

3) LATENCY
Software delays are defined by the time it takes to generate text from the original text using hardware [6] and the No. of clock cycles/block (at the time of encryption).

4) THROUGHPUT
Throughput is calculated in terms of original text processed/time unit (bps) at a frequency of 100 KHz, whereas in software, it is measured in terms of the average quantity of original text processed each CPU clock cycle at a frequency of 4 MHz [4].

5) POWER REQUIREMENTS
The volume of power Consumption by the circuit to implement the algorithm is Calculated in watts (W).

6) EFFICIENCY
It provides performance over resource demands. For hardware, this can be measured as follows [40]:

Hardware Efficiency = Throughput [Kbps]/physical memory

Similarly,

Software Efficiency = Throughput [Kbps]/Code Size [KB]
Algorithm size = code size.

A STRUCTURE WISE CLASSIFICATION OF LWC
Here both operations encryption and decryption take place at a fixed block size (64 bits or above) at a time in block cypher, and continuous streaming is utilized for input (or word-for-word) objects [4]. To develop a strong cypher, Claude Shannon [35, 40] recognized two key parts of any hidden lettering: confusion and diffusion. Confusion mix the text and s-box to make complicated cypher as possible [4, 35]. When compared

to single stream, the stream cypher uses only confusing material, while the block cypher uses both operations with a simple design. The block cypher has difficulty to direct reversing the encryption process to get the original text back, whereas the stream cypher uses XOR techniques to decrypt data that can be quickly restored to its original form.

Different types of structures:

Substitution-Permutation Network (SPN). In block cipher algorithms, permutation boxes or layers of substitution boxes (S-boxes) or No. of rounds are used to construct the cipher text block.

A Feistel Network (FN). Diffusion is applied to only one half part of the input block in each round after dividing it into equal halves. In addition, at the start of each round, two halves are swapped with each other.

The Generalized Feistel Network (GFN). The Feistel network is a version of the classic Feistel network that is more generalized. It breaks the plaintext into two equal halves sub-blocks and applies Feistel structure to each sub-blocks [41].

ARX. ARX is a secret key primitive design paradigm that uses Addition, Rotation, and eX-OR operations. When compared to Feistel ciphers and SPN, ARX is small and fast, but it has security limitations.

B STRUCTURE WISE LWC ALGORITHMS
1) SUBSTITUTION PERMUTATION NETWORK (SPN).

AES [24] is a well-known SPN-based method that is specified by NIST and works on 128-bit blocks with three key variants of 256, 192, and 128bits [24]. The minimal Gate Equivalent need for AES is around 2400 GEs [4], which is high for some minor real applications [35]. It proves that reasonably efficient performance when resources given more [38].

PRESENT is a highly efficient hardware and software algorithm. It is constructed on a SP network, and it use 64-bit block with two different key sizes: 128-bits and 80-bits, with requirements of 1886 and 1570 GE respectively. The minimal GE requirement of PRESENT is approximately 1000 GE (for encryption process) [4], with an appropriate level of security requiring 2520-3010 GE [35]. It takes a more time in software (permutation layer), thus it has to be improved [32, 35, 40, 42].

GIFT. In CHES-2017, an upgraded form of the PRESENT was introduced. It provides a slimmer S-Box with less physical space. In addition, the no. of rounds is reduced, resulting in higher throughput and a easier and quicker key scheduling. GIFT comes in two flavours: GIFT-64, which is a 28-round with a 64-bit block size, and GIFT-128, which is a 40-round with a 128-bit block size. A 128-bit key is used in both cases. GIFT64, a lighter variant, was also discovered to be more vulnerable than GIFT-128 [16, 24].

TWINE. As PRESENT, it obtains an excellent overall status while also overcoming lots of its employment difficulties. It uses 64-bit input with 128-bit and 80-bit key variations [16]. In comparison to AES, it needs roughly 2000 GE and a greater circuit size per throughput. In terms of speed, AES is quicker than TWINE when 1 KB or more of ROM is available, but in case of 512 bytes of ROM AES cannot be executed and operates 250% faster than PRESENT [11].

MIDORI. Medical implants, for example, were created with a low/tight energy budget in mind. Midori64 and Midori128 are the two versions available. Both of them [18] use a 128-bit key size of two distinct block sizes 128 and 64-bit, distinctly for 20 and 16 rounds.

mCrypton. "miniature of Crypton" [4] is a energy-efficient, lightweight and cost-effective version of Crypton [4], it is suited for both software and hardware deployments. It uses a variety of keys to conduct 13 rounds on the 64-bit block and 3 blocks of 128-bit, 96-bit and 64-bit.

Klein. Iterates through 20 (1528 GE), 12 (1220 GE), and 16 (1478 GE) iterations on 64-bit input utilizing 96-bit, 64-bit, and 80-bit keys. It was created with software implementation in mind, mostly for sensors.

LED [10] in this Algorithm PRESENT (S-box), a lighter variant of AES [16], and PHOTON (mix column method) [5] are some of the characteristics borrowed. Key scheduling is not available in LED, its unique and decrease chip space while increasing security risks such as associated key assaults [14]. It processes 64-bit input for 32 or 48 times using different keys such as 128-bit (1265 GE), 96-bit (1116 GE), 80-bit (1040 GE), and 64-bit (966 GE).

2) FEISTEL NETWORK (FN).

The lightweight **DES** is referred to as DESL. It uses a similar 64-bits block size, 56-bits key size and 16 rounds. DESL is distinguished from DES by the decrease no. of S-boxes. It requires 1850 GE, which is 20% compressed [4]. DESL lightens DES by removing the first and last permutations [18].

Tiny Encryption Algorithm (TEA) is appropriate for hardware that is very tiny, low-cost and computationally weak [4]. It completes 32 rounds [20] with GE needs of 3872 [21] using a 128-bit key on a 64-bit input. Its simplistic key scheduling may be subject to brute force attacks on occasion [16, 22]. Another constraint to claiming the tea sack structure is that it has three equal keys to decryption, rendering it defenseless against attackers [22]. The improved variant of TEA is (XTEA), which utilises the similar key and block size as TEA but has 64 rounds of iterations, requiring 3490 GE. [90]. It has a complicated key scheduling scheme with limited variation in the Shifting, exclusive-OR, and addition functions [24]. XTEA [24] was enhanced with XXTEA [24] to guard against related-key attacks on 36 rounds [24].

Camellia [25] is a recognised cypher by ISO/IEC, IETF, NESSIE, and CRYPTREC. Mitsubishi Electric Corp., Nippon Tele and Telephone Corp. Collaborated on its design. Camellia provides the same level of security by using key size and block processing like AES and has two itearation variations, 24 and 18, to choose from. It's noted for its quick software executions [26], while the hardware execution takes 6511 GE.

SIMON [27]. In hardware, this will be known as its small foot-shaped footprint. It provides multiple key sizes (256-bit, 192-bit, 144-bit, 128-bit, 96-bit, 72-bit 64-bit) across a block of 128-bit, 96-bit, 64-bit, 48-bit, 32-bit[95].763GE is required for execution in the smallest version [27].

SEA[28]. It is designed for small IoT devices, particularly those with limited memory space [28, 29]. For the most lightweight hardware variant, it makes use of a 96-bit key with two mandated block sizes of 96 bits and 8 bits, with the need of 3758 bits.

3) GENERALISED FEISTEL NETWORK (GFN).

CLEFIA offers a 128-bit input block with 256, 192, or 128 bit key via 26, 22, or 18 rounds [33, 34]. It demonstrates good performance and protection in front of different attacks [16, 33, 40], but at a significant cost, as the smallest version costs 2488 GE (for encryption) for a 128-bit key [4]. The dual confusion and diffusion qualities of CLEFIA are responsible for its high defence against security assaults. This, on the other hand, necessitates more space and limits its applicability in tiny applications [35].

Piccolo [39]. Piccolo is another ultra-lightweight cryptographic technique that can be used in devices with very limited environmental conditions (RFID, sensors, etc.). It use 128-bit and 80-bit s two key sets to process 64-bit input and, 31 and 25 two iterations using 64-bit input. The simplest hardware utilization (80-bit key) necessitates 432 GE, plus another 60 GE for decryption.

TWINE [19]. LBlock-derived code completes 36 iterations on a 64-bit state with two key size: 128-bit and 80-bit. TWINE consumes nibble (4-bit) permutation in its place of bit transformation in the popular tiny hardware implementation, which requires 1866 GE. It also employs only one S-box instead of the ten S-Boxes used by LBlock.

4) ADD-ROTATE-XOR (ARX)

SPECK [27]. SIMON's brother, created by the NSA, is a software-oriented cypher. It can execute 22, 23, 26, 27, 28, 29, 32, 33, and 34 iterations with the similar key sizes and block size as SIMON. The lowest hardware implementation is a 48-bit block and 96-bit key that requires 884 GE, whereas the most effective is a 128-bit key and 64-bit block that requires 186 bytes of ROM and 599 rounds [27].

IDEA [42]. Lai and Massey devised this system, which uses a 128-bit key on a 64-bit input to complete 8.5 rounds and is primarily utilized for high-speed data transmission [4]. It employs a 16-bit unsigned integer and doesn't require S-box or P-box to perform data operations like modular multiplication, XOR, and addition. It's noted for having the effective on embedded devices (like PGP v2.0) with a throughput of 94.8 Kb/s and memory requirements of 596 bytes [4].

HIGHT [4]. It uses simple computational techniques to execute compact round functions (no S-boxes) that uses 64-bit data 32 times using a 128-bit key. The smallest version [14] acquires 2608 GE for a throughput of 188 Kbps.

LEA [4] is a 32-bit common processor software-oriented cypher introduced by the ETRIK. It uses 256-bit, 192-bit, and 128-bit keys to interpret 128-bit input block and perform 32, 28, and 28 rounds, respectively. LEA runs at 326.94 iterations per byte on the ARM platform.

C. SOFTWARE AND HARDWARE PERFORMANCE COMPARISON

Many researchers have evaluated the performance of the well-known lightweight cryptography algorithms [4, 35, 40] [Appendix 1] utilising various platforms such as ARM [35], AVR [4], NXP [35] microcontrollers. Several characteristics were matched for different LWC algorithms in different platform (Python, Java, C, C++), message size, etc.) during these experiments, including logic process (m),area (GE), power consumption (W), throughput, latency (cycle/block), RAM/ROM (bytes) requirements and so on. The performance of the specified LWC algorithms on 0.35/0.18/0.13/0.09 m technologies (H/W utilization) and 32/16/8 bit microcontrollers (S/W utilization) platforms is summarised in Appendix 1.

As per the software efficiency (SE) performance SPECK, SIMON, PRIDE is good according to the graph (Fig. 2).

The following graph (Fig. 3) illustrates the first 10, most memory-efficient LWC algorithms, which can be analysed for memory (ROM and RAM) requirements by different LWC algorithms. With zero bytes of RAM and less than 200 bytes of ROM, SPECK and SIMON once again win the tournament, closely followed by PRIDE.

Latency and throughput, two significant software criteria, were again led by SPECK and SIMON, with the lowest latency rate (408 and 594 cycles/block) and peak throughput (470.5 and 323 Kb/s), respectively, followed by IDEA. ITUbee and PRIDE are also among the top ten performers on the list (Figs. 4 and 5).

Midori is first in terms of hardware efficiency, followed by PICCOLO, which is second with a tiny variation from GOST. The first 10 hardware efficient LWC algorithms are depicted in Fig. 7.

With a generally little square size (only 8 pieces), SEA wins the key and block size equipment proficiency race, trailed by Hu mmingbird-2 with a twofold size block (Biggest key in top 10), lastly KATAN/KTANTAN with a 4 times bigger block than the pioneer (Fig. 6).

PRESENT, EPCBC, PRINT, SIMON/SPECK, and RECTANGLE are all supported, using either a 64-bit or 48-bit block or an 96-bit or 80-bit key. With a tiny variance from PRINT, the graph (Fig. 7) shows that KTANTAN requires the least amount of space to implement (462 GE) (41 GE more). With fewer than 900 GE requirements, SPECK/SIMON appears in the top five listings. All of these results can be seen using either 0.18 μm or 0.13 μm technology. Based on energy consumption, Midori has the lowest demand (1.61 J/bit), followed by Piccolo, although both have varying performances in different situations.

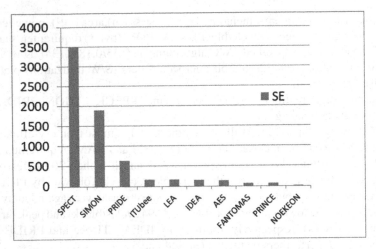

Fig. 2. Software efficient LWC algorithms (Top 10).

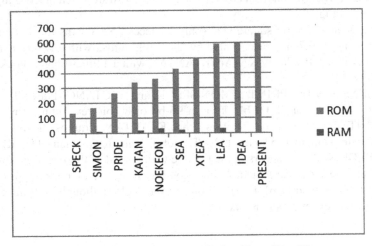

Fig. 3. Memory efficient LWC algorithms (Top 10).

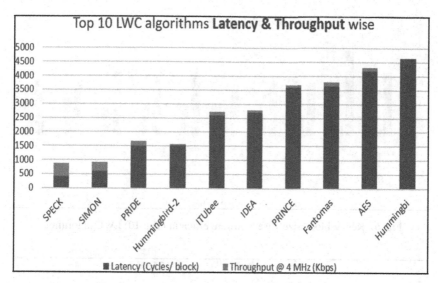

Fig. 4. Latency efficient (Top 10) LWC algorithms.

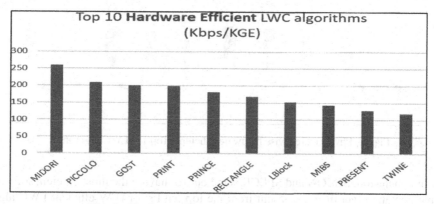

Fig. 5. Hardware efficient (Top 10) LWC algorithms.

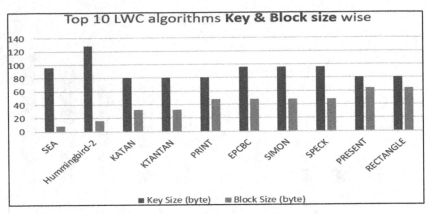

Fig. 6. Key & block size wise hardware efficient (Top 10) LWC algorithms.

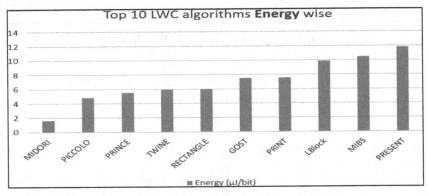

Fig. 7. Physical area wise hardware efficient (Top 10) LWC algorithms.

In conclusion, SIMON and SPECK stand out for having the most efficient software implementation, yet they are absent from the top ten list of H/W efficient LWC algorithms. In General, currently no one of the LWC algorithms satisfy all of the efficiency benchmarks for H/W and S/W.

4 Research Directions and Open Research Challenges

1. The perfect algorithm will strike a balance between performance, cost, and security. Implementing all three criteria is complex, but any two of them may be done quickly [4]. The performance of the method will suffer as the number of rounds or key sizes grows. These could be done by focusing design efforts on using a smaller amount memory and computational power, resulting in fewer Gates. Without compromising good security, equivalent (physical space) needs and minimal power (energy) consumption are required [35]. Based on the findings of the preceding study, we have identified the following research challenges that need to be addressed in order for LWCs algorithms to be effective in IoT security:

Table 1. Security analysis of LWC algorithms.

LWC Algorithm	Differential Cryptanalysis*	Linear Crypt-analysis	Integral/Square/Saturation Cryptanalysis	Algebric/Cube Cryptanalysis	MITM/Biclique	Related Key attack	Side-Channel/Differential fault attacks
AES	√[3]	-	-	-	√[4]	√[4]	√[7][8]
PRESENT	√[10]				√[28]	√[5]	√[7][8]
GIFT	√[41]		√[4]		√[13]	√[11]	√[16]
SKINNY	√[14]	-	-	-	-	√[14]	√[9]
RECTANGLE			√[16]	-	-	√[16]	√[16]
MIDORI	√[18]	√[18]			√[18]		
ICEBERG	√[15]						
PRINCE	√[4]						
PRINT						√[22]	
Klein					√[16]	√[16]	√[16]
LED	√[23]				√[16]	√[14]	
EPCBC				√[23]		√[16]	
TEA						√[22][16]	
XTEA						√[16]	
Camellia	√[26]						√[16]
SIMON	√[29]			√[30]		√[30]	
KASUMI	√[4]					√[18]	
LBlock	√[25][26]		√[19]		√[19]		
ITUbee						√[16]	
CLEFIA			√[26]			√[40]	√[40]
PICCOLO	√[28]				√[28]		
TWINE			√[4]		√[4]		
SPECK	√[26]					√[12]	
IDEA					√[4]		
HIGHT	√[26]	√[15]			√[26]	√[26]	
LEA							√[27]
HUMMINGBIRD-2						√[26]	
HUMMINGBIRD	Vurnable to several attacks						

2. Confusion, one of cryptography's two essential features, could be done by selecting an efficient and appropriate No. of S-boxes to display a proper stability between security and performance [15]. Designing fast and easy but powerful confusion (Substitution, S-box) and diffusion qualities with the suitable combination of security, cost and performance is of practical interest, for example, How to minimize.
3. Design key scheduling which is easier with smaller keys and sufficient strength.
4. Increase in the no. of rounds has a negative impact on performance and cost, therefore how can the number of rounds be reduced (or increased) without compromising performance or security?

5. We're now working on "SPN methods", with a particular focus on S-Box, in order to create a standard LWC algorithm that balances three key characteristics: cost, performance, and security.

5 Conclusion

IOT security is one of the biggest worries, owing to the apparent development in the number of IoT devices in numerous fields. As a result, lightweight algorithms with trade-offs between cost and performance, as well as security performance, are required. LWC is an effective approach to protect connections by exchanging data for IoT-restricted devices. The LWC's well-defined qualities (Security, cost and performance) are comparable, and this study highlights some of the research potential and open research challenges. According to the literature evaluation, the NIST has certified the brands PRESENT and CLEFIA for grounds of safety, appropriate performance, and cost. The strongly integrated applications of SIMON and SPECK are outstanding. New attacks are being recorded, however, as new LWC algorithms emerge, which is unavoidable and unending. The conflict between cyber security specialists and hackers is constantly a source of fresh research scope in the field of cyber security, particularly in the field of lightweight cryptography.

Appendix 1

Hardware and Software Performances of LWC Algorithm

The following table spans two groups: **Hardware Implementation** (columns Tech–Hardware Efficiency) and **Software Implementation** (columns Key Size–Software Efficiency).

LWC Algorithm	Key Size	Block Size	Tech (µm)	Area (GEs)	Power (µW)	Energy (µJ/bit)	Throughput @100KHz (Kbps)	Hardware Effi-ciency (Kbps/KGE)	Key Size	Block Size	ROM (byte)	RAM (byte)	Latency (Cy-cles/block)	Energy (µJ/bit)	Throughput @4MHz (Kbps)	Software Effi-ciency (Kbps/KB)
AES*	128	128	0.13	2400	2.4	42.38	56.64	23.6	128	128	918	0	4192	16.7	122	132.9
PRESENT*	80	64	0.18	1570	2.33	11.77	200	127.38	128	64	660	0	10792	43.1	23.7	35.91
RECTANGLE	80	64	0.13	1467	1.46	5.96	246	167.68								
MIDORI	128	64	0.09	1542	60.6	1.61	400	259.4								
mCrypton*	128	64	0.35	2594	4.66	138.61	33.51	12.91	96	64	1076	28	16457	68	15.5	14.41
NOEKEON*	128	128	0.35	2604	4.68	1362.21	3.44	1.32	128	128	364	32	23517	95.9	21.7	59.62
ICEBERG	128	64	0.18	5817	8.72	21.81	400	68.76								
PUFFIN-2	80	64	0.18	1083	1.62	314.74	5.2	4.8								
PRINCE*	128	64	0.13	2953	2.95	5.53	533.3	180.59								
PRIDE*									128	64	1108	0	3614	14.4	70.8	63.9
PRINT^	80	48	0.18	503	0.73	7.54	100	198.8	128	48	266	48	1514	6	169	635.34
Klein*	64	64	0.18	1220	1.83	59.18	30.9	25.32								
LED#	64	64	0.18	966	1.45	282.55	5.1	5.27	80	64	2164	368	35161	10.6	7.28	3.36
I-PRESENT	80	64	0.18	2467		370										
EPCBC	96	48	0.18	1008	1.51	124.74	12.12	12.02								
DESL*	56	64	0.18	1848	2.77	62.37	44.4	24.02	64	64	3098	0	8365	33.4	30.6	9.88
TEA*	128	64	0.18	2355	3.53	35.32	100	42.46								
XTEA*									128	64	648	24	7408	30.3	34.5	53.24
Camellia*	128	128	0.18	6511	9.76	33.57	290.1	44.55	128	128	504	0	17514	70	14.6	28.97
SIMON*	96	48	0.13	763	0.76	48.32	15.8	20.7	96	48	1262	12	64000	256	8	6.34
SEA*	96	8	0.13	2562	2.56	117.67	2.29	0.89	96	96	170	0	594	2.3	323	1900
KASUMI*	128	64	0.13	3437	3.44	29.9	115.14	33.5	128	64	426	24	41604	173.7	9.2	21.6
MIBS^	64	64	0.18	1396	2.09	10.47	200	143.26	64	64	1264	24	11939	47.6	21.4	16.93
LBlock^	80	64	0.18	1320	2	9.9	200	151.51	80	64	3184	29	49056	66.2	5.2	1.63
ITUbee^									80	80	976	58	18988	25.6	13.48	13.81
GOST^	256	64	0.18	1000	1.5	7.5	200	200	256	64	716	0	2607	10.4	122.7	171.37
Robin^									128	128	4748	190	10240	13.8	25.7	5.27
Fantomas^									128	128	1942	80	4935	6.6	103.74	53.42
CLEFIA*	128	128	0.13	2678	2.67	36.82	76	28.37	128	128	1920	78	3646	4.9	140.42	73.14
PICCOLO^	80	64	0.13	1136	1.13	4.8	237.04	208.66	128	128	3046	0	28648	114.5	17.8	5.84
TWINE#	80	64	0.09	1503	1.05	5.91	178	118.42	80	64	966	70	21448	28.9	11.93	12.35
SPECK*	96	48	0.13	884	0.88	73.67	12	13.57	64	64	1180	140	20505	11.93	12.48	10.58
IDEA*									128	64	134	0	408	1.6	470.5	3511.19
HIGHT*	128	64	0.35	2608	4.7	24.93	188	72.08	128	64	596	47	2700	10.8	94.8	159.06
LEA#	128	128	0.13	3826	3.82	50.22	76.19	19.91	128	128	5718	0	6377	25.5	40.14	7.02
KATAN*	80	32	0.13	802	0.8	64.16	12.5	15.58	80	64	590	32	5231	97.8	97.8	165.76
KTANTAN^	80	32	0.13	462	0.46	36.96	12.5	27.05	80	64	338	18	72063	289.2	3.5	10.35
Hummingbird^									128	16	10516	82	10233211	138814.8	0.012	0
Hummingbird-2^	128	16	0.18	2159	3.23	40.48	80	37.05	128	16	1822	50	4637	6.2	13.8	7.57

References

1. Regla, A.I., Festijo, E.D.: Performance analysis of light-weight cryptographic algorithms for internet of things (IOT) applications: a systematic review. In: Proceedings of the 2022 IEEE 7th International Conference for Convergence in Technology (I2CT) (2022). https://doi.org/10.1109/i2ct54291.2022.9824108
2. Lata, N., Kumar, R.: Analysis of lightweight cryptography algorithms for IoT communication. In: Sharma, H., Saraswat, M., Yadav, A., Kim, J.H., Bansal, J.C. (eds.) CIS 2020. AISC, vol. 1335, pp. 397–406. Springer, Singapore (2021). https://doi.org/10.1007/978-981-33-6984-9_32
3. Shah, A., Engineer, M.: A survey of lightweight cryptographic algorithms for IoT-based applications. In: Tiwari, S., Trivedi, M.C., Mishra, K.K., Misra, A.K., Kumar, K.K. (eds.) Smart Innovations in Communication and Computational Sciences. AISC, vol. 851, pp. 283–293. Springer, Singapore (2019). https://doi.org/10.1007/978-981-13-2414-7_27
4. Thakor, V.A., Razzaque, M.A., Khandaker, M.R.: Lightweight cryptography algorithms for resource-constrained IoT devices: a review, comparison and research opportunities. IEEE Access 9, 28177–28193 (2021). https://doi.org/10.1109/access.2021.3052867
5. Khalifa, M., Algarni, F., Khan, M.A., Ullah, A., Aloufi, K.: A lightweight cryptography (LWC) framework to secure memory heap in internet of things. Alex. Eng. J. 60(1), 1489–1497 (2021). https://doi.org/10.1016/j.aej.2020.11.003
6. Charmonman, S., Mongkhonvanit, P.: Internet of Things in E-business. In: Proceedings of the 10th International Conference on E-Business, King Mongkut's University of Technology, Thonburi, pp. 1–9 (2015)
7. The trouble with the Internet of Things. https://data.london.gov.uk/blog/the-trouble-with-the-internet-of-things. Accessed Aug 2015
8. McKay, K., Bassham, L., Turan, M.S., Mouha, N.: Report on lightweight cryptography (Nistir8114). NIST, Gaithersburg (2017)
9. Zhang, F., et al.: Persistent fault attack in practice. In: Proceedings of the IACR Transaction Cryptographic Hardware and Embedded Systems, pp. 172–195, March 2020
10. Bhasin, S., Breier, J., Hou, X., Jap, D., Poussier, R., Sim, S.M.: SITM: See-in-the-middle side-channel assisted middle round differential cryptanalysis on SPN block ciphers. In: Proceedings of the IACR Transaction Cryptographic Hardware and Embedded Systems, pp. 95–122, November 2019
11. Lightweight cryptographic algorithms for guessing attack protection in complex Internet of Things applications.
12. Dinu, D., Corre, Y.L., Khovratovich, D., Perrin, L., Großschädl, J., Biryukov, A.: Triathlon of lightweight block ciphers for the Internet of Things. J. Cryptograph. Eng. 9(3), 283–302 (2019)
13. Banik, S., et al.: GIFT-COFB. Submission Round 1, 29 (2019)
14. Liu, Y., Sasaki, Y.: Related-key boomerang attacks on GIFT with automated trail search including BCT effect. In: Jang-Jaccard, J., Guo, F. (eds.) ACISP 2019. LNCS, vol. 11547, pp. 555–572. Springer, Cham (2019). https://doi.org/10.1007/978-3-030-21548-4_30
15. Toshihiko, O.: Lightweight cryptography applicable to various IoT devices. NEC Tech. J. 12(1), 67–71 (2017)
16. Biryukov, A., Perrin, L.P.: State of the art in lightweight symmetric cryptography. Technical report 10993/31319, University of Luxembourg Library, Esch-sur-Alzette, Luxembourg (2017). https://orbilu.uni.lu/handle/10993/31319
17. Engineer, M., Shah, A.: Performance analysis of lightweight cryptographic algorithms simulated on Arduino Uno and MATLAB using the voice recognition application. In: Proceedings of the 2018 International Conference on Circuits and Systems in Digital Enterprise Technology (ICCSDET) (2018). https://doi.org/10.1109/iccsdet.2018.8821126

18. Okello, W.J., Liu, Q., Siddiqui, F.A., Zhang, C.: A survey of the current state of lightweight cryptography for the Internet of Things. In: Proceedings of the International Conference on Computer, Information, and Telecommunication Systems (CITS), pp. 292–296, July 2017
19. Adomnicai, A., Najm, Z., Peyrin, T.: Fixslicing: a new gift representation. In: Proceedings of the IACR, p. 412 (2020)
20. Hatzivasilis, G., Fysarakis, K., Papaefstathiou, I., Manifavas, C.: A review of lightweight block ciphers. J. Cryptograph. Eng. **8**(2), 141–184 (2018)
21. Kumarkushwaha, P., Singh, M.P., Kumar, P.: A survey on lightweight block ciphers. Int. J. Comput. Appl. **96**(17), 1–7 (2014)
22. Appel, M., et al.: Block ciphers for the IoT-SIMON, SPECK, KATAN, LED, TEA, PRESENT, and SEA compared. Technical report, Technical University of Darmstadt, Darmstadt, Germany (2016). http://download.mmag.hrz.tu-darmstadt.de/media/FB20/Dekanat/Publikati onen/CDC/2016-09-05_TR_SimonSpeckKatanLedTeaPresentSea.pdf
23. Andrews, B., Chapman, S., Dearstyne, S.: Tiny encryption algorithm (TEA) cryptography 4005.705. 01 graduate team ACD final report. Technical report 33695183, Rochester Institute of Technology, Rochester, NY, USA (2020). https://www.coursehero.com/file/33695183/ TEApdf/
24. Stallings, W.: Cryptography and network security: principles and practice (2017). https:// www.pearson.com/us/highereducation/product/Stallings-Cryptogra%phy-and-Network-Sec urityPrinciples-and-Practice-6th-Edition/9780133354690.htm%l. Suzaki, T., Minematsu, K.: Improving the generalized feistel. In: Hong, S., Iwata, T. (eds.) FSE 2010. LNCS, vol. 6147, pp. 19–39. Springer, Heidelberg (2010). https://doi.org/10.1007/978-3-642-13858-4_2
25. LaraNino, C.A., DiazPerez, A., MoralesSandoval, M.: FPGA-based assessment of midori and gift lightweight block ciphers. In: Naccache, D., Xu, S., Qing, S., Samarati, P., Blanc, G., Lu, R., Zhang, Z., Meddahi, A. (eds.) ICICS 2018. LNCS, vol. 11149, pp. 745–755. Springer, Cham (2018). https://doi.org/10.1007/978-3-030-01950-1_45
26. Sekar, G., Mouha, N., Velichkov, V., Preneel, B.: Meet-in-the-middle attacks on reduced-round XTEA. In: Kiayias, A. (ed.) CT-RSA 2011. LNCS, vol. 6558, pp. 250–267. Springer, Heidelberg (2011). https://doi.org/10.1007/978-3-642-19074-2_17
27. Lu, J.: Related-key rectangle attack on 36 rounds of the XTEA block cipher. Int. J. Inf. Secur. **8**(1), 1–11 (2009)
28. Aoki, K., et al.: Camellia: a 128-bit block cipher suitable for multiple platforms — design and analysis. In: Stinson, D.R., Tavares, S. (eds.) SAC 2000. LNCS, vol. 2012, pp. 39–56. Springer, Heidelberg (2001). https://doi.org/10.1007/3-540-44983-3_4
29. Satoh, A., Morioka, S.: Hardware-focused performance comparison for the standard block ciphers AES, camellia, and triple-DES. In: Boyd, C., Mao, W. (eds.) ISC 2003. LNCS, vol. 2851, pp. 252–266. Springer, Heidelberg (2003). https://doi.org/10.1007/10958513_20
30. Beaulieu, R., Shors, D., Smith, J., Treatman-Clark, S., Weeks, B., Wingers, L.: The simon and speck families of lightweight block ciphers. IACR Cryptol. ePrint Arch. **2013**(1), 404–449 (2013)
31. Standaert, F.-X., Piret, G., Gershenfeld, N., Quisquater, J.-J.: SEA: a scalable encryption algorithm for small embedded applications. In: Domingo-Ferrer, J., Posegga, J., Schreckling, D. (eds.) CARDIS 2006. LNCS, vol. 3928, pp. 222–236. Springer, Heidelberg (2006). https:// doi.org/10.1007/11733447_16
32. Mace, F., Standaert, F.: ASIC implementations of the block cipher sea for constrained applications. In: Proceedings of the 3rd International Conference on RFID Security, pp. 103–114 (2007)
33. Eisenbarth, T., et al.: Compact implementation and performance evaluation of block ciphers in attiny devices. In: Mitrokotsa, A., Vaudenay, S. (eds.) AFRICACRYPT 2012. LNCS, vol. 7374, pp. 172–187. Springer, Heidelberg (2012). https://doi.org/10.1007/978-3-642-31410-0_11

34. Kumar, M., Pal, S.K., Panigrahi, A.: Few: a lightweight block cipher. Turkish J. Math. Comput. Sci. **11**(2), 58–73 (2014)
35. Bhardwaj, I., Kumar, A., Bansal, M.: A review on lightweight cryptography algorithms for data security and authentication in IoTs. In: Proceedings of the 4th International Conference on Signal Processing, Computing and Control (ISPCC), pp. 504–509, September 2017
36. Shirai, T., Shibutani, K., Akishita, T., Moriai, S., Iwata, T.: The 128-bit blockcipher CLEFIA (extended abstract). In: Biryukov, A. (ed.) FSE 2007. LNCS, vol. 4593, pp. 181–195. Springer, Heidelberg (2007). https://doi.org/10.1007/978-3-540-74619-5_12
37. Dinu, D., Biryukov, A., Großschädl, J., Khovratovich, D., Le Corre, Y., Perrin, L.: FELICS–fair evaluation of lightweight cryptographic systems. In: Proceedings of the NIST Workshop on Lightweight Cryptography, p. 128 (2015)
38. Bansod, G., Raval, N., Pisharoty, N.: Implementation of a new lightweight encryption design for embedded security. IEEE Trans. Inf. Forensics Security **10**(1), 142–151 (2015)
39. Sallam, S., Beheshti, B.D.: A survey on lightweight cryptographic algorithms. In: Proceedings of the IEEE Region Conference, pp. 1784–1789, October 2018
40. Hosseinzadeh, J., Hosseinzadeh, M.: A comprehensive survey on evaluation of lightweight symmetric ciphers: hardware and software implementation. Adv. Comput. Sci. Int. J. **5**(4), 31–41 (2016)
41. Banik, S., et al.: Midori: a block cipher for low energy. In: Iwata, T., Cheon, J.H. (eds.) ASIACRYPT 2015. LNCS, vol. 9453, pp. 411–436. Springer, Heidelberg (2015). https://doi.org/10.1007/978-3-662-48800-3_17
42. Zhang, W., Bao, Z., Lin, D., Rijmen, V., Yang, B., Verbauwhede, I.: RECTANGLE: a bit-slice lightweight block cipher suitable for multiple platforms. Sci. China Inf. Sci. **58**(12), 1–15 (2015)
43. Atawneh, B., AL-Hammoury, L., Abutaha, M.: Power consumption of a chaos-based stream cipher algorithm. In: Proceedings of the 2020 3rd International Conference on Computer Applications and Information Security (ICCAIS) (2020). https://doi.org/10.1109/iccais48893.2020.9096730
44. Sleem, L., Couturier, R.: Speck-R: An ultra light-weight cryptographic scheme for Internet of Things. Multimedia Tools Appl. **80**(11), 17067–17102 (2020). https://doi.org/10.1007/s11042-020-09625-8
45. Aslan, B., Aslan, F.Y., Sakallı, M.T.: Energy consumption analysis of light-weight cryptographic algorithms that can be used in the security of internet of things applications. Secur. Commun. Netw. **2020**, 1–15 (2020). https://doi.org/10.1155/2020/8837671

Permissioned Blockchain-Based Solution to Document Processing in the Real Estate Industry

Vishalkumar Langaliya(✉) ⓘ and Jaypalsinh A. Gohil ⓘ

Department of Computer Application, Marwadi University, Rajkot 360003, Gujarat, India
vishalkumar.langaliya111484@marwadiuniversity.ac.in,
jaypalsinh.gohil@marwadieducation.edu.in

Abstract. For Blockchain Technology, Real Estate is a particularly excellent target since it has a complicated transaction process that is designed to prevent fraud and enable stringent ownership protection. The real estate industry demands these characteristics, and this is where blockchain excels. Blockchain Technology can be used to enhance System openness making it possible for regulators to identify and stop fraudulent activity. Blockchain technology and the fundamentals of the Indian real estate market are introduced in the first section of the article. The second section summarizes recent research in the area of interest and points out research gaps. The framework and suggested algorithms for document processing in the Indian real estate sector are shown in the third part. The implementation of the proposed algorithms with tools and technologies is suggested in the final section. Using the permission blockchain, the proposed algorithms can be put into practice as chain code. The suggested algorithm's ultimate purpose is to preserve transparency, record integrity, and trust factor in the targeted area to encourage openness, integrity, availability, and trust.

Keywords: Blockchain · Indian real estate · Chain code · Hyperledger fabric · Transaction processing

1 Introduction

1.1 Blockchain Technology

In 2008, Satoshi Nakamoto made the idea of distributed blockchains a reality. He modified the architecture by extending the chain without requiring new blocks to be signed by trustworthy parties. Multiple nodes retain a secure log of all data transfers, often known as transactions. Through a peer-to-peer network, each participant timestamps and validates each transaction. Without the necessity for a centralized authority, this is managed. Because of these developments, blockchains have evolved into the foundation of cryptocurrencies (Fig. 1).

A distributed database called a blockchain enables direct transactions between two entities without the requirement for a centralized authority[2]. This straightforward yet

S. Rajagopal et al. (Eds.): ASCIS 2022, CCIS 1760, pp. 217–231, 2022.
https://doi.org/10.1007/978-3-031-23095-0_16

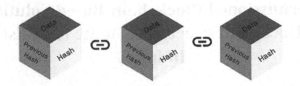

Fig. 1. Blockchain as a chain of blocks [1]

potent idea has broad ramifications for a variety of institutions, like banks, governments, and markets, to name a few. Any company or organization that relies on a centralized database as a competitive advantage could be disrupted by blockchain technology (Fig. 2).

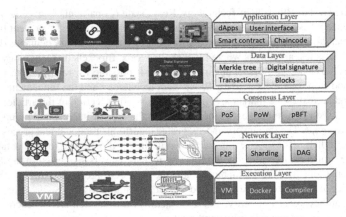

Fig. 2. Layered architecture of blockchain [3]

1.2 Indian Real Estate Sector

Real estate is defined as land, along with any buildings or structures on it, as well as the air surrounding it and the ground below it. A further name for it is real estate. Residential properties estate, business offices, public buildings, such as theatres, hotels, and restaurants, as well as retail establishments and industrial buildings, such as factories, are all included [4]. The purchase, selling, and construction of land, homes, and other structures are all aspects of real estate. Property owners, developers, designers, real estate professionals, renters, and buyers are some of the major stakeholders in the property industry. The real estate sector has gained importance in India since the country's economy was opened up (Fig. 3).

1.3 Impact of Blockchain Technology on the Indian Real Estate Sector

The real estate industry is currently adopting blockchain technology because it can streamline many of the industry's procedures. Documentation, recordkeeping, diligence,

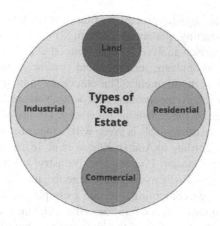

Fig. 3. Classification of real estate [5]

registration, and closure are all parts of these processes. Utilizing blockchain technology, the seller will provide the buyer with a password or private security key. The purchaser will have access to past property records, including ownership, upkeep payments, etc. The property buyer, after recognizing it, can also access the title documents, property tax, encumbrances, etc. Mortgages, payment transfers, and property registration may all be done extremely easily thanks to the digitization of data. As a result, blockchain technology streamlines accelerates, and improves the real estate process. The real estate industry would also gain from blockchain technology in many other ways, such as by eliminating title fraud, increasing tax revenue collection, eliminating corruption at the government level, reducing property disputes, lowering transaction costs due to the minimal use of intermediaries, and eliminating the need for physical storage of property papers.

Benefits of blockchain technology for the real estate industry

1. Blockchain makes it possible to view the data yet prevents tampering. This promotes data transparency and trust.
2. Because it will be "online," buyers will be able to simply search for real estateproperties online. Given the growth of internet portals and the demand for them, this will be extremely advantageous for the real estate industry.
3. Both speed and cost, which are big problems in the Indian real estate market, are solved by blockchain transactions.
4. In the blockchain, the usage of intermediaries is likewise constrained. This reduces unnecessary expenses and restricts fraud.

2   Related Research Work and Limitations

2.1   Summarization of Recent Research Work

In the year 2021, Fahim Ullah et al. [6] put their attention on a thorough design and engagement mechanism for real estate owners and users who are parties to a smart contract. Along with a step-by-step process for founding and terminating smart contracts, a list of functions for starting, generating, altering, or dismissing a smart contract is provided. To do a comparison analysis, Rohan Bennett et al. [7] use many frameworks, such as the strategic grid analysis, technological readiness and maturity assessment, and adherence to business requirements. The outcomes show that the hybrid approach enables adherence to the requirements of the land dealing organization and that proofs-of-concept are a crucial stage in the expanding trajectory. The use of blockchain technology and smart contracts in real estate deals is given with a maturity model in the conclusion.

In the year 2020, According to Adarsh Kumar et al. [8], a blockchain data network and intelligent healthcare system Processes in Industry 4.0 Internet of things (IoT), industrial Internet of things (IIoT), machine intelligence, intelligent systems, cloud technology, edge devices, edge computing, etc. are examples of 4.0 processes that offer transparency, quick and easily accessible, security, efficiency, etc. The issue with the manual method is that the accuracy of the information about a property is not transparent. Toqeer Ali et al. [9] developed a Transparent and Trusted Property Registration System on Permissioned Blockchain to address this issue. For example, the individual in charge could misrepresent the manual process to the stakeholders by manipulating the data in the database. To help election stakeholders, understand the potential dangers, security threats, important required qualities, and weaknesses that could be associated with adopting blockchain e-voting for national elections, Olawande Daramola et al. [10] proposed blockchain e-voting architecture was utilized as a basis. The study discovered that internal vote tampering and numerous security vulnerabilities may be avoided using blockchain electronic voting.

In the year 2019, It outlines concerns with the present land recordkeeping process, such as a lack of accountability, inconsistent data sets with many government departments referencing the same parcel of property, and delays, as well as how Blockchain Technology can be used to address these problems. The development of a system using Blockchain technology for land titling is also illustrated by Vinay Thakura et al. [11]. This technology will provide legitimate and definitive ownership rights and make land titles tamper-proof. The study suggests exploiting Blockchain's intrinsic profits, with a focus on smart contracts. Every transaction will be recorded by the system and securely documented, regardless of whether it concerns the selling of a property, an inheritance, a court order, the acquisition of land, etc.

Using the free software permissioned blockchain design architecture Hyperledger fabric, an experimental prototype was created in 2018 by Mayank Raikwar et al. [12]. They discussed the key design criteria and associated design ideas before encoding several insurance processes as smart contracts. Numerous tests were run to evaluate the framework's performance and the security of the suggested design and transactions centered on a blockchain-enabled platform. To build a blockchain-based electronic voting system, Friorik P. Hjalmarsson et al. [13] propose a fresh approach that addresses some of the flaws in existing systems and investigates some of the popular blockchain frameworks. They revealed a blockchain-based electronic voting system that safeguards voters' privacy while facilitating safe and convenient voting.

Blockchain and smart contracts are presented by Ioannis Karamitsos et al. [14] for the real estate industry. After presenting a complete design of a smart contract, a use case for leasing out homes and companies is considered. They offer a method for designing smart contracts that pave the door for the development of several Blockchain use cases. Comprehensive state finite processes and functions are defined for a specific use case that significantly contributes to the real estate domain.

2.2 Research Gap

We concentrated on the Systemic Literature Review of recent research conducted from 2018 to 2021 during the study and prepared a Proportional and Inclusive Review Analysis of Block Chain Applications in Different Domains [15]. According to a recent analysis, only a small number of industries, including the health sector, the insurance sector, the e-voting sector, and the land sector, have adopted blockchain technology. Future applications of blockchain technology with smart contracts include many untapped markets. The processing of real estate paperwork in traditional India is centralized, necessitating the obligatory involvement of an intermediary, and it lacks transparency, integrity, accessibility, and confidence. Additionally, the system lacks certain sophisticated business logic that may make it reliable and safe.

3 Proposed Research Work

In the field of Indian Real Estate Document Processing, the proposed framework will be used to address many issues, such as third-party trust, security, and integrity. Government agencies would handle and store Indian Real Estate Document Processing data using the proposed Hyperledger Fabric, a permissioned blockchain to process documents including sale deeds and mortgages. Participants in the transaction include the seller, buyer, mortgage agency, and insurance authority, while peers in the transaction include the registration authority, district magistrate (collector), court, and municipal authority. We are using permission blockchain rather than blockchain since the documents and data used in Indian Real Estate Document Processing are confidential. Direct negotiations between the seller and the buyer are an option for real estate transactions. They are equipped to launch blockchain transactions.

For fundamental operations, we developed three algorithms. The property registration process has one with business logic, the mortgage registration process has another with business logic, and the mortgage release procedure has a third with business processing. We advise using IPFS to store processed documents (InterPlanetary File System). The suggested model archives attribute such as security, privacy, and integrity. Additionally, it eliminates the chance of a single point of failure.

3.1 Designed Framework and Components

The suggested framework's three main, fundamental elements are listed below (Fig. 4).

- **PEERS** -Registration Authority, District Magistrate (Collector), Court, and Municipality Authority
- **PARTICIPANTS** - Seller, buyer, mortgage agency, and insurance authority

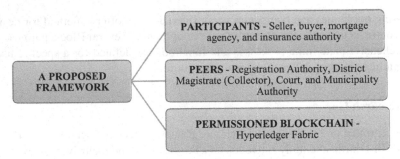

Fig. 4. Fundamental elements of the suggested framework

• PERMISSIONED BLOCKCHAIN - Hyperledger Fabric

1. Peers
    The registration authority's main services include adding new property registrations, transacting real estate, transferring ownership, issuing deed titles, and giving forth information about real estate and ownership. The District Magistrate is examining the property's legal component. The municipal authorities confirm the type of property and its condition; for instance, when registering an apartment, it is confirmed that the flat is finished and ready for registration.

2. Participant
    Any seller or buyer participating in the proposed framework is a direct user participant. The purchaser or vender may be merely the owner's authorized agent rather than the real owner of the property. Users include other organizations that authorize loans, insure properties, and approve mortgages by checking client information such as property ownership, type of property, and so on. These organizations include loan agencies/banks, insurance, and mortgage agencies.

3. Permissioned Blockchain
    It is a blockchain with limited network participation. The need of the government for control over blockchain network membership is therefore satisfied. Data, however, are controlled by multiple organizations. The most recent data set is kept in each peer's ledger. The blockchain is based on Hyperledger Fabric, which executes Smart Contracts (Chain code) to store and make accessible user-accessible data on property transactions. Owners of real estate are also given title deeds by executing a certain Chain code. The business logic that will be used to provide the service is contained in the chain code.

4. IPFS
    The Interplanetary File System is a peer-to-peer connection and distributed file system technology that enables data storage and dissemination (IPFS). Each file in the global namespace that links all computing devices is uniquely identified by IPFS through the use of content-addressing. In contrast to a centrally maintained server, IPFS is based on a decentralized system of user operators that each keep a fraction of the entire data. This results in a resilient data storage and sharing system. There is a cryptographically generated hash value for each item of data on IPFS. It

uses this one-of-a-kind hash to identify the data that is stored there. In IPFS, data is separated from transactions, which lowers communication and compute costs while maintaining privacy [16]. Due to the safe storage method offered by the IPFS protocol, it's a viable option for maintaining title deed records [17] (Fig. 5).

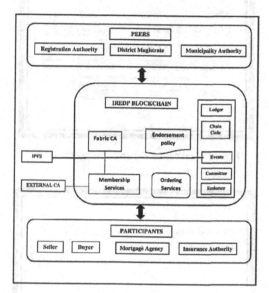

Fig. 5. Core architecture of the suggested framework

3.2 Core Transaction Process Flow

The three crucial processes for processing Indian real estate documents are the subject of the proposed framework:

1. The Registration of Real Estate

   Both the buyer and the seller agree to participate in the property registration process. This transaction will be registered at the registration office with the appropriate legal papers. The documents will be examined by the authorities, who will then approve the sale deed documents after receiving the required stamp duty fees (Fig. 6).

2. Registration Process for Mortgages

   To mortgage the property, the owner must apply the mortgage registration process. After the registrar authorities have confirmed the property's ownership, the mortgage will be registered and the mortgage registration notice will be sent (Fig. 7).

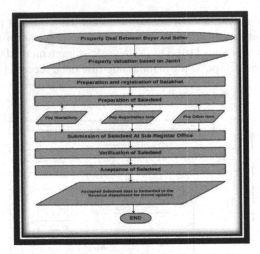

Fig. 6. Real estate registration process flow

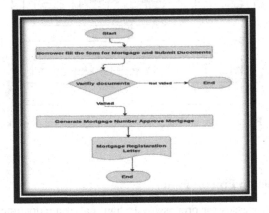

Fig. 7. Mortgage registration process flow

3. The Mortgage Release Procedure

The property owner must apply at the registrar's office without a form from a linked organization, like a bank, to have the mortgage freed. The Registrar Authority issues the mortgage letter to the owner after making sure that previous records are accurate and that no uncompleted forms are there (Fig. 8).

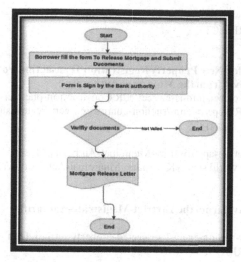

Fig. 8. Mortgage release process flow

3.3 Proposed Algorithms

Algorithm-1 for New Property Registration

Input Data: enroll-no, sign, Smart-Contract-id, transaction-proposal, owner-info, property-info, property-completion-info, Stamp duty-fee-paid

Result: Insert the Final Transaction in Blockchain Database.

Step 1: Participant verification and authentication
        if (enroll-no-exists=False OR sign_valid=False) then
                abort request;
        end if

Step 2: Access Verification of Participants

        if (enroll-no having the ability to invoke-Smart-Contract-id=False) then
                REJECT
        end if

Step 3: Examining the format and looking for duplicates Transaction
        if (Verify_whether_proposal_is_in_desired_format =False) then
                REJECT
        end if

```
        if (Verify_whether_transaction_is_Duplicate_or_Original =False) then
                REJECT
    end if
```

Step-4: Approval for New Property Registration Transaction from all authorities
a) Approval from the Municipal Authority
```
if (property-owner-info-is-correct OR Construction-plan-verified
        OR property-construction-completion-certificate-issued =False) then
            REJECT
Else
    transaction-approved-by-Municipal-Authority=True;
    update world state; (Key value: Municipal-Authority-Validation=True)
end if
```

b) Approval from the District-Magistrate-Authority

```
    If (Any-pettion-against-subjected-property==true) then
        REJECT
    else
        transaction-approved-by-District-Magistrate-Authority=True;
            update world state; (Key value: District-Magistrate-Authority-
    Validation=True)
    end if
```

c) Approval from the District-Court-Authority
```
    if(Any-Stay-order-against-subjected-property==true) then
                REJECT

    else
        transaction-approved-by-District-Court-Authority=True;
        update world state; (Key value: District-Court-Authority-
            Validation=True)
    end if
```

d) Approval from the Registration-Authority
```
    if (owner==FALSE OR Saledeed-transact-property-amount>owner-
    property-amount OR property-valuation==FALSE) then
                    REJECT

    else if (Stamp duty-fee-paid=True || Stampduty-fee-paid-
    amount=evaluated-fee) then
        transaction-approved-by-Registration-Authority=True
        update world state;
            (Key value: Registration-Authority- Validation=True, Fee-
    paid=True,
                owner=new-owner)
        Insert transaction to the ledger;
    else
        REJECT;
```

end if

Step-5: Final Sale deed transaction execution

if key-value (Registration-Authority-Validation=True, Municipal-Authority-Validation=True, District-Court-Authority-Validation=True, District-Megistrate-Authority-Validation=True, Fee-paid=True, owner-new-owner) then

Issue-title-deed and store to IPFS;
IPFS-address=location of title-deed on IPFS;
Calculate hash_deed=hash (Issued-title-deed);
Update world state (key-value: hash_title_deed = hash_deed, IPFS_location= IPFS-address);
else
REJECT
End If

Algorithm-2 for Mortgage Registration Process

Input Data: enroll-no, sign, Smart-Contract-id, transaction-proposal, owner-info, property-info, mortgage_details

Result: Insert the Final Transaction in Blockchain Database.

Step 1: Participant verification and authentication

  if (enroll-no-exists=False OR sign_valid=False) then
    abort request;
  end if

Step 2: Access Verification of Participants
  if (enroll-no having the ability to invoke-Smart-Contract-id=False) then
    REJECT
  end if

Step 3: Verification of Mortgage details

  if (mortgage_fees_paid=True AND property_details = True) then
    verify-property-details-with-records;
    update world state (key-value: verification-property-details =true);
  else
    REJECT
  end if

Step-4: Final Mortgage Registration transaction execution

  if key-value (Fee-paid=True, verification-property-details =true) then

    Issue-mortgage and store to IPFS;
    IPFS-address=location of the mortgage on IPFS;
    Calculate hash_deed=hash (Issued-mortgage);
    Update world state
    (key-value: hash_mortgage_id = hash_mortgage, IPFS_location =
  IPFS-address);
  else
    REJECT
  end if

Algorithm -3 for Mortgage Process Process

Input Data: enroll-no, sign, Smart-Contract-id, transaction-proposal, owner-info, property-info, mortgage_details

Result: Insert the Final Transaction in Blockchain Database.

Step-1: Participant verification and authentication

      if (enroll-no-exists=False OR sign_valid=False) then
          abort request;
      end if

Step 2: Access Verification of Participants

      if (enroll-no having the ability to invoke-Smart-Contract-id=False) then
          REJECT
      end if

Step 3: Verification of Mortgage Registration details

      if (owner_details=True) then
          verify-mortgage_details-with-records;
          update world state (key-value: mortgage-release-status=true);
     else
          REJECT
      end if

Step-4: Final Mortgage Release transaction execution

      if key-value (mortgage-release-status=true) then
          Issue-mortgage-release and store to IPFS;
          IPFS-address=location of mortgage-release on IPFS;
          Calculate hash_deed=hash(Issued-mortgage-release);
          Update world state
          (key-value: hash_mortgage_release-id = hash_mortgage-release,
     IPFS_location= IPFS-address);
     else
              REJECT
      end if

3.4 Deployment

To implement the provided framework and analysis, we constructed a mock small basic form of design with the bare lowest configuration. For deployment purposes, we made use of the following technical specification. Ubuntu v16.04.6 LTS, Node.js, curl, Docker, and NPM SDK. Hyperledger Fabric.

4 Conclusion and Future Scope

At the outset of this post, we discussed the importance of emerging technologies like blockchain. Additionally, we've outlined the six-layer architecture of the most crucial elements of blockchain technology and described their structure. We also talked about

Indian real estate, which is the country's most significant and influential industry, and provided a brief description of the various kinds of real estate that are offered there. The article's middle half discusses ongoing research as well as the significance of blockchain in the Indian real estate industry. Finally, we have shown the research hole that blockchain technology can fill. The article's proposed architecture for processing Indian real estate documents is a permissioned blockchain system with smart contracts. Peers, participants, and components are described, and a flow diagram is used to illustrate the three main processes' progress. An effective algorithm that can be used to implement the first three stages has been proposed. The article's conclusion lists the technical requirements for deployment. Even though the suggested framework has already been put into practice, a comparison analysis can still be done in the future to enhance the functionality of the system.

References

1. https://money.com/. What is a blockchain?
2. Profile, S.E.E.:Lecture Note on Introduction to Blockchain Introduction to Prepared and Compiled By Dr Md Ashraf Uddin Federation University Australia (2021)
3. Langaliya, V., Gohil, J.A.: KARAR : a smart contract enabled conceptual framework for Indian real estate document processing using blockchain technology, 3
4. 10th Planning Commission, Tenth Five Year Plan Report 2002–07, Source, pp. 829–846, 2002. https://niti.gov.in/planningcommission.gov.in/docs/plans/planrel/fiveyr/10th/volume2/v2_ch7_6.pdf
5. https://ibiene.com/real-estate/investing-in-real-estate-part-iii/, Investing in Real Estate
6. Ullah, F., Al-Turjman, F.: A conceptual framework for blockchain smart contract adoption to manage real estate deals in smart cities. Neural Comput. Appl. 1–22 (2021). https://doi.org/10.1007/s00521-021-05800-6
7. Bennett, R., Miller, T., Pickering, M., Kara, A.K.: Hybrid approaches for smart contracts in land administration: lessons from three blockchain proofs- of-concept. Land **10**(2), 1–23 (2021). https://doi.org/10.3390/land10020220
8. Kumar, A., Krishnamurthi, R., Nayyar, A., Sharma, K., Grover, V., Hossain, E.: A novel smart healthcare design, simulation, and implementation using healthcare 4.0 processes. IEEE Access **8**, 118433–118471 (2020). https://doi.org/10.1109/ACCESS.2020.3004790
9. Ali, T., Nadeem, A., Alzahrani, A., Jan, S.: A transparent and trusted property registration system on permissioned blockchain. In: 2019 International Conference on Advances in the Emerging Computing Technologies (AECT), pp. 1-6 (2020). IEEE.https://doi.org/10.1109/AECT47998.2020.9194222
10. Daramola, O.: Architecture-Centric Evaluation of Blockchain-Based (2020)
11. Thakur, V., Doja, M.N., Dwivedi, Y.K., Ahmad, T., Khadanga, G.: Land records on blockchain for implementation of Land Titling in India. Int. J. Inf. Manage. **52**, 1 (2020). https://doi.org/10.1016/j.ijinfomgt.2019.04.013
12. Lakshma Reddy, B., Karthik, A., Prayla Shyry, S.: A blockchain framework for insurance processes in hospitals. Int. J. Recent Technol. Eng. **7**(5), 116–119 (2019)
13. Hjalmarsson, F.P., Hreioarsson, G.K., Hamdaqa, M., Hjalmtysson, G.:Blockchain-based e-voting system. IEEE International Conference Cloud Computing CLOUD, pp. 983–986 (2018). https://doi.org/10.1109/CLOUD.2018.00151
14. Karamitsos, I., Papadaki, M., Al Barghuthi, N.B.: Design of the blockchain smart contract: a use case for real estate. J. Inf. Secur. **09**(03), 177–190 (2018). https://doi.org/10.4236/jis.2018.93013

15. Langaliya, V., Gohil, J.A.G.: A comparative and comprehensive analysis of smart contract enabled blockchain applications. Int. J. Recent Innov. Trends Comput. Commun. **9**(9), 16–26 (2021). https://doi.org/10.17762/ijritcc.v9i9.5489

16. Xu, J., et al.: Healthchain: a blockchain-based privacy preserving scheme for large-scale health data. IEEE Internet Things J. **6**(5), 8770–8781 (2019). https://doi.org/10.1109/JIOT.2019.2923525

17. Sun, J., Yao, X., Wang, S., Wu, Y.: Blockchain-based secure storage and access scheme for electronic medical records in IPFS. IEEE Access **8**, 59389–59401 (2020). https://doi.org/10.1109/ACCESS.2020.2982964

Automatic Evaluation of Free Text Answers: A Review

Nirja Shah[✉] and Jyoti Pareek

Department of Computer Science, Gujarat University, Ahmedabad, Gujarat, India
neerjasanghvi@gmail.com

Abstract. In the area of Artificial Intelligence where human-computer interaction is possible using natural languages like English, Hindi, Gujarati. NLP is used to summarize text, translation of text to other languages, accessing answer scripts of students, recognizing emotions, virtual assistance etc. In the modern era, evaluating answer scripts automatically with accuracy and consistency would be a great help for various Universities, Schools, Colleges and institutes. In this review paper we have given an overview of systems that have been developed and engineered till date. Also, we have discussed different approaches that are used and the accuracy that has been attained by the researchers. Though there are many systems which evaluate descriptive answers automatically with great accuracy for the English language, for Indian local languages.

Keywords: Natural Language Processing (NLP) · Text evaluation techniques · Automatic evaluation · Hindi text evaluation · BERT · Ontology · Machine learning · ANN

1 Introduction

Evaluation means determining to what extent has the person understood the topic or instructions. It is the proceeding by which the prior sequel and hence prompted actions are tested. Teaching and learning to play a vital role in evaluation process. It provides feedback to teachers about the learner's drawbacks or deficiency. Thus, Evaluation decides lots of important aspects of a student to the teacher in evaluating answer sheets with accuracy and consistency. [1] Fig. 1 is Bloom's Taxonomy Framework used to check the student's level of thinking.

Based on the above architecture and extracting the best of the learners, the Question paper can be designed of many different categories of questions, to test the knowledge of the student. Figure 2 displays the types of questions generally asked in an exam. Here the questions true and false, fill in the blanks, multiple choice, Match the following, etc. fall in the category of closed ended questions, whereas Descriptive answers, Comprehensions, Short answers and Essay fall in Open ended answers. Evaluating closed ended answers are quite easy as it has a limited words of correct answers. On the other hand, open-ended answers have a wide range of answers which can be correct. Evaluating these open-ended answers is time-consuming and costly.

S. Rajagopal et al. (Eds.): ASCIS 2022, CCIS 1760, pp. 232–249, 2022.
https://doi.org/10.1007/978-3-031-23095-0_17

In India, boards like State Board, CBSE, ICSE, IB, etc. are followed in schools. About 1.43 crores students appear for various annual examinations conducted by different board authorities. The students are also continuously evaluated for the chapters taught during the semester in different forms. While a class test normally includes only objective question types, the final exam question paper consists of various parts including all question types. Evaluating the objective part is easy as compared to the subjective part, as it has only one word as answers to evaluate. Whereas the descriptive part has a lot of areas to be checked like the tenses, the grammar, the punctuation, etc. Evaluating answer scripts are done manually, lacking in accuracy and consistency in evaluation. To evaluate and grade the papers a lot of valuable time gets consumed. Also, the evaluation and grading methods vary from teacher to teacher, leading to a lack of consistency and accuracy, ultimately leading to dissatisfaction among the students. In 2017, [2] wrote that about 9,111 CBSE students from Class XII filed for re-checking of their papers, out of which mistakes were found in 4,632 cases. Class 10 teachers of CBSE board are paid Rs 25 per paper and for class 12, they get Rs 30 per paper as remuneration. GSEB teachers who examine papers of class 10 and 12 science stream exams get Rs 6 per paper while those examining papers of class 12 general streams get Rs 6.50 per paper.

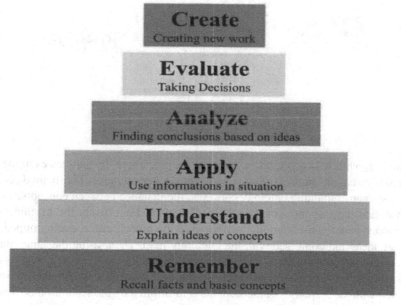

Fig. 1. Bloom's taxonomy - [1]

2 Related Work

Automatic Evaluation of answers have been an influence for educators in the past few years. In these pandemic situations virtual classes have been the only medium for education. Leading to online examinations, automatic evaluation of the answers can be implemented to declare the result quickly. Various online evaluation applications and websites are available for objective answers in English but evaluation of descriptive answers is provided by very limited applications. Various techniques have been used to evaluate descriptive answers with great accuracy. Figure 3 describes different techniques used for Automatic Evaluation.

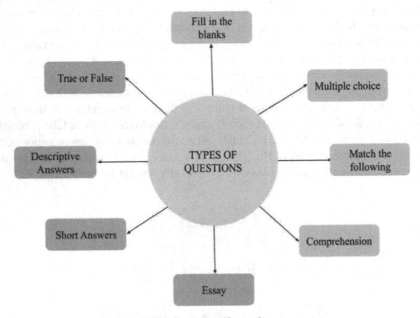

Fig. 2. Types of questions

Ontology with ML was used in a system by [3], where Techniques examined and executed showcased a high correlation with Human Performance. The method accepts a multi-hash map containing ontology concepts, the distance between concepts, a model response, and the responses of the students as input. First, using the machine learning approach under consideration, the phrases in the model response are grouped using Ontology ideas and combined with the Ontology map. Then, using the same machine learning approach, a connection between each idea and the students' responses is determined using the updated multi-Hash map. The total amount of ideas (q) that are positively correlated with the responses of the students is multiplied by the separation between the primary concept and the current concept. The final score is then calculated by dividing this value by the total number of ideas in the multi-Hash Map. The word- weight approach is applied to Ontology. Having followed the acquisition of the words from the ontology, the words in the model answer are combined with the concepts from the ontology, and the weight of each keyword is then deduced by dividing the entire frequency of each word in the students' responses by the total frequency of words in their responses. This work can be enhanced by using Ontology with ML technique. Students can be provided with feedback about the missing concepts in their answers.

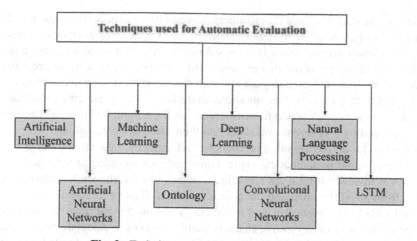

Fig. 3. Techniques used for automatic evaluation

In the initial years the system developed by researchers used to evaluate by just finding the similarity between model answers and student answers. A system was proposed [4] where the student answers are evaluated with the use of Natural Language Processing (NLP) algorithm and Artificial Neural Networks. A set of keywords and answers from evaluators are stored into the database as a dataset. Student answers are evaluated automatically using two algorithms of NLP and ANN. Pre-processing technique is applied first to the answers. With the use of artificial neural networks answers are compared and grammar is checked using NLP algorithms. In NLP some linguistic analysis is performed along with POS tagging and by the artificial neural networks' algorithm students' answers are compared with the staff answer and keywords. Marks generated from both NLP and ANN are stored in the database. Marks calculator is used to calculate total marks obtained by the student by finding the average of the result obtained in all the stages. By these methods they have achieved remarkable results. The limitation in proposed system is that the sentence order is not checked. Also, the answers are evaluated using similarity techniques.

Another system by [5], which works with syntactic relation-based feature production technique for pre-programmed assessment of narrative answers was proposed. A cognitive-based approach where answers are evaluated on the basis of their correctness and clauses deployed in the answer is used. The students are provided with feedback and marks so that they can overcome where they lack in the subject. An input of Questions along with its correct answer and student answers is fed. The process is classified into training and prediction modules. The training module includes: Question classification, Answer classification, Answer evaluation, Scoring and feedback. The system is provided with a Question answer Dataset, where the question and answer both are classified based on its features like Question/Answer type, Head word, Bigram count and LESK algorithm. These are used for fetching sentence meaning along with Naive Bayes' Classification method. Then the number of words matched are calculated where the semantic keywords and TF and IDF calculation is conducted. Further Jacquard similarity, Bag of Words are also checked and Score is calculated. At the end feedback is provided to the students. Here the classification algorithm has shown an accuracy of 95% precision. Limitation of the system is matching the keywords. Grammatical mistakes, Spelling mistakes are not taken into consideration. Also, the sentences in the answer should be in sequence of the model answer [6] engineered a system, where students' answers were evaluated by comparing it with the standard descriptive answer. At the very beginning they classified the questions on the basis of different criteria and samples of exam answers were collected from different universities and institutions. The answers were evaluated by 5 different evaluators and then these evaluated answer scripts were processed and analyzed by other teachers to understand the psychology of the evaluator. Diagrams and mathematical expressions were not included in the research. The system was divided into 3 main parts: the standard answer, the student answer which ranged from 80–100 words, and the comparison unit. First of all, domain related data was collected from e-resources and textbooks. Then the textual data was analyzed to find the occurrences of keywords, characters and sentences to calculate density using a data text analyzer. Based on the frequency of keywords they were divided into 2 parts HFV and LFV. Later, the matching algorithm where standard answer and student answer along with the domain corpus are provided to the algorithm. Using a bag of word and n-gram technique text is pre-processed. Term frequency is counted, followed by term weight where index termsare called from student answers in LSA and from corpus of this domain. Disintegration of singular value, cosine similarity and score calculation are then followed. They have used 1440 samples in electronic form. Performance measures like average score difference (ASD), Standard Deviation (SD) and a Pearson Correlation (PC) are applied between computer assessor (marks calculated using LSA and HPLSE technique) and Human Assessor. For answer category 'Why', domain computers 320 samples were used and an average score of 0.83 in HPLSE and 1.73 using LSA, whereas in 'What' category they have attained average score of 2.36 in LSA technique and 0.56 for HPLSE technique. For Electronic Domain with 'What' category they have attained an average score of 0.23 for LSA and 0.11 for HPLSE and for 'Write' category 0.76 and 0.48 respectively. Limitation of the system was it only checked for similarity and keywords. Another limitation of the system is the number of words, diagrams and mathematical formulas. Also, only Why, What and Write categories are checked for answers.

Evaluation using graphs, fuzzing string matching, grammar checking and many other similarity measure was proposed by [7] where the system implements evaluation of descriptive answers by automatically generating graphs related to sentences. In this approach Model Question, its expected answer, keywords and student answers are fed as input. The Model part of input is pre-processed and the questions are bifurcated in different types, and along with it summarization is performed and stored in Database. The student data is pre-processed and summarized after which different strategies are used to compare student answers with model answers. First Keyword and Similarity score where number of keywords are matched in model and student answer and its cosine similarity is also checked. Next, they checked the language score followed by the Fuzzy String Matching score of NLP that checks the matching of 2 string patterns and a matching score is obtained. Last is the concept graph score, here graphs of student answer and model answer are automatically generated and resemblance is checked using ontology learning for synonyms and antonyms of words. The final score is based on the type of question asked, and the cumulative score is calculated from all the modules. Limitation is Non-textual content like equations, diagrams and tables cannot be scored through this work.

A Transformer based language model to encode questions, answers and reference text was proposed [8]. The technique proposed has effectively helped in measuring the likeliness among the reference and an automatic generated answer, deceiving the question explanation. They built multiple large public and industrial paradigms where they examined to model, for edifying and testing AVA. They have built two types of: (i) linear classifier, which interprets and helps to verify their model conjecture and (ii) Transformer-based methods, which was profitably used in various language insight tasks. AVA-NQ and AVA-GPD has been used to edify and analyze models datasets. They have also checked for the point-wise performance on the WikiQA and TREC-QA datasets. Their experimentation has achieved up to 74.7% in F1 score in anticipating human judgment for single answers. Also, overall system Accuracy with an RMSE, ranged from 0.02 to 0.09, provided multiple references are available.

TF-IDF and KNN algorithms of machine learning are used in a system proposed [9]. Teacher creates a test question along with its descriptive answers, which would be stored in a database. The students will attempt the test and their descriptive answers will be compared with the answer set of teachers using Term Frequency-Inverse Document Frequency algorithm which will extract keywords from students' answers and then would be compared with the teacher's answer. Based on the resemblance of matched keywords, the marks of the test will be determined using the K Nearest Neighbour algorithm.

Using Machine learning techniques and models like NB, LR, SVM, and GBDT [10] has proposed a system where scanned student answers are first converted to a text file using OCR tool, and Answers graded by teacher are taken as input for pre-processing. NLP and NLTK tool kit is used for pre-processing the text semantics, TF-IDF based vector space mapping is applied on each pre-processed answer and key, and a score is generated which is compared with the cosine score, this process is followed by comparison and grading of answer using clustering techniques where keywords are extracted using graph-based ranking model. To conduct experiments on student documented answers, models like Naive Base, Logistic Regression, Support Vector Machine and Gradient Boosted Decision Tree are considered. Final score is generated on the basis of similarity between text using ML techniques. The correctness and accuracy of student answers is calculated on the basis of resemblance with model answers, existence of keywords, Vague and contradictory answers, the grammatical syntax, synonyms and the context of the answer. Limitation of the system is that only similarity between text and keyword occurrence is checked.

A combination of techniques like Artificial Neural network, NLP and feed forward Back propagation was used in a system by [11] along with keyword similarity, length of answer to evaluate the student answer. As the initial stage Image Acquisition is performed to scan the text and extract the answer in digitized format later using pre-processing Binarization, noise removal, skew correction, and slant removal implemented text is filtered. Segmentation is applied on the images and sub images using threshold method, edge detection techniques etc. Each character is represented as a feature vector in the feature extraction stage, later these vector characters are classified and recognized using feed-forward back-propagation Neural Network. At the end machine-readable text is extracted which then calculates the length of answer text and NLP techniques will be applied. Similarity percentage is calculated between the keywords extracted and provided. Also, the length is considered for grading. Limitation is that keywords are only matched. Sentences are not checked for meaning. Grammatical mistakes are also ignored.

Another combination of techniques like Machine Learning and NLP was used by [12] for evaluating Subjective answers. Here the system uses modules like pre-processing, similarity measurement, model training, result predicting, machine learning and final result predicting. Pre-processing is done using NLP techniques, next comes the similarity measurement module where WDM, MNB, TF-IDF, WordNet, Word2Vec and Cosine similarity is used to calculate similarity between sentences. The result is predicted by combining with multinomial naive Bayes model, pre-processed data of answer is given as input for similarity measurement using Cosine and WDM. Distance of cosine, WDM along with thresholds like COS_LOWER, COS_UPPER, WDM_LOWER, WDM_UPPER, are considered for evaluation. If score > best_score then best score is updated, and if not then current comparison score is calculated. The machine learning model is fed with the result and processed. A pre-trained word2vec model from Google consisting of 300 dimensions of around 100 billion words vocabulary is used for this experiment. An accuracy of 88% is achieved with WDM and 86% accuracy with cosine similarity. Also, [13] has developed a system where evaluation is conducted using ML and NLP. Features are extracted from answer sheets and given as input to machine learning algorithms. The system performs tokenization, stop word removal, stemming which results in a set of words called keywords. Based on the occurrence of keywords in the answer, marks will be assigned to students. The score then is compared with the human graded score and error is analyzed, the kappa model is used to check the statistics. Evaluation Measures like Recall, Precision, Accuracy, and F-measure were used and an accuracy of 0.88 is obtained.

Machine Learning's BERT algorithm was used for grading and evaluating student answers written in Indonesian Language by [14]. The methodology was divided into 3 parts 1) Dataset Collection 2) Pre-processing 3) Grading Process. In the first part a dataset was created from 60 responses of students which included 10 short random questions out of 100. Teacher answers were also taken which were implemented for training purposes. The answers were bifurcated in 4 categories namely: true, True not incomplete, contradictory, and incorrect. The question context text was combined with answers and were tokenized using base-BERT-uncased. Later fine-tuning adapted deep learning process to separate tokens between question and answers where BERT was assigned task of grading short answers. Cohen's Kappa and Confusion Matrix are applied to check the consistency between automatic evaluation and human evaluation. Cohen's Kappa Coefficient created 0.75 value, whereas Confusion Matrix produced Precision of 0.94, Recall value as 0.96, F1 score as 0.95, and Specificity value as 0.76.

A system was also proposed earlier where Hindi answers are evaluated by [15]. In this system researchers have proposed an implementation to translate the answer in English before evaluating it. There are a wide range of rules that are employed to extract all possible sets of answers from Hindi text for the input question. The focus of the system was basically on four kinds of questions of type What, Where, How many, and what time. On analysis of the system, the overall efficiency of the system was found to be considerable. An average accuracy of 68% has been achieved in the process. Limitation: The efficiency of the algorithm needs to be improved. Also, in place of using static data sets this algorithm can be extended for dynamic data sets present over the internet.

Evaluation based on similarity of words, text, topic was performed by [16]. In this system the author has used 6 different techniques. First of all complex and compound sentences are converted to simple sentences using dependency structure-based technique and co-reference resolution is also performed. Number of sentence, Answer length in words, Average sentence length in words, No. of unique words, No. of spelling errors, No. of noun, verb, adjective, preposition, Average number of clauses per sentence are considered for similarity measurement. To check the word similarity TF-IDF and LSA are used. Then comes the topic modeling-based similarity where Text Rank algorithm is implemented where a sentence related graph is generated and similarity is measured when contents intersect each other. Key sentence are than selected based on highest score, later the key sentence answer and student sentence are compared which results in score based on three things, exact match, position-specific word-by-word matching, and position independent matching. Which is followed by sentence embedding and Answer similarity using InferSent (based on bidirectional LSTM). Potential subset of a sentence is calculated by one-to-one mapping of sentences. Also, additional sentences are identified and are scored on the basis of their correctness.

[17] proposed technique leverages the question to make a well-informed decision when grading and assigning suitable marks. To investigate the context of the question, new representations for the two responses (predicted answer and student's answer) were produced using the Cross-Attention approach. Here they have used the question as the query and the answer as both, the value and the key. Their response grading model contains two modules: the Representational module and the Grading module. The model's operation is similar to that of a Siamese network, in that the two representational modules provide an output vector, which the grading layer then uses to accurately grade the response. During the answer grading phase, the reference answer is used to generate an appropriate score for a student's answer. Two representations are generated so as to compute a score for each answer. These representations include a representation of the expected answer with respect to the question. It is by comparing these two representations that answers can be effectively scored. This is the first time a comprehensive end-to-end model has been constructed, with a fully linked neural network layer serving as the grading layer. The model performed with an exceptional accuracy of 64.4% and a within-1 accuracy of 95.88% using this architecture.

[18] has developed a Deep learning LSTM network that rates student answers using word weights that highlight significant words/phrases and a knowledge base (KB) of typical answers. It employs three modules: input representation and embedding, knowledge base selection, and representation fusion. The element-wise product of the KB-based weight matrix, the TF-IDF weight matrix, and the word encoding matrix yields the input representation layer. The embedding module creates embedding for the knowledge base and questions and saves them in two matrices (memory vectors). The knowledge base

selection module gets relevant information using these two memory vectors. The representation fusion module combines the embedding of the student answer with the selected facts from the memory vectors to forecast the output of the Bi-LSTM network. This technique has an overall accuracy percentage of 83.37% and may thus be used to supplement hand grading.

A Semi-open-ended short-answer question evaluating model [19] in which students express their subjective ideas based on some facts in their responses is proposed. CBOW is incorporated for domain-general information from Wikipedia and domain-specific knowledge from graded student short responses to develop an automated grading model for semi open-ended short-answer questions, and they produced word vectors to feed LSTM-based classifiers. The research shows that combining domain-general and domain-specific information enhances automated grading performance on semi-open-ended questions substantially. Using LSTM to exploit word sequence information enhanced grading accuracy as well.

3   A Systematic Review

Based on a thorough literature review of recent works in automatic answer grading, this part provides a systematic evaluation of the various research works, the methodologies and procedures used, and the results/outcomes thereof.

Table 1. Summary of literature review

Reference	Method	Feature	Accuracy
[3]	Machine learning and Ontology	Singular value Decomposition (SVD) for LSA is performed in MatLab. Word- Net is used for synonym search.By adding n-grams to the LSA package, GLSA is implemented. BLEU is also implemented	90% correlation with human performance
[4]	NLP and ANN	The student answers are evaluated using ANN for comparison and use NLP to check the grammatical mistakes	95% correlation with faculty evaluation
[5]	Machine learning, Artificial Intelligence, and Semantic analysis	Feature extraction using NLP and generation of weights for the answers of candidates using ANN	90%

(continued)

Table 1. (*continued*)

[6]	HPLSE, LSA	Singular value decomposition, cosine similarity and score calculation are followed. They have used 1440 samples in electronic form. Three performance measures are implied to analyse the effectiveness of the technique such as average score difference (ASD), Standard Deviation (SD) and a Pearson Correlation (PC) between computer assessor and Human Assessor	Pearson correlation human assessor and system is 0.76
[20]	NLP, Deep learning	Extracts keywords from image and then evaluates the answer with the use of NLP and Deep learning concepts	0.72
[21]	Siamese Bidirectional LSTM, GloVe	Reference and student answers both are taken as input and are converted to MAE give 0.65, pre-trained GloVe word vec- 0.89, 0.61 point tors for embedding a layer which generates 300 dimensions. Distance between reference answer and student answer is calculated and sigmoid function is applied	Pearson, RMSE, and accuracy
[22]	Machine learning concept wordNet graph	Ideal answer WordNet graph is compared with the student answer graph and a similarity is counted	RMSE as 0.31

(*continued*)

Table 1. (*continued*)

[23]	Deep Learning, BERT	Feature extraction architecture and fine-tuning architecture are used. Feature Extraction Model student answer and model answer are given as input to embedding vectors and later calculates and combines the result of dot product and absolute difference of the vectors.Fine Tuning Model is implements BERT along with linear Regression layer where the student and model answers are tokenized	Pearson correlation coefficient of 0.73
[24]	Multiway attention networks, Deep learning	They use transfer blocks and attention mechanisms to extract answer matching information and understand semantic meaning	88.99%
[25]	LSTM, Machine learning, RNN, D-DAS	The system uses deep descriptive answer system model to extract similarity between answers	73%
[26]	NLP and ANN	Shallow parsing is executed to get the relevant words only from the extracted answers. Answers are then classified based on similar of marks	95%
[7]	NLP, Concept graph and Fuzzy string	Keyword Similarity, Language score, Fuzzy String matching, followed by graph generation	–

(*continued*)

Table 1. (*continued*)

[8]	Transformation based language and Linear classifier	Checks the similarity between reference answer and system generated answer	74.7%
[9]	TF-IDF and KNN algorithms of Machine Learning	Keywords are extracted from the student answer and using KNN the score of the answer will be predicted based on number of words matched	–
[10]	NLP, NLTK, TFI-DF	Student documented answers are evaluated based on models like Naive Base, Logistic Regression, Support Vector Machine and Gradient Boosted Decision Tree. The correctness and accuracy of student answers is calculated on the basis of resemblance with model answers, existence of keywords, Vague and contradictory answers, the grammatical syntax, synonyms and the context of the answer	–

(*continued*)

Table 1. (*continued*)

| [11] | ANN, NLP, Feed back propagation | Text is filtered after image capture, noise reduction, skew correction, and slant removal. Images and subimages are segmented using edge detection techniques, threshold methods, etc. The feature extraction stage uses feature vectors to represent each character. Later, a feed-forward back-propagation neural network is used to categorise and identify these vector characteristics | – |
| [12] | Machine Learning, Word net, Word Mover's Distance, bayes (MNB), and (TF-IDF) | This study suggests an innovative method that makes use of tools like Wordnet, cosine similarity, machine learning, and natumultinomial naive ral language processing. Answers are assessed using solution statements, and a machine learning model is developed to anticipate marks. Overall, the results indicate that WMD outperforms cosine similarity | – |

(*continued*)

Table 1. (*continued*)

[13]	Machine learning and NLP	Features are extracted from 0.8 answer sheets and given as input to machine learning algorithms for tokenization, stopword removal and keyword extraction. Based on the occurrence of keywords in the answer, marks will be assigned to students	0.88
[14]	BERT, fine tuning, Deep learning	In this system the answers were bifurcated in 4 categories namely: true, True not incomplete, contradictory, and incorrect. Later fine-tuning adapted the deep learning process to separate tokens between question and answers where BERT was assigned the task of grading short answers	Cohen's Kappa Coefficient = 0.75 Confusion Matrix produced Precision = 0.94
[15]	NLP	After translating answers from hindi to english there are a wide range of rules that are employed to extract all possible sets of answers from Hindi text. The focus of the system was basically on four kinds of questions of type What, Where, How many, and what time	68%

(*continued*)

Table 1. (*continued*)

[16]	LSTM, TF-IDF	Complex and compound sentences are reduced to simple sentences in this system by applying a dependency structure-based method, and coreference resolution is also accomplished. The key sentence is chosen based on the highest score, and the key sentence response and student phrase are then compared, yielding a score based on three factors: exact match, position-specific word-by-word matching, and position independent matching	78.44%
[17]	SBERT,Cross Attention,feed forward neural network	The evaluation is done in 2 phase the representation module and the Grading module. In representation module cross attention layer and feed forward neural network is applied. And in Grading module deep learning training is used	95.88%
[18]	Deep Learning using LSTM-RNN	Deep learning LSTM networks judge student replies accuracy rate of using word weights to favour keywords/answers and KB composed of conventional answers	The overall this system is 83.37%

(*continued*)

Table 1. (*continued*)

[19]	Deep Learning using LSTM network	The CBOW algorithm is used to manufacture features from domain-general and domain-specific sources.A probabilistic score vector is produced by the LSTM classifier	–

4 Discussion

In current history, there has been a rise in research on the subject of automated response grading, particularly in the automatic grading of brief responses. In light of the Covid-19 crisis and the extensive use of online classrooms and exams, this research has become more pertinent. We discovered that works in understanding the quality applied either a) similarity measures that use both basic and enhanced feature extraction for similarity measure and semantic similarity, or b) machine learning and deep learning networks like LSTM. Our study of the literature discovered that the majority of research in automated grading uses non-standard, self-generated datasets. Experiments using standard datasets improve model comparability. Techniques and procedures are evaluated in a realistic and meaningful manner. Although standard datasets such as Mohler et al. and SemEval datasets were utilized, their usage was limited, and the majority of the research relied on datasets created from internal sources such as school/college/university level evaluations.

From comparing student responses with reference responses, we discover that similarity measures (distance-based algorithms) produce favorable results for short, closed-ended responses. When students are asked to express their own opinions via open-ended questions or replies with fewer keywords, these strategies do not produce the best outcomes. For these queries, ML approaches in conjunction with KB display improved results. We think that classifying the questions into short/long and open/closed would help to focus the automatic grading process. For open-ended, lengthy queries, we advise applying summarizing techniques at the pre-processing step to get rid of redundant or similar content. Not all keywords or concepts are equally relevant to a given solution. Therefore, weighting words according to pre-established criteria or according to domain-specific KB can aid in improving grading performance. Our analysis suggests that more research on weighing methods is necessary.

5 Conclusions and Future Work

Colossal amount of research is being conducted for engineering an adequate model for automated evaluation of answers in English.

Summarizing the finding of our survey:

– One word answers, or simple answers are evaluated.

- A chief complication in the evolution of a QAS is dataset for regional languages.
- Utmost Question Answering Systems bank on smaller sized datasets.
- A reasonable judgment among these systems is tricky since they use individual data sets

Miscellaneous type of work has been done using sundry techniques like machine learning, Natural Language Processing, Neural Networks, Ontology, deep learning. Algorithms like Naive Bayes, LSTM, BERT, Li near regression, Logistic regression, KNN, K-mean, SVM, clustering, LSI (Latent Semantic Indexing), Text Rank, TF-IDF, RAKE, Bag of words, Bilingual Evaluation Understudy (BLEU) and many more have been used. It has been observed that BERT, Naive Bayes, LSTM, Ontology have given accuracy ranging from 85–90. Evaluating answers by string matching, or keyword matching lack in assessment as they do not check the grammatical mistakes, spelling mistakes, also the occurrence of sentence may vary in student answer. A system which checks all of the above mentioned drawbacks along with the grading accurately the answers still is a subject of research. Also, we can observe that very little work has been done in Indian languages like Hindi, Gujarati, Tamil, Marathi. Automated evaluation of answers written in local languages are evaluated by translating them to English, Translating systems are not ideal for long complicated sentences. A proper technique needs to be proposed where answers can be evaluated in the language itself. Grading of the answers is also required to be designed along with giving feedback to the students.

References

1. Shabatura, J.: Using Bloom's Taxonomy to Write Effective Learning Outcomes (2022). https://tips.uark.edu/usingblooms-taxonomy/
2. Yagnik, B.: Gujarat board teachers get Rs 6.50 per paper for examining answer sheets (2017). https://timesofindia.indiatimes.com/city/ahmedabad/gujarat-board-teachers-get-rs-6-50-per-paper-for-examining-answer-sheets/articleshow/57635117. Accessed 16 Apr 2022
3. Devi, M., Syamala, H., Mittal: Machine learning techniques with ontology for subjective answer evaluation (2016)
4. Lakshmi, V., Ramesh, V.: Evaluating students' descriptive answers using natural language processing and artificial neural networks. Int. J. Creative Res. Thoughts (IJCRT) 5, 3168–3173 (2017)
5. Patil, T.: Automatic assessment of descriptive answers for online examination using semantic Anal. J. Gujarat Res. Soc. 21(5) (2019)
6. Kaur, A., Kumar, M.S.: High precision latent semantic evaluation for descriptive answer assessment. J. Comput. Sci. (2018)
7. Bagaria, V.: An intelligent system for evaluation of descriptive answers. In: 3rd International Conference on Intelligent Sustainable Systems (ICISS), pp. 19–24 (2020)
8. Vu, T., Moschitti, A.: AVA: an automatic evaluation approach to question answering systems (2020)
9. Jadhavrao, R., Kulkarni, A., Deshpande, U.: Online score prediction system for descriptive answers. Mukta Shabd J. (2020)
10. Sanuvala, G., Sameen, F.S.: A study of automated evaluation of student's examination paper using machine learning techniques. In: 2021 International Conference on Computing, Communication, and Intelligent Systems (ICCCIS), pp. 1049–1054 (2021)

11. Bharambe, N., Barhate, P., Dhannawat, P.: Automatic answer evaluation using machine learning. Int. J. Inf. Technol. (IJIT) **7**(2) (2021)

12. Bashir, M.: Farrukh: subjective answers evaluation using machine learning and natural language processing. IEEE Access **9**, 158972–158983 (2021)

13. Tanwar, V.: Machine learning based automatic answer checker imitating human way of answer checking. Int. J. Eng. Res. Technol. (IJERT) **10**(12) (2021)

14. Wijaya, M.C.: Automatic short answer grading system in Indonesian language using BERT machine learning. Intell. Artif. **35**(6), 503–509 (2021)

15. Sahu, S., Vasnik, N., Roy, D.: Prashnottar: a Hindi question answering system. Int. J. Comput. Sci. Inf. Technol. **4**, 149–158 (2012)

16. Saha, S., Kumar, D., Rao, C.H.: Development of a practical system for computerized evaluation of descriptive answers of middle school level students. Interact. Learn. Environ. **30**(2), 215–228 (2022)

17. Oasis, A.S.: Question-centric evaluation of descriptive answers using attention-based architecture. In: 2022 12th International Conference on Cloud Computing, pp. 20–25 (2022)

18. Yang, S.: Deep automated text scoring model based on memory network. In: 2020 International Conference on Computer Vision, Image and Deep Learning (CVIDL), pp. 480–484 (2020)

19. Zhang, L.: An automatic short-answer grading model for semi-open-ended questions. Interact. Learn. Environ. **30**(1), 177–190 (2022)

20. Rowtula, V., Oota, S.R., Jawahar, C.V.: Towards automated evaluation of handwritten assessments. In: International Conference on Document Analysis and Recognition (ICDAR), pp. 426–433 (2019)

21. Prabhudesai, A., Ta, D.: Automatic short answer grading using Siamese bidirectional LSTM based regression. In: IEEE International Conference on Engineering, pp. 1–6 (2019)

22. Vij, S., Tayal, D., Jain, A.: A machine learning approach for automated evaluation of short answers using text similarity based on WordNet graphs. Wireless Pers. Commun. **111**, 1271–1282 (2020)

23. Awatzki, J., Schlippe, T., Benner-Wickner, M.: Deep learning techniques for automatic short answer grading: predicting scores for English and German answers. In: Cheng, E.C.K., Koul, R.B., Wang, T., Yu, X. (eds) Artificial Intelligence in Education: Emerging Technologies, Models and Applications. Lecture Notes on Data Engineering and Communications Technologies, vol 104. Springer, Singapore (2022). https://doi.org/10.1007/978-981-16-7527-0_5

24. Liu, T., Ding, W., Wang, Z., Tang, J., Huang, G.Y., Liu, Z.: Automatic short answer grading via multiway attention networks. In: Isotani, S., Millán, E., Ogan, A., Hastings, P., McLaren, B., Luckin, R. (eds) AIED 2019. LNCS (LNAI), vol. 11626, pp. 169–173. Springer, Cham (2019). https://doi.org/10.1007/978-3-030-23207-8_32

25. George, N., Sijimol, P.J., Varghese, S.M.: Grading descriptive answer scripts using deep learning. Int. J. Innov. Technol. Explor. Eng. (IJI- TEE) **8**(5) (2019)

26. Nandini, V., Maheswari, P.U.: Automatic assessment of descriptive answers in online examination systems using semantic relational features. J. Supercomput. **76**, 4430–4448 (2020)

Blockchain Federated Learning Framework for Privacy-Preservation

K. M. Sameera[(✉)], P. Vinod, K. A. Rafidha Rehiman, P.N. Jifhna,
and Sandra Sebastian

Department of Computer Applications, Cochin University of Science and Technology,
Kochi, Kerala, India
{sameerakm,vinod.p,rafidharehimanka}@cusat.ac.in

Abstract. Real-time data for machine learning introduced challenges, especially security and privacy issues, while sharing critical private data. The proposed unified federated learning system threaded with blockchain technology is a solution for personal communication over decentralized networks and challenges related to traditional machine learning. Federated Learning (FL) ensures the client's local data privacy. The blockchain part of the system helps the server to authenticate local models from the client and introduces a notion of trust. FL-based Logistic Regression, Support Vector Machine (SVM), and Artificial Neural Network (ANN) models have experimented on two different domains: network traffic and healthcare. To assess the system's validity, we have used three benchmark datasets-KDDCUP99, NSL-KDD, and Pima Indians Diabetes Database. Numerical results demonstrated that the proposed approach is efficient for reliable and private communication over a decentralized network. For KDDCUP99 and NSL-KDD dataset achieves 99% and for Pima Indians Diabetes achieves 65.88% accuracy using the Fl-based ANN model. Additionally, we evaluate the performance of the FL model integrated with blockchain for privacy and security.

Keywords: Federated learning · Blockchain · Privacy · Logistic regression · Support Vector Machine · Artificial Neural Network

1 Introduction

Data privacy is a critical issue in multiple domains such as corporate, education, healthcare, supply chain, IoT, etc.; at the same time, data is essential for machine learning and artificial intelligence-based research. Machine learning training poses several privacy risks to participant's data when it is shared in the public domain for processing. Privacy standards are continuously emerging to protect users' private data in ever-growing digital environments. Privacy preservation mechanisms are widely used to protect confidential data locally to avoid leaking sensitive information. The application of privacy preservation techniques using federated learning has recently gained much popularity and shares only machine learning models instead of sensitive data and user profiles. In 2016, Google introduced [1] Federated learning, an improved version of distributed machine learning

S. Rajagopal et al. (Eds.): ASCIS 2022, CCIS 1760, pp. 250–261, 2022.
https://doi.org/10.1007/978-3-031-23095-0_18

approach that facilitates collaborative processes by model building without disclosing sensitive data. Federated learning improves the accuracy of a model by customization and personalization in real time to offer trusted solutions and local data protection.

Integrating blockchain with federated learning gained the attention of researchers to utilize blockchain characteristics such as decentralization, anonymity, and trust for privacy preservation. The distributed ledger concept in the blockchain is unchangeable if appropriately configured and offers a high level of security, transparency, immutability, and tamper resistance.

In this study, we execute a proof of work for integrating federated learning and blockchain technology for preserving privacy. We used three publicly available datasets from different domains to experimentally prove that the integration of FL and blockchain is promising for security. These datasets are utilized for client-side local training with FL-based Logistic regression, SVM, and ANN as classifiers, and measure the performance based on accuracy and f1 score. The aggregated results together with a cryptographic hash value are stored in a blockchain for future reference and to prove the integrity of the information.

The following are the key contributions of this reach paper:

1. We proposed a federated learning framework threaded with blockchain for private communication over decentralized networks to ensure privacy.
2. Design and implement the federated learning system and use Flask server with postman APIs to create the blockchain network.
3. Finally, we evaluated the effectiveness of the suggested framework using the benchmark datasets KDDCUP99, NSL3-KDD, and Pima Indians Diabetes.

Organization of the Paper: The related works of blockchain and federated learning are described in Sect. 2. Section 2 elaborates on the proposed architecture. The suggested model's performance evaluation and results utilizing various performance measures are covered in Sect. 4. Section 5 concludes the work with recommendations for further enhancement.

2 Related Works

This part discusses the related research on federated learning, blockchain technology, and integrated solutions using FL and Blockchain.

Federated Learning: Federated learning is a communication-efficient model, and it trains the model across many clients in a decentralized manner. Instead of sharing sensitive data, the learning parameters of each participant are exchanged. The central aggregator of FL initially distributes the initial global model to each participant for local training, and each participant trains the initial model with its own local data. Then the participant shared the local model with the central aggregator for aggregation of the local models. The central aggregator distributes the new model to each participant, and the procedure was repeated until the global model converged. In FL, each participant carried out the entire training procedure cooperatively, reducing data transfer and assuring privacy concerns over personal information. The authors in [2] developed a paradigm for covid19 diagnosis using a cluster-based collaborative federated learning system without sharing relevant data or information on remote health-care institutions. Using a multi-modal ML model, they examined the system on X-ray and ultrasound images from various sources. The authors in [3] outlined a strategy for an intrusion detection approach using FL where each IoT device generated data is trained using the global model and communicates the model parameters to the server for aggregation. They investigated the experiment using the NSL-KDD dataset and obtained an accuracy of 83.09%. The authors of [4] used the FEDPAD algorithm in an FL scenario to detect anomalies in network traffic. The researchers extracted multidimensional features from session and packet levels, as well as smoothed the data using the Grubbs criteria. Their proposed system outperforms the ARIMA approach and Autoencoder with the RNN algorithm. The authors in [5] use medical DP-GAN to privately generate diverse patient data to solve the data availability issues and protect the training sample's privacy.

Blockchain-based Systems: Blockchain is an emerging technology that permits transactions in a chain of blocks and addresses security and privacy concerns in several domains such as healthcare, supply chain, smart cities, education sector, and many more [6–8]. Singh et al. suggested a BlockIoTIntelligence design by fusing AI with blockchain to establish a scaled and secured IoT with device intelligence, edge intelligence, cloud intelligence, and fog intelligence [9]. The authors in [10] proposed a framework for the healthcare industry to achieve privacy and security for patient data in the electronic healthcare record system using blockchain technology. With the help of blockchain technology, Makhdoom et al. [11] invented the PrivySharing technique for exchanging smart city data in a safe and private manner. According to their study, a multi-Ch blockchain system balances better than a single-Ch blockchain solution. In [12], Lizcano et al. assessed the potential of blockchain in the higher education sector. They employed distributed ledger technology to securely exchange educational materials, manage transactions, and assess training centers based on reputational capital.

Integration of Blockchain and FL: Integration of Blockchain and FL can provide integrity of trained models, thus preserving the privacy and security of the service. The authors in [13] employ a fuzzy hash function applied to the model parameters and store the hash value on the blockchain to protect FL algorithms in IoT systems. Blockchain-based threaded federated learning with multi-agent system architecture for IoMT was proposed in [14], but the time required for the execution was too high. The authors of [15] demonstrated a blockchain-based system utilized in the education sector to anticipate future job opportunities for students after graduation. They also provide the ability to verify the employee's recorded information, and students can exchange information with the e-portfolios platform. In [16], Qi et al. proposed an FL framework with blockchain that secures urban traffic while simultaneously defending against poisoning threats. Furthermore, they employed differential privacy to ensure the privacy of vehicle data and adapted the GRU design to the FL system to attain accurate Traffic Flow Prediction. The authors in [17] proposed an FL that uses blockchain technology to detect COVID-19 using CT scans. They employed data normalization approaches and segmented them using a capsule network to efficiently do classification while preserving the privacy of the medical data.

3 Proposed Methodology

This section elaborates on a unified federated learning system integrated with blockchain technology to guarantee confidentiality and privacy in a decentralized network effectively. Figure 1 illustrates the architecture of the proposed approach, consisting of two key components: Federated learning and blockchain. More importantly, the proposed model is developed using a federation of participants to collaboratively train a global model without sharing participant's local information. The following steps constitute the proposed system's workflow:

1. **Initialization Phase:** During this phase, the federated server creates an initial global model, distributes it among each participant, and then waits for updates from the participants.
2. **Local Model updation phase:** After receiving the initial global model, each participant trains the model using pre-processed local data to create a new local model and update the information to the server.
3. **Global Updation Phase:** The federated server aggregates the local models received from the participants to generate a new, upgraded global model using fedAvg [18]. Following that, the federated server distributes the new updated global model to the participants, who utilize the new global model for training. The procedure is repeated until the termination condition is fulfilled, which happens when the federation round expires or the model converges.
4. **Block Generation Phase:** Following a successful federation round, the federated server mines a block in the blockchain, and stores model parameters, timestamps, performance matrices, and the hash value. Every block has a (1) timestamp that shows the time it was mined, (2) a hash value that is the preceding block's hash encrypted with SHA256, (3) Nonce, used for computing the proof of work, and (4) transactions, which include the information about the algorithm used for training along with the parameter and record the performance of the system. Further, participants can use this global model stored in a block after verification to ensure privacy and integrity.

4 Performance Evaluation

4.1 Datasets

WE evaluated the performance of the various models on three benchmark datasets: KDDCUP99, NSL-KDD, and Pima Indians Diabetes.

1. KDDCUP1999: Researchers have extensively utilized this dataset for analyzing anomaly detection in network traffic [19]. It contains about 49,00,000 rows with 41 attributes and five labels named normal, Denial of Service Attacks (DoS), User to Root Attacks (U2R), Remote to Local Attacks (R2L), and Probing Attacks.

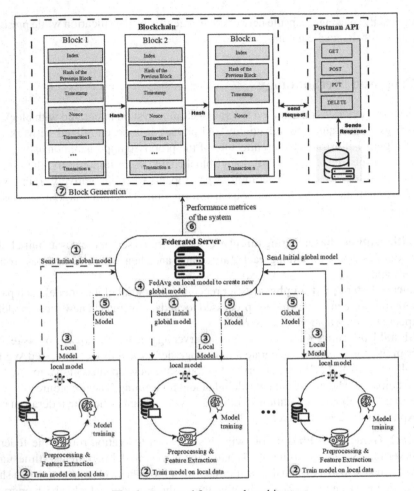

Fig. 1. Proposed framework architecture

2. NSL-KDD: This dataset [20] is a modified version of the KDDCUP1999 dataset, including internet traffic records. The dataset consists of 1,074,992 records, and 43 attributes, and each sample is classified as either an attack type or as normal.
3. Pima Indians Diabetes: The dataset is provided by the NIDDK [21], in which the database aims to diagnose whether a patient is a diabetic or not. The database consists of 768 records and 9 attributes and a class either diabetes or non-diabetes.

4.2 Simulation Setup

The proposed models experimented using PySyft and PyTorch on an Intel 8-core i9 processor running at 3.70 GHz with 32 GB of RAM.

Table 1. Simulation parameter setting

Parameter	Value
Total number of participants	$n = 2$
Number of participants for aggregation	$k = 2$
Federation round	$T = 20$ or $T = 100$
Optimizer	SGD
Learning rate	$\alpha = .01$
Batch size	$B = 100$ or $B = 1000$

Federated Learning Setup: To examine the effectiveness of the proposed model, we consider the number of participants $n = 2$, one federated server, and the selected participants for aggregation $k = 2$. We followed an IID data distribution (the total training data is equally randomly distributed among all the participants). We performed the preprocessing steps to minimize the system's computational complexity by replacing the categorical feature with numerical values and eliminating duplicate instances. Then, feature extraction techniques extract the relevant attributes and divide them into training, and test sets with a ratio of 8:2. Eight features are selected from the Pima Indians Diabetes dataset, and 33 different features are selected from the KDDCU99 and NSL-KDD datasets. The number of federated rounds for the KDDCUP99 and NSL-KDD datasets is set to $T = 20$ and Batch size $B = 1000$. For the Pima Indians Diabetes dataset, we use $T = 100$ and Batch size $B = 100$. Table 1 summarises all the parameters used in our simulations.

Initially, the federated server is empowered to select two participants for learning and share the global model. The federated server generates an architecture based on FL-based Logistic Regression, SVM, and ANN models and used FedAvg to aggregate the models.

Table 2 summarises all the model-specific hyperparameters used in our simulations. For the Pima Indians diabetes dataset, the FL-based ANN model contains eight inputs, 20 neurons in the hidden layer, and two output layers. For the KDDCUP99 it is 33 inputs, 20 neurons in the hidden layer, and 23 outputs. For the NSL-KDD dataset, follow the same simulation setup of the KDDCUP99 dataset for the FL-based ANN model except for the last layer which contains 2 neutrons. For each layer, we use ReLu as the activation function. For the FL- based SVM model, we utilize the kernel type 'rbf' and the default settings for all other parameters. For the FL-based Logistics regression, we set $C = 1.0$, $penalty =' l2'$, and the default settings for all other parameters.

Blockchain Creation Setup: We used a Python-based flask framework to simulate the proposed blockchain network. By mapping endpoints to Python functions, the Flask framework enables users to interface with the blockchain network using HTTP requests made with the POST and GET methods. The Postman application programming interface (API) tool simulates endpoints for blockchain APIs. The Postman API mining method is

Table 2. Model-specific hyperparameter settings

Dataset	Model	Hyperparameters
KDDCUP99 NSL-KDD Pima Indians diabetes	Logistic regression	C = 1.0 penalty = 'l2'
KDDCUP99 NSL-KDD Pima Indians diabetes	SVM	gamma = 'scale' kernel = 'rbf' C = 1.0
KDDCUP99	ANN	Layer 1: 33 × 20 Layer 2: 20 × 20 Layer 3: 20 × 23
NSL-KDD	ANN	Layer 1: 33 × 20 Layer 2: 20 × 20 Layer 3: 20 ×2
Pima Indians diabetes	ANN	Layer 1: 8 × 20 Layer 2: 20 × 20 Layer 3: 20 × 2

used to accomplish block generation requirements. To get information, GET methods are used, while POST methods are used to add information. The blockchain's Flask server receives the request for block creation and publishes the transaction in each block. The dataset used, FL training classifier, server global model accuracy, and f1- score are recorded in each block as a transaction. All functions employed in this research are accessed using the URL http://localhost:5000/ followed by the function name. We employ different methods, such as creating a new block, calculating the proof of work, and validating the chain on the network.

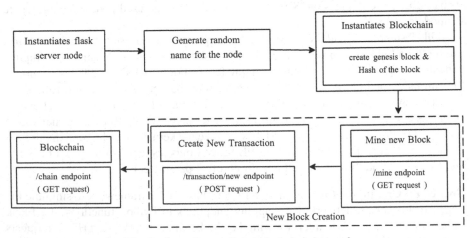

Fig. 2. Steps for creating a blockchain network

Steps for creating a blockchain using the flask server are shown in Fig. 2. To create a blockchain network, create a flask server node and generate a random name for the server. The blockchain is then instantiated, and a genesis block and hash of the block are created. We established a postman API to interact with Blockchain nodes. Following the execution of the POST request to the '/transaction/new' router of the Flask server, creates new transactions into the current block and mine a new block using the '/mine' router. Miners then use PoW consensus to validate the transaction and add it to the blockchain. The '/chain' router returns the complete list of blockchain instances along with the block length.

4.3 Evaluation Metrics

This section discussed the evaluation metrics to validate the system's performance such as Accuracy and F1-Score.

Table 3. Evaluation of the performance of proposed model

Dataset	Accuracy			F1-Score		
	Logistics regression	SVM	ANN	Logistics regression	SVM	ANN
KDDCUP99	97.95%	97.28%	99%	97.09%	98%	99.81%
NSL-KDD	84.95%	86.05%	99%	85%	86%	99.81%
Pima Indians Diabetes	65.88%	64.93%	65.88%	66%	65%	66%

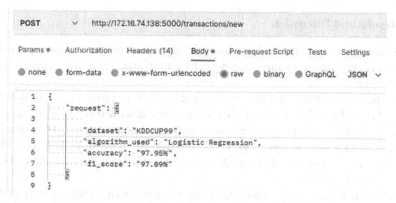

```
POST        ⌄    http://172.16.74.138:5000/transactions/new

Params ●   Authorization   Headers (14)   Body ●   Pre-request Script   Tests   Settings

● none   ● form-data   ● x-www-form-urlencoded   ● raw   ● binary   ● GraphQL   JSON ⌄

1  {
2       "request": {
3
4           "dataset": "KDDCUP99",
5           "algorithm_used": "Logistic Regression",
6           "accuracy": "97.95%",
7           "f1_score": "97.89%"
8       }
9  }
```

Fig. 3. A POST method request made to generate a new transaction using '/transaction/new' router.

Accuracy (ACC): Ratio of the number of accurate predictions to all of the classifier's predictions. The formula states as:

$$ACC = \frac{TP + TN}{TP + TN + FP + FN} \tag{1}$$

Precision: It is the percentage of true positive samples among those labeled as positive by the model. The formula states as:

$$Precision = \frac{TP}{TP + FP} \tag{2}$$

Recall The ratio of Positive samples accurately categorized as Positive to the total number of Positive samples is used to determine recall. The recall is mathematically expressed as follows:

$$Recall = \frac{TP}{TP + FN} \tag{3}$$

where TP denotes a true positive, TN represents a true negative, FP indicates it as a false positive, and FN defines it as a false negative.

F1-Score (F1): Calculated using the harmonic mean of the recall and precision of the model. The mathematical equation is as follows:

$$F1 = \frac{2 \times TP}{2 \times TP + FP + FN} \tag{4}$$

4.4 Results and Discussion

In this section, simulation findings from the proposed framework are discussed. To evaluate the performance of the model we employed evaluation metrics such as Accuracy and F1-Score.

The performance comparison of different models is summarized in Table 3. As observed from Table 3, in the KDDCUP dataset, the federated server's global accuracy for 96.42% in FL-based logistic regression with an F1-score of 97%. The accuracy and F1-score for FL-based logistic regression achieved by the NSLKDD are 84.95% and 85%, respectively. For Pima Indians Diabetes Dataset it reaches an accuracy of 65.88% with an F1-score of 66%.

For the FL-based SVM, the KDDCUP dataset achieved a global accuracy of 97.28% and an F1-score of 98%, it is 84.95% and 86% respectively for the NSLKDD dataset. For the Pima Indians diabetes dataset, the global server accuracy and F1-score in FL-based SVM achieve 64.93% and 65% respectively. In the FL-based ANN model, the KDD and NSL-KDD dataset got the accuracy and the F1-score as 99% and 99.81%. For the Pima diabetes dataset, the accuracy and the F1-score are achieved as 65.88% and 66%.

```
1     {
2         "index": 2,
3         "message": "New Block Mined",
4         "nonce": 45300,
5         "prev_hash": "77ed879b6511d9f1f999e97459a12139472665fa52d3a8a038ada8906f66ee68",
6         "timestamp": "2022-10-27 02:35:19.815659",
7         "transactions": [
8             {
9                 "algorithm_used": "Logistic Regression",
10                "dataset": "KDDCUP99",
11                "model accuracy": "97.95%",
12                "model f1_score": "97.89%"
13            },
14            {
15                "algorithm_used": "Logistic Regression",
16                "dataset": "NSL-KDD",
17                "model accuracy": "84.95%",
18                "model f1_score": "85%"
19            },
20            {
21                "algorithm_used": "Logistic Regression",
22                "dataset": "Pima Indians Diabetes",
23                "model accuracy": "65.88%",
24                "model f1_score": "66%"
25            }
26        ]
27    }
```

Fig. 4. A GET method request made to mine the block using the '/mine' router.

```
62            {
63                "index": 4,
64                "nonce": 16868,
65                "prev_hash": "6bff650cb12cc42ae4b582a438141d89dbe593c63d18d41e08fda5522cc8a4d1",
66                "timestamp": "2022-10-27 02:42:54.021318",
67                "transactions": [
68                    {
69                        "algorithm_used": "ANN",
70                        "dataset": "KDDCUP99 ",
71                        "model accuracy": "99%",
72                        "model f1_score": "99.81%"
73                    },
74                    {
75                        "algorithm_used": "ANN",
76                        "dataset": "NSL-KDD ",
77                        "model accuracy": "99%",
78                        "model f1_score": "99.81%"
79                    },
80                    {
81                        "algorithm_used": "ANN",
82                        "dataset": "Pima Indians Diabetes ",
83                        "model accuracy": "65.88%",
84                        "model f1_score": "66%"
85                    }
86                ]
87            }
88        ],
89        "length": 4
90    }
```

Fig. 5. A response from the flask server '/chain' router using the GET method for FL-based ANN models

According to this table, we concluded that, compared to other models, FL- based ANN attained the highest accuracy and F1-Score on the KDDCUP99 and NSL-KDD datasets. The table shows that for the Pima Indians Diabetes dataset, both the FL-based Logistic Regression model and the FL-based ANN model attain the maximum performance.

The Postman API mining method is used to fulfill block generation requirements. Figure 3 shows the POST method request is made to add a new transaction in the block. Figure 4 demonstrates the GET method requests made to the '/mine' router. The '/chain' router returns the complete list of blockchain instances along with the block length. Figure 5 demonstrate the response from the Flask server's'/chain' router leveraging postman APIs and the GET method with FL-based ANN models.

5 Conclusion

In this article, we proposed a unified federated learning system integrated with blockchain technology to guarantee the confidentiality and privacy of the distributed network effectively. The illustrative numerical results demonstrated that our blockchain-enabled data-sharing solution enhances security during the data-sharing process. Furthermore, incorporating federated learning offers a viable solution to enable secure and intelligent data exchange. The proposed framework's performance is assessed using three benchmark datasets and can allow the model parameters to be traceable and tamper-proof. In accordance with the examination of the results, the FL-based ANN model achieved the highest accuracy and result of each model stored in the blockchain network. For KD- DCUP99 and NSL-KDD dataset achieves 99% and for Pima Indians Diabetes achieves 65.88% accuracy using the Fl-based ANN model. In the future, we plan to develop a more sophisticated incentive scheme by utilizing a private blockchain network.

References

1. Yang, Q., Liu, Y., Chen, T., Tong, Y.: Federated machine learning: Concept and applications. ACM Trans. Intell. Syst. Technol. (TIST) **10**(2), 1–19 (2019)
2. Qayyum, A., Ahmad, K., Ahsan, M.A., Al-Fuqaha, A., Qadir, J.: Collaborative federated learning for healthcare: Multi-modal covid-19 diagnosis at the edge. arXiv preprint arXiv: 2101.07511 (2021)
3. Rahman, S.A., Tout, H., Talhi, C., Mourad, A.: Internet of things intrusion detection: centralized, on-device, or federated learning? IEEE Netw. **34**(6), 310–317 (2020)
4. Pei, J., Zhong, K., Jan, M.A., Li, J.: Personalized federated learning framework for network traffic anomaly detection. Comput. Netw. **209**, 108906 (2022)
5. Zhang, L., Shen, B., Barnawi, A., Xi, S., Kumar, N., Wu, Y.: FedDPGAN: federated differentially private generative adversarial networks framework for the detection of COVID-19 pneumonia. Inf. Syst. Front. **23**(6), 1403–1415 (2021). https://doi.org/10.1007/s10796-021-10144-6
6. Brisimi, T.S., Chen, R., Mela, T., Olshevsky, A., Paschalidis, I.C., Shi, W.: Federated learning of predictive models from federated electronic health records. Int. J. Med. Inform. **112**, 59–67 (2018)
7. Makani, S., Pittala, R., Alsayed, E., Aloqaily, M., Jararweh, Y.: A survey of blockchain applications in sustainable and smart cities. Cluster Comput. 1–22 (2022). https://doi.org/10.1007/s10586-022-03625-z

8. Rahman, M.S., Islam, M.A., Uddin, M.A., Stea, G.: A survey of blockchain-based IoT eHealthcare: Applications, research issues, and challenges. Internet Things, 100551 (2022)
9. Singh, S.K., Rathore, S., Park, J.H.:Blockiotintelligence: A blockchain-enabled intelligent IoT architecture with artificial intelligence. Future Gen. Comput. Syst. **110**, 721–743 (2020)
10. Tanwar, S., Parekh, K., Evans, R.: Blockchain-based electronic healthcare record system for healthcare 4.0 applications. J. Inf. Secur. Appl. **50**, 102407 (2020)
11. Makhdoom, I., Zhou, I., Abolhasan, M., Lipman, J., Ni, W.: PrivySharing: a blockchain-based framework for privacy-preserving and secure data sharing in smart cities. Comput. Secur. **88**, 101653 (2020)
12. Lizcano, D., Lara, J.A., White, B., Aljawarneh, S.: Blockchain-based approach to create a model of trust in open and ubiquitous higher education. J. Comput. High. Educ. **32**(1), 109–134 (2020)
13. Devrim, U., Hammoudeh, M., Khan, M.A., Abuarqoub, A., Epiphaniou, G., Hamila, R.: Integration of federated machine learning and blockchain for the provision of secure big data analytics for Internet of Things. Comput. Secur. **109**, 102393 (2021)
14. Połap, D., Srivastava, G., Keping, Y.: Agent architecture of an intelligent medical system based on federated learning and blockchain technology. J. Inf. Secur. Appl. **58**, 102748 (2021)
15. Shah, D., Patel, D., Adesara, J., Hingu, P., Shah, M.: Integrating machine learning and blockchain to develop a system to veto the forgeries and provide efficient results in education sector. Visual Comput. Ind. Biomed. Art **4**(1), 1–13 (2021). https://doi.org/10.1186/s42492-021-00084-y
16. Qi, Y., Hossain, M.S., Nie, J., Li., X.: Privacy- preserving blockchain-based federated learning for traffic flow prediction. Future Gen. Comput. Syst. **117**, 328–337 (2021)
17. Kumar, R., et al.: Blockchain-federated-learning and deep learning models for covid-19 detection using CT imaging. IEEE Sens. J. **21**(14), 16301–16314 (2021)
18. McMahan, B., Moore, E., Ramage, D., Hampson, S., y Arcas, B.A.:Communication-efficient learning of deep networks from decentralized data. In: Artificial Intelligence and Statistics, pp. 1273–1282. PMLR (2017)
19. Tavallaee, M., Bagheri, E., Lu, W., Ghorbani, A.: A detailed analysis of the KDD CUP 99 data set. submitted to second. In: IEEE Symposium on Computational Intelligence for Security and Defense Applications (CISDA) (2009)
20. Nsl-kdd data set for network-based intrusion detection systems. http://nsl.cs.unb.ca/NSL-KDD/, March (2009)
21. Smith, J.W., Everhart, J.E., Dickson, W.C., Knowler, W.C., Johannes, R.S.: Using the ADAP learning algorithm to forecast the onset of diabetes mellitus. In: Proceedings of the Symposium on Computer Applications and Medical Care, pp. 261–265. IEEE Computer Society Press (1988)

Path Planning and Static Obstacle Avoidance for Unmanned Aerial Systems

Pranshav Gajjar[1], Virensinh Dodia[1], Siddharth Mandaliya[1(✉)], Pooja Shah[2], Vijay Ukani[1], and Madhu Shukla[3]

[1] Institute of Technology, Nirma University, Ahmedabad, India
20bic048@nirmauni.ac.in
[2] School of Technology, Pandit Deendayal Energy University, Gandhinagar, India
[3] Department of Computer Engineering, Marwadi University, Gujarat, India

Abstract. The recent advent of computational intelligence and the field of deep learning has shown a significant application for the task of efficient navigation of automated and unmanned vehicles. The notion of a robot intelligently deciding a path based on minimalistic spatial knowledge and operating in a collision-free manner illustrates significant real-world importance. This paper offers a novel study for determining the best strategy for robust path planning in a simulated environment sufficed with static obstacles. The paradigm of behavior cloning and imitation learning is extensively explored, these techniques have depicted a better analogy to the human brain hence, justifying the experiments. This paper also conducts extensive tests on the existing technologies as baselines for an unbiased comparison, these algorithms include Rapidly- exploring Random Tree (RRT), A* search algorithm, and an improved rendition of the Ant Colony Optimization (ACO). The algorithms developed are centric to Unmanned Aerial Systems (UAS) however a correlation is also shown to unmanned ground systems and other automated robotics.

Keywords: Imitation learning · Behavior cloning · Collision avoidance · Deep learning · Unmanned aerial vehicles

1 Introduction

There has been a steady rise in the use of robotics and automated robots have become exceedingly common and utility-driven. Unmanned vehicles, especially unmanned aerial vehicles have shown significant improvements with regards to their computing facilities, further promoting and enabling the use of computationally demanding algorithms. The computing facilities implicate various companion computers that are capable of deploying various expensive algorithms [26]. This also promotes the use of multiple sensing platforms for extensive spatial awareness like Sonar [19], vision systems [9], and LiDAR [24]. Various algorithms and logical methods can be generated based on this sensor data, object tracking [16], advanced control mechanisms [12], and collision avoidance [11] are some such use cases. These systems do require an efficient and accurate traversal

© The Author(s), under exclusive license to Springer Nature Switzerland AG 2022
S. Rajagopal et al. (Eds.): ASCIS 2022, CCIS 1760, pp. 262–270, 2022.
https://doi.org/10.1007/978-3-031-23095-0_19

system that protects the mobile robot and guarantees a complete path and safe arrival at the designated endpoint. Hence, computing a safe trajectory and ensuring a collision-free and smooth motion of a mobile robot is a challenging and important task [5].

This paper offers a novel study for the task of collision avoidance and path planning for unmanned aerial vehicles, by leveraging various search algorithms, swarm intelligence, and imitation learning and delivers a comparative analysis for their computational efficiency. For making the study centric to unmanned aerial systems, the AUVSI SUAS competition, as referenced in [7] is taken as a situational baseline, the aforementioned algorithms are ultimately compared for their applicability in the competition. The competition offers a scenario where there are fixed waypoints and cylindrical obstacles, these obstacles may have an infinite height resulting in a sparse movement possibility. For this situation the only primary scope of movement is in the same plane, hence in this paper, a simulation platform is developed with circular obstacles, with a possibility of overlap to promote a similar scenario [3].

There have been developed various methods that assisted and inspired this study, and they are mentioned in the succeeding description. The paper [10] developed a novel A* based search approach, which depicted a 97% decrease in the execution time, when compared to the original baseline, that paper also leveraged these technologies for path planning and offered a proximate analysis in the MATLAB framework. The paper [27] proposed a modified and improved Ant Colony Optimization algorithm for a similar task, denominated as path planning for mobile robots. They combined the characteristics of MIN-MAX techniques and the A* search [27]. The research presented in the paper [29] proposed a novel methodology concerning an improved A* and greedy algorithm for path planning of a multi-objective mobile robot. The paper [30] offered a thorough comparative analysis between A* and RRT or Rapidly-exploring Random Trees for 3D unmanned aerial vehicle centric path planning. The paper [20] showed the applications of RRT or Rapidly-exploring Random Trees for an unknown environment, both simulatory and real-time experiments were shown, further justifying the experiments related to RRT here. A survey [18] was also examined on RRTs and their applications for path planning.

Comprehensive related literature also exists on behavior cloning, imitation learning, and the inverse reinforcement learning paradigm, these methods further bridge applied deep learning and human tendencies and work on the notion of learning a behavior policy from demonstrations [21]. The paper [6] leveraged conditional imitation learning for end-to-end driving, the simulation performed portrayed realistic 3D scenarios. The paper [2] proposed a sampling-based motion planning method for a nonholonomic system with a 100% test rate. The paper [5] also worked on imitation learning and catered it for Unmanned Aerial Vehicles (UAV). The article [28] leveraged reinforcement learning and proposed a novel pipeline for Comprehensive ocean information enabled AUV (Automated Unmanned Vehicles) path planning. The paper [15] also worked towards creating a novel and improved path planning algorithm with an emphasis on deep reinforcement learning. These publications and the abundant related literature accounts for a thorough understanding of the associated utilities of imitation learning and also symbolize the importance and significance of this problem statement. The subsequent sections provide a thorough understanding of the said technologies and the scope of this paper.

This section is followed by Methodology, results and the obtained empirical inference, and the conclusion and future work.

2 Methodology

This section offers a deeper insight into the underlying technologies and the approaches used in this comparative and empirical study. The algorithms and techniques are thoroughly elucidated along with their implementation attributes. These algorithms can be grouped into three portions, the conventional approaches which consist of the A* search and RRT, the swarm-based methods, and the deep learning methodologies associated with imitation learning.

2.1 A* Search

This section contains a condensed explanation of the A* search algorithm and the principal technologies which contributed to the algorithm [10, 27, 31]. It also includes the comparison to the baselined Dijkstra's algorithm [14] for a thorough understanding and for justifying its inclusion in this study.

When presented with the challenge of finding the shortest path between two nodes, the A* search method relies on the ideas of Dijkstra's shortest path algorithm to produce a speedier solution. It accomplishes this by using a heuristic element to assist in determining the next node to evaluate as it progresses down the path. The A* method, in addition to being quicker, differs from Dijkstra's by searching just the shortest path between the start and goal nodes.

Heuristics, also comprehended as heuristic functions, are utilized to provide acceptable solutions to exceedingly complex problems where finding the ideal solution would take too long. When you use heuristics, you sacrifice precision, correctness, and exactness for speed. One of Dijkstra's algorithm's shortcomings is that it may examine paths that will never provide the shortest path. The A* algorithm makes use of a heuristic function to help it determine which course to go next. The heuristic function discovers the shortest path between a given node and a given destination node. The procedure will add the actual cost from the start node to the expected cost from the destination node, and the result will be used to select the next node to analyze.

2.2 Rapidly-Exploring Random Tree

Using random samples from the search space, an RRT generates a tree rooted at the beginning configuration. As each sample is drawn, the algorithm attempts to link the sample to the nearest state in the tree. If the link is viable, the new state is added to the tree. The likelihood of extending an existing state is proportional to the size of its Voronoi area when the search space is uniformly sampled. Because the greatest Voronoi regions correspond to the states on the search's frontier, the tree preferentially extends towards huge unsearched areas. A growth factor typically limits the length of the link between the tree and a new state. If the random sample is further away from its nearest state in the tree than this restriction permits, a unique state at the most extensive distance from the tree along the line to the random sample is utilized rather than the random sample itself.

The random samples may consequently be thought of as directing the growth of the tree, while the growth factor governs its rate. This preserves the RRT's space-filling bias while restricting the extent of the incremental expansion. By raising the likelihood of sampling states from a given location, RRT growth can be skewed. Most realistic RRT implementations use this to direct the search toward the planning issue goals. This is achieved by adding a modest probability of sampling the target to the state sampling technique. The greater this likelihood, the more eagerly the tree grows toward the target. This summarized description and its corresponding implementation are based on the papers [22, 18]. A flowchart depicting the methodology of RRT [1] is mentioned in Fig. 1.

2.3 Ant Colony Optimization

The Ant colony optimization is an algorithm that is heavily inspired by the phenomena of ant foraging. From the starting location to the foraging path, each ant leaves a certain concentration of pheromone. With time, the pheromone will progressively dissipate, and the ants will utilize the pheromone concentration as the foundation for path selection. The higher the pheromone concentration, the more likely the path will be chosen. As time passes, the higher the concentration of pheromone left by the shorter path owing to more ants traveling, the greater the likelihood of ant selection on the higher concentration path and the greater the concentration of pheromones left. The shortest path will be found rapidly after many iterations, achieving the path planning aim. The ant colony method is essentially a parallel algorithm that is simple to construct and has high global optimization capabilities. However, as the environment grows larger, the computational volume grows exponentially, making it simple to slip into the local optimum. The implementations and the associated details are based on the papers [4, 8, 13]. Through extensive experimentation, the best hyperparameters are chosen for ensuring a thorough comparison.

2.4 Imitation Learning

Imitation Learning is a model for learning a behavior policy through demonstrations. Demonstrations are often portrayed as state-action trajectories, where each pair demonstrates the action to be taken in the state being visited. The shown behaviors are often used in two ways to teach the conduct policy. The first method, known as Behavior Cloning (BC), comprehends a generalized mapping from states to actions by considering the actions to be the target labelings for each state in a supervised learning paradigm. Another approach, known as. Inverse Reinforcement Learning (IRL), considers the exhibited behaviors as a sequence of decisions and seeks to develop a reward function that optimizes the demonstrated decisions. This paper focuses on leveraging the existing technologies for self-driving agents and works on a collision avoidance algorithm to clone the policy generated by the RRT baseline in a fully observed environment. Two main neural network strategies, a Convolutional Neural Network (CNN) [23] and a CNN-LSTM, where LSTM implicates Long Short Term Memory [17] (are used. The

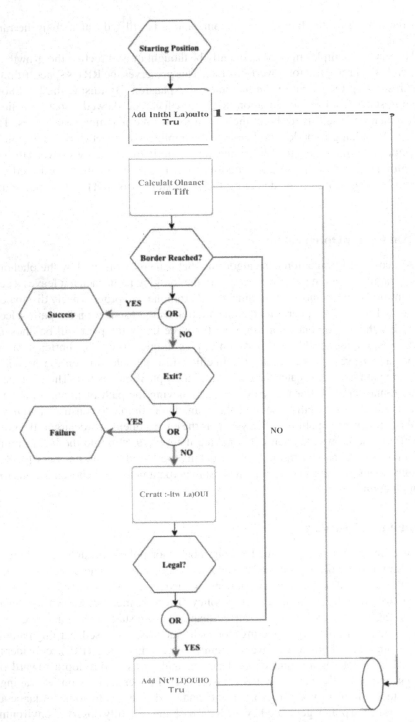

Fig. 1. Flow of information and methodology concerning the RRT paradigm as depicted in the paper [1]

addition of a recurrent network may allow the agent in terms of advance preparation. The training metric used for these networks was the percentage avoidance success rate, which was obtained as 93 and 86 respectively. As the deep learning models potentially function on local information, their computational efficiency should surpass conventional approaches which are forced to frequent replanning in dynamic and changing environments. The above-mentioned description can be comprehended as condensed information from the papers [2, 5, 6, 21].

3 Results and Discussion

This section presents the empirical data of the above methodologies, these methods were assessed based on their average computational efficiency or execution times. The same obstacle map is used for comparing all the algorithms, ensuring a fair and impartial comparison.

Table 1. The algorithms and their execution times, the algorithm names follow the previously mentioned abbreviations.

Algorithm	Execution time (Seconds)
RRT	1.641
A*	1.459
ACO	10.725
CNN	**1.342**
CNN-LSTM	1.384

From this table, it can be inferred that the imitation learning-based algorithms have a justifiable use case for mobile robot path planning, as the standalone CNN outperformed the other tested approaches. The swarm-based optimization approaches, though being a legitimate candidate, resulted in a computationally expensive experience. In the conventional approaches, RRT and A* gave a similar performance, but the A* search was efficient by a percent margin of 11.1. For the deep learning approaches the LSTM augmented network gave a comparatively higher average execution time, but still possessed a 7% higher success rate, deeming it to be a better tradeoff. Though the use of imitation learning was proved successful, it will still be associated with the initial algorithm that was used for training. So the choice of the working algorithm should be based on the availability of data and the specific utility. The ACO algorithm did give a poor performance in terms of computational efficiency however this aspect can be improved by using it in conjunction with other related methods [25].

As the motion of the agent is in a two-dimensional setting, these algorithms and trained structures can also be leveraged for other unmanned systems. The below mentioned Fig. 2 depict a graphical description of the aforementioned algorithms on various real-world scenarios pertaining to the competition. Here (a) represents a sample path generated by the CNN-LSTM model on a random obstacle test, (b) depicts a sample path generated by the CNN model on a test simulation, where overlapping obstacles are present which accurately resembles the competition's scenario. The image (c) depicts a sample path generated by the RRT algorithm, on a variably sized obstacle map, made according to one of the competition's possibilities.

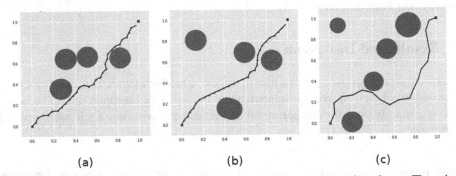

(a)   (b)   (c)

Fig. 2. A sample path generated by the CNN-LSTM model on a random obstacle test. The points red and blue depict the start and the end points.

4   Conclusion and Future Work

This paper aimed to obtain an efficient and robust path planning approach for collision-free traversal of an Unmanned Aerial System centric to the AUVSI SUAS competition. After thorough experimentation on justified algorithms, a comparative analysis is provided. Due to the planar motion and simulation nature of these experiments, the study can also be leveraged to other automated systems, like Unmanned Ground Vehicles (UGV) and Automated Underwater Vehicles (AUV). Furthermore, the authors aim to work on real-time implementations for a better comparison and also on more robust systems for collision detection and global motion planning in various mobile robot paradigms.

References

1. Aguinaga, I., Borro, D., Matey, L.: Parallel rrt-based path planning for selective disassembly planning. Int. J. Adv. Manufact. Technol. **36**, 1221–1233 (2008). https://doi.org/10.1007/s00170-007-0930-2
2. Banzhaf, H., Sanzenbacher, P., Baumann, U., Zollner, J.M.: Learning to predict ego-vehicle poses for sampling-based nonholonomic motion planning. IEEE Robot. Autom. Lett. **4**(2), 1053–1060 (2019). https://doi.org/10.1109/lra.2019.2893975
3. Chapter, A.S.: Suas 2022 rules (2022). https://www.auvsi-suas.org/competitions
4. Chaudhuri, A.: A dynamic algorithm for the longest common subsequence problem using ant colony optimization technique (2013), http://arxiv.org/abs/1307.1905v1
5. Choudhury, S., et al.: Data-driven planning via imitation learning. Int. J. Robot. Res. **37**(13–14), 1632–1672 (2018). https://doi.org/10.1177/0278364918781001

6. Codevilla, F., Muller, M., Lopez, A., Koltun, V., Dosovitskiy, A.: End-to-end driving via conditional imitation learning. In: 2018 IEEE International Conference on Robotics and Automation (ICRA). IEEE (2018). https://doi.org/10.1109/icra.2018.8460487

7. DeGroote, N.S., Barnes, E., Burton, J., Terry, M., Ouwerkerk, J.N., Cohen, K.: A solution for the challenges presented by the 2020 AUVSI SUAS competition. In: AIAA Scitech 2021 Forum. American Institute of Aeronautics and Astronautics, p. 0522 (2021). https://doi.org/10.2514/6.2021-0522

8. El-Dosuky, M.A.: CACO: competitive ant colony optimization, a nature- inspired metaheuristic for large-scale global optimization (2013). http://arxiv.org/abs/1312.4044v1

9. Causa, F., Fasano, G.: Improved in-flight estimation of inertial biases through CDGNSS/vision based cooperative navigation. Sensors 21, 34069288 (2021). https://doi.org/10.3390/s21 103438

10. Guruji, A.K., Agarwal, H., Parsediya, D.: Time-efficient A* algorithm for robot path planning. Procedia Technol. 23, 144–149 (2016). https://doi.org/10.1016/j.protcy.2016.03.010,

11. Wu, J., Luo, C., Luo, Y., Li, K.: Distributed UAV swarm formation and collision avoidance strategies over fixed and switching topologies. IEEE Trans. Cyber. 34951860 (2021). https://doi.org/10.1109/TCYB.2021.3132587

12. Yan, K., Wu, Q.: Adaptive tracking flight control for unmanned autonomous helicopter with full state constraints and actuator faults. ISA Trans. 34865842 (2021). https://doi.org/10.1016/j.isatra.2021.11.012,

13. Yang, L., Fu, L., Li, P., Mao, J., Guo, N., Du, L.: LF-ACO: an effective formation path planning for multi-mobile robot. Math. Biosci. Eng. 19(1), 225–252 (2022).https://doi.org/10.3934/mbe.2022012

14. Levin, G.M.: Dijkstra's method of program construction. Encyclopedia Softw. Eng. (2002). https://doi.org/10.1002/0471028959.sof093

15. Li, J., Chen, Y., Zhao, X., Huang, J.: An improved DQN path planning algorithm. J. Supercomput. 78(1), 616–639 (2022)

16. Luigi, P., Spagnolo, P.: Object tracking in multiple cameras with disjoint views. In: Object Tracking. InTech (2011). https://doi.org/10.5772/14220

17. Murugesan, R., Mishra, E., Krishnan, A.H.: Deep learning based models: Basic LSTM, bi LSTM, stacked LSTM, CNN LSTM and conv LSTM to forecast agricultural commodities prices (2021). https://doi.org/10.21203/rs.3.rs-740568/v1

18. Noreen, I., Khan, A., Habib, Z.: Optimal path planning using RRT* based approaches: a survey and future directions. Int. J. Adv. Comput. Sci. Appl. 7(11) (2016). https://doi.org/10.14569/ijacsa.2016.071114

19. Santamaria-Navarro, A., Loianno, G., Sol'a, J., Kumar, V., Andrade-Cetto, J.: Autonomous navigation of micro aerial vehicles using high-rate and low-cost sensors. Auton. Rob. 42(6), 1263–1280 (2017). https://doi.org/10.1007/s10514-017-9690-5

20. Tian, Y., et al.: Application of RRT-based local path planning algorithm in unknown environment. In: 2007 International Symposium on Computational Intelligence in Robotics and Automation, pp. 456-460. IEEE (2007). https://doi.org/10.1109/cira.2007.382896

21. Torabi, F., Warnell, G., Stone, P.: Behavioral cloning from observation. In: Proceedings of the Twenty-Seventh International Joint Conference on Artificial Intelligence. International Joint Conferences on Artificial Intelligence Organization (2018). https://doi.org/10.24963/ijcai.2018/687

22. Tsardoulias, E.G., Iliakopoulou, A., Kargakos, A., Petrou, L.: A review of global path planning methods for occupancy grid maps regardless of obstacle density. J. Intell. Robot. Syst. 84(1–4), 829–858 (2016). https://doi.org/10.1007/s10846-016-0362-z

23. Vestias, M.P.: Convolutional neural network. In: Research Anthology on Artificial Neural Network Applications, pp. 1559–1575. IGI Global (2022). https://doi.org/10.4018/978-1-6684-2408-7.ch077

24. Wallace, L., Lucieer, A., Watson, C., Turner, D.: Development of a UAV-lidar system with application to forest inventory. Remote Sens. 4(6), 1519–1543 (2012). https://doi.org/10.3390/rs4061519

25. Wen, Y., Haiying, W., Zhisheng, Z.: Obstacle avoidance path planning of manipulator based on improved RRT algorithm. In: 2021 International Conference on Computer, Control and Robotics (IC- CCR), pp. 104-109. IEEE (2021). https://doi.org/10.1109/icccr49711.2021.9349398

26. Wyder, P.M., et al.: Autonomous drone hunter operating by deep learning and all-onboard computations in GPS-denied environments. Plos One 14(11), e0225092 (2019). https://doi.org/10.1371/journal.pone.0225092

27. Dai, X., Long, S., Zhang, Z., Gong, D.: Mobile robot path planning based on ant colony algorithm with a* heuristic method. Front, Neurorob. 13, 31057388 (2019). https://doi.org/10.3389/fnbot.2019.00015

28. Xi, M., Yang, J., Wen, J., Liu, H., Li, Y., Song, H.H.: Comprehensive ocean information enabled AUV path planning via reinforcement learning. IEEE Internet Things J. (2022)

29. Xiang, D., Lin, H., Ouyang, J., Huang, D.: Combined improved a* and greedy algorithm for path planning of multi-objective mobile robot. Sci. Rep. 12(1), 1–12 (2022)

30. Zammit, C., Van Kampen, E.J.: Comparison between a* and RRT algorithms for 3D UAV path planning. Unmanned Syst. 10(02), 129–146 (2022)

31. Zeng, W., Church, R.L.: Finding shortest paths on real road networks: the case for A* 23(4), 531–543 (2009). https://doi.org/10.1080/13658810801949850

Comparative Study of Various Algorithms for Vehicle Detection and Counting in Traffic

Anand John[1,2](✉) and Divyakant Meva[3]

[1] Department of Computer Applications, Christ College, Rajkot 360005, Gujarat, India
anand_john@yahoo.com
[2] Marwadi University, Rajkot 360003, Gujarat, India
[3] Faculty of Computer Applications, Marwadi University, Rajkot 360003, Gujarat, India

Abstract. Now a days massive traffic queues and accidents are very much there in the Indian roads. Traffic Management is a critical issue which influences us all things considered, regular. Use of knowledge, for example, IoT and picture dealing with can move a smooth traffic supervision structure. To avoid clashing of vehicles during the signal, we can analyze the traffic crowd conditions and arrange the movement of the vehicles in the cross road in such a way that there should not be any collision and the traffic in each side of the road should get equal priority. If the traffic is less in any side of the road, then there is a need to change the priority and the side where the traffic is higher is given higher priority for movement. These traffic movements can be analyzed by taking the photos in the cameras and the pictures can be checked by using the fastest algorithms of object discovery. In this paper various comparison is done for analyzing the traffic movements by using the different kinds of object discovering algorithms like YOLO v3, YOLO v4, YOLOv5, YOLOv6 and YOLO v7.

Keywords: Traffic management · Object detection · Convolution neural network · Deep neural network · YOLO v3 · YOLO v4 · YOLO v5 · YOLO v6 · YOLO v7

1 Introduction

Vehicle discovery in a picture or video is a very difficult job in the endurance of different environment. Vehicle discovery and location in pictures has become one of the most significant purposes for everybody to ease person, save time and to achieve perfection. The primary target of learning and looking for computer vision is to propose the lead and method of natural eyes straight by utilizing a computer and later on change a framework that lessens human actions. In this paper, several models are implemented for discovery and trailing in jupyter notebook environment. This is a method of perceiving and positioning an object which is in motion with the help of a camera.

Traditional traffic flagging works by time set in any electronic equipment, in each crossing point for each approaching traffic. The main issue is that even when there is no traffic in a road, traffic of other roads has to wait till the timing for the preceding road

© The Author(s), under exclusive license to Springer Nature Switzerland AG 2022
S. Rajagopal et al. (Eds.): ASCIS 2022, CCIS 1760, pp. 271–286, 2022.
https://doi.org/10.1007/978-3-031-23095-0_20

becomes zero. We can design a framework that eliminates the issue by dealing with the number of vehicles on a road. Similarly, the framework gives the benefit that police stall need not be involved all through the roads of the city and traffic dealing can be more fruitful.

Traffic regulation breaking is one of the significant descriptions behind mishap. To lessen this, vehicle discovery technique can be used to detect the violating vehicle. By scrutinizing the different vehicles and traffic movement on the road, the situation and position of the traffic can be known and correct information can be provided so as to manage the traffic in the most efficient technique. In our planned method, we are going to use real time traffic facts from CCTV cameras, we are going to processes that data, and by extracting expressive evidence from real time traffic data such as vehicle types, mass of traffic. Various traffic signal periods are being specified ac- cording to density at that specific road [1]. To tackle this issue, a single-phase method has been proposed for vehicle location, which is you-just look-once (YOLO) structure. Single phase method is fast and can discover vehicles in real time model. We can use YOLO model as the main location calculations to change the objective recognition issue into the regression issue by AI. Classifiers are utilized for photograph characterization and counting [2].

Here, we investigate the possibility of vehicle discovery by means of five advanced algorithms. Apparently, we relate the precision and usage of different YOLO algorithm forms like v3, v4, v5, v6 and v7for the purpose of vehicle finding using these object revealing algorithms.

2 Literature Review

2.1 YOLO Real-Time Object Tracking

YOLO is very fast, meticulous in finding vehicle in an image or video. Initially, photographs are captured from real time traffic zone and we apply the YOLO algorithm. The photograph is divided as grids of 3×3 matrixes. Subsequently, each grid undergoes classification and localization of the vehicle object. The assurance score of each grid is found. If no accurate vehicle is discovered in the frame area, hence the assurance score of the frame area will be zero or suppose an accurate vehicle is discovered in the frame area, then the confidence score will be one. Similarly, anchor boxes are used to augment the exactness of vehicle discovery [3].

The traffic density is discovered on the basis of the counting of vehicles which is discovered and the threshold value. The threshold value can be given as per the requirement [4]. These models are stranded on the Tensorflow with keras platform to discover the best accurate results.

The paper [5] explains various algorithms for vehicle counting and use tiny-YOLO because of limitations of hardware. By comparing various models, it achieved the results that YOLO was the best model for vehicle discovery. In the case of poor light conditions, the vehicle discovery is limited which is done for a custom dataset using YOLOv3 model especially during the night hours. It also states that instead of using tiny-YOLO, YOLO should be used for performance discovery of vehicle counting. The accuracy in vehicle discovery through YOLOv3 is explained in paper [6]. The methodology helps to generate good information regarding the traffic in order to control the real time problem. Still many problems are yet to be addressed in this paper. In the method OpenCV library of python is being used for different vehicle discovery.

In the paper [7], Alexey and his team had demonstrated comparison of different results using YOLOv4. They have stated by the comparison results that YOLOv4 is the fastest than all other previous algorithms of YOLO. Likewise, the accuracy is shown to be increased in YOLOv4 by the authors.

In the paper [8], Yidan Chen and Zhenjin Li has addressed certain problems occurred in identifying the vehicles using deep learning in effective traffic conditions. They have shown that using artificial intelligence, even various vehicles can be discovered accurately and speedily because everything is done by the algorithm itself. So, by using the current advanced technology, the vehicle detection method and vehicle counting in real time traffic conditions can be improved. The related methodology and its performance for effective vehicle discovery and the test results are discussed in this research paper.

3   Methodology

3.1 YOLOv3 Architecture

YOLOV3 method operates neural system to discover items in pictures, videos etc. The YOLOv3 method simply does a single check through a neural system to distinguish items. Assuredly, the vehicle discovery from the whole photograph is finished in just one method execution. YOLOv3 use darknet-53 engineering which contains 53 layers as the pillar for feature separator [9]. YOLOv3 applies continuing links and selection. YOLO v3 applies a several label approach which lets vehicles to be discovered more precise which has the highest discovery percentage values (Fig. 1).

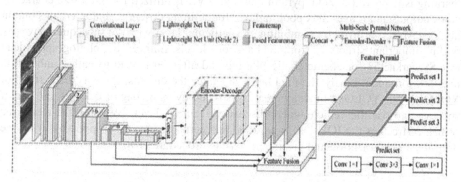

Fig. 1. YOLOv3 network architecture (source: https://viso.ai/deep-learning/yolov3-overview)

The discovery is performed at three dissimilar balances. It is very effective in discovering smaller objects, still it takes persistent release time as related to the previous method of YOLO. YOLOv3 uses self-determining calculated object finding method and paired statistical loss calculation for the vehicle discovery while testing. So, we can use difficult real time datasets for YOLOv3 method preparation. We can also create dataset for discovering vehicles in the photographs.

3.2 YOLOv4 Architecture

YOLOV4 architecture uses CSPdarknet53 as a pillar. YOLOv4 is the most exact continuous neural network on MS COCO dataset. The YOLOv4 design operates head and neck which comprises of spatial pyramid pooling extra section and Path Aggregation Network (PANet) way combination. The neck works as an intermediate joining the backbone and the head.

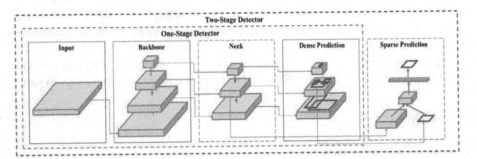

Fig. 2. YOLOv4 network architecture (source: https://iq.opengenus.org/yolov4-model- architecture)

   In this model Cross Stage Partial Network as displayed in Fig. 2. is applied as a support for characteristic extraction and it is obtained from densenet. It joins the characteristics from the particular layer to the following layer in the dense block. Using densenet the problem of gradient values disappearing is reduced and the gradient layer learning is improved. Spatial pyramid pooling layer is utilized for fixed size characteristics outputs and it uses max pooling layer for defining different characteristics output layers. PANet is utilized for combining the particular layer with the subsequent layer by finding important structures from the backbone levels. Initially, the photograph is lead to CSPDarknet53 for characteristic filtering and afterwards lead to path combination network for union. Lastly, the final layer generates the outputs, same as the method of YOLOv3. The YOLOv4 model increases its speed by using bag of freebies and bag of specials and rise the vehicle object discovery accuracy level. By using the technique of bag of freebies the IOU loss is adjusted and certain areas are dropped by using the dropblock regularization and diverse increasing procedure [10].

3.3 YOLOv5 Architecture

The work of head in one phase finder is to accomplish decisive discovery which is composed of matrices comprising rectangle box values: breadth, length, item name, and object possibility. Foremost, the photograph is led to darknet53 for characteristics removal and subsequently led to feature pyramid network for characteristics addition. Lastly, YOLO gives the outputs.

   Yet, YOLOv5 operates PyTorch in its place of darknet. As shown in the Fig. 3. YOLOv5 consists of backbone CSPDarknet53 as support which tackles the identical

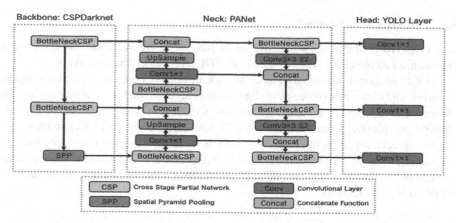

Fig. 3. YOLOv5 network architecture (source: https://doi.org/10.48550/arXiv.2205.11830)

gradient data, neck PANet and yolo head layer. CSP (cross stage partial network) filters the feature layer and takes required information from it to increases accuracy, and decreases the limitations. PANet (path aggregation network) implements a feature pyramid network that includes different layers having hierarchical layers. This improves the proliferation of low-level strong features in the model. The feature pyramid network identifies the vehicles in the photograph even though it may large or regular. Path aggregation network works on the localization in lower layers, which improves the exact position and discovery of the vehicle in the photograph. Furthermore, the head in YOLO v5 generates three dissimilar output of characteristics layers to achieve different measures of estimate. It also helps to increase the prediction of different size vehicles proficiently in the network. The picture is given to CSPDarknet53 for characteristics filtering and again given to path aggregation network for characteristics combination. Lastly, the YOLO layer will create the output [11].

The YOLOv5 model consists of focus construction and CSP network as the support. The three layers of focus architecture are joined as single layer. Furthermore, as displayed in Fig. 3. Conv. is convolution layer in the network. Spatial pyramid pooling is a pooling layer that takes random size of photograph and converts into proper size output, so it eliminates the proper size limitation. The fusion layer is changed to get an accurate layer. Concat is used to separate the preceding layer. The final three convolution layers are prediction modules used in the head of YOLOv5 algorithm.

The neck holds both spatial pyramid pooling area and PANet. YOLOv5 is designed in python software design language. This enables the fixing and addition of internet of things equipment simple [12].

Using YOLOv5 algorithm, we discover the vehicles in the picture and also count the number of vehicles. The different vehicles are also segregated. Using all these information, we can analyze the traffic movements and situation of that road and we can direct the traffic to the right path. In these YOLOv5 algorithm, it is tested with the yolov5s.pt weights using the inference and with a picture resolution of 640*640 with a confidence score of 0.25 and with an epoch 300.

3.4 YOLOv6 Architecture

The YOLOv6 fundamental was delivered in June 2022 by Meituan, and it has great presentation on the COCO dataset standard. YOLOv6 model has 295 layers.

YOLO v6 model is a solitary phase item identification structure engaging to manufacturing applications and processing stable well thought out plan and outrageous accomplishment. YOLOv6 accomplishes the discovery of objects using different weights like yolov6n.pt, yolov6s.pt and yolo6t.pt using COCO label structure. YOLO v6 characterizes the model limits straightforwardly in python. YOLOv6 is made from accompanying techniques: - Easy device response design for support and neck to filter out fine characteristics in YOLO v6. It uses the intersection over union loss to increase the accuracy of vehicle discovery (Fig. 4).

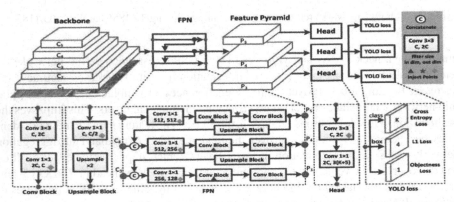

Fig. 4. YOLOv6 architecture based on PP-YOLO (source: https://arxiv.org/pdf/2007.12099v3. pdf)

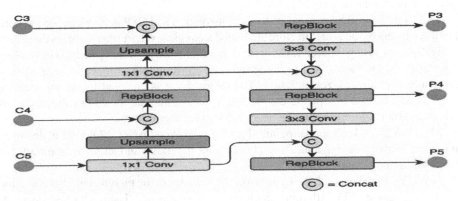

Fig. 5. YOLOv6 Rep-PAN neck (source: https://blog.roboflow.com/yolov6)

YOLOv6 repeats through the backbone and uses Rep-PAN neck as shown in Fig. 5 to reform it with the device in observance familiarizing which is called Efficient Rep-backbone. Similar to the evaluation of YOLOv6, there's an inference script that comes with the source's tools. This inference program lets us to send a group of photographs in a specified directory on which the YOLOv6 model will run its predictions.

In addition, this inference utility also comes with a number of arguments we can pass for things like displaying the labels on the predicted images, modifying the confidence level and NMS thresholds, and setting max detections. Although, YOLO v6 is displaying the different vehicles in addition to other items, the number of vehicles is counted and results is displayed using python programming logic. In YOLOv6, the confidence threshold is made about 0.25 so as to discover the vehicles exactly.

3.5 YOLOv7 Architecture

YOLOV7 was created by Chien-Yao Wang, Alexey Bochkovskiy, and Hong-Yuan Mark Liao, remembering the memory required to keep layers alongside with the distance required for a feature to back-spread through the layers. The smaller the feature, the more powerfully the model will learn. The last layer combination selected was extended efficient layer aggregation network (E-ELAN), a high level rendition of the ELAN calculation unit. The model was measured in deepness and breadth for getting good performance while connecting layers together. This algorithm keeps the structure best while leveling for unlike sizes. YOLOv7 practice feature flow spread paths to see the segments in the system get the training re-characterization plans [13]. YOLO v7-tiny is used to test small models and it can also be executed in devices like mobile (Fig. 6).

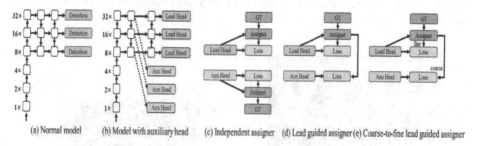

(a) Normal model (b) Model with auxiliary head (c) Independent assigner (d) Lead guided assigner (e) Coarse-to-fine lead guided assigner

Fig. 6. YOLOv7 network architecture (source: [13])

YOLOv7 model has 415 layers. The YOLO model head makes the ultimate discovery for the system, yet at this point adding a supporting head to the bottom of the system that lies near the middle can be worthwhile. During testing, the detection head and the head that make predications is supervised. The YOLOv7 model draws rectangle boxes more accurately than the preceding versions at identical inference speeds. The inference is tested in YOLOv7 and it gives good accurate results and higher speed as revealed in the photographs given below in the results. The photographs are taken from real traffic area at the crossroads of the city.

4 Results and Discussion

All the test are done using the different versions of YOLO algorithm for discovering the vehicles in the real-time traffic environments photographs. The versions of YOLO algorithm tested for traffic photographs are YOVOv3, YOLOvv4, YOLOv5, YOLOv6 and YOLOv7. Around 500 pictures were captured from real-time traffic conditions in the Rajkot city of Gujarat state and tested using the different algorithms specified above and some of the test results are shown as below in the corresponding section.

4.1 YOLOv3 Test Results

The Initially, we test with YOLOv3 by using the COCO labels and the yolo weights by reading through the WeightReader method and we are giving the class threshold value to 0.6. When the YOLOv3 algorithm is drawing the bounding box in the photo- graphs, the labels are checked for any vehicles and also the vehicles are counted. The method for counting vehicles is shown below.

```
vehiclecount=0
    for i in range(len(vv_boxes)):
        if vv_labels[i] =='bicycle' or vv_labels[i] =='car' or vv_labels[i] ==
'motorbike' or vv_labels[i] =='truck' or vv_labels[i] =='bus':
vehiclecount+=1
print('Total Count of vehicles', vehiclecount)
```

So, by counting the vehicles, we can find out the traffic density in that specific zone. Hence, we can evaluate and take appropriate measures based on the results we have attained (Fig. 7) (Table 1).

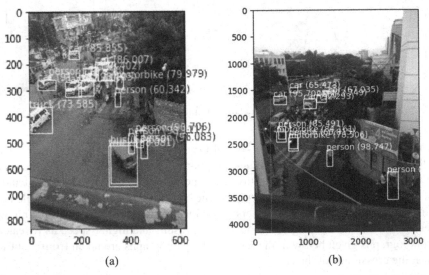

(a)   (b)

Fig. 7. Vehicle discovery using YOLOv3 model:(a) Traffic picture1; (b) Traffic picture2.

The test results using YOLOv3 model has found some cars with above 90% confidence score, while some cars were found between 60 and 90% confidence score. The

Table 1. Vehicle discovery in percentages and total count using

Traffic picture1 results		Traffic picture2 results	
truck	68.08127164840698	car	65.47337174415588
car	86.00677847862244	car	67.0352578163147
truck	73.58483672142029	car	95.70233225822449
bus	63.650232553482056	car	73.74858856201172
car	85.85494756698608	car	92.2930359840393
car	90.40185809135437	motorbike	84.16067361831665
motorbike	79.97893691062927	motorbike	78.50607633590698
car	91.96276068687439		
car	98.1052577495575		
car	97.44498133659363		
Total vehicles count: 10		Total vehicles count: 7	

model has also found motorbike with above 75% confidence score and truck with above 65% confidence score. We have also calculated the total number of vehicles present in each photograph so as to analyses the traffic condition.

4.2 YOLOv4 Test Results

We test with YOLOv4 model by loading the YOLOv4 weights and providing all the COCO classes to discovery the vehicles in the photographs. All the photographs to be tested are passed in the predict function of YOLOv4 model and hence we can count the number of vehicles in each photograph and display the total vehicles in each of the photographs. Through this method, we can find out the traffic density in that part of the lane (Table 2) (Fig. 8).

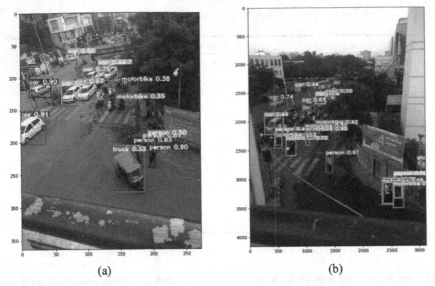

(a)   (b)

Fig. 8. Vehicle discovery using YOLOv4 model: (a) Traffic picture3; (b) Traffic picture4.

Table 2. Vehicle discovery in percentages and total count using YOLOv4.

Traffic picture3 results		Traffic picture4 results	
car	0.970512	car	0.741080
car	0.967665	motorbike	0.718357
car	0.907120	motorbike	0.633398
car	0.900991	car	0.625823
car	0.882398	car	0.583182
car	0.752723	motorbike	0.581094
truck	0.565538	motorbike	0.569125
car	0.496997	car	0.439149
car	0.438577	car	0.435957
motorbike	0.379568	motorbike	0.419850
motorbike	0.347711	motorbike	0.399142
truck	0.330366	motorbike	0.320439
		car	0.300715
Total vehicles count: 12		Total vehicles count: 13	

The test results using YOLOv4 model has found cars were found above 40% confidence score. The model has also found motorbike between 30 and 75% confidence score and truck with above 30% confidence score. It is found that vehicles are discovered more than in YOLOv3 model. The accuracy is YOLOv4 in vehicle discovery was found much higher.

4.3 YOLOv5 Test Results

The traffic photographs are tested for vehicle discovery based on the COCO labels using YOLOv5 model using PyTorch Hub inferences. Also, the inference is tested using detect command by loading the YOLOv5 weights yolo5s.pt and by providing the directory which contains all the photographs. The confidence threshold is given 0.25 and the photograph resolution is given 640 * 640. Using YOLOv5 model, we can also simply discover certain vehicles by giving the class values as parameters while running the detect python program, so other items in the discovery method is skipped while running the inference (Table 3) (Fig. 9).

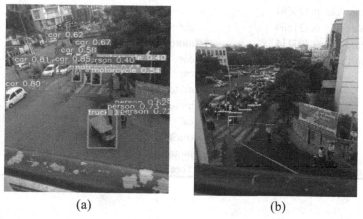

(a)   (b)

Fig. 9. Vehicle discovery using YOLOv5model: (a) Traffic picture5; (b) Traffic picture6.

YOLOv5 gives more vehicle discovery than YOLOv4 as we see the output the confidence score of cars and motorcycles is above 30%. So, a car of small size in the photographs is also discovered. The inference of YOLOv5 model is executed and the results are saved in a text file by providing the parameters as a text file name with detect program in the inference execution. Besides, we can also save the configuration in the results by passing the save-conf parameter. By reading the text file, we can count the number of vehicles for each photograph in the directory and hence the traffic density can be found and suitable management can be done to ease the traffic.

Table 3. Vehicle discovery in percentages and total count using YOLOv5.

Traffic picture5 results		Traffic picture6 results	
car	0.845577	car	0.841095
car	0.806192	car	0.560038
car	0.797309	car	0.537799
car	0.761327	car	0.522617
car	0.672858	motorcycle	0.497498
truck	0.659157	car	0.471674
car	0.619150	car	0.421760
car	0.583353	car	0.371542
motorcycle	0.540684	car	0.348025
motorcycle	0.431869	car	0.341984
motorcycle	0.397115	motorcycle	0.333556
motorcycle	0.304913	car	0.306483
		car	0.288184
		motorcycle	0.276817
		motorcycle	0.275135
		car	0.262143
		truck	0.255200
		motorcycle	0.254657
Total vehicles count: 12		Total vehicles count: 18	

4.4 YOLOv6 Test Results

The real-time traffic photographs are tested for discovering vehicles using YOLOv6 model based on the COCO datasets. The inference of the model is executed and the results are automatically saved in the inference directory and inside it as an exp directory. If the inference directory is not there, it is automatically created. For executing the inference, we run the infer python program by loading the YOLOv6 weights yo- lo6s.pt and by providing the source directory which contains all the traffic photographs. The results containing vehicle discovery are shown in the traffic photographs given below in Fig. 10 (Table 4).

(a)   (b)

Fig. 10. Vehicle discovery using YOLOv6 model: (a) Traffic picture7; (b) Traffic picture8.

Table 4. Vehicle discovery in percentages and total count using YOLOv6.

Traffic picture7 results		Traffic picture8 results	
car	0.250037	motorcycle	0.254078
car	0.279445	motorcycle	0.26282
truck	0.313929	car	0.267813
bus	0.354841	car	0.378036
car	0.369597	car	0.389138
truck	0.385803	car	0.42073
motorcycle	0.419476	car	0.583188
car	0.453297	motorcycle	0.690425
motorcycle	0.502152	car	0.778198
car	0.516931		
truck	0.546826		
car	0.619221		
car	0.655627		
car	0.685368		
car	0.789172		
car	0.826889		
Total vehicles count: 16		Total vehicles count: 9	

The confidence threshold is given 0.25 and accurate discovery of vehicles is done using this algorithm. The traffic photographs are also tested using yolov6n.pt weights and the discovery is done more accurately than yolov6s.pt weights. The number of vehicles is counted from the text file created after executing the discovery method. The speed is higher in YOLOv6, but in discovery of vehicles in YOLOv6 is not always better than YOLOv5. In some cases, YOLOv6 is giving less discovery of vehicles than YOLOv5.

4.5 YOLOv7 Test Results

The YOLOv7 model is also tested using PyTorch for vehicle discovery in real-time traffic condition based on the COCO model. It is tested in video as well as in a list of traffic photographs which is put in the images folder. The testing is done by executing the detect program of YOLOv7 and loading the yolov7.pt weight. The confidence threshold is given 0.25 and image resolution is given as 640*640. The results are put in a text file and the number of vehicles is counted and the traffic conditions are analyzed (Table 5)(Fig. 11).

(a)   (b)

Fig. 11. Vehicle discovery using YOLOv7 model: (a) Traffic picture9; (b) Traffic picture10.

YOLOv7 is the latest algorithm found for discovery of vehicles and other items. Using this algorithm, the results we got for the photographs are many cars are discovered with above 40% confidence score and also motorcycle above 40%.

YOLOv7 is discovering vehicle much better than YOLOv6 and YOLOv5. The inference speed is higher and accuracy of vehicle discovery is larger.

The truck detected are actually auto-rickshaws. The execution of YOLOv4 gives great discovery accuracy and great speed. The application can be created to apply traffic control framework by producing complete vehicle detail and vehicle types [14].

Consequently, from the above results it tends to be deduced that along with the assistance of different sensors and photograph handling procedures a rough degree of traffic can be figured out that is comparable to continuous movements of traffic. These facts assembled can be utilized to evaluate and control the traffic progressively relying upon genuine densities of traffic [15].

Table 5. Vehicle discovery in percentages and total count using YOLOv7.

Traffic picture9 results		Traffic picture10 results	
truck	0.272673	motorcycle	0.268157
truck	0.320351	motorcycle	0.268157
car	0.325014	truck	0.288303
motorcycle	0.446728	car	0.293766
car	0.492529	car	0.297999
motorcycle	0.502315	motorcycle	0.306219
motorcycle	0.562611	car	0.310756
car	0.585348	motorcycle	0.322571
car	0.635469	truck	0.332648
motorcycle	0.667393	motorcycle	0.394485
car	0.864376	car	0.395993
car	0.865841	motorcycle	0.424088
car	0.86938	car	0.432432
car	0.874343	car	0.49499
		car	0.567261
		truck	0.592834
		car	0.613747
		motorcycle	0.615285
		motorcycle	0.615878
		motorcycle	0.630688
		car	0.735706
		car	0.762048
		car	0.882188
Total vehicles count: 14		Total vehicles count: 22	

5 Conclusion

Many vehicle detection algorithms like YOLOv3, YOLOv4, YOLOv5, YOLOv6 and YOLOv7 are being discussed and compared. Initially, all the algorithms architecture is shown and then their detection results are displayed. By using these systems, we can decrease the amount of traffic overcrowding on the road in our city. The vehicles are counted and from that traffic analysis can be done. From the test, it is found that YOLOv3 is showing very accurate results but it is slow compared to other YOLO algorithms. YOLOv3 is better than YOLOv4 in speed as well as in accuracy for vehicle detection. But, YOLOv5 is much more improved than YOLOv4 model in speed as well as in accuracy. YOLOv6 is improved than YOLOv5, but in some cases YOLOv6 is not giving accurate detection as YOLOv5 for detecting vehicles and counting. On taking the average, YOLOv5 is found better than YOLOv5 as per the test conducted in this research paper. YOLOv7 is the latest model version and it is extremely fast than YOLOv5 and YOLOv6. It also gives accurate results with significantly higher speed in detecting vehicle detection and counting. Using YOLOv7 model, we can detect multiple vehicles and count the vehicles and we can add our labels and real- time photographs. But still, we have limitations in the YOLO algorithm. Small vehicles like motorcycle which are together, as shown in the traffic photographs using YOLOv7 are not detected.

References

1. Lin, C.-J., Jhang, J.-Y.: Intelligent traffic-monitoring system based on YOLO and convolutional fuzzy neural networks. IEEE Access **10**, 14120–14133 (2022)
2. Huang, Y.-Q., Zheng, J.-C., Sun, S.-D., Yang, C.-F., Liu, J.: Optimized YOLOv3 algorithm and its application in traffic flow detections. Appl. Sci. **10**(9), 3079 (2020)
3. Shinde, P., Yadav, S., Rudrake, S., Kumbhar, P.: Smart traffic control system using YOLO. Int. Res. J. Eng. Technol. **6**(12), 967–970 (2019)
4. Godse, S.P., More, N., Surana, A., Patil, P., Kamble, S.: Traffic density detection with vehicle identification for smart traffic monitoring. Int. J. Res. Eng. Technol. Sci. **8**(10), 1–6 (2019)
5. Abdullah, A., Oothariasamy, J.: Vehicle counting using deep learning models: a comparative study. Int. J. Adv. Comput. Sci. Appl. **11**(7), 697–703 (2020)
6. Khazukov, K., et al.: Real-time monitoring of traffic parameters. J. Big Data **7**(1), 1–20 (2020). https://doi.org/10.1186/s40537-020-00358-x
7. Bochkovskiy, A., Wang, C.-Y., Sun, S.-D., Yang, C.-F., Liao, H.-Y.M.: YOLOv4: Optimal Speed and Accuracy of Object Detection. Preprint at http://arXiv:2004.10934 (2020)
8. Chen, Y., Li, Z.: An effective approach of vehicle detection using deep learning. Comput. Intell. Neurosci. **2022**(2019257), 1–9 (2022)
9. Lin, C.-J., Jeng, S.-Y., Lioa, H.-W.: A real-time vehicle counting, speed estimation, and classification system based on virtual detection zone and YOLO. Math. Probl. Eng. **2021**, 1577614 (2021)
10. Bochkovskiy, A., Wang, C. -Y., Liao, H.-Y. M.: YOLOv4: optimal speed and accuracy of object detection. ArXiv:2004.10934v1 (2020)
11. Nepal, U., Eslamiat, H.: Comparing YOLOv3, YOLOv4 and YOLOv5 for autonomous landing spot detection in faulty UAVs. Sensors **22**(2), 464 (2022)
12. Ali, S.M.: Comparative analysis of YOLOv3, YOLOv4 and YOLOv5 for sign language detection. Int. J. Adv. Res. Innov. Ideas Educ. **7**(4), 2393–2398 (2021)
13. Wang, C.-Y., Bochkovskiy, A., Liao, H.-Y.M.: YOLOv7: Trainable bag-of-freebies sets new state-of-the-art for real-time object detectors. ArXiv 2207.02696v1 (2022)
14. Hasibuan, N.N., Zarlis, M., Efendi, S.: Detection and tracking different type of cars with YOLO model combination and deep sort algorithm based on computer vision of traffic controlling. Sinkron **6**(1), 210–220 (2021)
15. Jacob, S.M., Rekh, S.G.M., Paul, J.J.: Smart traffic management system with real time analysis. Int. J. Eng. Technol. **7**(3.29), 348–351 (2018)
16. Katsamenis, I., et al.: TraCon: A novel dataset for real-time traffic cones detection using deep learning. ArXiv 2205.11830 (2022)

Correction to: Mitigation and Prevention Methods for Distributed Denial-of-Service Attacks on Network Servers

Kwitee D. Gaylah and Ravirajsinh S. Vaghela

Correction to:
Chapter "Mitigation and Prevention Methods for Distributed Denial-of-Service Attacks on Network Servers" in:
S. Rajagopal et al. (Eds.): *Advancements in Smart Computing and Information Security*, **CCIS 1760**
https://doi.org/10.1007/978-3-031-23095-0_5

In the originally published version of chapter 5 the reference line was not complete. The 30th reference line in chapter 5 has been updated.

The updated original version of this chapter can be found at
https://doi.org/10.1007/978-3-031-23095-0_5

Author Index

Printed in the United States
by Baker & Taylor Publisher Services